FIFTY STRONG

Four Decades of US Veterans and Families Share
Their Combat and Post-War Experiences

JOHN MAINO

Fifty Strong

Four Decades of US Veterans and Families Share
Their Combat and Post-War Experiences

© 2021 John Maino

First Edition
All Rights Reserved. The author grants no assignable permission to reproduce for resale or redistribution. This license is limited to the individual purchaser and does not extend to others. Permission to reproduce these materials for any other purpose must be obtained in writing from the publisher except for the use of brief quotations.

Disclaimer
The views expressed in this work are solely those of the individuals interviewed and do not necessarily reflect the views of the publisher, and the publisher hereby disclaims any responsibility for them. In the event you use any of the information in this book for yourself, which is your constitutional right, the author and the publisher assume no responsibility for your actions.

Front cover photo:
Rich Karki (from left), Norman Calcote, John Wheeler, and Terry Quick pose for a photo in Vietnam while smoke rises behind them. (Rich Karki collection)

Back cover photo:
Three boys from the orphanage that Larry Ebsch and other members of his unit visited while in Korea (Larry Ebsch collection)

ISBN: 9798739143679

Design by M&B Global Solutions Inc.
Green Bay, Wisconsin (USA)

DEDICATION

This book is dedicated to all of those who said yes, they were in fact willing to raise their right hand and defend their country with their life.

And to those they left behind.

FOREWORD

Storytelling has always been one of John Maino's passions and gifts to all of us. John's personality is bigger than life, whether he is keeping us company on the radio, broadcasting on TV, supporting a local charity, or authoring a book just like this one.

But what really sets John apart is his patriotism and how he honors the American veteran. Within the pages of this book, he shares the stories of the men and women who have served this country in uniform and remembers their sacrifice.

These stories are those of courage by our local veterans who, by choice or by chance, fought in three different wars spanning over seventy-five years to preserve the very freedoms we enjoy today.

President Ronald Reagan once said, "Those who say that we're in a time when there are no heroes, they just don't know where to look." Look no further. Thanks to John Maino, this book is full of them!

Doug LaViolette
US Army Veteran
President, The Brian LaViolette Foundation

PROLOGUE

There are two questions I get asked on a pretty regular basis: How many vets have I talked to about their experiences and is there anything they all have in common. One is impossible to answer, the other is pretty easy.

As for a total number, I couldn't even come up with a guess that would be close to accurate. You could add up the number of profiles I've done in my four books but that would only be scratching the surface.

Some of the most insightful, compelling, spellbinding, heartbreaking, heartwarming, joyous, funny, sad, compelling, informative, and irreverent conversations I have ever had with veterans were in the most basic settings with neither a notepad nor tape recorder to be found.

It's the second question, about what they all have in common, that is easy to answer. There are two elements: mutual respect and deep personal pride in having served their country.

Now, did many of the veterans I have spoken with have issues at times with their branch of service, other branches of service, training, weapons, officers, battle plans, food, equipment, lack of sleep, tour of duty, medical treatment, post-service services, etc.? Yes, many of them did and there are post-service issues that still affect many veterans years after their service.

Some of my greatest memories are of Iraq/Afghanistan veterans sharing stories and possibly beverages at small-town VFWs and American Legions with WWII, Korean, Vietnam, and Gulf War veterans. It doesn't matter who was relating an experience; whether it was a twenty-two-year-old talking about the dangers that came with driving a Humvee through Baghdad in the middle of the night in 2006 or a ninety-two-year-old talking about the fear he felt walking through hedgerows in France in the summer of 1944. Each paid rapt attention while the other was speaking. It was during these times that I would watch their eyes; the eyes of those speaking, and the eyes of those listening. I felt as though there was a silent form of communication taking place that only those who had spent time in a war zone could decipher.

With that, I wish to give a sincere "thank you" to all who so graciously shared; not only their military experiences but also - in brutally honest fashion - experiences that intrinsically became a part of their post-war lives.

I had a Korean War veteran tell me something I will never forget. He said that when he was in Korea the only thing he could think of was how, if he made it home, life was going to be, *A big bowl of cherries.* That he was going to put the war in the rearview mirror and move on. He then admitted that after a couple of months back home his biggest concern was, *How in the hell am I supposed to live the rest of my life when I'm thinking about the war all the time?*

I try to show, whenever possible, how one's wartime experiences can also affect those around them. In some cases, the battles at home were as hard-fought emotionally as those in steamy jungles or on top of snow-covered ridges.

I am at a loss for words when it comes to thanking the spouses who shared the silent, (although in some cases, not so silent) battles they fought during the post-war years. Their story needs much more attention and appreciation than I can give in this one volume.

Thankfully, at least as of this writing, no veteran needs to stand alone. There are some incredibly dedicated veterans' organizations who, day or night, will lend a hand at a moment's notice. Their mantra is simple; "Please just ask. We will take it from there."

Man or woman, young or old, physically damaged or completely unscathed, there truly is a brotherhood standing watch out there who, as they so often say in modern war zones, "Have your six."

Some of the names in this book - although none of the individuals profiled - have been changed. Nothing else has been altered in any way. This is exactly what they remember and, in many cases, have tried to forget. As many told me, in one form or another, "Maybe getting everything out from start to finish will put some of those bad days to rest for good."

Okay, one last quick confession; yes, something has been changed. You won't find much profanity in this book. Not that it wasn't used during the interviews, but when given the option to, let's say, soften their language, basically everyone took that route. It fell under the umbrella of, "I would rather not have my grandkids and great-grandkids read the book and see me using that kind of language. They don't know I used to talk that way."

Their secret is safe with me.

John Maino
February 2021

CONTENTS

World War II introduction 1

Richard Stolz 3

Wilfred Carriveau 9

Richard Jenkins 15

Jack Kraszewski 21

Bob Plummer 29

Korean War introduction 37

Hubert Robenhorst 41

Edwin Wilber 47

Bill Koch 55

Jim Jolly 63

Stanley Mott 77

Don Bettine 81

Lee Frangquist 93

Lewis White 101

Chet Caine 109

Dick Baeten 117

Larry Ebsch 127

Jerome Scray 135

CONTENTS

Vietnam War introduction **139**
Gerald Gerndt 145
Linda Gomlicker, Lt. Col. ASAFR 157
Jim Barlament 163
Ron Umentum 175
Steve Aznoe 187
Chuck Wellens 195
Hubert "Hub" Joski 211
Ken Vanden Heuvel 219
Rich Karki 233
Richard Konitzer 257
Jim Jaklin 265
Cletus Ninham 275
Lee Piechocki 287
Joe Resop 297
Jack Shavlik 305
Mike Berzinsky 319
Clyde "Blackie" Rosin 329
Bill Enz 339
Randy Truttschel 351
Col. Judith Lisa, Ret. 361
Donna and Paul Boehm 367
Gold Star Families **375**
David Dellangelo 377
John Gmack 381
Mikal Sullivan 393
1st Lt. Tom Shaw 399
Acknowledgements 407
About the Author 409

WORLD WAR II
1941 - 1945

They were adolescents of the Great Depression. A generation who grew up knowing America not as a world-wide leader, but as a country struggling within itself to survive. This was survival at the most basic level. A steady job that would provide the absolute necessities: food on the table and money to pay the rent or mortgage was the new American Dream.

Volumes have been written about America's lack of concern for political upheaval in Europe and the Far East during this time. It's been said that the military rumblings in those lands should have spurred the US to better prepare itself against those foreign threats. When I mentioned that very idea to one World War II veteran, he explained to me that the only rumblings he was concerned with were the ones in his stomach.

It's documented that the US military, near the start of the war, ranked below even Romania in manpower and readiness. Ironically, many vets I've spoken to have said they would have gladly joined the military during the Depression, but in their words, "The Army wasn't hiring either."

This is the backdrop upon which America assembled a massive military force, shifted its industrial might to a near-total war effort, and within five years defeated two of the most massive and well-prepared military powers in world history.

With all due respect to the industrial giants and military strategists who played a major role in defeating the Axis powers, it was those kids of the Depression, the ones who went face-to-face with the enemy and in over 400,000 cases lost their lives, who truly deserve the nation's highest accolades.

Richard Stolz displays a model of his ship, LST 50.

RICHARD STOLZ

Signalman
Landing Ship, Tank
US Navy
World War II

For the United States military during World War II, sea-land invasions, while potentially extremely costly, were the main form of large-scale assaults on enemy-held regions. The two largest of the war, in fact in modern military history, were the invasion at Normandy, France in June of 1944 and at Okinawa in April of 1945.

Nearly a half-million Allied personnel played a role in those endeavors. Over seventy-five years later it would be hard to find more than a handful of veterans who took part in each of those two historic invasions.

A 1942 graduate of Green Bay East High School by the name of Richard Stolz is one such person.

I enlisted in the Navy in February of 1943. After graduating from boot camp I went to signalman school in Farragut, Idaho. In November of that year, I was sent to New Orleans and assigned to LST 50 (Landing Ship, Tank). We had a crew of 127 men.

In December of that year, we put to sea and traveled up to Boston, where we joined a convoy of over forty ships and headed across the Atlantic. Maybe we were too naive to understand everything. At that age, you think nothing will happen to you because you were so young. But everyone was young. The skipper might have been in his early thirties. Everyone else was around my age, eighteen or nineteen. We were just a bunch of young guys who spent most of our time clowning around.

We were screwballs. There were big loudspeakers on the ship and they would play music, all the big music of the day, while we worked. It didn't seem that what you were doing was all that unusual because everybody else your age was doing the same sort of things. It was a very unique time. I've said it many times, it made a man out of me.

The one time I didn't screw around is when I was on duty as chief signalman. I would be up on the conning tower receiving messages and relaying them to the officer of the deck. This was a no-nonsense job. If I wasn't on duty I made sure the other guys knew exactly what they were supposed to do.

Richard Stolz collection

You had the convoy commodore leading the columns of ships with submarine chasers circling all around the whole thing to protect us.

Once you were at sea we were not allowed to send out radio transmissions. There were German submarines all around us and if we sent out any kind of electronic signal they would be on us right away. So, you communicated with lights, semaphore, or flag hoist. Those were the only means of communication we could use. With semaphore, you have a flag in each hand and each position of the arm is a letter. You spelled the words that way. This was used regularly and you really had to be on the stick to read that stuff. In fact, you didn't even need flags, you could do it with your hands and communicate that way. But yes, all the outgoing communication had to be visual.

With flag hoist signaling, all the various flags that were hooked to the halyard meant a certain thing. We had a codebook that told what each hoist meant.

A lot of times we would be in formation, one ship after another all in line, and the lead ship would send us hoists. The hoists might be saying something like, "forty-five degree turn to starboard." You could refer to the codebook for every display and what it meant.

Signal lamps were used at night. We had a secret book for that too. The orders would come from the convoy commodore. He would put up different lights on his halyard. It might be red over green over yellow, and then it would be changed on a different day. Those would be the directions you needed to follow.

You had to really be on the ball to do this or you could have a catastrophe. There was one night where the commodore gave the signal, but the ship that was following along in the next column read it wrong and two ships ran into each other in the middle of the ocean. I'm standing there watching it through my binoculars and I told myself, *They're going to hit!* All of a sudden there was a terrible crash and they collided. It ended up being pretty bad.

We first landed in Belfast, Ireland, and then went to England in March of 1944.

In England, we hid out in an estuary in a beautiful little town called Salcombe for at least a couple of months before D-Day. It was on the southern coast of England. We were ready to go at any time. We were already fully loaded with everything we needed before we left the States.

You never knew when the call would come, but all of a sudden one day we were told to head out. We knew it had to be the big one because of all the activity. We hadn't seen anything like that before. We got into formation with all these other ships; thousands and thousands of them. We were absolutely amazed by the whole thing.

I was on the bridge of our ship. It was a very dark morning, just dark and gloomy. The sea was actually rather calm. As far as you could see, all around you, there was nothing but airplanes and ships on their way to Normandy. The battlewagons would sit a few miles offshore and send shells over our heads to the beach. Then there were the destroyers. My God, just tons and tons of ships and materials.

We headed to Normandy and sat there until they needed us. Our cargo consisted of troops, trucks, heavy trucks, tanks, jeeps, just all kinds of things. They would drive the vehicles right onto the beach from our lower deck. When we got close to shore it really started getting bad. We didn't hit any mines – luckily.

On one of the many trips we made that day, I was watching from the main deck. We were in a two-ship column. I'm looking at the ship next to us. All of a sudden it must have hit a mine because it just exploded and started to sink. We couldn't stop, we had to just keep moving towards the beach. The only time we ever stopped to help was when we came upon a Liberty ship that was sinking. It was loaded with tanks and everything else. They must have been torpedoed or hit a mine because it was severely damaged. There wasn't anything you could do to save the ship. All we could do was take the guys off and put them on ours.

Those poor Army troops that were on our ship...oh boy. The doors would open and they would climb out. Those guys were scared. We were scared too, but those guys were more scared of being on our ship than on dry land. They knew ships were being blown up around us. They wanted to get out and take their chances on shore. I wouldn't have traded places with those guys for anything and those guys wouldn't have traded places with us. Everybody was scared to death. It didn't matter where you were located. It was terrible.

We couldn't tell exactly how it was going for the guys on the beach. The Germans had concrete bunkers up on the hill and they were firing at us. Our guys had to fight their way up and charge those bunkers. The Germans had 88s (88millemeter: *A very high-velocity artillery piece that could be used as an anti-aircraft or anti-personnel weapon. Arguably the most devastating, effective, and correspondingly, feared weapon in the Nazi arsenal.*)

They were firing at our ships. Those were terrible things that could destroy just about anything. Our guys just had to go up, kill the Germans, and knock out those guns. Our destroyers would come in close and fire the heck out of them but a lot of the destroyers got shot up, too. So you had people getting killed both ways all the time. You really couldn't tell who was winning or losing. It was just a mass of firing.

That entire day was spent traveling back and forth along the coast while the fighting was going on. We saw ships sunk, guys drowning, dead guys floating in the water...it looked like those poor guys on the beach were in a terrible situation, just terrible.

Once we unloaded our cargo we would load up with wounded troops. We made many trips; many, many, back and forth from the French coast to England.

We had three or four doctors on our ship and they had an operating room. You felt so bad for the poor guys they were working on. They maybe had an arm blown off, but they were fighting to stay alive. The doctors would have to cut off what was left of something and throw the parts over the side. There would be parts and everything floating in the water. It was not a nice thing to see.

We would put those poor wounded guys on stretchers, three to four high along the walls of our tank decks and attached to the bulkhead. You just felt terrible for those guys.

We had many other missions after Normandy. In August of 1944, we took part in the invasion of Southern France, near St. Tropez. One of our jobs was to go to Africa, pick up French troops, and drop them off at Marseilles. Well, the French troops didn't want to go. They thought it was a better deal to just sit on our ship. Just around the time it started getting tense, a ship behind us got hit badly. Oh man, you've never seen people want to get off a ship quicker than those guys did.

We went all through the Mediterranean: Sicily, Corsica, Sardinia. The job was pretty much the same; dropping stuff off and picking stuff up. The thing I remember most was just the devastation. The unbelievable number of wrecked ships and cities.

The worst day of my life in the war didn't have anything to do with a battle. It was the time we got caught in a typhoon. That was a terrible, terrible thing. The waves were over thirty-five feet high. You would dip down and all you could see were walls of water on both sides. The bow would go high in the air and then come crashing down. We were in a convoy, but those waves were so big you couldn't see any other ships around you. It's like you were being buried by water out in the middle of the sea. The boats hanging from the sides of the ship were hitting the ship so hard that cracks started forming and water started coming in. It's the worst storm I've ever seen; the worst thing I ever experienced during my time there.

In October of '44 we were sent back to the States for a thirty-day leave and to be refitted for our next mission which was in the South Pacific.

In April of 1945, we left Saipan and headed to Okinawa, where the Army and Marines had kicked off a huge invasion. We carried materials and supplies onto the beach. There were a lot of wrecked ships but going in wasn't hot and heavy like it was at Normandy.

I do know it was really bad for the guys who had to go in and do the fighting. It was terrible for them. The Japanese would come out of those hills and they wouldn't give an inch. It was do or die. Our guys would just plow on day after day. They would see their guys getting killed all the time and they just had to keep going forward. That's when our people really knew the Japanese weren't going to surrender - weren't going to give up. I wouldn't have wanted to be one of those guys fighting on that island for anything.

We were back at Pearl Harbor when the atomic bombs were dropped. We got sent to a little town in Japan called Wakanora. We

The LST 50, Richard Stolz's ship during World War II. (Richard Stolz collection)

anchored there and worked as shore patrol. Our job was to keep our sailors away from the local population. We first had to find out if the locals were going to be nice to us or not. We were afraid, we really were. We knew how incredibly fanatical the Japanese soldiers had been, how they were so willing to die for their country. We didn't know if the local populace would be the same way.

We were the first Americans in this little town. The local people looked at us very curiously. The area was quite primitive. We had our SP belts on and we patrolled all around. We didn't have any trouble at all. The local citizens were all very nice to us, very submissive, very polite, not the least bit belligerent towards us. They turned out to be simply very, very nice people.

When I came home, I was happy as heck. I just wanted to put on my old clothes from my high school days and meet up with my friends. I wanted to return to the life I left. I was just very, very happy and pleased to be in my home. It was just wonderful.

I did my first semester of college in Green Bay and then went to Madison and graduated from the University of Wisconsin. I just dug in and carried on with my life. My roommate at school had been a paratrooper at Normandy, but we never talked about the war. I'm sure he had some very bad memories or nightmares because of what he went through, but he kept them to himself. Most of the returning veterans were that way. We all had the same attitude, that we did what we had to do and that's just the way it was. You were happy to be home in one piece and there was no need to talk about it.

It wasn't until years and years later that people started asking about the war. Up until then I rarely spoke about it.

Maybe it's because we were so young that we were able to move on the way we did. I mean when you're still in your teens and you look over the side of your ship and see some bodies floating by or parts of bodies, well, maybe it takes a young kid to put up with all that crap and move on. The one thing I still think about is those poor young guys heading into the beaches. I still feel sorry for those guys. Those are the guys I thought about when I did think about the war.

I'm ninety-six years old now. A lot of things happened behind me, but I'm still here. That's just the way the Lord made it I guess.

WILFRED CARRIVEAU

85th Regiment
10th Mountain Division
US Army
World War II

It's a historical misfortune for the soldiers who slogged their way from Sicily to the top of the Italian boot that the greatest moment of the Italian campaign - triumphantly riding into Rome and wresting it from the Nazis - happened to occur on June 5th, 1944. It goes without saying that D-Day, the invasion of France - which occurred just a few hours later - captured the front pages, while the self-proclaimed "dogfaces" of the Italian Campaign were once again relegated to the back. It's something they were accustomed to.

Legendary war correspondent Ernie Pyle did his part in trying to capture the courage and carnage of the fight for Italy. It was perhaps best captured in his haunting story, "The Death of Captain Waskow." That article brought to light the essence of this campaign. There were few broad-stroke battles with war college-strategies such as those fought on the great plains of Europe.

For the most part, this battle consisted of tired, shivering, young GIs going up one steep, muddy, mountain after another while trying to dislodge well-entrenched, experienced German troops. The gains were small; the cost was high.

Wilfred Carriveau of Lena, Wisconsin, left behind a wife and young son to join that fight.

John Maino

I was homesick before I even left town. May of 1944 is when they drafted me and sent me to basic training at Camp Blanding, Florida. Being from the north they figured I had been a skier so I was assigned to the 10th Mountain Division. Well, my skiing experience was nothing like what these guys had gone through in training. The only way I came to a stop was by falling down.

They trucked me right to my unit in Italy as a replacement. You hear about a lot of guys who have a real hard time as replacements, but the guys in my unit – the 85th Regiment, 2nd Battalion of the 10th Mountain Division – were really good guys. They accepted me right away.

There was heavy snow but it was a different type of snow than it was back home. It's like it was drier. You could lay in it and it wouldn't melt.

We were in action right from the start: Monte Belvedere, Po Valley, Lake De Garda. It seemed like no matter where we were, the Germans were looking down at us. We never seemed to get the high ground. If we took a mountain or hill, there was another one that was higher and they were up on the next peak. They knew exactly where we were all the time. That's kind of a scary feeling knowing you're being watched that way. That's why most of our patrols were at night. A lot of the patrols were to try and capture prisoners. That was a tough assignment. Those were rough experienced soldiers they had there. They were all SS troops. They knew what they were doing. The local civilians hated them and were scared to death of them. The Germans had taken everything the civilians had: cattle, horses, everything.

It seems like it was never really dark in the mountains; like the moon was a big spotlight shining down. We would be walking on a patrol and all of a sudden you would hear a flare fired off. As soon as you heard that you just froze, just stood there stiff as a board, hardly breathing until it went out. The best thing we had going for us was that the Germans weren't being supplied very often. They were low on ammunition for their artillery and mortars. They wouldn't fire unless they knew exactly where we were. They were very selective but very accurate. When you attacked, they would have those mortars marked right down on top of you, and then when you got close to them they would fall back and there would be another line all set up. They kept leapfrogging back that way. It's like there was always another line waiting for us. As I said, they knew what they were doing up there.

During the day we would hide as best we could in our foxholes. That's how you lived. Sometimes they would fire airburst shells that would send shrapnel right down on top of you. My chum and I decided we needed some cover for our foxhole so we went to this barn and took the door off, carried it back, and put it over our foxhole. Then we put dirt and stuff on top of it for protection. When the captain came by he asked where in the hell did we get that door. So we told him. He said,

"Didn't you know you walked right through a minefield to get there?" We didn't know. We just walked right through it. The Lord was with me every step that day.

There was one time when I went through a minefield on purpose - the only time. The captain told us that a patrol was trapped and almost out of ammo. We knew that once the Germans found them they would be slaughtered. They wouldn't be taken prisoner. He said we had to find out exactly where they were and get some mortar fire around them to keep the Germans off. I volunteered.

They gave me a packboard with communications wire. I got through the minefield; praying every step of the way. I got there and set them up with the wire. Then I laid another wire on the way back in case the first one got busted. When I got back, the captain dropped to his knees and started crying. He knew what would have happened to those guys. They wouldn't have had a chance. They called in their position and our mortars blasted that whole side of the mountain, which allowed our guys to get out of there. They gave me a Bronze Star for that.

> **Bronze Star Award To Pfc. W. Carriveau**
>
> Special to Press-Gazette
>
> LENA, Wis.—Pfc. Wilfred Carriveau of Lena, member of the 85th Mountain Infantry, has been awarded the Bronze Star "for meritorious service in combat on April 15, 1945, near Serra d'Aiano, Italy." Carriveau entered service May 30, 1944, and went overseas Nov. 30. His wife and child live here, as does his mother, Mrs. Fred La Rue.

Mines were the scariest thing. It didn't matter who you were. One wrong step and you were gone. There was a civilian who had his barn a pretty fair way from his house, but with the way our minefield was set up, he had to go way around the side of the mountain to get there safely. One day he told our captain he was going through the minefield. The captain said no, he couldn't go. The man started yelling, telling the captain that it was his property and that he would walk in the same footsteps that one of our guys had walked. The man said if he didn't get to his cows, they were going to die or the Germans were going to take them. So he went. He didn't get 100 feet when he stepped on a mine and got blown up.

Everybody says war is hell, but that doesn't even come close to how bad it really is. If you are on the front lines, you are scared all the time because you knew you could get killed or wounded real bad in the blink of an eye. Mines, mortars, snipers, artillery shells, you couldn't protect yourself from all of them. There were guys who might be standing around talking to their chums and the next thing you know a shell comes in and kills them all. They wouldn't know what hit them. One second you're talking about home and the next second you don't exist in this world. It didn't matter how deep you dug your hole, a shell could land right on top of you and sometimes they did. Then you would hear wounded guys crying out; "I don't want to die! I don't want to die!" It was just a terribly helpless feeling.

The strain got to everybody. It helped a lot if you had guys who would help you out. I remember when I first got there and I dug my foxhole under a tree. One of the guys told me I shouldn't do that because if a shell hit that tree, every splinter of wood would be like shrapnel. I was digging another one when a guy said to come over to his hole. It was big enough for both of us. I left all my stuff by my hole and crawled over. A little while later a shell landed right next to my hole; right where I had been. My rifle, my cartridge belt - everything was blown up. I told the captain I might as well go home because I didn't have anything left to fight with. He told me to look around; there were plenty on the ground to choose from.

One of our missions in the Po Valley was to try and capture a hill in the middle of the night. They told us to take the ammunition out of our rifles. No firing on the way in, bayonets or grenades only. That way, if there was a rifle blast, you knew it was a German.

We caught them sleeping. The fight was personal - vicious hand-to-hand fighting. Both sides were throwing grenades; the only light was from the flashes. I remember being in a fight with a big German. The next thing I knew I was waking up. A German potato masher (hand grenade) had come flying in, hit me on the side of my forehead, and knocked me out colder than hell before rolling off the side of the hill and going off. My buddies had grabbed me, pulled me between some rocks, and then went back to the fighting.

When I came to, I was bleeding from my nose and my ears. My head was hurting like hell. The medic said I had to go back to the aid station. I said no. My buddies were there and they said they would take care of me. The medic said, "No, this is too serious, he's going back" I told him no. There was no way I was going back. I was staying with my buddies. He gave me a handful of pills and said, "Take these, you're going to need them." Boy was he right; my headaches were just something awful.

The medic left. He didn't register me as wounded because I didn't go back to the aid station. Because of that, I never received a Purple Heart. I still have a dent in my forehead from where it hit. I've had all kinds of problems since then including being classified as 100-percent disabled and pretty much going blind because of it, but it doesn't matter. The Army just won't give me a Purple Heart. That still bothers me.

When we got to the Po Valley there was a big hydraulic plant on the river. They wouldn't let us cross it on foot because they said it was boobytrapped. So we got in boats and started paddling across. A German plane started strafing us. There were only one or two of them, but that was enough. Guys were paddling like crazy. Some of the boats turned over and got in the current, taking the guys down. We were lucky to get to the other side. We crawled up the bank and all of a sudden we could hear guns going off. It was our own artillery firing at us from where we had just left. They didn't know we had made it as far as we did. The captain got on the phone and told them to cease-fire before they wiped us out. Actually, I think it was the British that was firing. They were with us a lot. The thing is, they were so accurate, they could drop a shell right where they wanted. Lucky, this time, most of them were going over us.

We found a place to sleep in a house alongside the road. The lady told us to go upstairs. There was a wooden sawhorse with planks laying on top. I fell right asleep. The next morning the captain is going all over the area rounding everybody up. When I went downstairs, I gave the lady a pocket-full of sugar packets. She went and bought me an egg. I thought, *What am I going to do with that egg?* Well, she goes back into the kitchen and fries it up. The captain came in and said, "Where the hell did you get a fried egg from?" I said, "The lady gave it to me for some sugar packs." Well, he tore into his bag like you can't believe for some sugar packs so he could get a fried egg. We laughed and talked about that for a long time. Just sitting down at the kitchen table and eating fried eggs right before we went back to fight. It's almost like for a few minutes we weren't in a war where your next meal might be a raw potato you picked up going across a field.

In the spring of 1945, the Germans were still up in the Alps, but there wasn't any real reason to go up and get them. They had had enough. They were coming down and surrendering. In a couple of days, the war in Italy was over.

When we saw how they were dug in, we were glad we didn't have to go in and dig them out. They had been there for years and had tunnels everywhere. It would have taken a lot of time and a lot of men to get them out of there.

One of the guys we captured was an SS officer. The captain told me to take him back to headquarters. The guy had a pair of binoculars and a Beretta pistol. I go to take the pistol and he goes, "No! No! No!" He was so arrogant. The captain said to take him back, but to not do anything until I was out of his sight. So we start walking and pretty soon I stop and take his binoculars, then his pistol and a leather case with artillery maps in it. We were walking down the trail, which had communication wires strung along the ground from headquarters to the front lines. He was walking kind of strange. Then I realized he was trying to cut the lines with his hobnailed boots. I stopped him again, put my bayonet right to his gut, and said, "If you try that again, you're a dead duck!" He started swearing and spitting right in my face, "You dirty swine! You dirty American! You dirty so and so...!" Just cursing me out right in my face. When I came back the captain said, "How far did he make it before you taught him a lesson?"

There was a time after the war when some guys were putting together a trip to Italy, to the places we had been. They asked me if I wanted to go. I said no. They asked why not. I told them I had too many bad memories and that I didn't want them to start coming back. My wife can tell you. I had to have my own bedroom. I was fighting the Germans again in my dreams. My wife can tell you stories; she knows better than anybody. The hand-to-hand fighting, crawling on your belly hoping you didn't get spotted, guys being sick with dysentery, the smell of blood, of gun powder - no I didn't want that.

The movies have the noise and the pictures but not the smell. It was horrible, horrible. I never knew the human body could stand so much. A lot of guys cracked up. I think the thing that kept me going was my family back home. That was all I kept thinking about; staying alive so I could get back to my wife and my little boy.

When I came home, my little boy kept running around; didn't pay any attention to me. Finally, somebody said, "Where's your daddy?" He ran into the bedroom and came out with a picture of me.

RICHARD JENKINS

8th Armored Division
US Army
World War II

There are those who have the great fortune of being impeccably trained for the climate and conditions they will be sent to fight in. Some - not all.

Richard Jenkins, from one of the most isolated regions in the Upper Peninsula of Michigan, spent most of his training in the Deep South enduring incredible heat while eluding alligators and rattlesnakes. This, as many a veteran would understand, would play no role in where he was sent.

I was born about twelve miles north of Watersmeet, Michigan, a place called Bruce Crossing. We lived in an old log cabin back in the woods. On the night I was born my grandma had to walk two miles on snowshoes to deliver me. It was pretty crude living in that territory back then. There weren't too many people around. If you had a good rabbit hound, a 12-gauge shotgun, and some snowshoes you were in business.

My dad had been an Army mechanic in World War I. I didn't have any thoughts about becoming a soldier; no way. There were still guys around who had lung problems from breathing in gas over in France in the first war and there wasn't any VA (Veterans Administration) to take care of them.

One Sunday afternoon, one of my brothers and I were outside working on a car when my mother came out and said, "Pearl Harbor has been bombed." We looked at each other and said, "Where in the hell is Pearl Harbor?" Within a couple of years, all three of us boys were in uniform, my brothers both in the Air Corps and me in the Army.

As soon as I graduated high school I went to Detroit to make some money before they grabbed me. That's when I got my letter, "Your friends and neighbors have selected you to represent them in the Armed Forces of the United States." Well isn't that wonderful?

When I was inducted they asked a bunch of questions about what I did. I told them I was a mechanic and they said, "Good, you're going in ordnance." They placed me in the 8th Armored Division and sent me down to the swamps of Leesville, Louisiana to train. What a terrible place that was. It was like that TV show where they go hunting alligators. One day I was walking through this swampy area and I stepped over a log and there was this long black thing laying there and it started wiggling. Somebody said, "That's a water moccasin!" Well, they weren't very nice to have around. I got the hell away from him in a hurry. Then at night when we were out in the boonies you would get all set up in your sleeping bag in the pup tent and start to sack out and you would get woken up from wild pigs trying to get in and grab our food.

Richard Jenkins collection

We got sent to England for training and then on January 5th, 1945, we loaded up on LSTs (Landing Ship, Tank) and went across the straits of Gibraltar. In France, we went up the Seine River to the town of Reims. This was near where the armistice was signed at the end of World War I. It was cold, damn cold, coldest winter in Europe in forty years.

They sent us right up to the Battle of the Bulge; Holland, Belgium, those areas. You would see whole masses of kids walking around. When we were driving along the little kids would be running alongside us, "Cigarette for papa? Choc-o-lat for mamma?" And like GIs have always done, we dug into our bags and gave them everything we had. Those kids were just like kids anywhere else, just doing whatever they had to do to survive.

By the time they offloaded us, out in the boonies someplace, we were freezing our butts off. They took some big barrels, half-filled them with water, and put them over a fire. Then they took a whole bunch of little cans of weenies and beans and tossed them in there. When they were hot enough they pulled them out and said, "Here, this is your supper."

We didn't have good winter clothes. The sleeping bag was canvas on the outside and a blanket on the inside. You would scratch out a place in the snow and put the poncho down first. That was the best thing we carried. Those helped in a lot of different ways. So you would put the poncho down in the snow, then you would take your shoes off and put them in your sleeping bag. You would have on every article of clothes you owned, but you would still freeze all night long.

You could see how completely unprepared our military was for that attack. Nobody thought the Germans would be able to come through the thick forest and attack with tanks. But they did. It caught our intelligence officers completely off guard. They just knocked the hell out of the Americans. It was terrible intelligence and anticipation on our part.

I got there about the time the Americans started pushing back. You would see dead Germans lying all around in the snow, Americans GIs too. I was a mechanic, so I didn't have to shoot anybody. We had different details of guys for every job there was. If somebody got killed in a tank and we had to fix it, there was a detail that would go inside and clean it out. We had one tank that had been hit right by the porthole that an officer was looking out of. An 88mm shell hit it. That poor guy's brains were blown all over the interior of the tank. It made me sick to my stomach. Just seeing it and knowing what happened inside there. It's like anything else; you don't really believe it unless you see it.

You didn't feel anything when you saw hundreds of dead Germans lying around. You couldn't. They were the bad guys. At least that's how you felt in the middle of a battle like that. You were too worried about trying to stay alive yourself. We always said we wouldn't talk about the gory stuff when we got back. Even though we weren't doing the killing, you couldn't help but be around it all the time.

We slept in the flatbeds of trucks most of the time. Once in a while, we would sleep in a house or barn where we could burrow in the hay. I acquired a sheepskin vest from someplace and wore it inside my other clothes to keep warm.

We were pushing them back through the Hürtgen Forest (near the Belgian border with Germany). There had been really hard fighting there for a few months. It had been a thick forest with huge pine trees, but now it was all blown apart. We saw where artillery, tanks, and other things had stood their ground, firing as long as needed. Each emplacement had a lot of snow piled around it with empty casings all around. It was cold as hell there too.

Our job was to keep the tanks running. One of the biggest jobs was just trying to make sure they had enough fuel to keep going. A lot of times the track of the tank would get hit by a shell. We would take it off, lay it out and get the tank back on it. We also had big wreckers to help move them. The one thing the tanks struggled with was turning on ice. We were going down this icy hill in Belgium and had to make a left turn. Well, the tracks were steel and rubber, but sometimes they wouldn't grip. The tank went right through the side of a house. The barrel was sticking right into the living room. Those people didn't like us very much that day.

The German tanks were far ahead of ours because Hitler put a lot of money into them. The first place the American tanks met up with the Germans was North Africa and the Germans kicked the hell out of them. We had the M4 tank. They call them Shermans now, but we never called them that. The Germans had two things that we didn't have an answer for. One was the 88mm. It was first used as an anti-aircraft gun, but then they realized how effective they were when lowered and used as a ground weapon. They killed a lot of people trying to cross the Rhine River with that thing. Their shells would go through our tanks like they were made of butter. Just punch a hole through them like there was nothing there.

The other thing was the Panzerfaust. We had bazookas but the Panzerfausts seemed more deadly. They would sneak up with those things, get close, and fire a shell that would burn a hole right through six to eight inches of steel. The most vulnerable part of the tank was in the back where the door to the engine was. If they put one through there, it was sayonara. No questions asked. Those things raised hell with our tanks.

The way we kept going was by out-producing them. We started sending so much equipment that along with the Air Force we overwhelmed them. Once they started losing their armament they couldn't keep up. The biggest mistake the Germans ever made was invading Russia. If they had left Russia alone, there is no way in hell we would have ever set foot in France.

The weapon which turned the tide at the Bulge was the P-47 Thunderbolt. Once the fog lifted those things turned anything that moved into dead meat. They had four .50-caliber machine guns on each wing and fired rockets. They just knocked the crap out of the Germans. Patton gets all the credit, but it was those pilots in the P-47s who were really the difference makers in the Bulge.

We would set up someplace and just watch hundreds upon hundreds of B-17s fly over us at about 15,000 feet. They just filled the skies day after day. When we got to the town of Aachen in Germany we saw the damage they could do. There weren't two bricks on top of each other. That city was so flattened it was unbelievable. It had been wiped off the map. But you know, you would still see people crawling out of the rubble and finding a way to survive. Just scratching and clawing and surviving.

Another day, we were on one side of a river and were told to stop because the British Air Force was going to soften up the other side. We heard them coming over. They were Lancasters. We later heard that there were 400 of them. They weren't made for flying daylight raids because they were slow. All of a sudden we saw this explosive ball of flame and a trail of smoke heading to the ground. We counted thirty different explosions like that. It's hard to say if anyone ever got out before the crash. The Germans shot them down like they were ducks in a row.

We didn't know what was going on. We were just peons who went where they told us to go. The people of Holland and Belgium were so grateful to see us you can't believe it. The Dutch especially were very special people. They hated the Germans so much. They had suffered mightily ever since the occupation.

But you know, when we moved into Germany, the people there seemed happy to see us too. At least they could see that the war was coming to an end and maybe they would survive after all. We weren't supposed to fraternize with the civilians, but nobody said you had to follow every order. The normal German citizens were human beings just like us. They hated war as much as we did. I got to be friends with one of the German families. I don't remember exactly where it was, but they were hurting for food. I had gotten a hold of a 30.06 rifle and went out to find something for them to eat. I shot a big fat spruce goose and brought it to them. They fixed up a big meal and invited me.

In May of 1945, we went into the Sudetenland of Czechoslovakia, the 8th Army helped in the liberation of the country. They still celebrate that today over there. There's one day I will never forget. We were told to load up on our trucks. We didn't know where we were going. They took us to a mass grave. The local Czechs had rounded up the citizens who had been sympathizers with the Nazis and a few of the Germans who were still there. They made them dig out this big pit and get right in and uncover bodies. There was something like 250 Czechs who had been slaughtered just before the Germans left. The people were down in this mass of mud and dead bodies. They were up to their chests in it. Some had shovels - others had to use their bare hands. The Czech civilians had guards with guns standing all around the pit. Every victim was taken out and cleaned up by the sympathizers so they could be identified. The regular Czech citizens in the Sudetenland suffered quite a bit under the Germans. That was one of the first places Hitler annexed. The Nazis bled it dry.

The Czech people wanted to throw a huge parade in the city of Pilsen to celebrate their freedom from the Germans. My job was to get a car ready for one of the dignitaries. Well, the car we got ahold of had been one of Hermann Goering's convertible Mercedes. The only problem was that the transmission was shot. So we stole a transmission from a different car and got it running for the parade. The dignitary was Jack Benny, the comedian. After the parade all these newspaper guys went up to him, they were all over the damn place, and asked him what he thought about Goering's Mercedes. He said, "Well, it was alright, but not as good as my old Maxwell back home." That was the car he always talked about on his radio shows.

People ask me about my biggest impression from the war. Here it is. People are just people, damn it. Get away from the politicians and the generals and you can get along with anybody. If you're nice to somebody, they will be nice to you. I don't care what else is going on. And when you're caught in a war zone, the civilians suffer just as much as the soldiers do. We saw terrible situations the citizens went through: starving, hurt, and killed from bombings, little kids without parents, war orphans. They had it every bit as bad as the people doing the fighting, but nobody ever talks about their sacrifice.

EUGENE "JACK" KRASZEWSKI

553 Anti-Aircraft Battalion
9th Division
US Army
World War II

There are popular tours in Europe that transverse the route taken by Allied forces from the summer of 1944 through the spring of 1945. They start in France, travel through Belgium, the Netherlands, and end in Germany. The brochures often mention quaint hotels and picturesque scenery.

A young man from Pulaski, Wisconsin, once navigated that route. His accommodations consisted of ice-filled trenches. The scenery, bombed-out cities and the sight of atrocities that would shock the outside world.

When I got drafted in 1943 the war in the Pacific was going strong, but you didn't hear as much about what was going on in Europe. You didn't have any choice on where you were going though. They sent me to Camp Hulen, Texas, and put me in an anti-aircraft battalion. We were trained on 40mm guns. They would tow a big target behind a plane and we would fire at it. We didn't use explosive shells like we did in the war. When the plane would land we could see how many holes we put in the target. I'm not so sure we were real good shots on some of those days.

This base was right on the border, about three miles from Mexico. Every time we got a pass we would head over there. You'd be in one of the dark night clubs and pretty soon the MPs would come in and kick you out, telling you it was off-limits. I guess they didn't want us hanging around those shady girls.

Private Kraszewski
(Jack Kraszewski collection)

I was a corporal and was the top guy on the gun. One day I was made acting tech sergeant and was put in charge of a group of guys. We all got some passes and went out. We came back later with a bunch of booze and built a big fire. We must have made a lot of noise because at daybreak a guy opened my tent flap and said the captain wanted to see me. I was sicker than hell. I walked in and said, "Corporal Kraszewski reporting." All he said was, "It's now Private Kraszewski." End of conversation.

After we finished training they gave us a week off, but I stayed and went right through. I'm glad I did. I got sent to Europe; all those other guys I hung out with were sent to the South Pacific.

It took us eighteen miserable days on the USS *Washington* to get to Scotland. They put you in a little nine-foot-wide cubbyhole with four rows of bunks on each side. If somebody on the top bunks started heaving from seasickness it got pretty nasty. People were sick all the time. That was a long trip.

We were in a convoy with destroyers alongside us. They said there were German submarines all over and they would try to pick off the last ships in line. I don't know if that was true or not, but you didn't want to be that last ship.

We docked in Scotland, then went to England, and then took LSTs to France. This would have been the late summer or fall of 1944.

That trip across the English Channel was rougher than the one coming across the ocean. The waves were high as the ship. It felt like it was going to bust in half. Our battalion consisted of four batteries with 200 men in each and eight squads with twenty men to a squad. The guns were on wheels so we could tow them behind our trucks. We also had four .50-caliber machine guns in the turrets. That's what I was on.

The worst thing was the damn cold. We tried to find places to stay whenever we could, maybe an old barn or something, but it didn't happen very often. One night we stayed in this old chateau with a big fireplace. We went out and cut down trees to keep that thing burning. But most nights we slept in slit trenches. You would put your raincoat down first and then cover up with two blankets but two blankets don't do too much when it's below zero. If we were lucky, there was a haystack someplace close by that we could crawl into or take some straw and put down in the hole first.

Our feet were cold and wet all the time because our boots were leather. We didn't have rubber boots like they have now. Once our boots got wet they never dried out. You would try and keep one pair of socks under your armpits all day so maybe you would have a dry pair of socks to put on. That would help a little bit, but your feet were freezing all the time. Some guys got frostbite. That was pretty miserable.

You were always dirty and you were always cold. But, what could you do? If you found a little stream it probably had ice over it and the water was ice cold. I think I had one shower in about six months. We came across a cement-making factory and our officers went in and asked if we could take showers there. That was the only time.

The French people didn't have anything – nothing. But one day after sleeping out in the cold and the snow some French people brought us hot vegetable soup. I think it's the best soup I've ever eaten.

A couple of days later we went through a town and a lady brought us a bottle of Calvados brandy. Three of us drank it on the way to our next spot. By the time we got there, none of us were able to walk around. Oh, it was wicked stuff.

We saw our most German planes in Holland. It was pretty exciting when they would come down spraying their machine guns all over. We would have sixteen guns firing at the same time. You didn't know who was actually hitting the planes. Just my gun alone could fire 300 rounds per minute and that's with shooting in bursts. No one person or gun got credit for hitting the planes. We weren't very far apart and we all opened up.

A lot of our time was spent guarding bridges and things like that. The Germans always wanted to knock them out to slow us down on our way to Germany. You'd be sleeping in your trench, maybe you had finally gotten warmed up a little bit, and then somebody would wake you and you'd have to get up and go stand guard duty. Those were scary

Jack Kraszewski (second from left) and his buddies pose with a downed German plane. (Jack Kraszewski collection)

nights. You're standing out there in the pitch dark. You'd hear something walking around and you didn't know if it was a Kraut or a cow. When we stood guard back in Texas, I was always worried about rattlesnakes crawling around. I hated those things too. Maybe I just hated guard duty.

We didn't sit around and cry and worry, didn't talk about getting shot or anything like that. We had twenty guys who were like brothers. We were all together and figured what comes, comes. I guess that's how we looked at it.

One night we're sitting there and we could hear this plane overhead. It started dropping incendiary bombs. They were small bombs that lit up everything like it was daytime. One of those things landed about ten yards from me. They didn't explode, they just burned until they went out. That was scary because we knew bombers were going to be next. Pretty soon one came over but even with all that light he still missed the bridge.

Another thing they had in Holland was those buzz bombs. The Dutch people called them "Fleekie Boom." They were loaded with explosives and only had a certain amount of fuel in them. After they fired them off, they would go a certain distance and then come down. During the day you would listen for the motor to stop and you knew it was coming down. At night you would see the flame trailing it and when that went out, the same thing, down it would come. They had them pretty well-timed for how far they wanted them to go. Some went right over us; some stopped short of us.

When the Battle of the Bulge started in the middle of December we were near the Rhine River. We didn't know anything was going to happen. The only problem was the weather – the coldest nights we had seen. During the day it was cloudy, foggy, and snowy but we were relaxed. Things were pretty quiet. When the Germans hit our front lines they just pushed our infantry straight back. I don't know how many miles it turned out to be. I know we had to keep moving up through deep snow for three days straight. They told us to be on alert for anything; on the ground, in the sky, it didn't matter. Anything comes our way, shoot it. From what we could tell the Germans weren't stopping for anything.

They told us to stay in the middle of fields, not in villages or towns, because we had to be able to see the German planes coming over. If there was even one tree in a field we would wrap a primer cord around it and knock it down so it didn't get in our way.

I will say this though, it's a miracle with the way they kept us fed. We had a lot of hot meals. I don't know how they kept up to us with food and supplies and everything, but they did. If they couldn't cook something, they made sure we had rations at least. Those supply guys, food and ammunition guys, those guys were unsung heroes.

As soon as the weather cleared our bombers and fighters came in, and I will tell you, they just blew that place apart. They attacked for two-three days straight. The sky was black with them going over during the day and you could read a newspaper at night from the light of so many bombs exploding.

When the Krauts started fleeing they blew up the bridges behind them. Our Army engineers had to build pontoon bridges. They did it at night and were under attack the whole time. They would build them in one day. The infantry and tanks went across first. We were right behind them.

Once we were in Germany, we went through the Black Forest. That was a tough-looking area. Those pillboxes they had there were about three feet thick. Our tanks took care of them. The big thing you had to worry about were mines all over the place.

One day we came upon a concentration camp. We could smell burnt flesh before we even got to it. It was full of displaced people: Jews, Polish, Italian, all different nationalities. They were people who had been healthy and strong enough to work for the Germans. Now they were so skinny there was nothing to them and all they had on was rags. I was fluent in Polish, so I started talking to them. They told me they got one meal a day, hot water with a piece of beet in it. It was the type of beet we used to feed our cows in winter.

We took care of them and fed them, but some of them were just too far gone. They were beyond help. We didn't know these kinds of camps existed. We went to a crematorium. Some of the bodies weren't completely burned yet. There were piles of bones. It was terrible. You could see the empty canisters of the poison they had dropped down onto the people who thought they were going to be taking showers.

We would ask the German people what happened, about why they killed all the Jews and those other workers. Nobody admitted to knowing anything about that stuff. They keep saying they had no idea. All they said was that Germans wouldn't do anything like that. Pretty soon, word of mouth got to us that there were big pits around where the Krauts had lined up people, shot them, and then covered them up with bulldozers. Other people said the guards would build big woodpiles and put the bodies on them and set them on fire. But the German citizens kept saying they didn't know anything about it. I don't know about that.

One day one of the Polish prisoners asked me if I could get him some potatoes. So I brought him a couple of bags. I figured they were going to eat them. He wanted them to make moonshine with. I don't think it was a week before they had it made. They gave me some but warned me not to drink too much. It was powerful stuff.

We had two young Italian boys that we kind of adopted. They had been doing forced labor for the Nazis. Oh were they glad to be with us. They were so friendly. They would do anything for us, always wanting to help. We made sure they

Jack Kraszewski poses with an American jeep while in Europe. (Jack Kraszewski collection)

put all their weight back on before they left. I don't know where they were sent, maybe the Army sent them home.

The Germans didn't want to talk to us too much, especially the girls. They would be driving their cattle and I would try talking to them, but they would turn the other way. They must have been told to not fraternize with the Americans.

The best job I had was as a chaplain's assistant. He had his own jeep and when he was done with whatever he had to do, it was all mine. I traveled all over the place. Went into some of those towns that were just piles of bricks and rock, everything was destroyed. I don't know why I didn't take a camera with me. Looking back on it, those would have been some pretty interesting pictures of what happened over there.

When I came home I saw the Statue of Liberty. I hadn't seen it on the way over. I got

Jack Kraszewski collection

a pretty big lump in my throat knowing I had made it back.

When I got to Pulaski I got off the bus and walked the rest of the way home. It was about 2:00 in the morning. The door was unlocked so I went in. I heard my dad from upstairs say, "Who's there?" I said, "It's me." So they got up. That was it. That was my homecoming. I was back at my old job at the cheese factory a few weeks later.

About twenty years after the war we had a reunion. Oh, it was so good to see those guys again. As I said, we were like brothers. We never talked about the war. We talked about the times we had together. Those were good memories.

We all said the same thing, we wouldn't do it again if you paid us a million dollars, but it was worth a million dollars to go through that experience with those guys.

BOB PLUMMER

B-24 Engineer/
Gunner
13th Air Corps
US Army
World War II

If there was one branch of the United States Armed Forces that used style and fashion as a recruiting tool during WWII it was the Army Air Corps. Recruiting posters showed dashing pilots with neatly trimmed mustaches, scarves, and stylish leather flying jackets leading the way while raining death and destruction from the air.

But what the posters didn't show was that for every pilot and copilot, there were at least eight guys in the bowels of the mighty bombers in cramped, uncomfortable, oftentimes
near-freezing conditions who played extremely vital roles in every mission over flak-filled enemy territory.

I was only seventeen years old when I graduated from Fond du Lac (Wisconsin) High School in 1943. I had to wait until July 10th to sign up in the Air Corps. I was interested in any aspect of it really, either pilot training or mechanical.

The schooling was quite extensive. They sent us to an aircraft mechanics school in Biloxi, Mississippi, then up to Ypsilanti, Michigan, to see the production of the B-24 bombers. That was really something to see. They had 4,000 people working there and were rolling out one plane per hour. What was interesting is that many of the test pilots were women. I hadn't known that at the time. I don't think many people did.

Then we went to gunnery school in Texas. At this point, my goal was to be a flight engineer on the B-24.

The last two training spots were Lincoln, Nebraska, and Boise, Idaho. This is where you were assigned to a crew and started flying practice missions. One day we would theoretically bomb Walla Walla, Washington, or Salinas, California. Unfortunately, quite a few planes went down on those missions. Whether it was from inexperience on the part of the crews or mechanical issues, no one ever really knew. Personally, I think many of them may have been caused during the fuel-transfer process. If you have someone inexperienced and does it wrong or forgets how to do it the plane simply runs out of fuel and crashes. Chances are, there was still gas in the auxiliary tanks but it wasn't transferred. You wouldn't think something like that could happen, but it did. I was told there were more people killed in the Army Air Corps than all other branches combined. If something catastrophic happened, you would lose ten guys at a time. In fact, that very thing happened to one of the B-17s. I was good friends with the pilot. His plane was sitting at the end of the runway when another plane came in and landed right on top of him. Twenty guys were killed in an instant.

The idea was to get the crews comfortable with the plane and their assigned jobs and then fly that plane overseas. Well, just before we were set to leave, they took our plane away from us because our radar crew was transferred to another plane. So now, instead of flying, we had to take a troopship all the way to the Philippines. That was pretty gruesome, thirty days with over 5,000 men on board. That was no pleasure cruise. You would be stuck down in the bowels of the ship where it was blazing hot and smelled horrific. We couldn't wait to get off.

We docked at Manila Bay, it was about the size of Lake Winnebago. There were so many sunken ships there that that's what you tied up to.

There was still fighting going on around the outskirts of the city, so one night we decided to sneak over and see what was going on. We went a little further than we should have. We encountered a Japanese officer with a pistol in his hand. We just froze. One of our guys shot him. We lost all interest in doing any more exploring right then and there.

In June of 1945, they flew us down to Morotai Island in Indonesia. The Australian Army had control of the island, but Japanese troops, who were starving in the hills, would come down to steal food. There were also Nepalese, Gurkha troops with the Australians. They would go out at night looking for Japanese troops and if they found them, would cut their throats. We had to wear special markings to let them know we were friendly. The Aussies said those guys would cut your throat so fast and so clean you wouldn't even know what hit you.

We started flying bombing missions to Formosa. They would last anywhere from twelve to sixteen hours; over water the entire time. Fortunately, the Japanese were running out of fighter planes and pilots. We encountered very few, although the ones we did face were absolutely fearless. They would come right at you. They also had extremely accurate anti-aircraft fire. So the less time you spent over land, the better.

There wasn't really a good place to go down. We did have eight-man inflatable rafts and some emergency kits, things like that. A lot of the islands were uninhabitable. There were some crews that went out on missions and just disappeared. They just vanished; no idea where they went down or what happened to them.

Some of the guys carried what we called a "passport to China." It was an American flag with instructions on how to be compensated for rescuing Americans. Each one had a code on it that could be traced. You pretty much had to sign your life away to get one. I've heard that there were guys who were shot down, picked up by submarines, and then gave the flag to someone on the sub as a thank you. I later heard the FBI would try to find who had the flag. That's how seriously they took those things.

We did missions to bomb the naval aircraft bases in Formosa. We also flew missions to Borneo, where the Japanese had big oil refineries. We were told that if we went down there the locals would try to get to us right away and take care of us. One of our planes did go down and one of the only survivors made it back to our base. I had a talk with him in the mess hall. He had gone a little batty. He said there were headhunters on the island and the Japanese would pay them for American heads. Well, due to the Australian missionaries being there before, the natives realized that the Japanese were the bad guys and the Aussies and Americans the good guys. Some of our guys were taken care of by these natives. He said the locals would go out at night and come back with Japanese heads in a sack and give them as gifts. He said one of them came back with a head one day and when he took it out, it was an American. He said, "No, No this is an American!" The native said, "He pom-pom my Mary." Mary is the name they gave their wives from the lessons of the missionaries....he had caught him in bed with his wife.

We had some interesting times. We flew a different plane almost every time we went up. Part of my job was transferring fuel. We had tanks in the wings. They all went into a manifold where I could direct fuel flow. I was the busiest guy on the crew. On one mission we used about two-thirds of our fuel on the way to the target. On the return flight we were past our alternate landing field and realized that although we might not run out, we were going to be very close. I wasn't working the pumps that day. The pilot had been transferring it himself. Half an hour from our base the gauges showed no fuel at all. The commander ordered us to fly over the base, make a big circle, and come in one at a time. I said, "We don't have enough fuel to even do that!" We always

Bob Plummer (far right, front row) poses with a B-24 crew in the Pacific Theater, World War II. (Bob Plummer collection)

carried a flare gun to signal that you were under duress. There was a hole in the wall of the plane with a jar lid you could screw off. I told our radioman, "Open that hatch and fire that gun!"

By this time we were in a landing pattern. We started going into the crosswind to begin our approach and we lost our first engine. We lost another one heading into our final approach, and then just as we were about to land we lost our third. We landed but didn't even have enough fuel to taxi in. A tractor had to come out and tow us. That last engine would have conked out in a minute or so. It's amazing we didn't crash land.

Ditching in the ocean was our biggest scare. The B-24 was not a good plane to ditch. It was too boxy. The bomb bay doors were the weakest spot on the plane. If you didn't land perfectly, those doors would buckle, the plane would come to a violent stop and lurch nose-first into the water.

We didn't have consistent crews. You would be working with different guys on a regular basis. On one flight I was sitting in my normal spot right behind the pilot and copilot. I transferred all my fuel to the spare set of tanks that were feeding all four engines. I had gone a long time without sleep. I told them I was going to even out the fuel and level off our load. Then I was going to take a nap. I told them how long it was going to take for the fuel to transfer and strictly told them to not let me sleep past that time. When I woke up, it was total silence. All four engines were out. They forgot to wake me. That scared the hell out of me. They were on autopilot so they were probably both asleep themselves. We had dropped below 10,000 feet. It was the quiet that woke me up. Luckily the blades were windmilling and we got the engines to restart. That episode shook me up. I always thank God, I got out of that one.

We carried twelve, 500-pound bombs. If we took fire from anti-aircraft units we would mark out an area about the size of a football field and drop clusters of twenty-pound frags (fragmentation bombs.) Honestly, we were not very accurate with our bombs. Nowadays you can take one fighter and do the job of an entire squadron; they hit anything they aim at.

When we came in for an approach on a target I had several jobs. We carried about five boxes of aluminum foil. My job was to drop those to clutter up the screens of the Japanese radar so they couldn't read our altitude.

I was also the top turret gunner. I only fired the gun one time. A Japanese fighter was coming in, but we put out so much firepower that he turned and got out of there. Another time I was climbing out of the upper turret and I felt something hit my head. I looked down in my lap and here was a little piece of flak. It had busted through the Plexiglas. I kept that in my pocket for years. The pilot wanted to put me in for a Purple Heart, but I said, "Nah." Actually, I was supposed to be wearing a helmet and wasn't. They got the bleeding stopped. I was fine.

About every other mission I was also squadron photographer. I enjoyed that very much. We would open the hatch as soon as the bombs were away and I would start clicking. I still have a collection of photos that I took.

We had an outdoor theatre at the bottom of a hill. They had cut the trees down and set up lights, kind of a nice set up to show movies. One night the base commander ordered the movie stopped. He got up and explained that an atomic bomb had been dropped over Japan and had evaporated a city. He tried to explain a little bit about it. We thought, *Okay fine, that's one less city to worry about.*

The second bomb was very good news too. The end was within sight. Our missions now were to fly to Russia, over the line into Manchuria, and provide ground support for the Russian troops. I almost feel like the main thing we did was help the Russians put a lot of people behind the Iron Curtain.

Three days after the armistice was signed, our assignment was to fly to an island and pick up some troops so they could catch a ship heading for home. It was September 5th, 1945. A
pitch-black, drizzly early morning. We were breaking in a new pilot. I was kneeling between the pilot and the copilot, which I did on every

takeoff, calling out airspeed, watching instruments; my usual duties. For some reason, the plane started veering to the left of the runway. We ran too close to the edge and blew a tire; the landing gear collapsed and the prop came flying into the cabin. The navigator and I sat so close to each other that my left foot was touching his right foot. His name was Hank. He was a great guy, just the kind of guy that everyone liked.

The prop missed me by about a foot and hit him. It took off his arm and crushed his skull. Props came off of two more engines. I remember the sound of the engines screaming as I tried getting out of the plane, it sounded like a thousand chainsaws. The plane was breaking apart, leaving a gap just wide enough to crawl through. The pilot and copilot got out. The radio operator, Sam, didn't come out with us. I turned around to see if he was coming, but the plane burst into flames.

I yelled to the pilot and copilot, "Where in the hell is Sam!" We hear a scream coming from the plane and one of the guys tries running back in. I grab him around the ankles to try and stop him. Then he goes, "Look...look!" It was Sam. He was climbing out of the plane with his clothes on fire. We grabbed him and got the flames out. A Navy jeep raced out to us. The copilot miraculously wasn't injured. The pilot had a hole in his leg. We got everyone, including Sam, on the jeep.

Sam was screaming in pain. I went to the hospital with him. No doctors were there yet, I told the corpsman, "Give him some morphine, please!" He said, "I can't, the cabinet is locked up." I said, "Give me an ax; I'll get into it!" About that time a Navy doctor comes in. He said, "Everything is going to be all right. We're going to get your friend some morphine and take care of him. Everything is going to be okay." Sam kept saying, "Hit me! Hit me, Bob! Knock me out! Please knock me out!"

I started to leave and the doctor said, "Where are you going?" I said, "I'm going to see what happened to my friend Hank." He said, "You're not going anywhere," and pointed to a mirror. I thought at first that I was looking out a window and there was this strange person looking back at me all covered with blood and mud and everything. It didn't look like a human being at all. He gave me two shots of morphine to knock me out.

I lost a full day. I guess it was around 10:00 the following morning that I woke up. I still wanted to go back to the plane, but they said it had all been cleared out. There was nothing to see.

I felt so sorry for Hank, and for his parents. To know that he survived the war and still wasn't coming home. He was a Polish kid from Hamtramck, Michigan. I think he was the only guy on the crew that I never heard swear. He had a sister that used to write to him all the time.

The parents suffered mental health issues over the years because of it. I know they were very bitter. They needed someone to blame. I'm sure they had been thinking how wonderful it was that the war was over and their son would be coming home.

I didn't talk to them until well into the 1950s. I had a layover in Detroit and I called his sister. I wanted to explain how it happened. I told her he never knew what hit him, which was true. This was ten years after it happened, but it didn't help. It was almost like it happened yesterday for her.

After that crash, I lost all desire to ever get into a plane again, but I took a job that involved lots of traveling. One time I was stranded in Grand Rapids, Michigan, and the only transportation was a North Central Airlines flight. I started flying again, but I was a white-knuckled flyer for about a year.

In 1969 I faced my biggest fear. I got my pilot's license and bought a Cessna. I've flown ever since.

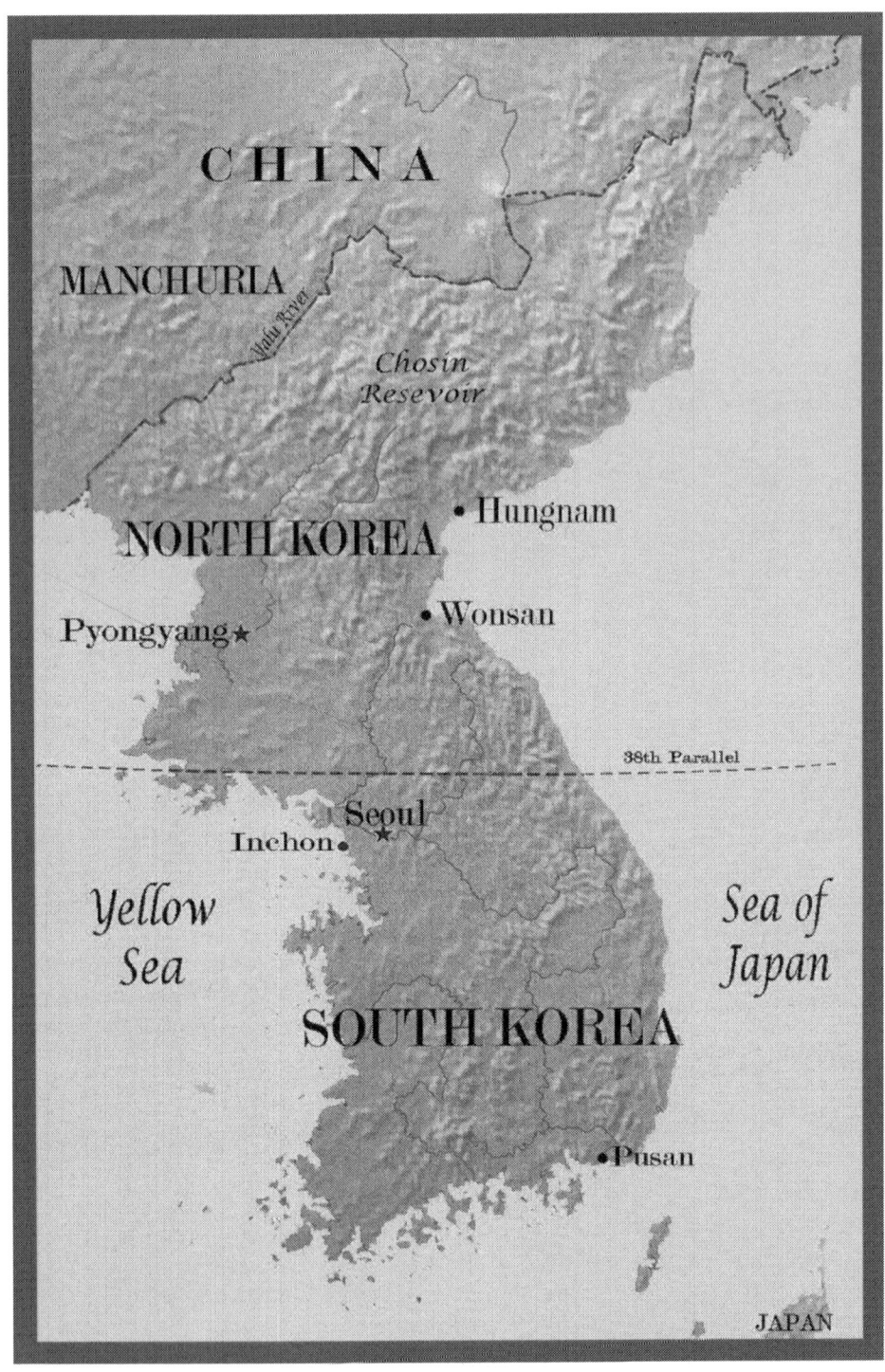

KOREAN WAR

1950 - 1953

After seeing the results of just two atomic bombs dropped on mainland Japan in August of 1945, you have to assume that when US military strategists began sketching future defense plans, they began with an eye towards the sky.

With such incredible firepower being delivered in one swift blow and nary a worry about casualties of their own, perhaps the days of slogging through ground battles, with high casualties and a supply train of everything from bullets to beans, was no longer going to be the standard by which the US went to war.

Certainly, US ground forces would still have a presence around the world. Missile bases (especially those in European countries that rubbed shoulders with Soviet Bloc counterparts) had to stay on constant alert. Tank battalions in Germany were vigilant and trained to respond with lethal force at the first sign of Soviet T-34 tanks rumbling through the Bavarian countryside. In Japan, soldiers, sailors, and Marines kept watch over the "defensive perimeter of the Pacific." In talking with many military members who were stationed there, duty, and in fact, life in general, was really quite comfortable.

The idea that a country would take on one of America's allies in a ground war seemed as outdated, remote, and had as much chance of succeeding as the tragic WWI horseback cavalry charges against twentieth-century machine guns.

With the formation of an autonomous United States Air Force in 1947 and the successful detonation of an atomic bomb by the Soviet Union in 1949, an arms race had begun. Aeronautical designers worked around the clock trying to stay in the lead by developing aircraft that flew higher, faster, more stealthily, and delivered more destruction with fewer bombs than ever before.

American soldiers march over a mountain during the Korean War.

One would think that just the sight of eight-engine B-52s lumbering down runways with payloads that could wipe out millions would be enough to discourage even the most upstart and aggressive enemy.

In some ways, the US military may have been banking on that very thought.

If a hostile country did get the notion to start a cross-border skirmish, there was always the sixty-member United Nations to call on and help get the situation under control.

In the years immediately following WWII, huge numbers of deployed military personnel clamored to shed their uniforms and return to civilian life as soon as possible. Their job was done. They had, in their minds, saved the world and it was time to enjoy the fruits of their efforts. Theirs was not a quiet request. Loud demands were made to local congressmen to do their part in bringing the boys home. At foreign bases, massive protests sprung up demanding a change in the military's plodding "points system" which charted one's homeward course.

Perhaps for the first time in US military history, military brass capitulated to the demands of those in uniform. A massive demobilization program called Operation Magic Carpet was an incredible success. In the summer of 1945, the US military had over twelve million men and women in uniform. Less than two years later; in June of 1947, that number was slightly more than 1.5 million, a drop of nearly ninety percent.

Between 1945 and 1950, US military numbers held steady at around 1.5 million. It was also during this time that many budgets were slashed. Much of the equipment, weapons, and ammunition that helped defeat the Nazis and the Imperial Japanese, were put in mothballs. Young, inexperienced draftees, filled the ranks of departed, experienced, veterans. This military was a shell of the one which had defeated two incredibly large, vicious foes just five years before.

Following World War II, both the Soviet Union and America stepped into Korea to lend a hand in ridding the country of the oppressive Japanese invaders who had taken residence in 1910.

The Soviets took over north of what was simply an agreed-upon line on a map marked as the 38th parallel. From day one they showed no inclination of only "lending a helping hand" and heading home. Communism was now going to be the way of life in North Korea.

The Americans worked south of the 38th parallel and, with a wary eye on their former comrades to the north, also lent a military presence in the form of a small contingent of troops and roughly 500 military advisors.

It was on June 25, 1950, that an estimated 90,000 Soviet-trained North Korean troops crossed over that map line and unleashed massive attacks. Within four days, the capital city of Seoul was in Communist hands.

The invaders were relentless as they rampaged throughout the southern peninsula. Their stated goal was to "unify" the country. Their modus operandi was the wanton slaughter of anyone who resisted, or in the case of thousands of innocent civilians, even those who did not.

The South Korean Army, loosely numbered at around 65,000, had neither tanks, artillery, nor air power to slow the horde. Soviet tanks, the same model which proved so effective against the Nazis, rampaged at will throughout the country. It was a complete rout.

For America, the unthinkable had just occurred. An aggressor had invaded a US ally and - nuclear threat be damned - had goaded the US into a ground war. The timing could not have been worse. In the words of Lt. General Matthew Ridgeway, "We were in a state of shameful unreadiness."

For those with boots on the ground in this alternating sweltering/freezing, inhospitable, foreign land, it would be a long, miserable, frustrating, and bloody three years. Over 33,000 American troops who faced combat on Korean soil during that span would never again see their homeland. Over 100,000 others would earn a Purple Heart. The military was not prepared and, for the most part, the folks back home were not interested. Yet this war, forever burdened with the yoke of a "police action," moved forward.

HUBERT ROBENHORST

99th Field Artillery
1st Cavalry Division
US Army
Korean War

It's a mistake to assume that being assigned to an artillery unit assures safe passage in a war zone. In reality, there is no more enticing target for the enemy than crew members of artillery pieces that could wipe out huge numbers of troops from miles away.
From his very first moments in Korea, a young artilleryman from Suring, Wisconsin, discovered just how fanatical this enemy would be.

I was only seventeen years old when I joined the Army in 1947. I was gung ho to be a paratrooper. We trained with the 101st Airborne Division at Fort Breckenridge, Kentucky. They had us jumping off of towers and stuff like that. I loved every minute of it, but I never got to jump out of a plane. They switched us over to an artillery unit. Just like that. And there wasn't a damn thing you could do about it. They shipped us to Japan and just like that, we were artillerymen with the 105mm howitzer.

I don't remember any big announcement or anything when they said we were going to Korea. It was just a hassle getting everything moved. I mean, loading up all these artillery pieces and shells and stuff, that's a major project.

We landed there in July of 1950. It was kind of a bad deal from the beginning. We hooked up our equipment and everything and headed toward the front lines. We bivouacked in a river bed. Well, around two in the morning, all hell let loose. The North Koreans were set up on the side of a hill and started firing. We were like fish in a barrel. They blew us apart with mortars. It lasted about three hours. We fought back with the three artillery pieces that were still active. We finally chased them out of there. When daylight hit we saw that we had lost twenty-five to thirty guys out of the sixty who landed. Arms and legs were lying all around. Half of our equipment and trucks were just junk. That was our very first day in Korea. We had a couple of guys who went wacky. They couldn't take it. I don't blame them. What the hell, these were close friends who had lived together in Japan for a year and a half. What a terrible, terrible night. I still have nightmares about that.

I've always believed that we had been set up. I had been around artillery long enough to know how it works. You usually fire at least one round to get range; they didn't do that. The fire came in right on target from the very first round. They somehow knew exactly where we were going to be set up. I found out later there were a lot of spies. You certainly couldn't tell the difference between a North Korean or a South Korean. I still think somebody passed information along to the North Koreans on that hill.

Hubert Robenhorst collection

We moved out with what we had left and met up with the 2nd Marine Division at the Han River. They had North Korean bodies piled up around them, but when they left they had three truckloads of dead Marines stacked like cordwood in the back of their trucks too. It was a damn bloody fight for both sides. We were wondering what in the hell we were getting into.

We had to wait until all the Marines got out of there. There was only one bridge that they could cross so we had machine guns and everything covering them. We were there for about two weeks and just about starved to death. We had lost everything in that ambush the first night. They finally dropped some food and ammo to us. It's a good thing the North Koreans didn't know how low we were on ammo; they could have run right over us. We would fire a couple of shots every day just to let them know we were still there, but we didn't have much to waste.

Our second major battle wasn't much better. We were going across a field with one tank in the lead. They had an ambush set up. They blew up the tank and then came swarming out from an oat field. We were sitting ducks. The only thing I had was a .45 pistol. We had to run like hell. We didn't have anything to fight back with. I took my entire gun crew and we headed out to a river. There was another bunch of guys crossing. They had all their clothes on. This was November 2nd, 1950. I told my guys to take their clothes off right down to their shorts. As bad as it was crossing like that, at least we had dry clothes to put on when we got to the other side. We made it out that time. The other guys were freezing to death in their wet clothes.

You always wanted to have infantry around you but that wasn't always the case. There was one time that the infantry was on the ships offshore and we got cornered. When we got attacked all we had behind us was water. We had to fight day and night to hang on. That's where I got a piece of our own shrapnel in my knee. Everybody says, "Why didn't you get a Purple Heart?" I tell them, "Because there wasn't a medic around to do anything." I just powdered it with sulfa and wrapped it up and that was it. The reason I think it might have been our shrapnel is that they were so close to us that we had to elevate the barrels of our artillery pieces as close to ninety degrees as possible so the shells would land right around us. I'm almost positive the shrapnel was from one of the shells we fired.

They came after us in one big wave. I remember our guy on the radio calling for some help and he was told they couldn't send help, but for us to fix bayonets. We were an artillery unit on our own. We didn't have any rifles to put bayonets on! All we had were some carbines and sidearms. I would like to know who in the hell came up with that brilliant idea.

You never really relaxed over there. I don't care how tired you were, you couldn't let your guard down. We kept someone on the gun twenty-four hours a day. There were times when you would hear of someone getting their throats slashed. Guys would be buried in their sleeping bags because it was so damned cold, but then they were helpless if somebody attacked them. I started sleeping with my arms crossed in front of my neck. I still sleep that way.

I don't remember how it happened exactly, but I became a forward observer. Well, that was a little slice of hell and back, I'll tell ya.

We wouldn't go out any further than seven miles because with the 105s that was the range. A couple of times we had to call in airstrikes with the F-80s. They always sent a young officer along to call them in. I went through so many lieutenants . . . three of them got killed. I still think it was because of that stupid bar on their helmets. It seemed like every time they raised their heads a bullet would come their way. It was too easy of a target. One time the captain said to me, "I'm putting you in command out there, I'm making you a lieutenant." I said, "The hell you are. You're not putting that bar on me, not after what I've seen happen to the other guys."

There were four of us that would go out on those missions. In the daytime, we would hide. At night we went out and hunted, as we called it. Just sort of scout around and see where the action was. You learn a few things when you do that. A lot of people don't know this, but when it's dark, if you shut your eyes tight for a while and then open them, you would be surprised how good you can see in the dark.

We took prisoners when we could. We couldn't just shoot them. But believe me, the Chinese and the North Koreans didn't feel that way. The worst thing I ever saw was one day when we came down off a hill after a fight and there were a couple of US Army trucks smoking. The trucks had been loaded with wounded soldiers. They were all shot. Some of the guys were tied to the side of the truck and burned alive. OK shooting guys in war, that happens, but torturing guys that way? What makes a person do that? Can you imagine what was going through those poor guys' minds?

One of my interpreters was also my radio operator. He got shot through the chest by a sniper. It blew the radio right off his back. We went to this little village, just sort of snooped around to see if there was any sign of enemy activity. We came upon this Korean woman in her twenties. I tried to speak a little bit of Korean to her. She said, "That's all right, I can speak English." So I explained to her that my interpreter had been shot and asked if there was someone we could use. She said she would do it. So she was our new interpreter in the field. Once a week we had to go back to headquarters, give reports, and get a hot meal. I thought, *What the hell am I going to do with her at headquarters?* So she put her hair up, we put a helmet on her and tried to pass her through. Well, we were standing in the chow line and some guys started screwing around and they bumped into her. She got knocked down and her helmet flew off . . . oh geez. It wasn't two minutes later that I was standing in front of the captain in his tent. I explained the situation and he said. "By right, I could court-martial you, because you didn't ask permission to use her."

He said, "I can't let her go back up with you." They kept her there. I found out later she went all the way to battalion headquarters and worked as an interpreter. So she ended up with a good job.

There were a lot of ways to get killed over there. When you found a dead soldier, or even if you went back to get some equipment that you had left behind, you always had to be careful because they used to booby trap everything they could. Even our dead bodies, you had to be really careful when you turned them over. On our jeeps, we had to put a piece of angle iron with a hook on top because they would string wire across the road to try and take your head off.

When we called in airstrikes, they would go right over the top of us first to see where we were, then make a pass around and go hit the target. I remember one time when they were coming in and I saw that bomb come out of the plane. I'll tell you, I think I stuck my head two feet into the ground. I thought I had screwed up and they were dropping them on us, but it went right over the top of us and into the hillside where the North Koreans were.

I think about things a lot. I wonder how many people I killed by calling in airstrikes. There were times when we would drop leaflets in an area we were going to bomb, warning the civilians to get out before we leveled it. There was another time when the North Koreans were dug in on a mountain and I called for the planes. They came in and dropped napalm on them. Can you imagine . . . think of that. They get burned up. It's what you had to do. I mean it really was you or them, but it's still something that makes you think long and hard after the war is over. It's no wonder people who have been in wars go goofy sometimes.

Hubert Robenhorst (3rd from left) poses with his artillery team. (Hubert Robenhorst collection)

The things you try to think about, more than anything else, are the times you can laugh about. We were set up on a river bed and British troops were up on the hill in a big barn. Me and two other guys were on an outpost right below and decided we should go check out what was going on in the barn. You know, for security reasons. So we go up there and have a few drinks with the Brits. You got to remember, we were living on K-rations and they had a room full of hams. I mean just the most delicious-looking food hanging from the rafters. I said, "When we leave here, grab everything you possibly can and take off!"

We were just about back to our outpost when we saw the captain walking up to us. He said, "I knew something was going on!" He chewed us out pretty good. He said, "I could have every one of you court-martialed for leaving your post, and besides, I could smell you guys coming a mile away with all those hams you're trying to hide." We had to turn them all over to our cooks. That's the only thing that saved our hides.

I was in Korea for 361 days and spent Christmas of 1950 there. We were told they had a spot all cleared out for a big Christmas dinner. They had turkey and everything set up. Tanks and minesweepers had cleared the area. Well, as it turned out, they missed a few. We'd be eating dinner and you would hear an explosion. Somebody who was on his way in would go flying in the air. . .boy oh boy.

When I got home I realized that people didn't pay that much attention to the war. People were like, "Where've you been?" You would tell them, "Korea," and that was it. They didn't want to hear anything about it. That was a common thing. They had no idea how rough of a road it was.

I would like to meet the first guy who called it a "police action." I still dream about it. I still think about friends I lost. One of the guys killed, that hit me the hardest, happened in Milwaukee. He went through all that hell over there and went home a little ahead of me. I said, "Give me your address. When I get home I will stop by. We can have a good time and not worry about getting shot at." So, not long after I got back, I drove down to Milwaukee to see him. I rang the bell; his sister answered and said, "I'm sorry to tell you this, but right after he got home he stepped off a streetcar and got hit by a car, he was killed."

That's another one you just try to put in a box and move on. I think guys from wars have to do that a lot.

Hubert Robenhorst (far left) and his team during the Korean War.
(Hubert Robenhorst collection)

EDWIN WILBER

8th Regiment
1st Cavalry Division
US Army
Korean War

Volumes could be written on experiences endured and honors bestowed on the Native American Veterans of Wisconsin. It's a long legacy, it's a proud legacy, and it's one into which Edwin Wilber etched his name by leading the way through some of the toughest mountain battles of the Korean War.

When I got my draft notice in November of 1950, I already had three months of combat under my belt in Korea. I asked my commanding officer if I could go back to the Shawano County courthouse and straighten it out.

I didn't mind being in the Army. I signed up in 1950 and was actually kind of anxious to go in. My dad, my uncles, cousins; seems like everybody was in at one time or another. You have that kind of patriotism when you're young. We believed in the Pledge of Allegiance and everything. We were proud to wear the uniform. One time a representative presented a citation on Memorial Day to recognize how many people from Keshena and the reservation fought in the wars. He said that for its size, we had more people fight in WWII than anyplace in the United States.

I landed in Korea on Christmas Day 1950. The first thing you thought of was that it was damned cold and we were a long way from home. The first time I got hit was January 25th, 1951. A grenade came tumbling down the hill and guys were yelling, "Grenade! Grenade!" I

Edwin Wilber (right) sets up a defensive position after capturing a hill in Korea. (Edwin Wilber collection)

ducked away but still got hit in the back of the neck. The metal is still in there. They sent me to an aid station near Pusan for twelve days. It was like being on vacation. It was run by Swedish medical people. They gave me a real bed. I was okay with staying there for the rest of the war. When I was going to leave, I noticed all the supplies stacked in a tent. The sergeant turned his back on me and I stuffed all the socks and gloves I could get my hands on in my pack. I could barely close it. When I got back to my squad I dumped it all out and said, "Here you go fellas, help yourself."

We spent all of our time patrolling in the mountains. Only headquarters and staff were on flat ground. Somebody decided they should make the Indian the point scout. That was the most dangerous spot. I didn't ask to be there.

On one patrol we walked up to a North Korean outpost. I don't know why the medic was right up next to me, but they sprayed him with a machine gun. I got down and the bullets were kicking up dirt right in front of my face. I got up, I didn't pay any attention if they were still firing or not. I picked up our medic and put him over my shoulder. He weighed over 200 pounds and I was about 160. This little Korean guy that we adopted into our unit got up to help me, but they pinned him down. He couldn't come over to help me. Later on, I thought about how all the big guys - the squad leaders, the sergeants - all ran away and left me there. I'm not trying to brag or anything, but it doesn't matter how important someone thinks they are because of rank. It doesn't mean a thing about how they're going to act when you come under fire.

Once I got him off the hill, me and another guy slipped off our field jackets and got some poles to make a stretcher. Can you believe the other guys wouldn't even lift a finger to cut down poles with their machetes to help out? And this was the medic who was wounded - a guy who would risk his life to help any one of them!

We went up to another unit's outpost with the medic. When you came up to our lines you had to yell to let them know you were coming in. So I hollered, "Send somebody down to help. Our medic's been hit!" Finally, they came down with a tank. Their officer said to our lieutenant, "Great job." He hadn't done a thing, not a damn thing. I told him, "You want to take the credit for saving him, go ahead."

Sometimes we would go on night patrols. Those were always spooky. You don't have any say in the matter. It was just, "Wilber, saddle up your squad." Sometimes we would come upon North Koreans who had been killed by our artillery or planes. You would see them lying there and think, *My God, they're just kids ... fifteen or sixteen years old!*

One of the main things the veterans had to do was to keep new officers from getting us killed. One time we were in our foxholes on a hill and a new lieutenant came to my hole. I said, "Sir, I saw a light in that area over there last night." He says, "Point it out to me on the map." So I did and he goes, "OK, well we are right here." And I go, "No, no sir, we are over here!" I had to show him exactly where we were and exactly where they were. If you didn't double-check, they could call artillery on your own position. The next day a Piper Cub flew over, we called them mosquitos, they were looking for that area. Pretty soon the jets came in and raised hell.

The foxholes were a lot smaller than they looked in movies. We just made them big enough for two men, as small a target as possible. We would fill our helmets with snow, try to melt it with a little flame, and then put instant coffee in there. It was never hot, but you would do anything to try to feel a little bit of warmth.

My sergeant and I hated each other. One time one of the guys who was always raising hell got into another fight. I was tired of bailing him out so I grabbed him. The sergeant came up, grabbed me from behind, and spun me around. I swung and he went down. He went kind of crazy and started yelling about having me court-martialed. I knew he would try.

An officer came up to investigate. I explained that someone grabbed me from behind and I didn't know who it was. So I swung but missed and he went down anyway. The officer talked to other guys in the squad and they backed me up; so he said forget about it. I knew that the sergeant would try to get back at me the first chance he had. Now, here's the funny part. He got transferred to another unit. One night he was on guard duty and they caught him sleeping. They busted him down and sent him back to the line and put him in my squad. I was assistant squad leader so now he was under me. Wow, did he suck up to me like you wouldn't believe!

One day we got orders to clear out some bunkers and trenches. I started tossing grenades at the bunkers. I got to about six or eight feet of this one bunker and they started throwing grenades back. It was okay being that close because their grenades were going over me. My guys were tossing me grenades and I kept tossing them where I thought the Koreans were hiding. I had fired some rounds already; it was an eight-shot clip and I had probably fired five rounds. What I did then was to jump in the trench. If I could have put my rifle down, I could have grabbed them and thrown them out of there, they were that small. I picked up one of their burp guns and killed everyone in the trench. It wasn't a lot different than some of the other days we attacked their lines, but this time somebody important must have seen it because I ended up getting a Bronze Star.

CITATION: *PFC Wilber, assistant squad leader was advancing up the rugged slopes of the objective. When the rest of his squad was immobilized by a heavy concentration of fire PFC Wilber exhibited exceptional courage, moved out to silence the hostile emplacement which was obstructing the advance, crawling to within grenade range of an enemy bunker, he silenced it with two accurately thrown grenades, then working his way to a connecting trench, PFC Wilber entered a second hostile position and killed its occupants with a Chinese automatic weapon.*

One day they just told us the enemy was up in the hills and we had to go clear them out. One company went up first and got the hell kicked out of them. Then we went up, leapfrogging through them. We were always grabbing grenades and extra ammo from our dead guys. I went to take a bandolier of ammo off one guy laying there and he woke up - scared the hell out of me. I go, "Hey, this guy is still alive over here!" I took his grenades anyway. I needed every damn one I could get my hands on. There were a lot of grenades being thrown and a lot of gunfire on our flank. About halfway up, the radioman came up to me and said, "You're supposed to call in artillery." I had never called artillery before.

I said, "Where are the sergeants?" He said, "Gone." I said, "Where in the hell are they gone to? Dead? Wounded? What?" He didn't say anything, just handed me the phone. So we took out the map and figured out where we were. We called in the coordinates, dropped back about twenty yards, and watched the rounds hit above us. They peppered the hell out of that hill and we headed up again. The North Koreans that were left up there started throwing grenades at us.

Years later I visited one of the guys who was going up that hill with me. He was an Indian too, from Oklahoma. He said, "Do you remember the day we were throwing their grenades back? Holy cripes what a dumb thing to do!" But I said, "What else could we do? You just reached down and picked them up and threw them back."

Finally one came in that I didn't see. It landed right behind me and blew up into my legs. I was blown over backward and landed on another grenade. My buddy grabbed me and dragged me down out of the way. They put me on a stretcher and four guys started carrying me out. A bullet came flying right over me and hit one of the guys in the hip,

Edwin Wilber sits in a wheelchair after being wounded in Korea. (Edwin Wilber collection)

he went down and so did I. I laid there for a hell of a long time before somebody came and grabbed me by the back of my neck and got me out of there. The North Koreans on that hill kept trying to finish me off. One of my guys later said they were bringing guys down and putting them in one of three lines: guys who weren't hurt too bad, guys who were hurt real bad, and dead guys. We went up with 120 men, I believe only around thirty didn't get wounded or killed.

They put me in one of those little capsules on a helicopter. They had given me some morphine; it was really hurting. When I got to the MASH unit they put me on a cot and I waited my turn. They were operating on different guys; a lot of wounded were coming in. I just kept waiting and waiting and they just kept bringing in more guys. The guys who were hurt the most were taken care of first. Boy, I was hungry too. I told the nurse, "I'm so hungry, can I get something to eat?" She said, "No, because you're going to be operated on soon." But a little while later she came back with half of a candy bar. Did that ever taste good! It was over a day before they operated on me, that's how many guys they had come in hurt worse than me.

I had lost so much blood that I couldn't even raise myself up off the stretcher. Then they set me up with an IV and I just watched that blood going in me. I thought that had to be a good sign, at least some was going in instead of it all going out. I didn't know it at the time, but either way, that was going to be my last day of fighting. The orders for me to rotate home had already been issued, but they hadn't told me yet. Maybe it's better that I didn't know.

One of my buddies told me later it was a damned good thing those grenades weren't very powerful. He said he saw my body get lifted up. He said I got hit by two grenades. I said, "That's what I kind of wondered. I couldn't figure out how I could have been so wounded above and below by one grenade." My arm was useless and my fibula was broken. I got hit on October 10th and released from the hospital in March. The funny thing is since I got wounded on the last day of my rotation, I didn't get out any sooner than I would have. This wasn't one of those "million dollar wounds."

You know, the night before we attacked that hill, we were waiting in our foxholes and getting mortared. There were these two other guys about 100 yards away. A shell landed by their hole and caved it in on them. They both cracked up. Before that even happened, I had been telling people to get one of them out of there. I thought he was half-nuts. We got them out of there and he's still screaming and yelling and mortars were still coming in. It made me mad as hell with the way he was carrying on. I gave him a good hard slap in the face and kicked him in the ass. I said, "Get the hell out of here before you cause more guys to get hit!" I never saw him again. Guys would crack up like that.

After the war one of the guys from my squad said, "Remember the night before that big battle when you sent our friend Charlie down to my foxhole? Did you ever know what happened to him?" I said, "No." He said, "He took a mortar round right in the chest, killed him right away." Charlie was the nicest guy in our squad. He was a really great friend of mine. I remember he had a really tender voice; he used to sing opera songs. Man, he was good. I remember one night when I was living in Keshena years later and got a phone call from another guy from my squad. He was crying on the phone. He said, "Wilber, remember Charlie, the great singer, the really great guy? Why did this have to happen to a guy like that? You're lucky you didn't see him, Wilber. I wish I hadn't. They blew his head off with that mortar. I still see it, I can't get it out of my mind."

A lot of times over the years you would think about things. Think of things that maybe you could have done better. One other thing I always think about is how our artillery would just pound those hills and the P-51 planes would bomb them and you would think there couldn't be a single thing alive. But you go up there and they fight back like hell.

Sometimes you laugh at things. We went on a reconnaissance patrol and got pinned down. We got out of there but realized we were missing a man. Everybody was like, "Where's Smitty? Has anybody seen Smitty? Did Smitty get hit?" The last thing in the world you wanted was to be taken prisoner, so we headed back. My squad is walking down the road when we look and here comes Smitty walking right toward us. We're like, "What the hell happened?" He said, "I don't know, I think I fainted or something and just woke up."

One time I was helping the medics with a guy who had his stomach ripped open from a fragment. When the medic put iodine on it the guy passed out from the pain. I thought he had died on us, but the medic said, "No, he will be okay." The problem was, the gash was so big he didn't have bandages big enough to hold everything in. He told me to take my poncho off. So we wrapped it around his stomach, taped him up with it, and sent him back. That's just stuff you did, you didn't even think about it.

I got two Purple Hearts and a Bronze Star. At least I've had a chance to look at them with my family. There's a lot of guys I was with who didn't make it out and those medals are the only thing their families have of them. They call the Korean War the forgotten war. Try telling that to the 33,000 families who lost someone there.

BILL KOCH

1st Battalion
7th Regiment
1st Marine Division
Korean War

If you study the history of the Korean War, one aspect is abundantly clear: he who held the high ground was king of the valley. Untold numbers of Allied, North Korean, and Communist Chinese troops fought and died trying to conquer and hold on to those most valuable pieces of property. A young Marine from the lakeshore region of Wisconsin experienced the sacrifice it took to claim one of those top spots first hand.

The Korean War got started just after I graduated from Washington High School in Two Rivers. I really didn't know what to do. I had broken up with my girlfriend who I had gone out with for two years. I didn't have anything going on. I was sort of lost. So I thought, *What the hell? I might as well enlist in the Marine Corps.* When I told my dad he said, "The Marines? Are you crazy?"

A lot of guys went to San Diego but I got sent to Parris Island, South Carolina. I got there in October of 1950. As soon as we pulled into the station, a little red-headed corporal put his foot on the railing and said, "Welcome boys, you are now cannon fodder." Normally they would have thirteen weeks of training but they needed guys in Korea so bad that they cut our training to eight weeks. It was pretty intense. I went in at 156 pounds; when I went home on leave a few months later I weighed 186. They put thirty pounds of muscle on me. I remember when my sister first saw me. She was like, "Oh my God, what did they do to you?"

It's funny but when my brother joined the Marines he went to boot camp in San Diego. I always gave him crap about that. I told him the only thing Hollywood Marines do is run on the beach for the movie cameras. The real Marines go to Parris Island. Although I have to admit, Parris Island isn't called "the hell hole of the South" for nothing.

As soon as we were done with all of our advanced training they shipped us right to Korea. This was May of '51. The only stop we made was Kobe, Japan. They said we had seven hours of liberty. Well, the first thing my buddies and I tried to do was get our money exchanged so we could buy some beer. When we got to the line, it was three-four blocks long. We said, "The hell with this, liberty will be over by the time we get our money." A little Japanese guy heard us. He said, "Follow me I can get it exchanged." So we followed him. Just block after block, now we're getting into a pretty seedy area. We get to a bar and go in and he says, "Wait here, I'll be right back with your money." So we waited and waited, finally, we went into the back room. The only people in there were sitting around smoking opium. He was gone. We were so mad; we wrecked that place, overturned the big heavy bar, did lots of things. Then we heard the police sirens heading our way so we ran out of there in a hurry. But now we're stuck. We only had a few hours to go before we head into war and we have no money. So off came the watches and anything else. We headed to a pawn shop and got some cash. We found a bar, had a good time and a few days later we were on the front lines in Korea.

We landed in Pusan and went to a staging area where you were assigned to a unit. I was sent to Charlie Company, 7th Regiment. They transported us up north and we started marching. We just marched day after day. Finally one of the guys asked the sergeant, "How far are we from the front lines?" The sergeant said, "Front lines? Hell, you're twenty miles in front of them."

Our first mission was called Operation Mousetrap. Really, our only job was to be used as bait. Our planners had figured out that there was only one way for the Chinese to attack us, and when they did, our other units would spring the trap.

I remember it being a very hard climb up the side of a mountain. A lot of the mountains we climbed were like that. You would get to what you thought was the top and there would be another one right behind it that you had to climb. We would sit there at night and listen for any sign that they were crawling up toward us. We had tin cans and everything strung in the wires, but you couldn't really sleep. Maybe that's why I still have sleep problems now, from that.

The trap worked perfectly, our guys slaughtered them. When we came down off the mountainside, bulldozers were just covering mounds of dead Chinese. But that didn't even make a dent in how many they had in the country.

After that, we went to a rest area for a few days and then were sent into another operation up north. Our objective was to take a hill that had a bunker on top and a Chinese trench below it.

We fought our way to the trench and were trying to figure out how to knock out the bunker. We started going one way in the trench and "POW," the first guy was shot in the head. So quick, we turned around and started going the other way, "POW!" Same thing, shot in the head. Now we didn't know what to do...which way to move. All of a sudden this guy comes out from on top of the hill, an American - no idea where he came from. I still remember he was wearing a T-shirt that was all ripped apart. He just stood there and started yelling at us, telling us we were a bunch of chicken-shits for not attacking the bunker. So I thought, *What the hell? The longer we sit in one spot, the more certain the Chinese would start dropping mortars on us, and if we go to either side we will be shot.* So, I went up with him. Everything happens so fast. You charge up a hill and the guys behind you could be getting shot but you don't know it. You're just trying to move as fast as you can while always keeping an eye out for a place to take cover. You have your objective, but there's always self-preservation in your mind too.

We got to the bunker and threw in some grenades, while the rest of the platoon charged straight ahead. We eventually overran the position.

When it was over, a lieutenant from a different unit came in and started setting up machine-gun emplacements. His name was Eddie LeBaron. He became a quarterback in the NFL. I remember years later when I would be listening to a game and hear his name and remember him on that mountain in Korea.

Our lieutenant said he was putting me and the other guy who helped knock out the bunker up for Bronze Stars. We didn't get them, but Eddie LeBaron did get one. We always thought maybe it was because he was a lieutenant and a star quarterback and we were lowly privates. We didn't know for sure, but we always liked to joke about it.

Editor's note: Eddie LeBaron spent twelve years in professional football between the Canadian Football League and the NFL with the Dallas Cowboys and Washington Redskins. He was awarded a Bronze Star and two Purple Hearts during his service in the Marine Corps in Korea.

When you take a mountaintop like that, the first thing you do is set up your position for the night, or for however long you're going to stay there. You don't dare go any further forward because your artillery would be bombarding that area all day. But, the one thing you said to yourself more than anything, once you were on top, *Thank God, that's one less mountain we have to climb.*

Looking back, you sometimes wonder how you did it; climbing mountains, attacking positions when they're shooting down on you. But you didn't stop. You just kept going. That's why they wanted young guys, nineteen-twenty years old. We were physically capable of doing it and we didn't ask questions. Attitude is the big thing that came from the tough training. You were trained to act instantaneously to an order - no hesitation. That's what helped you overcome nerves when facing fire.

(Bill Koch collection)

Before you pushed off, they would bombard or napalm the hell out of a hill. You're thinking, *How can anybody survive that?* But they would still be there. It was still a scary thing, climbing those mountains with them up above you, but you're a young kid and you don't really think about it. You just moved up. I do remember this, if the BAR (Browning automatic rifle) guy went down, you dropped your M-1 and grabbed that gun. The firepower of a BAR was amazing.

Some guys did struggle with doing those things day after day. We were on one operation where my best friend Bob was ahead of me. He suddenly fell down. I said, "Bob, what's wrong? What's the matter?" He just sat there and said, "Bill, I can't take it anymore. I just can't take it." He just couldn't go on. His nerves were shot. They had to take him off the front lines and send him to a supply unit.

My son and I watched a World War II movie where something like that happened and he asked me if that was true. And I told him. "Yes, it was. That does happen in war."

In training, they tried to instill such hate for your enemy that I think some guys took it too far. There was a time when we were walking up a hill and a Marine came down with a couple of Chinese prisoners. One guy turns to me and says, "They're not going to make it." And I said, "What do you mean?" Turns out, the guy who volunteered to take them back, did it so he could kill them. Nowadays you would be court-martialed for something like that. But in war, back then, nobody thought that much about it. It sounds terrible now, but that's how it was.

I felt bad for some of the replacements we would get. To be thrown into the situation we were in unprepared had to be hard. I remember this one guy, he was from Wisconsin, he had to be about five-foot-five and 200 pounds. He wasn't in any sort of shape for the kind of walking we had to do, up and down mountains and everything. I remember we would put him at the front of the patrol to start and by the time we got to where we were going he was at the back. He just couldn't keep up.

One of the things that can really get to a person during war is the smell. You can't describe it. There was one mission that had us walking through a town on the way to our objective, but it smelled so terrible, the entire area, from dead horses, dead bodies, everything. We had to walk around the outskirts of it. It was that bad.

There was a unit near us that lost a man - just disappeared. For a week they sent out patrols looking for him. Finally, on the seventh day, they found him. Well, guess whose group got picked to go and pick him up? We get there and he's full of maggots. His head was in one place, his body in another, and the maggots had been eating him for a week. The smell was just unbelievable. We got him on the stretcher and took our T-shirts off and tried to cover him up so maybe it wouldn't be so bad.

Me and a guy, named Hawkeye Hilton, were in the back carrying him. When we got to the base of the mountain, we were so weak from the smell that we couldn't carry him any further. They sent some big guys down to carry him up the rest of the way. They finally got him to the top and sent his remains to an aid station. That was one experience that wasn't too nice.

When we weren't going out on missions, we were dug into the side or top of a mountain. We lived in holes and bunkers. A lot of our time was spent just watching, keeping an eye out to see if the Chinese were going to make a move. That actually can drive you nuts. As bad as it might be, you would rather have action.

One thing about the Marines, they are known for being a very lightweight outfit. The heaviest gun we had was a 250mm howitzer. If anything happened, like the Chinese breaking through American or South Korean lines, we got called down to patch it up. We would just jump in the trucks and take off. We were a reactionary force. Once we got there and secured the position we would hand it over and go back to our place on the hill.

The best times were when they would send us back to reserve for a few days. I would volunteer to work in the supply tents. When the officers would come around looking for grapefruit juice, I would tell them that I would trade it for some of their vodka. That's how we used to barter. It was the same thing with C-rations. Some guys couldn't stand the Phillip Morris cigarettes or the beef stew; so guys were trading all the time.

There was one time we were told we would be in reserve for a week. One of the guys I was with knew how to make what they called "raisin jack." That stuff was wicked. He would take a five-gallon can and fill it with water, raisins, and yeast. Then he would let it sit for a week to ferment. Well, after a few days, we got word that we were going back. We certainly didn't want to leave that behind for someone else, so we drank it before it was ready. Oh my God, I got so sick I thought I was going to die! A couple of guys had to help me to my pup tent. When I woke up, the guy I shared the tent with was gone. I may have thrown up a few times in there during the night.

On my last operation, we were going up the side of another mountain in a leapfrog maneuver. We had Charlie, Baker, and Able companies supporting each other. One would go up ahead, set up a base of fire, then the next group would go ahead, and so on. It was our turn to go next. We were all set to go when three rounds of recoilless rocket fire hit us. You never heard them coming. They were such high velocity, that you would only hear the whistle after they hit. There were thirteen in my squad. Three were immediately blown to bits and nine were wounded.

Here's exactly what I remember. I was in the air and trying to yell for help, but nothing would come out. It wouldn't come out until I hit the ground. Now, and this is something I remember distinctly. People can take it with a grain of salt. I don't care. I'm just telling you exactly what I remember. Again, this all happens in an instant, but it must have been when I was flying in the air. All I saw was pure white and absolute calm. White as white can be, and so calm, just so calm. Every once in a while I look back and wonder if the Lord decided maybe I should live. If it happened, it happened, but in my mind, that's what I remember.

When I came out of my concussion, I got up and ran to the corpsman. He looked me over and started to send me to the aid station. Then all of a sudden he said, "Oh I gave you plasma. I wasn't supposed to since you have a head wound." He said, "When you get down there make sure you tell them you received plasma." I said, "Okay." He said, "Can you walk down there on your own?" I said, "Well, I ran here." So I got up, tried taking one step, and went right down. Shrapnel had gotten into my upper leg and hit a nerve. They had to carry me down on a stretcher. I have no idea how I ran to the corpsman in the first place.

They patched me up a little bit and then flew me to the hospital ship in Pusan. That's where I got operated on. I got hit in five places: head, left arm, right shoulder, and both legs. They took a piece of shrapnel out of my shoulder that was about an inch and a half square and pretty thick. They said if it had been an inch, either way, it would have smashed up my collar bone or hit an artery.

When I woke up the next morning I looked around and started laughing. I said, "You guys don't look so good." One of them said, "Maybe you should look in the mirror yourself."

It was a ward full of head wound patients. We were a rough-looking bunch. One guy had a piece of his skull, right in front of his head, that had been cut out and it moved in and out with every heartbeat. We looked pretty bad.

I asked one of the people working there if I could visit one of my squadmates, a man named Johnson, a Black soldier from Chicago. They took me down, and I couldn't believe it. His legs were both amputated near the waist. I said, "How are you doing?" He said, "I'm fine, I'm alive, I'm going to be okay." He had such a great attitude. I thought to myself, *What do I have to complain about after seeing him?* You had to admire that so much.

From there they sent me to the Army hospital in Osaka, Japan. One day when the doctor came around he asked me how I was doing, I said, "Fine, but how long before I can go back to my unit on the front lines?" He said, "Front lines? Hell, that head wound is your ticket home."

They sent me to Hawaii, then to San Francisco, and finally Great Lakes Naval Station. They opened up my arm and did what they called a banjo technique. They attached a piece of wire with rubber bands attached to it, to straighten my fingers, which weren't working right. Eventually, the feeling came back to them, except for my thumb. My only regret is that I scored high in the mechanical aptitude test and wanted to work in that field, but because of my thumb, I couldn't. So, I learned to tie a shoe without using my thumb and went into the shoe business for the rest of my career.

I like to say I served three, six-month hitches: six months training, six months fighting, and six months recovering.

When I came home I did a lot of drinking. I think a lot of the veterans did. Maybe it was to try to forget stuff. Finally one day my dad opened my bedroom door after a long night and said, "That will be enough of that." That's all he had to say. That's the type of respect I had for him. Right then and there I realized, *Okay, it's time to settle down and get a job.*

My philosophy on the Korean War is this; I fought on the front lines for what I thought was the betterment of humanity. We were told we were there to stop communism, which I believe we did.

We didn't have any sort of psychological test or anything when we got out. When I was discharged they handed me a beer and said goodbye. The one thing I took away from it, and I told this to my kids, nothing opens your eyes more than facing death. You go through that and you become an altogether different person.

JIM JOLLY

2nd Battalion
1st Regiment
1st Marine Division
Korean War

While technically classified as a retreat, the breakout at the Chosin Reservoir is held in the highest esteem in military circles. Incredibly outnumbered by an enemy that held the high ground, the mixed bag of Marine, Army, and British troops, slogged their way through nearly eighty miles of hostile territory en route to the port city of Hungnam, North Korea. For Jim Jolly, and most certainly many of his fellow Marines, it was an experience that would stay with them for the rest of their lives.

I wasn't a very good kid growing up around my hometown of Elba, Michigan, which was near Lapeer. I got into all sorts of trouble and it stayed that way right into my teens. Some people told me I was heading for jail. The town leaders thought that my best friend and I were such trouble makers that they put in a special curfew just for us. We put up with that for one day and skipped town.

We just started hitchhiking south looking for work on farms. It wasn't long before he got homesick and I was on my own.

I got ahold of my stepbrother near Carbondale, Illinois, and stayed with him for a while. Then I decided I wanted to join the Marines. But here's the funny part, because I was only seventeen years old, I needed my mother's permission. I said, "There's no way I'm going back to Michigan to get her to sign." The recruiter said, "Don't worry, we will have a local recruiter up there take care of it."

So anyway, the Michigan recruiter called back to the Illinois recruiter and said, "Did you know the FBI is looking for your recruit?"

Jim Jolly collection

As it turns out, my "friend" who went back home, told this wild story that we had both been kidnapped, and that's the reason we left town. The FBI was looking for me and the kidnappers. That is God's honest truth. Can you believe that? Anyway, they got it straightened out, and the next thing I knew I was on my way to Marine Corps Recruit Depot, Parris Island, South Carolina.

Even though there wasn't any sign of war at the time, they trained us harder than hell. Our DI was a veteran of the fighting in the South Pacific, and he told us, war or not, he was going to teach us how to fight and live, not fight and die. I enjoyed it. I won top honors on the rifle range and was promoted to PFC (Private First Class) right out of boot camp. That was a pretty big deal, mainly because I got a $15 per month raise.

My first duty was something most people would kill for, Honor Guard Detachment in Washington, D.C. I mean, this was all spit and polish, dress blues, the whole thing. We were at some of the most prestigious events in Washington. When President Harry Truman gave his inauguration speech, I was standing just below him.

The only bad thing was that I had been trained to be a real Marine, and despite all the glamour and everything of this duty, it wasn't my idea of what I wanted to do. I guess that after all the tough training in boot camp, my idea of a Marine was a guy who had been trained for one thing, and that was to fight.

Nobody could believe I asked for a transfer from such great duty, but I did. It wasn't long before I was sent to a .30-caliber machine-gun squad at Camp Lejeune.

One day a lieutenant came up to us and said, "Guys start packing.

We're heading to Korea." We were like, *Why in the hell would they send us to Korea?* This was in the early summer of 1950. He said that South Korea had been invaded by the North Korean Army and had overrun the American and South Korean troops there. We spent the next couple of months getting new equipment and replacements. They also started training us on getting in and out of helicopters. They were a new thing around that time. We started getting pretty excited about getting into the fight, but it took us almost three months to get everything squared away equipment-wise. Everything was in mothballs. There hadn't been the foggiest notion that we would be called into action.

They saved us for the big invasion at Inchon - September 15th, 1950. Our first objective was to take this little island that controlled the harbor. One regiment went in, while we sat back and watched the action. Artillery and planes were bombing the hell out of the area. It was incredible to watch. Just the firepower of those planes and artillery and everything was amazing. You have to see something like that in person to understand how awesome it really is.

Our objective was a spot called Blue Beach. We started heading in at 4:00 in the afternoon. We were in amphibian vehicles with a back hatch. About ten minutes out from the beach we came to a sudden stop. We had hit a sand bar and were stuck. We got orders to crawl out the top hatch. Bullets had been pinging off the sides so we weren't sure what to expect. I got out and was just about to jump into the water when the guy next to me got shot in the arm, I turned to grab him, lost my balance, and dropped completely underwater. I had eighty-five pounds of gear on me and the machine gun in my hand.

I struggled to shore and got into a ditch with some other guys. That ditch was our only cover. We couldn't figure out how, with all that tremendous fire show we watched, there was still a concrete bunker with at least two machine guns going strong and focusing on us. They were so zeroed-in that we couldn't lift our heads above the ditch without a great chance of getting them shot off. Thankfully one of our flamethrower guys crawled up through ditches close enough to let loose with a stream of napalm. That silenced the bunker.

Our only objective for the rest of the night was to set up about a quarter-mile inland and see what the North Koreans were going to do. Nobody had any idea if they were going to attack or if they had all taken off into the hills - absolutely no idea. That made us even more nervous, the fear of the unknown, so to speak.

Our mission was to get to Seoul. A captured North Korean said he had been part of a unit whose only job was to slow us down, the bulk of their troops had moved back to Seoul to set up defenses. The closer we got to Seoul, the more fire we took. Now we started taking casualties. You just got a feeling that the closer we got to the city, every step closer, things were going to get that much tougher.

After five days we had made our way to one of the main roads heading into the city. We set up our machine gun overlooking the road. Me and another guy were on watch until midnight. There hadn't been a sound, not even a stray sniper shot. That was unusual. Then two other guys took over for us.

About 2:00 in the morning all hell broke loose. Our machine gun was firing non-stop. We jumped up and there was a Russian T-34 tank about thirty-five feet in front of us. Then a truck appears, our machine gun opened up and the truck starts burning and exploding. It was a North Korean ammunition hauler. Now the tank starts backing up to get out of there, but it backed into a deep ditch and went straight down with its guns pointing up. It was like a turtle on its back.

We started firing illumination mortars. It looked like the entire rice paddy in front of us was moving. There had to be hundreds of North Koreans coming toward us. We started firing, just firing at anything in front of us; throwing grenades, dropping mortars on them. It was just a constant fight all night long. Two more Russian tanks started coming in, but once they saw what was going on, they backed out and took off. As soon as it started getting light, the North Koreans disappeared. Just like that.

It was close to a full battalion, which is around 1,000 men, that had attacked us. We only had one guy killed. They lost an incredible amount of men.

We captured the crew of that tank that went in the ditch and turned them over to our translators. The tank was in perfect condition. It ended up getting shipped back to Camp Lejeune. They still have it on display there with a sign explaining how it was captured.

A few days later we were told to push out again. We came to a roadblock that was loaded with anti-tank mines so they (the tanks) had to stay back while we went on ahead. It was tough fighting, but we pushed so hard that we ended up a mile ahead of the rest of our lines. That can be a problem because the radios were garbage and if you didn't let your other units know where you were you, might get an airstrike called on you. We sent a runner back to let the other company know where we were. In the meantime, we found an abandoned building. Naturally, we went in to get some rest while they caught up.

We went upstairs in one of the buildings and looked ahead to the hills in front of us. There had to be at least a battalion of North Koreans digging foxholes. They had anti-tank guns, machine guns, the whole works. At first, we thought about waiting for the other platoon to join us. But it just didn't seem right to let those North Koreans work so peacefully. I told the sergeant: "You know, that machine gun can work just like a sniper rifle. I can clamp it down, fine-tune the adjustments and I can nail a few of those guys. If I set up in the back of the room, they won't even know where it's coming from." He thought it sounded like a good idea. We set it up. He started pointing out officers and I started picking them off one by one.

After I nailed five or six of them they realized there's only one place it could be coming from, so they opened up on us, and we opened up on them. Well, in the meantime our other unit was now close to us. They could hear the firing and assumed it was North Koreans in the factory. So they opened up on us. We had to send a guy out with an American flag to let them know who we were. The guy who ran out with the flag got shot in the neck, but he survived.

Our next big mission was the fight for Seoul itself. Gen. MacArthur had pretty much said that if we kicked the North Koreans out of Seoul, the war was over and we would be going home for Christmas.

They got us across the Han River in amphibs and we set up on one of the main streets in the city. It looked like they were expecting us. Everyplace you looked there were sandbags: in windows, doorways, on street corners. This didn't look good. We got orders to wait until all the units were on line. It looked like we were going to need everybody we could get.

On the first day, my gunner got shot and had to be taken out. Now I'm the gunner and one of the ammunition carriers moved into my old spot as the assistant gunner. There was heavy fire from pretty much every building across the street from us. We got orders to get across that

US Marines fight on the streets of Seoul, South Korea.

street first thing in the morning. During the night some tanks moved into position behind us. That helped immensely because they started blasting away at any place that looked like North Koreans could be hiding.

Early the next morning, it was time for us to move. I would carry the tripod and a can of ammo, the assistant gunner would carry the gun, the ammo carriers would follow. It sounded like a pretty good plan. Well, I got across the street and dove into a ditch with three dead North Koreans in it. It seemed like every gun on the block opened up on me. None of the other guys could get across. Thank God those tanks started blasting away and slowed down the firing.

That's the way it went, block after block. When we got to one of the last ones they started mortaring us. We got behind some sandbags and curled up as small as possible. You never knew where those mortars were going to land. They started hitting all around us. One hit right next to our wall of sandbags. It threw me and the gun backward about ten feet. A corpsman checked me for holes, but other than being dazed and a bloody nose I was okay.

It wasn't too long after, that we started seeing groups of Marines standing around on corners. They weren't taking any fire. Then we heard that US Army and South Korean troops had moved from Pusan up to the 38th parallel. As far as we were concerned, that was it, the war was over. We did what they said we had to do and now they are going to send us home.

We had a victory parade. A shop owner was handing us bottles of wine. MacArthur came in and handed the city back to the president, Syngman Rhee. That was it, a bunch of nineteen and twenty-year-old kids had landed at Inchon and won the war in three weeks. That was pretty heady stuff. Now we figured it was just a matter of getting back on the boats, head to Japan for some R&R, and then enjoy a nice voyage home for Christmas.

We were on board ship, drinking that good Navy coffee when we got the news - terrible news. Instead of going to Japan, we were heading for a place called Wonson on the northeast coast of North Korea to cut off the retreating North Koreans.

They had us make a big production out of it. An amphibious landing, whooping and hollering, the whole deal. I don't know who we were trying to scare. Bob Hope was already there getting ready to put on a show.

There wasn't anything going on around Wonson, so now we got word that Army, Marine and British troops were going to be sent to a place in the middle of the peninsula called the Chosin Reservoir. We also heard that some units had already moved up to the Yalu River, right on the Chinese border.

None of these reports were making us think we would be home for Christmas.

We loaded up hundreds of trucks and made the drive to the Chosin. It was about an eighty-mile drive and other than some mud huts, here and there, it was nothing to make you think this was any sort of prime territory.

The farther we drove the colder it got. It was heading towards November and we hadn't seen this type of cold before. We didn't have gear for this kind of weather. We were only supposed to be in the country for three to four months.

We kept getting news and none of it was good. There were rumors that both Army and Marine units were getting hit hard on the western perimeter. We didn't know if it was true. It was usually from chatter our radio guys would pick up.

The ground was so frozen that our engineers had to blow holes in the ground for the gun emplacements. We could barely scratch the surface with our tools so we gathered rocks and built our fighting holes above the ground. When you packed snow around it, it would freeze and turn solid. It at least kept the wind from cutting right through you. But it was still incredibly cold. The only good thing we had were down sleeping bags. You got inside of those every chance you had. Even with that, we would climb out and run around or do some exercises to get our blood flowing. It's hard to describe the cold we felt. Even though I've lived in northern states, I've never felt anything like that.

Our spotter planes were out every day, but they couldn't find anything unusual. There was no sign of life beyond us. Our commanders decided to split us up. One regiment would go to a town called Yudam-ni, which was right by the Chosin, another went to it Hagaru-ri, and we stayed at Koto-ri.

We seemed to have drawn the best straw. We were right on the route back to Hungnam, which was the port city, and where all the supplies were supposed to come from.

It seemed like it got colder every day. The boots we had would make our feet sweat. That wasn't good, because once the socks got wet and then froze again, there was a good chance of getting frostbite. You had to change your socks every chance you had. When we took off a pair we would wedge them between our clothes and our bodies to dry them out. But you would be out there in thirty-degree-below-zero weather, barefoot, trying to change your socks. It wasn't a good deal any way you looked at it.

We still didn't think anything was going to happen. We couldn't figure out why we were wasting our time sitting there when we could have been in Japan. We kicked the North Koreans out of the country. They didn't want to face us again. They weren't coming back.

Those thoughts lasted until right after Thanksgiving and our first hot meal. That's when we got the news that the Army unit to the west of us had been hit hard, and no matter what MacArthur and his people had been saying, it was Chinese troops that had attacked.

That Army unit was retreating back to the 38th parallel. Now we didn't know what in the hell was going on. The only news we got for about a week was bad news. All the units: Army, Marine and British were getting hit hard. Now there wasn't even a debate - by Chinese troops.

The whole discussion about whether it was Chinese troops or not came to an end when an officer and two platoons of Chinese soldiers came up to our line with a white flag. They wanted to surrender because they were freezing and starving to death. They had been given one ball of rice to last a few days and their feet were frozen solid. There was nothing for them to lose by surrendering. They also said their orders were to wipe out the 1st Marine Division and take no prisoners.

This was about the same time that some Chinese units behind us blew up the bridge - the only one linking us to Hungnam. Now we knew what their plans were: attack on the sides, push everybody toward the middle, take away our only avenue of escape, and attack with overwhelming numbers.

The Chinese were getting supplied with about half of the stuff that our planes were dropping. Some would float over to their lines, others to ours. It was a race to get to them. One of the best parts about those drops is that we used the parachutes to line our bunkers. It was now dropping to at least thirty to forty below zero at night.

When we looked into the mountains around us we could see Chinese moving around, but they were never there long enough to fire on. It was quiet for a few days. The kind of quiet that made you nervous. The Marines at Hagaru-ri weren't that lucky. They started getting hit hard. Our Commander, the legendary Chester Puller, said if the Marines there didn't get some help, they would be wiped out.

Part of our Marine tradition is helping others, so my Battalion, the 2nd, loaded up a bunch of trucks and a few tanks and we headed north toward Hagaru-ri.

We were stretched out for about a mile and a half. We hadn't been gone more than maybe twenty minutes before we got hit.

They opened up from the hills with machine guns and mortars. They knocked out a few of our trucks in the middle of the convoy to trap the rest of us behind them.

Then they started swarming down from the hills. We jumped out of the trucks and into the trenches. We opened fire. We were lucky in that we were near the back end of the column. The guys near the trucks that were burning had it the worst. It became hand-to-hand fighting for them.

The Chinese got into our lines between us and other Marines. You wanted to try and be careful where you fired but you really couldn't because they were all over. This lasted for about two hours. It is indescribable; trucks burning, Chinese running up and down the line killing Marines...some of whom never even made it out of their trucks.

If they had concentrated on the back half of the convoy, I don't believe I would be here today. Luckily for us, they moved toward the head of the column to try and knock out the tanks before they could get away. That saved our lives.

The column was now split in half. We couldn't go forward. For the next couple of hours, we picked up our dead and wounded. The poor wounded were half-frozen from lying out in that snow and freezing cold for hours. But you know what? They didn't complain. They were so tough, so stoic, for lack of a better word. We filled trucks with them and returned to Koto-ri. I lost many, many friends that day. Our entire sister squad was wiped out.

The tanks did make it to Hagaru-ri and helped prevent the Marines there from being wiped out.

That night at Koto-ri was the worst night of my life. Many of my friends were dead or wounded. I felt guilty because I didn't do more to save them. We did everything we could to keep the wounded from freezing, but how were we going to get them out? The Chinese were swarming over the mountains and it was like a gauntlet every time you tried getting through. I can still see the faces of those brave young Marines when we wrapped them up.

The next day, Colonel Puller held a meeting. His first words were, "Gentlemen, we are totally surrounded, which simplifies our problem." He went on to say that there were approximately 120,000 Chinese troops around us. Which means we were outnumbered at least 10-1. He ended his speech by saying, "We have seventy-eight miles of hard road to go, let's get at it."

That night, it was almost like the Chinese wanted to give us a reminder that they weren't going away. They attacked our northeast perimeter. They got inside our lines. They were running around. We kept killing them until they headed back to the hills.

We had to wait for the other Army and Marine regiments to reach us from the north. We heard that one of them got hit hard in the same place we had been a few days earlier. That area developed a nickname, "Hell Fire Valley."

While we were waiting for the other units, hundreds and hundreds of civilians started showing up on the roads. We had been told that there were probably Chinese guerillas in the mix and to be very careful. One woman that was searched was found to have two mortars hidden

American GIs and Marines gather in the cold prior to the breakout from Koto-ri.

under her coat. After that, no civilians were allowed through our lines.

I spent time manning a post that night. The roadblock we set up for the civilians was about 100 yards away. The temperature was at least thirty below. I could hear the women and children screaming from the cold. That was heartbreaking. Absolutely, incredibly heartbreaking.

The other units we had been waiting for finally got to our lines. That was the first sign of optimism. All of our units that had been strung out over hundreds of miles were back together. We knew from Hell's Valley how rough it was going to be, but at least now we were going out together.

Some people have said we should have taken a different route to get out of the Chosin. I've seen maps showing how we could have taken routes through different mountain passes. I've read where Chesty Puller is criticized for the way we went out. Okay, well none of the people writing those articles were there.

Here's the thing, we were not going to leave our wounded or our dead. Trying to move just our wounded on stretchers through those mountains would have been incredibly hard. Not only would that have made it harder on them, but harder on those trying to carry them.

There is no question, if the able-bodied had decided to take that route, they probably could have gotten behind the Chinese and made it to Hungnam unopposed. We didn't even consider that. We were in it together. If we all died because of our loyalty to our wounded and dead, well then so be it.

While we were preparing to go, the weather turned even worse. Now there was a blizzard to go along with the below-zero temperatures. Just loading the trucks was extremely hard. We were so cold and worn out at this point that everything was a struggle.

The convoy was at least six miles long. When we got to the ravine and saw the bridge, I felt somewhat uneasy. It was about thirty feet long and each track was about two feet wide. They always tell you to not look down. But everybody does. I don't think anybody could see the bottom from where we stood.

One side was a sheer drop. On the other side were hills with dug-in Chinese. Our patrols would go out ahead and try to clear some of those foxholes. I wonder if they were put in place too early. Some of the Chinese we came across were so frozen they were barely able to move.

We just kept moving, taking fire, and going into the hills to find the Chinese. We had no radio communication; which was normal. Those radios were terrible. We were probably halfway to Hungnam when a spotter plane flew over us. That was a great sight.

The further we marched, the better the weather got. Word got around to the military brass that we had broken out of the Chosin trap. Until now we had been written off. With the better weather came air support. Now we were getting Corsairs and other planes dropping napalm and rockets on the hills. When we got to within about ten miles of Hungnam we started hearing the Navy ships firing artillery into the hills. I can't even describe the feeling. It's something I can't put into words, to think that we might survive... just incredible. Even after all these years I still get choked up.

When we got close and could see the harbor, oh my. It was full of ships. Big, beautiful Navy ships. For the first time in a long time, I could put my rifle down and not be concerned with how quickly I would be able to pick it back up.

They had coffee for us. Good hot coffee. I spread out my sleeping bag, crawled in, and slept for I don't even know how long; until I woke up, let's just say that.

We thought maybe because of everything we had gone through they would send us home. No deal. We were sent back to the front lines. It became the same drudgery - walking up one hill after another. The fighting was a lot smaller but the Chinese still kept to their strategy of throwing as many men at us as possible.

They would mass at the bottom of the hill. We would call in Marine or Navy planes and they would just unload on them. The Chinese never changed their strategy. Although, it didn't seem like they were ever running low on fresh bodies either.

Korean War veteran Jim Jolly (left) with Iraq veteran William Kocken enjoy a Green Bay Packers game 2016.

One morning, my assistant gunner and I were spotted by a sniper who was determined to ruin our day. He kept hitting almost the exact same spot right in front of our machine gun. It was kicking up dirt into the gun which could make it jam. I crawled out of the foxhole to pull out the ammo belt. Right away I felt something hit my face. The sniper's bullet hit me just below my left eye. It traveled through my face, my neck, out my back, and then hit the assistant gunner.

I woke up in a MASH unit with my head covered in bandages. I spent three weeks there. I got to talking with one of the other wounded from my unit. He said he heard that our unit was going to be rotated back home, but you had to be with the unit at the time to be included. My head was still all green and black, but I convinced the doctors to let me rejoin my unit. They thought I was nuts, but they let me go.

When I got back nobody had any idea what I was talking about. We weren't going home. The guy who told me that was full of it. I never saw him again. Believe me, I wish I had.

Those days at the Chosin were like a nightmare that just won't go away. For many years I couldn't even think about it without going batty. It took a long time before I could even talk about it. The only ones I could really talk to were other guys who had been there. So many of the guys I started with at Inchon were dead, wounded, or just disappeared and I never heard from them again. I will say one thing; the night we were getting set to leave the Chosin, while we were loading the dead and wounded into the trucks, a star came out. It was the only star in the sky. It was so bright that I could read my Bible by it. None of us had ever seen something like that before or since.

We called it the star of Koto-ri. Many of us felt it was a sign that God was watching over us. If you don't believe that, that's fine. I'm just telling you how many of us felt and what we believe.

Years after the war we started up a group called the Chosin Few and our symbol was a pin representing the star of Koto-ri.

STANLEY MOTT

57th Field Artillery
7th Division
US Army
Korean War

Over the past 70 years, the story of incredible hardships, courage, and the subsequent breakout from the Chosin Reservoir has been chronicled in great detail. Much lesser known is the plight of units such as the US Army 7th Division which was fragmented, cut off, and relentlessly attacked by Chinese forces in an isolated region on the east side of the reservoir. This Division would incur terrible losses before joining the other allied groups for the final puch from Koti-ri to Hungnam.

Stanley Mott had endured some harsh winters while growing up with his family of seventeen in Marabel, Wisconsin, but nothing could have prepared him for what he was about to face during this bleak and brutal period in US military history.

I had six brothers in the service during World War II. One was wounded at Normandy, another was on a ship that got hit by a kamikaze, but they all made it home. That was a tough time for my mother. Every day she would write a letter to one of them.

There wasn't anything going on war-wise when I joined up at seventeen in 1949. A lot of us got sent to Japan. That was really good duty. It

The Mott brothers were well-represented in the U.S. military during World War II, prior to Stanley Mott's enlistment. Pictured here (from left) are Raymond, Eugene, Milton, Omar, Melvin, and Sidney. (Stanley Mott collection)

was like being back in Wisconsin, with all the snow we got. One night I had to walk guard duty, the type where you walk straight toward another guy, and then you turn and walk back. When I got close enough to see him I realized that it was one of my old neighbors from down the road in Larrabee, Wisconsin. We had a good laugh about that.

When we got word that fighting had started in Korea, they had us dig foxholes right around the barracks. They figured we would be getting attacked from Russia.

In October 1950, I was part of the landing at Inchon with the 57th Field Artillery of the 7th Infantry Division. The First Marine Division was ahead of us. It was a big gamble, but it worked out pretty well. We fought our way to Seoul. Then it was pretty much house-to-house fighting and everybody was a rifleman until we got through there.

We kept pushing them north through a bunch of different towns, all the way up to their border on the Yalu River. We figured that's it. We're done. We're going home for Christmas. We did exactly what MacArthur told us to do. No one had any idea the Chinese were sneaking across the river and setting up behind us. They crossed over at night. We didn't even know they were there. We found out about it on November 27, 1950. We were trapped.

It seems like it was right about then that it started turning cold, real cold, coldest weather they had in years. We had shoepacs which were supposed to keep your feet warm, but your feet would start to sweat and then they would freeze. That's how I got frostbite. There were some days it was so cold you almost wished somebody would shoot you to put you out of your misery. You figured that was better than freezing all night long.

There wasn't much you could do except crawl in a foxhole at night while they fired at you from the high ground. You never saw them during the day. They had white uniforms and blended right in. They would bark at you all night long: whistles, bugles, anything just to make guys jumpy. There were something like 120,000 of them out there and you hardly ever saw any of them. We didn't have anything close to that many guys.

They had more troops than they had guns. You'd shoot one and ten more would take his place. They were in tennis shoes. They had a lot of guys freeze to death. We did too. During the day, if the weather was right, we had air support. There might be forty planes in the air, but you never knew if they were hitting anything. We had machine guns set up. They used burp guns. They had artillery too. They would pull their artillery by hand or by horses. Our infantry guys would try to get close enough to call in fire missions for our artillery. We'd put it point-blank to where they called it, but, like with the planes, you never knew if you were hitting them or not.

They tried dropping us food from planes, but a lot of it went to the Chinese. It all depended on which way the wind was blowing. We had C-rations and K-rations left over from the Second War. It was something to eat. You didn't have any choice. The only hot food we got was when we would take a can of franks and beans and put them on top of the engine block while the trucks were warming up.

We were finally told to hook up with everybody else: the 1st Marines, the Brits, the Turks. We were on one side of the Chosin, the Marines were on the other. They wanted to get everybody together at Koto-ri and then try to break out to Hungnam.

Before heading out from there we loaded up the trucks with our dead. We would stack them five deep and then put the wounded on top of them. You didn't pack much, just what you could carry, and started walking. We started moving and got hit pretty much the entire time we were on the road. They were all over the place in the hills.

We just kept moving through all kinds of small towns. We got attacked just about every night. Whenever one of our guys got hit, the medics would get there as quickly as they could, but then a lot of times they would be picked off. They would be wearing red armbands and everything, but the Chinese didn't care. They didn't have any regard for human life no matter who you were.

Every time the Chinese set up a roadblock or blew up one of our trucks, the entire march would come to a stop. You'd take a truck or whatever and push it over the side, down a 300-foot drop. While we were doing that, they were trying to pick us off. The road was all ice, the trucks were loaded with the wounded and dead. Some of our infantry guys would go up ahead and try to clear out the Chinese ahead of us. As I said, it's a good thing we were young and didn't ask too many questions. You just did what you were told and kept moving along with everybody else.

At night you would get to a small town and wait for a day or two - wait for the entire line to form up before starting again. We never figured on ending up in such a tight spot as this.

Stanley Mott, back row fourth from right, with his unit while serving at Camp Crawford in Sopporo, Japan.
(Stanley Mott collection)

For us, the whole thing started on November 27th and we got to Hungnam on Christmas Eve. When we landed in Korea we had I believe, some 800-900 troops. I was later told that 103 of us walked on to the ships to take us out.

I didn't know it at the time, but my brother was working on one of the LSTs that helped take thousands and thousands of refugees out of there. They would have been slaughtered if they had been left behind.

After we rested a little bit, they sent us back to the fighting up near the 38th parallel. At least now we didn't have that feeling like there were thousands of Chinese in the hills just trying to annihilate you. When they told me I was going home I was glad to get out of there, that's for damned sure.

When I got back I tried to forget about it. I did to a certain extent. I didn't talk about it for a long, long time. When we would go to a Chosin reunion, my wife couldn't believe how many guys had fingers, feet, or hands missing. It was mostly from the frostbite.

We never talked about the war at those reunions. We talked about our families and things like that. If you were there, you didn't have to talk about it. You knew it was a matter of surviving. That's all it was.

DON BETTINE

7th Infantry
3rd Division
US Army
Korean War

The South Korean Army's early efforts in the war were unquestionably an unmitigated disaster. In their defense, they were also the victims of poor leadership, limited training, and scant weaponry.

Once given quality leadership, training, and up-to-date weapons, many fought nobly alongside their allies.

A young Army sergeant from Green Bay, Wisconsin, was given the arduous task of taking a company of ROKS, (Republic of Korea soldiers) and turning them into a legitimate combat unit. Their first assignment, helping the beleaguered Chosin survivors make it to their final destination.

The GI Bill was a big reason so many of my friends from the Green Bay Catholic Central class of 1947 enlisted in the military. We didn't think anyone would ever mess with the United States anymore, not after what we did to Japan and Germany. Joining seemed like a great way to see the world a little bit, and then come home and have your college schooling paid for. You couldn't beat it.

Little did I know I would spend twenty-one years in the Army and thirteen months in combat.

It seems like almost everybody I knew was stationed in Japan or Germany at some point during those years. I got sent to the Tokyo Ordnance Depot of the 8th Army. That's where I started. Then I moved around to different areas. Most of the Japanese civilians were very pleasant. Just nice friendly people. They seemed to accept occupation as well as they could. Some of the older men had a hard time accepting the westernization rules we brought with us. On most trains, they would have one car for GIs only. We would ride in those and then transfer to regular cars. In the regular cars, the men would sit and, if it was crowded, the women would stand. But when we rode, that was turned around. We made sure the men stood and the ladies sat. They didn't like that very much.

We liked going to Hiroshima because it was so modern. That might sound crazy, with it having been leveled to the ground just two years earlier, but they built that city right up from the ground in beautiful fashion. There were modern movie houses and great restaurants. They were very industrialist. You could stop at roadside stands and buy tiles with leaves embedded in them from the atomic bombs. They were selling them as souvenirs.

It was good duty. I was there for two years. I was on a troopship back to the states, four days out of Yokohama, when the Korean War broke out. By the time I got to the States my hitch had ended. I was discharged. But then I got a letter for the job I had really wanted as an instructor at the ordnance school in Aberdeen, Maryland. So I turned around and reenlisted, just for that job. Only, somewhere along the line, they changed my orders and instead of going to Maryland, they sent me to Korea.

They were in such a hurry to get guys there that they put me on a commercial flight to California and then to Hawaii. From there they flew me back to Japan. So I went from Japan to the US to Japan to Korea, just like that.

When I got to Japan with the 3rd Infantry Division, I found out it was so below strength that to build it back up to fighting strength, they filled it with South Koreans.

So we took the ROKs in Japan and ran them through basic training. When that was done, they put us on a troopship and sent us to Hungnam, North Korea. As soon as we got off the boat they loaded us in trucks and took us right up to the front lines and into a blocking position.

This is December of 1950, when the Marines and Army 7th Division were trying to break out of the Chosin Reservoir and get to the harbor where they could be evacuated.

They sent us up to a ridgeline along the road the guys from the Chosin would have to travel to get to Hungnam. It was cold as hell in the mountains. If you saw the Olympics a few years ago, you would know what I mean. It wasn't too bad in the flatlands, but as soon as you got into those mountains it was horrifically cold. They hadn't prepared us for that at all. We didn't have any sort of special winter clothes. They just sent us up there and told us what our job was. We were told to block the Chinese and North Koreans from getting into Hungnam and to keep the road open for our guys.

We took the high ground whenever we could and built bunkers and foxholes. We wanted to make sure we could see everything going on down below. We took over one place high above a river, which of course was frozen, and saw columns of Chinese troops in white overcoats.

Marine Corsairs like this provided support between Chosin Reservoir and Hungnam.

There had to be thousands of them, at least that's what it looked like to us, walking down the river. We put in a call and it wasn't long before four Marine Corsairs showed up. Those things were perfect for a mission like this because they could slow down and stay over a target. The jets were really terrific too, but they would make one pass, and whoosh in a heartbeat they were gone.

So the Corsairs come over and start hitting the columns. I will never forget this; instead of breaking ranks, the Chinese just squatted down and stayed right in place. Maybe they were told that the planes wouldn't be able to see them in their white uniforms. The Corsairs just raked those columns. When it was over we were sent down to assess the damage. We walked down to the riverbank and there was nothing but dead Chinese. The line seemed to stretch out for over a mile. We just couldn't figure it out. I mean at some point you'd think, just by human instinct, that you would break ranks and try to save yourself. They stayed right in formation. That was a little disconcerting in itself because you certainly realized the discipline those troops had.

We used to say, "Those Corsair pilots must not be married, because look how low and slow they go." If the Chinese or North Korean troops were dug in on a hillside, they would drop tanks of napalm and give it a little time to penetrate the area before another Corsair would come in with tracers and ignite it.

We were positive about one thing, if those Corsairs hadn't shown up, we never would have stopped them. They would have overwhelmed us. That was the thing about fighting the Chinese. You either killed them or they just kept coming. There was no in-between or anything like that and you never knew how many they had. There were times during the war when you would think the war could go on forever because no matter how many we killed they would just send in more. It seemed like an inexhaustible supply. That was something we certainly didn't have. We were scrounging for replacements all the time.

We patrolled the roads and the ridges every day. The main thing was to not let the Chinese or the North Koreans get behind us. That would have been bad, just really bad for everyone. That would have meant our men coming back from the Chosin would be walking right

Korean refugees pack rescue boats during the evacuation from Hungnam harbor, an event known as "The Christmas Miracle."

into a trap. And that's not even considering what would happen to the civilians.

Thank goodness we had tremendous firepower support. One of our most valuable assets was having a couple of Naval artillery observers with us. We wanted a fire mission one time so they called in the battleship *Missouri,* which was twenty miles off the coast. I remember the first time they fired those sixteen-inch guns over us. Those shells came over and my goodness what a racket. When they landed they blew holes so big it looked like craters on the moon. We sure were glad to see them and know they were on our side. We just prayed they would never have a short round.

It was only a few weeks, but it was a pretty miserable existence in those hills for everybody. You would have given anything for one day of being warm or to even have a warm meal. All the mess halls in our area had already packed up so the only thing we had to eat was cold C-rations. Eating all that cold food led to stomach problems. Then dysentery hit almost everyone, which was a different type of misery in itself. I went to one of the medics one day and he said, "Which end do you want me to fix? You can only pick one."

Those poor guys that were trying to get through to us had it even worse. We didn't really know until we got to talking with them later on just how bad it was on that trip. They had their own special sort of hell. Korea in November and December of 1950 was a truly godforsaken place and I don't think it mattered which side you were on.

The best sight in the world was on Christmas Day when we finally had everybody loaded up on the ships to go to Pusan. The "Christmas Miracle" they called it.

Once they blew up the wharf and the piers in Hungnam Harbor I knew it was over. The blast was terrific; all of our leftover artillery ammunition and things like that, we weren't going to let it fall into the hands of the enemy.

We were the last ones out. It didn't matter if you were first or last, just getting out of there was all that mattered. It was a great feeling to know that we not only helped those poor guys from the Chosin get out of there, but also thousands and thousands of South Koreans who were desperate to escape communism.

Once we got to Pusan we got reorganized with new uniforms, new equipment, all those sorts of things. My unit was still almost ninety percent Korean. These were the guys I had trained in Japan. I got along really well with them. You have to remember, until the end of World War II, the area was pretty much occupied by the Japanese. Many Koreans could speak the language. I had spent two years in Japan on occupation duty so I could speak it somewhat as well. They would come to me with their personal problems and things. We got along just fine.

The biggest problem was that the other GIs couldn't remember nor pronounce their names. Our solution was to give everyone a number that would be their name within the unit. We lined them all up, went down the line, and stenciled the numbers on their jackets. In fact, my right-hand man, a young Korean about nineteen years old, was number 82 to everyone. It worked out fine.

There had been reports that the South Korean soldiers would run as soon as the shooting started. We had heard about that being a big problem at the beginning of the fighting. But my guys were just like anyone else. Some guys would stand toe-to-toe during a fight. Other guys would disappear. You never knew how a guy would react. I had GIs who were model soldiers in training and then as soon as the fighting started you couldn't find them. As soon as the fighting stopped they magically reappeared.

Sometimes it wasn't a matter of a guy's courage. It had more to do with what they had gone through. It's like one fellow in my platoon, Louie, from Flint, Michigan. We were on the banks of the Han River, just outside of Seoul, a big flat area. Our job was to patrol the riverbank, make sure nobody got across. We sent some guys down to patrol the banks and Louie tripped a booby trap. It flew up and Louie started running so fast he outran it. The shrapnel didn't hit him. After he outran two of those, he was wiped out mentally. We had to get him out of there.

Battle fatigue seemed to happen to guys who had been there for a while and had seen their friends become casualties, either wounded or killed. Everybody thinks it's going to be the other guy who gets it, but when it's a good friend, the realization hits that you could be next, and it kind of bores a hole in your mind.

It happens to everyone sooner or later in war. I had a situation that was very, very hard. I had four friends who were standing together and a shell came in and killed them all. It was one of ours. "Friendly fire" as they called it. I really dislike that term.

People have asked me about the different little towns we fought in, but other than fighting in Seoul and some of the other big towns, I honestly can't say. When I started out as a lowly corporal, the captain, or whomever, would show me a spot on a map and say, "Clear out this town." You didn't ask questions. You didn't learn anything about it. You just went forward and did what he told you to do. Years later, or even when I went back and was stationed in Korea, I would look at maps and try to figure out where we had been. But at the time, you were more concerned about what was right in front of you, or even all around you, than you were about any real significance of why you were there.

There was a night we were in a reserve position just outside of the 38th parallel, and were ordered to load up on trucks. We had no idea where we were going but we went all the way across from the west coast to the east coast of the peninsula. Several Chinese divisions had broken through the South Korean lines so we were sent to stem the tide as they say. We ran into a lot of Chinese, suffered some casualties, but held our own. We took the high ground from the Chinese and waited for another unit to fill in the rest of the gap.

That's not the type of fighting anyone wants to do - fighting uphill. It's a pretty disheartening feeling when you're at the bottom and they're looking down on you with rifles and machine guns and hand grenades. There was one hill that was so high and steep that we had a hard time even climbing it much less fighting. There wasn't any sort of decent trail. We had to fight our way while crawling over rocks and everything while they were firing down on us. The really bad part of being on a hill like that is trying to get your wounded down. We would strap them onto stretchers, but the footing was so bad and so steep that if one guy stumbled everybody would go tumbling down to the bottom, the wounded included.

Sgt. Donald Bettine

If we had a full infantry platoon we would have three rifle squads and a weapons squad. You would just try to utilize the weapons you had for maximum advantage against the enemy. I carried a carbine, but I didn't care too much for those. As soon as the shooting started I traded my carbine for an M-1.

People might not realize how good of a weapon the M-1 really was. There was one time we were dug in above a big dam and a Chinese soldier, possibly on a suicide mission, was trying to run across the top of it. You could see the bullets hitting all around him. I had instructed a long-range shooting course. So I took the M-1, put the sights on him, adjusted, and knocked him off that dike.

If you knew how to manually adjust the sight on the M-1, it was very accurate at long range. It's been a long time but I seem to remember it being twelve clicks for 100 yards. That was very important because much of the fighting was at that range. You could have your sight set dead center on a target, but if you didn't adjust the sights, you would be far short of the mark.

The main weapon the enemy had was a small submachine gun that we called a burp gun. We had problems because, after battles, some of our guys would pick them up and keep them. When a fight would start they would sometimes use them instead of their carbines. The burp gun made a real distinctive ripping sort of sound. I wouldn't know if we had enemy troops inside the lines or if it was our guys firing them. I had to go around and take all their magazines away. I told them they could keep the damn guns as souvenirs, but they weren't going to be firing them in battle.

When the Chinese wanted to take a hill they would line up as many troops as possible and just start walking and climbing. You would see them coming, wave after wave. When they got close enough we found out only about half of them had weapons, the rest had hand grenades. By the time they got close to us, a lot of them had been hit, but some still got through. There were times when you would have to clean them out of your own positions. They would get right in around the foxholes. I've had them come within six feet of my position. I carried a .45 pistol with me just for that reason. Their numbers were amazing. They just kept coming and coming. Some guys had to get involved in hand-to-hand fighting. I personally never did.

Once fighting got this close it got pretty unconventional. Our weapons squad decided to use a little GI ingenuity as they called it. We had the 60mm mortars with us, but they weren't of much use when the fighting got close. So what they would do is take a mortar shell, attach it to one of the rifle grenades, and fire. The inertia would arm the mortar. It wouldn't go very far, but if that's all you were trying to do is get it over the lip of the hilltop and drop it down on those coming up, it worked really well. We broke a few rifle stocks that way but it was worth it.

We had a BAR man in the platoon who, during one fight, was mowing them down as they kept coming. He finally climbed out of his foxhole and fired from the hip. He cleared off the top of that hill before being killed. He was later awarded the Medal of Honor.

I guess my highest accolade was a Bronze Star with a V for valor, but I didn't think I did anything all that unusual or heroic to earn it.

My platoon was advancing toward a wooded area near what we called "The Big Walled City." There were these stone walls with a big gate and inside was a Shinto shrine which was like a temple. The Chinese were on top of the wall, firing at us. We had to get them off there, which we did. Before that, we were advancing into a wooded area and had received a lot of fire. We continued forward, killed a lot of Chinese, and kept moving. I was platoon sergeant at the time. I was directing my guys but some of them just weren't responding the way I wanted them to. They seemed a little too concerned with the sniper fire coming our way.

That's about the time I decided somebody needed to take charge and set an example. I started running toward the Chinese, shooting as I went. I was in pretty decent shape at the time. Maybe the Chinese were shocked or unnerved to see an American running straight at them like that and started surrendering. We rounded up the survivors and took them as prisoners. I will say this, the Chinese soldiers that were left behind, the ones that surrendered, they weren't the sharpest looking soldiers in the war, which may have helped.

A Green Bay Press-Gazette clip announcing Sgt. Donald Bettine's Bronze Star medal. (Donald Bettine collection)

I was totally surprised when they said I was getting a medal. One day the 1st sergeant of the company came down in a jeep and said, "Hey Sarge, I have to take you to regimental headquarters." So I went with him and that's where I received it.

This is my favorite part of the story. When I was in the Army of Occupation on an island off the coast of Japan, before Korea, I became great friends with one of the Australian soldiers. He was a gem. We did all sorts of crazy things. We had been writing letters back and forth. He was now in Korea and I told him about the medal. Who shows up at regimental headquarters, but him and his brother in a jeep with a big bullseye painted on it. We had a great time drinking the Colonel's whiskey for the rest of the night.

Those are the things I like to remember best about Korea. Or like the time they said they were cutting back on our beer allowance because of some sort of temperance movement back in the States. So what we did was dig a hole about four-five feet deep and put a top on it. Every time we got our beer allowance we would bury it until the hole was full and we had enough to spend one day just getting snockered.

My best day in Korea was leaving Hungnam Harbor, not just with the Chosin survivors, but with over 100,000 innocent Korean citizens. My worst day without question was the day my four friends got killed from that one shell.

I spent thirteen months in Korea. When I came home I was assigned to an Army Reserve unit in northern Idaho to fill out my hitch. I met a young lady I really liked, but then I had to go back to Green Bay. Well, it wasn't long before I decided I wanted that girl. So I went back and convinced her to move to Wisconsin. We loaded up the car and drove from northern Idaho to Green Bay. We got there on Christmas Eve.

I ended up reenlisting again and we both pretty much made the Army our life, being sent to Germany and back to Korea. It was tremendously gratifying to see how South Korea rebuilt after the war. There were beautiful skyscrapers, kids were going to great schools. It made you feel very proud of what our country did to help them. I could only imagine how brutal life would have been for those people if we had allowed the Communists to rule them.

Another wonderful thing that happened when I was there, was meeting a Korean man who spoke good English. He introduced me to a couple of Korean Catholic priests. They both had been part of the evacuation from Hungnam. To think that I would meet a couple of people we evacuated that day was really special.

South Korean soldiers like these fought side-by-side with American GIs.

One of the most enjoyable times of my life was being in charge of the ROTC program at Green Bay Premontre High School for many years. The friendships I made with those young men, many of who are great friends to this day, is something that I will cherish forever.

I will admit that I still have a very soft spot for the ones who suffered the most from the war, the orphans. They broke my heart. We did some things to try and help them out in many different ways through an orphanage in South Korea, but you never felt like you were doing enough. You always wanted to do more.

When I was back in Korea in 1960, I dug out my old platoon roster to see if I could look up some of my former soldiers. Unfortunately, I hadn't recorded their names, just the numbers we gave them. I guess I will never know what became of 82.

LEE FRANGQUIST

45th Infantry Division
US Army
Korean War

During the late stages of any war, it's only human nature for those on the front lines to count down the days left in their tour or to the end of the fighting altogether. But as so many tragically discovered, until all guns are silenced, a war zone is still the most lethal place on earth.

Nobody knew the Korean War was coming. At least none of us in the class of 1950 at Green Bay West High School. We had some guys who had joined the Marines before graduation. They would strut their stuff walking around school in their uniforms. Well about two weeks after graduation, the war started. They were the first to go. They got thrown into the thick of it right away. Some of them got shot up; one of them lost a leg. We were just dumbfounded. It just happened so quickly. We all felt so bad for those guys. I mean, who would have expected something like this to happen?

I got drafted in December of 1952. I was working as a mechanics helper at a mill in Green Bay at the time. I really liked the job, but I figured sooner or later it was going to happen. I think everybody figured that if you got drafted now, you were heading to Korea. With the way things were going over there it seemed like they needed every man they could get. Although, I had one friend whose family was German. He got drafted and got sent to Germany. He used to say, "This Army life is great. I'm loving it!"

Never in a million years did I even imagine Korea would be as bad as it was.

I got sent to Indian Gap, Pennsylvania, with the 45th Division. One of the weapons they trained us on was the 57mm recoilless rifle. They had set up an old tank as a target. It was probably about four blocks away. Everybody had a chance to fire at it. All these country bumpkins from down south were shooting at it. Nobody was hitting it. Finally, it was my turn. I hit it broadside. I think I was more shocked than anyone. The sergeant was like, "Do that again." I did, and hit it again. It was a heavy gun that you could fire from a tripod or the shoulder, and if you had a really good scope on there you could be pretty accurate.

My dad had taught me to be a great shot for deer hunting. I learned how to shoot a deer on the run if it was chasing a doe. How to anticipate where it was going and react quickly when it got in your sight. Maybe that carried over with the 57mm, I don't know.

When I got to Korea the Master Sergeant said, "You're going to be my gunner on the recoilless." I said, "How come?" He said, "Because it's on your record." So apparently that day back at Indian Gap followed me.

During our stays at the main outpost, I would be on it for probably twelve out of the fifteen days. The thing is though, it had such a backblast that it would kick up huge amounts of dust. So once you fired, you became a pretty good target yourself. We would have to pick it up and move after every couple of shots.

Enemy troops were our main targets. You would get information on where they were gathering or something and start firing at them. We had two types of shells, explosive and canister. We called the canister shells "lawnmower shells" because they would just mow down the enemy like you were shooting at them with a giant shotgun. They were actually filled with buckshot.

We landed way down south in Pusan. It was just a blur when I got there, total bewilderment. They transported us in these little rickety trains. I was twenty years old and just wondering where in the world I was. What was I doing in this strange country?

My first stop was a place called Sandbag Castle in the Kumsong River Valley. It was in the general area of a place called Christmas Hill. A buddy I had trained with, Edwin from Green Bay, had been assigned as a driver for the deuce-and-a-half trucks. It's funny. We used to pick raspberries together behind Ridge Road when we were kids. That's how we first met. When he dropped us off he goes, "Adios Lee!" and left. Years later when he passed away I went to his funeral and at the meal afterward, I told his family. I said, "Old Eddie brought me to a place called Christmas Hill, a place I almost got killed."

Right after we got there we had to go to an outpost on top of the hill. They had built a steep set of stairs going up sometime before. We knew they were probably sending us to a place where we would be right in front of the enemy. We were on the military crest; that's the backside of the hill, but then there was a long finger of land that went out beyond there with a ridge that tapered down.

It was pretty quiet during the day because neither side wanted to reveal themselves. There was a mortar platoon down below us. They would fire on a regular basis and we would get it right back.

We had 180 men in the company, five men to a bunker. I don't think they were built for that many. If all five were in there at the same time you couldn't lay on your back. Everybody had to lay on one side and then roll over when everybody else did. It rained all the time. This was early May, their wet season. We hung a poncho liner up near the roof of the bunker. It would fill up, but it did the job. We stayed pretty dry. One night I had to go outside and take a leak. Well, I bumped it somehow and the entire poncho, filled with cold water, came down on those sleeping guys. I don't think there is a swear word in the history of the US military that wasn't thrown at me that night.

Even though the recoilless rifle was my main weapon, I still took my turn on a listening post in the middle of the night. That was terrible duty. Nobody enjoyed doing that. I always carried a .45 pistol with me and would borrow a carbine from one of the guys. So I went out and found a hole someone had dug next to this big stump. I crawled in there and just watched and listened. Well, again, I had to take a leak but didn't want to do it in the hole. That was my home for the night. I tried being as careful as I could, but the enemy had spotters and they must have seen some movement because the next thing I know three of them come walking towards me.

I had a big piece of burlap with me so I got back down into the hole and pulled it over the top of me to hide. There was just a sliver to look through and I could see they were definitely Chinese troops from the type of caps they were wearing. You could also tell that they were new guys from how clean their uniforms were. Their rifles were still slung over their shoulders and they were bunched up together. If the first guy stopped, the other two would ram into each other and they would start jabbering at one another. That was a sign they were just as scared and nervous as I was. They had sent their rookies out there. Let the rookies get killed first. That's how our side did it sometimes too.

I knew I could open up and get a couple of them, but I wasn't 100 percent sure I could kill all three. I knew their comrades were sitting up there watching. The odds of me killing all of them and getting out of there alive weren't good.

They turned and made the mistake of walking toward one of our machine-gun nests which was manned by some very grizzled veterans. Sure enough, about twenty minutes later, bruuuuup! They took care of those guys.

I believe there were times when I either got knocked out or blacked out. You could never sleep out there, that was pounded into you. But there were times when mortar rounds would start coming in and hitting so close that the next thing you knew, the sun was coming up and you didn't really know exactly what happened.

We were on Christmas Hill for two weeks and then got sent back to our lines. We were relieved by Kilo Company. We got to take showers and dry out our clothes. The bunkers here were sturdy and dry. I had been on guard duty out in the rain; we were always in the rain, always wet. You would try to wring out your socks and put them against your belly to dry out, but you just accepted the fact you were going to be wet outside of your bunker.

After my watch I went back inside the bunker, took my socks off, and thought, *Oh, this is heaven.* I was laying there just starting to doze off when the guy who had taken my place on guard duty came running in. He said he heard on the radio that K Company was getting hit hard. They had been hit by about 1,500 troops. That would make it 1,500 versus 160. They wouldn't have a chance.

This was July 15, 1952, just two weeks before the armistice.

We got word to assemble and mount a counterattack. We headed out right around daybreak. We started making contact with the enemy. Since I was with the heavy weapons unit, I was more in the rear of the column. The guys up front were in heavier contact. The thing I will never forget is the sight of so many of our guys dead in the trenches. We had to walk around them. They had been massacred.

One of the survivors said they had been attacked at night and just completely overwhelmed. It was terrible to see what happened, just unbelievable, a total meat grinder.

I've thought about this many times. If we hadn't been relieved, it would have been us. You can't say it was a blessing because it was your fellow man who was wiped out. I guess it was a mini blessing for me personally, but you can't feel good about it either way.

I saw one of my buddies sitting there. He had been hit in both knees and was bleeding badly. I went looking for a medic. I found one and asked him if he could come to look at my buddy. He came over. He said, "I need you to help me with him." We put tourniquets on both legs and wrapped him with a lot of gauze. I told the rest of my guys, "Go on up ahead I will catch up with you." That's the last thing I remembered.

I woke up with rain hitting my face, my raincoat all torn up, blood running out of the holes of my arm, and hurting like you can't believe. The first thing I did was to pull on my arm to make sure it was still there. I'm pulling and pulling and thinking, *Well that's a good sign, it's not coming off.* But I started coming to my senses and realized I might die real soon. So I said the shortest prayer I knew from the Bible, *"Thine will be done. Thine will be done."*

I started looking around for the other guys. It seemed like we had all been blown in different directions. The hole from the impact of the mortar was only about fifteen-twenty feet away. In fact, I crawled in for a little protection. I started looking for the other guys. I yelled, "Medic! Medic!" He was about fifteen yards away, looking at me while trying to get to his knees. I realized, *Oh Lord, he's in terrible shape!* Much worse than I was. He slumped back down to the ground. I crawled over to him and checked his pulse. Nothing. He was dead. I looked around for the other guy. Found him . . . he was dead too.

I was alone and knew I had to make it to the other guys. I just kept crawling through trenches until I got over the hill to an aid station. Oh my gosh, I was so happy when I saw it. It's the first time I thought I might actually make it out of there. It was just a heavily fortified bunker made out of logs and sandbags, but they had lights in there and operating tables and regular doctors. They couldn't do anything extensive. Just patch you up and send you on your way. I just sat there waiting for somebody to come and take a look at me. There were dead bodies lying on stretchers outside the bunkers. A doctor started yelling, "I need a stretcher!" Well, I was the only one out there. I went over to a stretcher with a dead body on it and with one hand tried to flip him off and bring in the stretcher.

They finally brought me in and started working on me. After they cut off my raincoat I saw how ripped up my flak jacket was. The doctor said if I hadn't been wearing it I would be a dead man. With the way the shrapnel hit me on the left side, it would have torn my heart out. They patched me up and put my arm in a sling. Then I had to make my way back to Christmas Hill. When I got there I looked down and there were all these Army ambulances. That was a great sight. They loaded me up in one of them with some dead guys strapped in there and took me to the 46th Evacuation Hospital.

I waited outside for most of the day because there were helicopters coming in steady with more serious casualties. There was one guy who got off, this big burly guy. I thought, *Could that be our master sergeant?* So I went over and took a better look at him. Sure enough, it was him. He had bandages on his head that were soaked with blood and had tubes running out of him. It looked like a really serious head wound. Now, here's the ironic part. When we were getting ready for the counterattack, one of our South Korean soldiers, just this tiny little guy who we had nicknamed "Badass" was running around saying, "I lost my helmet. I lost my helmet!" Maybe he was saying that to get out of going on the mission. I don't know. But anyway the master sergeant said, "Here take mine," and threw it at him. I have no idea if that made a difference. I mean a helmet can only stop so much, but I always wondered if giving his helmet away could have cost him his life.

Once they got me inside they gave me a bathrobe and pajamas. I'm lying there and another helicopter comes in and out steps this finely dressed officer. It was the General of the 45th Division, Phillip Ginder. He had a fancy pistol on. He was all spit and polished. He talked to some people and then came over to my bed. He said, "I've heard you've been waiting here a long time." I said, "Yes sir." He started asking me about the counterattack and what had happened back there. I told him about everything I had seen. He turned to someone with him and said to go tell his attendant to come in. The guy comes in with an attaché case, takes out a little box, and opens it. Inside was a Purple Heart. The general took it out and pinned it on me. That was one of the proudest moments of my life.

They evacuated people for the trip to Pusan in stages. The first hospital was a bombed-out schoolhouse they had converted. Well, they had this little PX sort of place there where you could buy some things. So I went in to look around. I looked over to the side and, oh my gosh, there was my assistant gunner, a fellow from Tupelo, Mississippi. He had gotten hit in the ass. I teased him. I said, "You sure as hell didn't get that from charging!"

Then I ran into one of my ammo bearers. He was from North Carolina. His shoulder was all blown to hell. He turned out alright though. In fact, he came and visited me in Green Bay years later.

I asked them how it all ended up. One of them said he only knew of six guys that weren't killed or wounded. In a book I read, it said that eighty were killed or wounded. So I don't know exactly.

I got sent to the 382nd General Hospital in Osaka, Japan. There was a doctor there who was a 2nd lieutenant. He looked at all the X-rays and everything and said, "I'm going in there. I think I can save your arm."

The operation didn't turn out very good. My arm was still sort of useless. I told him I would rather have it amputated than a dangly arm for the rest of my life. He felt really bad. I could see that. He said he wasn't going to quit trying. Finally, after the third operation, I started moving my fingers and my arm. He had saved it. The only thing missing was feeling in the tips of my fingers. That never really came back, but I worked around it.

I remember one thing that happened when I was in the hospital. I had been engaged to a girl back home. One day I received a "Dear John" letter. That was pretty devastating. That's a very hard thing for guys in those situations. I know I wasn't the only one that happened to.

I served the rest of my tour in Japan and then got sent home. I remember taking the train from Milwaukee to Green Bay. There was a girl on there that had attended the same church as I did. We sat together and talked the entire way. It was so nice to talk to somebody like that. That made me feel like I was really going home.

I still remember taking a cab to my house where I lived. I dropped the duffel bag, ran up the stairs, and pounded on the door. My parents came down. It was wonderful, just really wonderful.

There was one thing I didn't expect. Now they call it Post Traumatic Stress. Back then they called it anxiety. I would get short of breath and be very nervous in certain situations. I was afraid to take a deep breath because it felt like I would have a heart attack if I did. I didn't realize that things from the war would stay with me the way they did.

The nights were very bad. There were certain things that seemed to haunt me. One was of the medic who helped me with my wounded buddy and was then killed by the mortar shell. Instead of remembering it as just asking him if he would come over and help my buddy, my mind was telling me that I said to him, *"Will you come with me to your death?"*

I didn't know the term "survivor's guilt." His death haunted me for a very long time.

I tried to push everything to the back of my mind. When I was working and raising a family it was easier to do. Keeping busy and my mind off of the war seemed like the best way to do that. But once I retired and had more free time on my hands it started up again. I described it to a counselor one time that it was like a vulture was sitting on my chest just waiting to pounce on me. I'm sure that's why I never wore a military cap or anything like that. I didn't want to be reminded of those things.

It took a lot of years, but I finally found some counselors who really helped. I told them things that I hadn't even shared with my wife. They really got me to open up. They were the first people I told about a nightmare I had been having for years and years. It just kept coming back. The dream was that my bed was in my backyard and I'm lying there sleeping and all of a sudden coming out of the ground are mothers and fathers and children of people I had killed. They kept asking me why? *"Why did you kill our son, my husband, my father? Why? Why did you do that?"*

I still go to the Veterans Center in Green Bay. It's all combat veterans. You can say anything you want and no one is shocked or offended because they've all been there. The one thing we all came to realize; if you were in serious combat, you were wounded. You might not bleed, but your mind has been wounded and it can take an awfully long time to heal.

It's almost like when you are with your guys in combat. You laugh together. You cry together. You joke with each other. We're all pulling on the same rope together, but now we're doing it at home instead of over in some other country. It's funny how you can take a bunch of guys from different situations and put them together and see how well they can work together. It's even more incredible what they will do for one another. That's the thing I take with me, the unity of guys like that.

Those sessions have helped change my life. Now I'm proud to wear my Purple Heart jacket. It has more meaning to me than anyone would realize.

LEWIS WHITE

Waist Gunner
28th Bomber Group
US Air Force
Korean War

The Korean War has never been defined as an air war - at least not where bombers are concerned. Unlike the massive carpet-bombing of Germany and Japan less than ten years before, the Korean bombing strategy was more target-specific, aimed at war production and sometimes vital dams.

However, if the Air Force had been given the green light for more intensive missions, they certainly had the firepower to do so with a fleet of the massive B-29 bombers at their home base in Okinawa. These were the Superfortresses that had delivered the world-altering payload on Hiroshima and Nagasaki in 1945.

Manning a set of innovative .50-caliber machine guns from a waist gunner position in one of those B-29s was a young man from Keshena, Wisconsin.

A young fella gets out of high school and he's kind of restless and doesn't know what to do. I thought joining the Air Force sounded like a pretty good idea at the time. I enlisted in 1951, right after graduating from Shawano High School.

When I was born in the Keshena hospital I was named Louis Washinawatok. But my grandfather was an orphan and raised by some people by the name of White. When I was in grade school they changed my name automatically to Louis White.

Lewis White collection

There was a time in the Air Force when I had to get high-level security clearance. They were doing background checks on everybody. The FBI must have come up to Keshena to check and see if Louis White was born when he said he was. But the hospital didn't have any records of it. So they called my base, which was Biggs Airfield in El Paso, Texas, and said to hold me there. They took everything away from me and wouldn't let me leave the barracks. I asked the guys holding me what I did wrong. They said they didn't know, only that they had orders to hold me. A few days later they came back and said to release me.

What happened was that when they went to the hospital they looked in the records and there was nobody named Louis White born there on the date I said. But they did have a Lewis Washinawatok. They got it figured out.

When I came home on leave my dad said, "I have to ask you something. What kind of trouble did you get into that the FBI was up here checking on you?"

In basic training, you had to fill out what you wanted to be. They had three lines for options. I put down "gunner" three times. I didn't know what some of those other jobs were anyway.

I still laugh about the first day of basic training. The sergeant says, "I know you guys have heard stories that we can make you do anything we want you to do. Well, that's not true. We can't make you do anything you don't want to do. But we can make you Goddamned sorry if you don't do exactly what we tell you to do!"

I was trained as a left gunner on the B-29 and the B-50 bombers.

We didn't have guns like they show in the movies. We had gun sights and buttons for triggers that fired two .50-caliber machine guns. I could control the front two and the back two. It was set up so if something happened and we let go of our switches, a different gunner could take control of your guns. But as soon as I pushed my switch again, I could take back control. We had gunners on the right and left, a tail gunner had three guns, the central control guy had two and the bombardier could control the top four. We had a lot of firepower. The MiGs (Soviet-built fighter planes) didn't want to come too close. We weren't too worried about their machine guns, but their cannons could do a lot of damage.

We were based in Okinawa and flew missions over North Korea. I still have the flight records for every mission I flew, all twenty-eight of them. Some were day missions, but also a lot of night missions. On the night missions, you would see the tracers coming at you and you would shoot back at where they were coming from. On the ground they had these great big spotlights that would search for us and when they found you the whole plane would light up.

If we were bombing just across the 38th parallel the trip would be about eight to nine hours total. If we had to go way up into North Korea, it would be maybe twelve to fourteen hours. There were a couple of times when we flew over China. I was reading one time where it said US planes never flew over China. Well, that's bullshit.

One time we were on a mission to drop bombs right alongside the Yalu River, which was the border between North Korea and China. They were shooting at us and we got hit by flak. One of our wings started on fire. We were trying to get it out when the captain said to the bombardier, "Get rid of those bombs, drop them now!" We dropped them and then got the fire out. The captain said, "Did anybody see where the bombs landed?" We all said no, we were too busy. He said, "Well I hope they didn't land in China, but don't say anything to anybody. When we land I will find a way to take care of it."

When we were in combat I never thought of anything other than doing my job. That's how you were trained. If something happens, you react and do what you were taught to do. Like if there was a MiG coming at us and shooting, you didn't stop and think about getting hit. You do your job and then if you do get hit, you do what you were trained to do in that situation. They trained us for everything that could happen up there.

I laugh when they show you in these movies where guys are shooting at a plane and they're shooting all over. Well, when you're flying in a tight formation you would have just as good of a chance at hitting one of our planes as theirs. We had a tight window to shoot in. If a MiG came through that area, you shot at him. We would yell to each other.

The other gunner was named Huff. I would yell, "Look out Huff, you got one coming in underneath!" He would do the same for me. But in the movies guys are shooting all over the skies.

We didn't worry as much about MiGs as we did the flak from ground fire and the surface-to-air missiles. We had escorts that would chase the MiGs off most of the time. Years after the war I ran into an old friend, Bill from around here. He was a fighter pilot stationed in South Korea. I asked him what he did. He said he flew escorts for the bombers. I said, "You might have flown on my missions." He said he probably did. They flew F-85s and F-86s. Those were big planes in those days. Somebody would send out, "We've got MiGs spotted on radar!" And you would hear back, "You guys stay in formation, we'll take care of them."

There was a time when our engines were on fire and they couldn't put them out so the captain called back and said, "Prepare to bail out!" So we all lined up to jump. We had never jumped before. They just told us how to pull the cord to get the chute to open up. The door was open. You could feel the wind and everything. I wasn't scared about jumping. I was more concerned with what was going to happen once I got on the ground. Nobody was too excited about getting captured by the North Koreans. We had heard stories about what that was like. We had some training on what to do, but basically, once you hit the ground you would be on your own. All they really told us was to stay off the main roads and make our way back the best we could. If we were on a mission way up north that would be a long walk home.

Whenever a plane got hit bad, they tried to make it out over the ocean. That way it would be easier for our rescue planes to pick them up. We had two eight-man rafts on the plane and each guy had his own individual raft that he could deploy.

I had a buddy who spent five days out there. "Oh boy, hungry!" he said. When he got picked up by the plane the first thing he said was, "You guys got anything to eat?"

But anyway, when we had that fire, we were all ready to jump when the captain radioed the radarman who was the only one with a headset and could communicate. The captain said, "Hold on, we've got the fire under control!"

So the radarman grabbed the first guy in line with a big bear hug and pulled him back, knocking all of us down. He said he thought that if he just tapped the guy on the shoulder that the guy would think it was a signal to jump.

We would go out with three squadrons. Usually, it was about thirty planes. They would tell us in the briefings what the target was. Mostly we carried 500-pound bombs. We would carry forty of them. We would drop them anywhere from between 20,000 to 30,000 feet. Sometimes we would go after factories. There was one way up in the mountains we

An American B-29 bomber drops its payload over a target.

went after one time. Then other times we would go after their airfields. When we hit the airfields, we would drop bombs with fuses on them, drop them right on the runways. Some would go off right away, some maybe an hour later, others might be twenty-four hours later. That way they never knew when a bomb was going to go off.

Sometimes we would drop anti-personnel bombs. When they wanted to get North Koreans out of the caves, the fighters would go in first and drop napalm. That would suck all the oxygen out of the caves and then we would come from behind and drop those bombs on them.

One of our biggest missions was trying to knock out a big dam. In the briefing, they said anybody who knocks it out gets a case of whiskey. We hit it but the photos showed that it didn't break. Another outfit went up. They hit it too, but it still didn't break. They sent an outfit from Japan to do it, still couldn't do it. So they loaded us up with 1,000-pound bombs and this time we got it done.

Whenever a new crew joined us they would be given the easiest runs to break them in. They would go around the 38th parallel on what we called "milk runs." The North Koreans didn't pay too much attention to what was happening there. There weren't any major targets. We gave the crew a hard time, teasing them about what an easy mission they had compared to what we had to do.

Well, we didn't know it but the North Koreans must have brought in all sorts of new weapons in that area. The crew came back and they were like, "Holy cripes! They threw everything at us! MiGs, heavy anti-aircraft fire, flak all over the place!" They asked, "If it was that bad for us, how bad was it for you guys up north?" We just laughed and said, "We didn't have any problems." I don't think they believed anything we said for a long time after that.

When our planes got hit, well that's a completely different story. I lost a couple of really good friends. One guy had a radio. It's what they called a transatlantic radio. You could pick up everything. I had a nice record player and a bunch of 45 (rpm) records. He and his guys would come down to my room when they weren't flying and say, "Hey you want me to take that now just in case you don't come back from your next one?" And I would say, "No you leave that son-of-a-bitch alone."

Lewis White mans his .50 caliber machine gun as a waist gunner on a B-29 bomber in Korea.
(Lewis White collection)

When he was flying I would do the same to him about his radio. I would say, "Give me that radio. I might as well take it right now."

Then one day some of his buddies came to my room and said, "You can take the radio. He's not coming back." Oh boy, that hurt.

I remember times when I would be writing a letter to my folks and someone would say, "The truck's here, we have to go!" So I would write in the letter, "I have to go, will finish when I get back." Then I started thinking, *That's a dumb thing to do.* What if that letter gets sent to them and that's the last thing they ever hear from me? That would be really hard on them.

The hardest thing for me right now is when I watch something on TV with planes in a war and they start coming in for a landing. I have to turn that off or leave the room. When they're in combat and everything it's okay, but when you see them landing, I have to stop watching. It's like you get that feeling of what it was like all over again. I would get the same feeling as if I was in that plane and everything the guys went through, how they would be feeling. I don't like reliving that part of it. I never said anything but my wife noticed it. She said, "How come when you see a plane landing you get up and walk out of the room?"

When we landed after missions we would sit and watch the others coming in. If they were shot up badly or had wounded, they would come in first while the rest circled. As soon as they landed, the trucks would run out to get them.

We had really good ground crews. As soon as we got back they would come to us right away and ask us questions, ask if anything was wrong with the plane. They took real good care of us.

One day the plane of the ground crew next to ours didn't come back with everyone else. Someone told them to go back to their barracks and wait. They said no, that they were going to stay there on the runway and wait. Finally, someone told the captain to go and talk to them. I don't know if it did any good or not, but they still wouldn't leave. They said they were going to wait there until the plane came back. It never did.

There was one mission when one of the planes got hit bad and the captain had his mic open. He must have thought he was just talking to his crew, but we could hear him. He didn't know it was going out over the air. He said, "We're hit and going down, bailout, God help you!" That's the last we heard of them.

One day we were sitting there getting ready for a mission and the captain came in and said, "Unload the plane. The war is over!" That was good to hear.

I still had time left to serve so they put me in a different SAC (Strategic Air Command) unit. Now I was on a B-50. They don't have those anymore. Both the B-29 and B-50 are gone.

We were trained in case we went to war with Russia. We had a special bomb. It wasn't an atomic bomb, but it was big, and we had one specific target to hit. With the way they had it planned, we would get to our refuelers over the state of Washington. If something happened and we couldn't refuel, we were to keep going. We would have enough gas to make it to our target and then about five minutes over the ocean on the way back. After that we were going down and on our own again.

I did see an atomic bomb go off. In 1954 they sent us from Biggs to the Bikini Islands. We were at 20,000 feet and twenty miles away. I was on the pilot's side so I had a good view. We had big heavy curtains over the windows and were supposed to wear these big heavy glasses, but me and another guy decided not to wear them. When that bomb went off it was so bright that I had to throw my hands over my eyes, and I swear to you I could see the bone structure in my hands. I held them there and when I took them away, the plane was white, just pure bright white.

When I looked at the curtain, it was bright red, and then somebody said, "Look at the mushroom!" It was all different colors from the sun hitting it, and cripes it was pretty. And then, I don't know who it was said, "Here comes the shock wave." When that hit us it was like somebody took a big baseball bat and started banging on the plane. I think we were up there for four hours. It would have been nice to take pictures but they told us ahead of time, "Do not bring any cameras and do not talk about what you see. If we find a camera on you or find out you've talked about it, you will be going to jail." I believed them.

I didn't talk about it until years later when I saw it on TV. That's when I first told my wife, "I was there. I saw that happen." That was the last one they set off there.

When I came home I took the train from Chicago to Green Bay and hitchhiked to Keshena. The war was over. Nobody seemed to care one way or another. A guy with a bakery truck from Green Bay picked me up. He dropped me off and I walked the rest of the way with my bag.

For my part, I thought the US did a good job in Korea, a very good job. I wouldn't be afraid to go again if I was younger. I would go. I think about the kids going off to war over the years, what they must think. I have three grandsons who went to Iraq and those places. They came back and never mentioned too much about it, just little things that happened. I was the exact same way.

CHET CAINE

Chet Caine poses with one of the more than a dozen military vehicles he has restored.

160th Regiment
40th Infantry
Division
US Army
Korean War

There are many different routes and circumstances that often come into play in determining how, when, and where a soldier ends up in a combat zone. But Chet Caine of Lowell, Wisconsin, may have taken one of the more direct routes you will ever find.

One day he was attending a dance in Missouri, and within a very short time was manning an automatic rifle with a group of strangers on the front lines in Korea.

My father was a WWI veteran, very proud of his service, very patriotic, and loved his country. I felt the same way and still do. He was my role model growing up. That's who I wanted to be. It sounds crazy, but in looking back, I was somewhat disappointed that I was too young to enlist before WWII ended.

I think it really bothered my mom a lot when I was finally drafted into the Army in May of 1951. She had lived through hard times with my dad in the first war and didn't want to go through that experience all over again. I could see that in the letters she had written.

But I still had that feeling that it was time to do my part. This was my generation's war. The Communists were on one side of the line, and it was our job to stop them from taking over the rest of Korea. We had to do something, and we did.

When I was in the 5th Armored Division at Fort Leonard Wood, Missouri, they would send guys who had been fighting in Korea back to our base to fill out the rest of their hitch. I think it was just more or less a way of getting them acclimated to being back in the States before sending them home. To tell you the truth, I really admired them. I wanted to hear what it was really like over there.

There was one guy I got close to. He had been wounded and now had a glass eye. When he got drunk he would pop it out. Well, he would leave on a Wednesday and not come back until Sunday night. I would have to wring the booze out of him so he looked somewhat respectable for Monday morning. He got drunk as a skunk, but with some of the things he went through I started to understand why.

The "Old Man" (company commander) wanted to send me to officer's training school, but I didn't want any part of being an officer. So then they sent me to NCO (non-commissioned officer) school, which was fine with me.

The people in that area were just fantastic to the soldiers. I was having a great time. I had my own car. I had met a nice young lady in Springfield, who I would take to church on Sundays. After services, there would always be two-three invites to come over to their houses for dinner.

Things were going really well until one night there was a dance. One of the lieutenants, who I never got along with, came over and asked me if he could dance with my friend. I said that it was okay with me, but it was up to her. They danced, and she came back and said she didn't want to dance with him anymore. Well, he had been drinking pretty heavily and came over and told her he wanted to dance again. She said no. Now he started talking pretty smart, so I told him that maybe we should go outside and talk about this. So we went outside. One thing led to another and I whipped him pretty good - which was a pretty serious thing to do. It's a capital offense to strike an officer during wartime.

A couple of weeks later I'm in front of the Old Man and he said he had two choices, have me court-martialed or ship me out. So that's how I ended up getting shipped to Korea.

The 40th Infantry Division had taken some heavy losses so they sent me there as a replacement with the 160th Infantry Regiment. My first assignment was manning a BAR on an outpost in the Kuma Valley. We had to walk up a steep mountain. It took a long time just to get up there. But we did it, carrying packs and rifles. I went back to that same spot in 2016 and looked up that mountain and wondered, *How in the world did I do that?* It looked impossible to walk up. You forget what kind of shape you had been in.

They assigned me to Baker Company, 1st Platoon, and put me on that outpost for thirty days. We were halfway between the American lines and the Chinese lines. It was interesting. It's different if you go over as a unit. You've trained together, you've formed friendships, but when you're a replacement you don't know anyone. You're kind of an outcast. It's pretty hard to fit in.

They just handed me a BAR and said, "There's your position." Your watch would be two hours on and two hours off. On the second or third night I heard something moving around in the empty C-ration cans we would throw down the hill. I woke up the other guy. He wasn't happy. He said, "It's just rats!" He went back to sleep. It still didn't sound right to me. A little while later I woke him again. Now he was really angry. About an hour later I still heard something that didn't sound right so I started pitching grenades. Well, that of course alerted the whole company. Flares started going up. The Old Man called, "What in the hell is going on out there?" The other guy said, "Oh the new kid is scared to death. He's pitching grenades at the rats down the hill."

When it was daylight we went down to check it out. The Chinese had cut the wires to our trip flares and had cut a path through a barbed-wire fence. Whether they had planned on hitting us that night or the next night we didn't know. We didn't find any blood, but at least we made them back off and think it over.

The enemy was about half-a-mile away. They would play music every night, Big Band music. They would also get on loudspeakers; "Hey sergeant so and so." Yup, they would call guys out by name. How they got that information we never knew. "Who's sleeping with your girlfriend tonight? Why don't you leave us poor people alone? You have no business over here. Go on home or come over here with us. We will take great care of you. Lay down your weapons. It's not your war. It's a big shots war." Then they would play some very nice Big Band music again.

They were close enough that you could get shot by their snipers. You never wanted to be silhouetted against the skyline. We would send out listening posts, reconnaissance patrols, but you always kept two guys in the observation bunker. In the early days of the war, you heard stories of guys being killed in their foxholes or bunkers. The enemy was all around you. There was a certain feeling that no matter which way you were facing they were behind you.

I know we had it easier than the guys who came before us. We lost guys on patrols and things but it wasn't like a few months before when companies got overrun and wiped out. I will be the very first to admit that a lot of the hard work had been done by the time I got there.

One thing everybody in Korea had to deal with were the rats. They would drive you crazy after a while. You would hear them digging through your pack at night and you knew they were carrying every disease around with them and they were absolutely not afraid of any man. They basically lived on the flesh of dead North Koreans and were just grotesquely fat.

One morning I saw my friend, Perez, and his hand was just raw. I said, "What in the hell happened to you?" He said, "The goddamned rat was running along the beam of my bunker so I reached up and grabbed him with my bare hand, smashed his head against the wall, and threw him down the hill. But the entire time I was doing that the rat had his teeth dug into my hand and tore it apart."

There was a spot where there were fifteen to twenty dead North Koreans. They had obviously been killed by napalm called in by a unit who had been there before us. The rats had feasted on them. Somebody had taken one of the heads and hung it on the fence post. Every day the rats and birds would gnaw on that thing until it was picked clean. That bothered me. I still see that damn head on that fence. That has actually bothered me more than some of the other things I saw. I couldn't see any sense in doing something like that.

Chet Caine collection

There's so much going on around you, along with your own concerns with self-preservation that it can be overwhelming. You try to look past it. It's like you see it, but you don't. You don't want to let it sink in. That's why when people ask me exactly when and where I was, I have a hard time remembering. I do remember the first casualty I saw, but it seems like it was a dream, like it wasn't real. I finally snapped out of it when I heard someone yell, "Caine, Caine! Come on, we gotta get out of here!" I was in some sort of a trance; maybe your mind tries to protect you.

There was a day when one of the officers asked me what I did in real life. I told him I drove trucks and fixed them. His exact words were. "So you're a half-assed mechanic?" I said, "Yes sir, I am."

They sent me back to Battalion Headquarters as a truck driver and mechanic. We had fifty-seven vehicles to take care of. A lot of stuff there was chickenshit. They had a rule, if you did something to screw up one of the vehicles, it would come out of your pay. That was unbelievable. But you know, I heard that a lot of the units in the rear were that way. It wasn't like that at all on the front lines.

We were short of everything. We couldn't get fuel oil, couldn't get antifreeze. We were even short of grenades. That's why I caught hell for throwing those grenades that one night.

When it was freezing cold, some thirty degrees below zero, I would start up the jeeps and keep them running because if they froze up, I would get charged. Total bullcrap.

One night one of the blocks on a truck froze up and busted. I went down to another company and asked their chief mechanic. I said, "Pappy what should I do? I don't want to get in trouble and have to pay for it." He said, "I'll tell you what. You go down to the mess tent. You tell the cook you want a big box of black pepper and condensed milk. You mix it up in sort of a gruel, get the engine good and hot, and pour it in. It will seal the block right up; at least long enough so you don't have to pay for it."

I got so tired of dealing with stuff like that, that I volunteered to haul ammo up to the MLR (main line of resistance). That's how bad it was in the rear.

Those were pretty scary trips. We only ran at night. We drove with what they called cat-eye headlights and blacked-out driving lights. There were times when it was almost impossible to see the road, between the darkness and the dust; which in the summer was atrocious. You would have fifteen to twenty trucks moving along bunched up tight in a row. It wasn't unusual to go on a mission and see a wrecked truck at the bottom of the mountain. The drop was about 1,000 feet. I did that for quite some time until I got sent to another area. But I didn't want to turn in the truck I had because it was a great truck and a lot of them were piles of junk.

I remember one time when I needed a part for my truck. My buddy Jim and I decided we would go and try to get what we needed off a wrecked truck that was at the bottom of the mountainside. We knew it was an area that wasn't the best place to be. We drove our jeep down as quiet as we could and hid it under some bushes. Then we walked down to the wrecked truck. The part we needed had to be chiseled off. As soon as we hit the chisel with a sledgehammer it sounded like a cannon went off. Obviously, we knew the noise would attract attention. Pretty soon Jim grabs me and goes, "Stop! Stop! I hear something!" We heard people talking, lots of people, and they weren't talking English. We hid in the bushes and didn't make a sound until we couldn't hear them anymore. We just hoped they had gotten tired of looking for us. For years we both talked and eventually laughed about how we could actually hear our hearts beating. We were so scared.

We didn't dare turn on the jeep lights when we got back to it. I walked in front and would motion to Jim which way to steer. We went that way for about two miles on that mountain road until we felt safe enough to really get out of there. That wasn't the smartest thing we ever did. You know, it's one thing to get killed doing something courageous; it's another thing to get killed doing something crazy.

Korean refugees stretch as far as the eye can see.

When you're in a war, you never really know what decisions can save your life or put you in really serious danger. You just never know.

There was one time when I heard about a position with an S-2 Intelligence Reconnaissance team. I was just a corporal at the time and if I got the spot, I would be promoted to sergeant. I went to the lieutenant in charge of the motor pool and asked him if he would put my name in for it. He said he would. So I waited and waited; never heard a thing until I was told someone else got the spot. I don't think my lieutenant even turned my name in because he would have had to find a replacement for me. I wasn't happy about it. As it turned out, the guy who took my place was captured on his very first mission. That was everybody's biggest nightmare, getting captured. We used to debate what you would do, fight to certain death or surrender? I've thought about that a lot, but you really can't say for sure until you are in that situation.

I remember being in Seoul, which changed hands something like four times. It was just bombed out and you would see civilians walking with everything they owned on their backs. There were just miles of them. It was mostly women and kids. The men were gone. If there were men, you were suspicious that they were infiltrators.

We had Korean kids around one of our bases that we tried to take care of. They were five or six years old. Everybody would tell people back home to send them gifts. You would see these kids in cowboy hats and chaps, with cap guns. Cutest kids you've ever seen. We gave them little jobs. We loved them.

One time when I came off the outpost and went to the chow line I saw a mama-san (GI slang for elder Asian woman) with two little boys standing there with pails. I kept an eye on them. After we got done eating we would dump our leftover food in big pails. So I decided to follow them. She took the scraps from those pails down to this spot under a bridge. There had to be thirty kids under there. She took all the scraps and threw them in big pots of boiling water. That's how she was feeding the kids. That was the saddest thing I've ever seen, seeing these suffering kids. I remember one poor kid; his lower jaw was missing. Some of them had suffered burns. It was just terrible. That story is never told well enough or often enough, how civilians suffer every bit, if not more, in war than the ones doing the actual fighting.

When I came home Ma, Pa, and my dog were the only ones happy to see me. We went out to a tavern. The bartender goes, "Hey Chet, where've you been? Haven't seen you for a while." I said, "I've been fighting in Korea." "Oh," he says, "What can I get you?" That was it.

One thing that I think led to people being so unconcerned about the war; there were no Ernie Pyles over there. News People weren't going to climb those hills and sit in below-zero weather. Nobody really

This military ambulance is one of fifteen different types of military vehicles Chet Caine has restored.

knows what Korea was like unless you experienced it. And it got to the point where if you were there, you didn't even try explaining it. You just moved on.

I've still got the letter from my mom where she said she was praying to God for her son's life. Well, you're not going to tell her, "Yeah, I hope so Ma, because it's hell over here." You don't do that. You just say, "Don't worry, everything is fine. I'll be out of here before you know it."

I've had people say, "Well Korea, the war started at the 38th parallel and it ended at the 38th parallel, what was accomplished?" I tell them the difference is between communism and capitalism. South Korea is the eleventh richest country in the world and North Korea can't even feed its own people. We stopped communism from expanding into the South. I think that's the victory right there.

I belong to the 40th Infantry Division Korean War Veterans Association. We each donate $600 a year to provide scholarships for poor Korean kids that graduate from a school in Gapyeong that our division built during the war. The Gapyeong area had been devastated. In 2016, I was invited by the South Korean government to attend the graduation at the school. It was a beautiful experience. The kids were so grateful to be there. Those are the types of things that make you feel it was all worth it.

I always loved cars and trucks and decided I would like to get a military jeep and restore it. Well, that was the start. Next thing you know I've got fifteen different types. It's a labor of love. They are such fine machines and so simple. You don't have to be a mechanical genius to keep them running. And no one is going to take it out of my paycheck if I break one.

DICK BAETEN

9th Rangers
187th Airborne
US Army
Korean War

For impressionable young men growing up during WWII, the word Ranger conjured up images of the trained killers who led the way in daring missions in both Europe and the Pacific. It was one of the most hazardous jobs of the war, but also one which carried immense respect and prestige.

Much to the disappointment of a ready, willing, and able Ranger/paratrooper from De Pere, Wisconsin, the terrain and battle strategy of Korea just wasn't conducive to using small, elite units on a regular basis.

Although a member of The 9th Rangers and 187th Airborne, (nicknamed "Rakkasans," the Japanese word for falling umbrellas) this trooper was destined to fight the war with his boots on the ground, if he survived airborne training.

I was too young for WWII, so I figured I had it made. I had a great job, I was president of the Paperworkers Union at the mill I worked at. The next thing I know, I was at Fort Jackson, South Carolina, learning how to fire 105mm howitzers with a bunch of guys from Mississippi, Georgia, Alabama, the real Deep South. They didn't care much for guys from the North. They had sent a whole bunch of us from Wisconsin, New York, New Jersey to fill in the unit. We were Yankees to them. They still wanted to argue about the Civil War. We never would have given it another thought. I think one of the main reasons we were sent there is because we were White. This definitely was not a segregated outfit.

I was only there about three weeks when I started thinking that I had to find a way out. It seemed like me and some other guys from the North were the only ones not related to each other. Our company commander and 1st sergeant were uncle and nephew. A couple of the corporals were cousins. It was crazy.

I got word that they were starting up a new Ranger division. There had been one that had been sent to Korea but they got hit hard.

I jumped at the chance. Anything to get the hell out of Fort Jackson and that unit I was in. I was sent to Fort Benning, Georgia, for jump training. Wow, those guys running the school did everything they could to get you to quit. It's like they just wanted to get rid of guys. A lot of guys were out of shape when they came in and those instructors just went after them with everything they had. You could see that some guys just couldn't handle the mental part, having someone right in their face telling them they were stupid, they were weak; every insult you can imagine. I was fine with it. I kind of laughed about it. I don't know why. I really kind of enjoyed it.

Dick Baeten collection

After they weeded out the guys who couldn't make it physically they started teaching us about jumping. They would draw us up in these towers that were 250 feet high. They called them Coney Island Towers. They would drop you to give you that first sense of having a chute open and coming down to land. Some guys got hurt, in fact, one guy got killed. A gust of wind came up and blew him back into the tower and his chute collapsed.

The first real jump I ever made was also my very first plane ride. They get you so prepared that you just move. You don't even think about it, which is how they planned it. The first jump is what they call an individual tap-out. You get to the door; they tap you on the behind and say, "Go!" So, that was okay. We did five jumps in four days. You graduate after your fifth jump. Then came the best part, the extra fifty dollars per month in your paycheck.

Then we went to Ranger training and did four more jumps. On the ninth one, the last one, we were going to try and land by this big T marker on the ground that had been placed there by the Pathfinders. Well, we started to jump and there must have been some sort of problem because the plane started banking and I'm on the side that's going up. We could hardly get out the door. I finally get out and land on a guy's chute below me. That's one of the last things you want to have happen. They told us what to do if that ever happens, "Double time off," and that's what I did. You have to run right off of his chute. You have very little time to get off him before your chute collapses.

So I'm on top of this guy's chute, I remember his name was Miles, he was a big guy. Most guys were between 150-170 pounds, but he was a lot bigger. I am right on top of him, sinking to about my knees. So I lifted my legs high like they taught and ran off of his chute, just ran right off it so my chute could get air. I got off him and we both landed safely, but we may have been knocked off course because I can still hear him - that big body crashing through the trees. He must have hit every branch. I landed in the trees as well, but it wasn't too bad for me. You wonder how many guys really got seriously hurt or killed in practice jumps over the years.

Our last stop for training before being sent to Korea was Japan. They stressed getting as many guys out of the plane as quickly as possible. They called it a nine-second daisy. They only wanted it to take nine seconds for twenty guys to get out of the plane. On one occasion the brass was there and someone wanted to impress them. They wanted to see twenty guys on each side of the plane go out in tandem. One of the things was everybody had to get out in a hurry before the plane went over water. Well, the weather was bad, real windy for jumping. They said stand up, hook up, check your equipment, shuffle up and stand in the door, and then it was waved off. Everybody moved back a little bit. We were already hooked-up. They made several passes but still no green light. They made nine passes before we were cleared to go.

We had been standing there all hooked-up wondering what in the hell was going on. When we did jump, I looked out and saw that we were over the ocean. We had Mae West vests on, but to activate them you had to drop your reserve chute with a quick release and keep your arms in so you don't fall out. The winds were about thirty miles per hour; higher than we were supposed to jump in. It blew us back over the blacktop. One thing they stressed was to not peek when you're going to land. Well, I peeked - and hit hard. My helmet liner split in two. I had a machine gun strapped to my side that banged me up pretty good. We

The 187th Airborne conducts a practice jump in Japan.

had one guy killed. Now, this is the part that still bothers me. It was all because some hotshot wanted to see a big drop and someone else wanted to impress him. There was no concern for the guys jumping in thirty-mile-per-hour winds. We never should have been given the green light. But because they wanted their big show, one of our buddies was dead.

There was another time when the entire stick didn't get out. The BAR man, another big guy, was about to go, but his BAR slipped and got caught in the door. So he's hanging out there by a strap, just hanging outside in space with the plane going about 100 miles an hour. We were watching from down below. They couldn't get his strap free so they finally dropped a line down to him and pulled him back in. This is after his entire body was hanging outside the plane as it made its passes. This is the part where I would have said, "Go to Hell!" They took the BAR off him and next pass they still made him jump. Not me, I can guarantee you that.

So now we were in the 9th Rangers, but before we got sent to Korea they disbanded us. You see, when they started up the Ranger units for Korea the idea was to send in small units; twelve to fifteen guys jumping behind enemy lines. Carry out your mission, basically disrupt something, and then make it back on your own. Well, they must have reconsidered because by the time we were set to go, in 1951, the fighting was pretty brutal and it was all big-unit type of operations. They were losing a lot of guys. The unit was being used as regular infantry and that's not what we were trained for. Finally, they said no more Rangers. That was a real letdown. They said we could go back to our original units, but that's the last thing I wanted to do. So I ended up joining the 187th Airborne stationed in Japan.

Our first action was actually on the island of Koje (now Geoje-do Island). They had a big POW camp there of North Korean and Chinese prisoners. They had been causing some serious problems. So a general and two of his aides went inside to calm things down. They were held hostage for a few days. We heard about it and just started laughing, "Dumb asses," that sort of thing. The next thing you know we get orders to go in and take back the camp. I think they called it Operation Flex Muscle. They put us through special training, even made us learn the Geneva Convention rules on what we could and couldn't do. They said we were going in to break up the compound. They positioned a tank right in front of the gate. My company, Gold Company, was the first to breach the wire. We went in with fixed bayonets and strings of concussion grenades. We wore gas masks because we were going to use tear gas on them. They had dug trenches and had made spears for weapons.

We weren't supposed to shoot anyone unless someone's life was definitely on the line. We went in. One of our guys had a flamethrower. He lit up one of the big buildings to get the prisoners out. We started rounding them up. The first guy I pulled out only had one hand. His other hand had been amputated. It had a fresh bandage on it. We figured maybe it was for stealing from other POWs. I'm not sure what in the hell he could have stolen in that place. The guys in this building were basically peons like us, just privates and stuff. Then there was another unit across the road where the officers were. We parked a tank directly in front of it and announced that we were taking a break for lunch. They would have until we got back to come out. By the time we got back, they were lined up at the gate ready to go. We did lose one guy on the operation. He was a flamethrower who was on the line with me. One of the POWs ran up and stabbed him in the side with one of those spears. That was our first experience with North Koreans and Chinese POWs.

It wasn't long after, we were assigned to transport thousands of POWs to another island. I was assigned as one of the guards. There were twenty-one of us and thousands of them on an LSD (Landing Ship, Dock.) So we were up above guarding them with our M-1s, but also thinking about what in the heck is going to happen if they decide to try and take over the ship. We were out about two miles and the guys running the ship dropped the ramp down into the water, just to let them know what would happen if they tried anything. They didn't.

Our first spot on the mainland of Korea was about ten miles from the 38th parallel. You knew the enemy troops were all over the place, but they wouldn't attack until the time was right. Every day we would see a group on a hill just observing us and then when it got dark they would disappear. Sometimes you would see the headlights of their trucks going through the hills. We were that close to each other.

A couple of the lieutenants put together a plan of surprising them by sneaking up on both flanks in the dark. One of the groups was supposed to go all the way up and the second group was supposed to stay below the hill and block them from coming down. Pretty soon we heard a firefight going on. Turns out the Koreans were gone, but the group that was supposed to be the blocking force decided they would rather go to the top of the hill too. So we hear all that shooting. Turns out the two squads had a firefight against each other. Each squad thought they were fighting the North Koreans. As I said, there were a lot of, for lack of a better word, dumb things that happened.

Our line of bunkers was pretty stationary, but we would pull patrols about three-four times a week. I always wanted to walk point. Maybe I was the most cautious one, I don't know, but I felt more comfortable doing that than putting my fate in someone else's hands. I learned from a great soldier, Sergeant Rollins. He had a third-grade education but he knew what was going on. He would go out with me and tell me that I was in charge, but if anything goes wrong he would be a couple of steps behind me. It was a really big loss when he rotated back. The new sergeant who took his place had been a cook. The first patrol I took out he said; "If you get into any trouble out there, give me a call, I will be in my bunker." I thought to myself, *If we get in trouble, you're the last person I'm going to call. I will figure out a way to get our asses out of there myself.*

We were dug in along a hill with a path that cut through a minefield in front of us. Well one night around 3:00 a.m., a reinforced platoon with about forty guys armed to the teeth started walking through our lines. They planned on setting up a big perimeter ambush down below us.

Around 9:00 a.m. a Piper Cub spotter plane was flying over the area and started taking fire. Okay, the North Koreans are showing their hand. That's what we've been waiting for. The pilot marked the area with smoke and then dropped out a dummy in a parachute. It was to lure the Koreans out of hiding so our guys could ambush them when they went out to capture the guy. We didn't know any of this at the time.

We were up in our bunkers watching and thinking, *Holy cow, they hit the plane and the pilot bailed out!* All of a sudden a call went out for smoke rounds from artillery. They filled that entire valley with thick smoke. We heard all sorts of fighting going on, it sounded like a serious battle. Later on, those same guys from the platoon came back through our lines. We were told to gear up and grab about a dozen stretchers. Our job was to pick up the dead and wounded, ours and theirs. Okay, well this can be pretty tricky. We could be walking into an ambush. We only went with about twelve guys. And I'm thinking, *Well this seems sort of dumb. Those guys were loaded for bear and they bugged out.* So we went down there and couldn't believe what we found...nothing. Not a damn thing except the dummy in his parachute. It was just a different sort of war.

We always went out in the darkness and came back in darkness. We moved slow, real slow. Sometimes it would take over an hour just to get out 800-900 yards. The only light we had was a soft green glow from the compass azimuth. We would get in our position, a little dip in the ground or something, and just stay low and quiet all day waiting for them to come to us. I honestly think there were North Korean or Chinese units ahead of us doing the exact same thing. Once in a while, one of their green flares would go off, which pretty much told us that

Dick Baeten in a foxhole in Korea (Dick Baeten collection)

GIs keep watch on a mountaintop outpost in Korea.

they knew somebody was out there. I think they were as jumpy as us a lot of times.

There were orders you would get sometimes that you just had to scratch your head over. One day one of our patrols went down to set up an ambush. It was dark of course, but the point man saw somebody just up ahead of him. This was just below us. Some of the patrol hadn't even gotten out of our minefield yet, so the point man goes up to ask him what in the hell he's doing ahead of the line. He gets close and realizes it was the tail-end guy of a North Korean patrol. They were heading back to their lines; most likely from an ambush they had set up for us. Our patrol of twenty-five guys had to fight its way back. So what does our officer do? He sends my squad of eight or nine guys back down. Twenty-five guys couldn't do the job so you send eight of us against thirty? And they know you're coming? That made a hell of a lot of sense. So we went down and started taking fire, but our light machine-gunner, a young guy named Berkley, was really good. We fired red tracers; they fired green tracers. He rigged his ammo belts so he had four or five tracers in a row. It looked like a stream of fire going out which made it a lot more accurate. Every time he saw a concentration of green tracers coming our way he would unload his tracers right in the middle of their fire. That made all the difference. It still bugged me though, that they sent us into a situation where you were outnumbered like that. A lot of times guys on the line had to figure out ways to overcome bad decisions by officers.

Our bunkers were really good. They had thick layers of sandbags on the top. They were two-man bunkers. There wasn't a lot of room in them but we were okay with it. We would get shelled, I would say, about three days out of five. They would shell us on schedule from 11:00 a.m. to 1:00 p.m. They wanted to catch us outside of our bankers heading for chow. We would have to stagger it, one guy going, the other staying in the bunker. You would hear those shells just whistle over while you were eating. The bunkers were good and sturdy, but I had one friend who was killed because they put a round right through his doorway. Normally they were more in back and off to the side, but this round got right inside the bunker and killed him.

Even in the bunkers guys were spooked pretty easy at night. We used to get beer sometimes. It was supposed to be one can a day. When you finished your beer you would toss the can down the hill in front of you. The unit that had been there before us did the same. You could always tell when a new guy had joined us because all night long they would be hearing the cans rattle and they would toss grenades down the hill. The only thing they did was kill a lot of rats that way.

We had a new forward observer come to our unit. Well doesn't he bring a big airstrike panel to put on top of the bunker. That was to let our pilots know we were friendly. It seemed like that turned out to be a bullseye for the North Koreans. They zeroed-in on those panels. We had three guys killed right away. I went out and pulled that thing down. I told him they had never been that accurate before and I wasn't going to take any chances.

When William Westmoreland, later, a General who became famous for Vietnam, took over our unit, he figured that if we went out another 4-500 yards and dug in on a ridge, the 187th would be the furthest unit over the 38th parallel in all of Korea. So he moved us up near Hill 1066. That was a crock of BS. We had to leave those sturdy bunkers for an area that was solid rock and hard sand. We dug holes that we could barely flop into. They were watching every move we made. The first day they shelled us hard, luckily they weren't very accurate. All that new trouble just to move a pin on a map. I had trained as a sniper and I would sit on a hill and watch the hill just a few hundred yards away from us for any sign of movement, but I never got a shot off. You knew they were out there looking down on you, but you could never catch them watching.

We used to have a colonel who always pushed for us to capture prisoners, but then he would say, "Yeah we want to catch one of those guys, but they don't know any more than you guys do. So I don't know what in the hell they would be good for." That was true. We didn't know anything. We were just guys in a bunker. We didn't know the big picture.

Dick Baeten's 187th Airborne patch

In October we got pulled out and sent back to Japan. We had baseball leagues, football leagues, things like that. Duty there was great, but my goal was to get out of there and be home for Christmas. One morning I got a call to report to Westmoreland's office. He said, "Sergeant, would you like to try out for the Honor Guard for President Eisenhower's inauguration in Washington? I thought, *I'm not going to make it. I'm not tall enough or polished enough or whatever they were looking for.* So I said, "No sir, I'm hoping to get out of here and get home by Christmas." He said that's fine, good luck, or something like that.

Here's the way I look at the Korean War. It was almost like a test by Russia and China to see if we still had the will to fight after World War II. If we had just let them go, what would stop the Communists from taking over any countries they wanted to?

China got a taste of whether or not we still had the will to fight. At least half the prisoners we had at Koje were Communist Chinese. Well over 100,000 others were killed.

They knew.

LARRY EBSCH

545th General
Dispensary
US Army
Korean War

There is absolutely no greater authority on the mental and physical price paid by those sent to battle than someone in the combat medical field. But as a young medic from Menominee, Michigan, discovered, it's not just those in uniform who suffer or need a helping hand.

I had hopes of joining the Marines, like my brother, who served in the Pacific in WWII, but my eyesight just wasn't good enough. Jobs were really scarce around Menominee in 1949, so I sat back and waited to be drafted. I never regretted doing that.

I was sent to Fort Sheridan, Illinois, like so many young men from Wisconsin and the Upper Peninsula of Michigan. This was in 1952. The Korean War was in full swing. When we finished basic training I was sent for additional infantry training at Fort Pickett, Virginia, and then to Fort Sam Houston, in Texas, for medical training. I have no idea how I was picked to be a medic. I don't recall filling out anything on the test they gave us that would leave anyone to believe I had any medical experience. In fact, if anything I thought maybe I would be made company clerk, or in a quartermaster company if not a rifleman. But I was made a medic and was damn proud of it.

Once you were selected for that program you were given very extensive training. From Fort Houston, I went to Fitzsimons Army Hospital near Denver, Colorado, and then to Fort Lewis, Washington.

It was from Fort Lewis that we were sent by ship to Korea. Now, here's something kind of funny. Here I was the medic and I was seasick before we left Puget Sound. I had no idea what Dramamine was, so the medic was the sickest guy on the ship.

It took thirteen days to get to Koje Island, off the coast of Korea. Our medical facility was a converted Quonset hut.

There was a huge POW camp there with over 150,000 North Korean and Chinese prisoners. That was a very rough place. There were riots there that were quite extreme. We would have to put our gas masks on at times because that's what our MPs and troops would use to stop the rioting. I was told the story of the general who had gone in there as a negotiator and was held hostage for several days.

There were times that we had to take care of the POWs and they were just very violent, very fanatical. They were just a miserable lot. I remember even when the war was winding down and there were some prisoner exchanges, they would come off the LSTs that they had been transported in and would throw things at our people. Here they were,

A guard watches over the UN's POW camp on Geoje Island, Korea.

Civilians pick through the rubble of a bombed-out Korean city.

going home, and were still just plain violent toward us.

The soldiers that were sent to us were so young, just eighteen or nineteen years old. I was just twenty-one myself, but gee whiz, these guys seemed like kids. You know, these kids didn't realize what they were getting into. There were so few jobs to be found around the country in the late 1940s that a lot of young men figured the military would be their salvation for a few years and then go back home and start over. They never expected to be tossed into the middle of a war like this. Especially since we were only five years removed from the end of WWII.

The wounded would say things like: "Doc are you going to take care of me?" I'd say, "Yes soldier I sure am." "Doc, please don't let me die." "I won't soldier. I won't." "Doc, how is my mother going to find out that I've been hurt...who's going to tell her?" "The Red Cross will take care of it soldier, don't worry about a thing."

Despite being kids, they were very, very brave soldiers that the American people have every right to be very proud of.

The conditions they fought in were very brutal; just terrible, and the medics didn't have the type of equipment they have today. Of course, I'm sure WWII medics wished they had what we had. But when I see how well-trained and equipped these medics are today, I can't be any happier for them and for the soldiers they're treating.

There was so much artillery used in that war, partially I think because it was such mountainous terrain. So much of the fighting was to take over hills. I know at one time the Korean War had the record for the most artillery shells ever fired in any American war. You stop and think about the lives that were lost and the men who were wounded just to take that one hill out there in no man's land, it was very sad. But that's the way the war was fought. Take one hill and move on to the next.

The patrols could be pretty brutal. I didn't have to go on any night patrols, but sometimes they would send a medic out with them if they thought they might be heading into a tough situation. They were usually nine-man patrols. They would be sneaking around out there in total darkness. The only light coming from artillery overhead. They would go out trying to find the enemy's location in the dark. Oftentimes they would get too close and there would be a pretty good skirmish.

When I was sent to Pusan in South Korea, we treated soldiers who were recovering, but scheduled to be sent to a different hospital. You can't believe how beat up some of those poor guys were. We had them come to us with toes off, limbs off, burned. In fact, the burns were the worst. I believe flamethrowers are now outlawed in war, but back then we used them on the enemy and they used them on us. We had guys that were burned terribly. Those were the absolute worst cases.

We had a warrant officer who crash-landed his helicopter. He was taken to us, just burned to hell. We used all the Vaseline gauze we could on him, gave him as much morphine as we could, and then shipped him out.

You know though, that war really showed how valuable helicopters could be for future wars. We would strap two litters on the outside. It would be just the two patients and the pilot, no machine guns or anything for support. They would take them out of the field and right to a MASH unit.

As a medic, we weren't really supposed to stitch patients up. But there was such a shortage of doctors and so many patients at times, that we did it anyway. The only thing we really weren't supposed to do was stitch head wounds or wounds close to the eyes. But there were times when we either stitched them up or they would bleed to death so we did what we felt had to be done. We weren't violating anything. We were told if it was an emergency situation, do what you had to do to save the patient.

Aside from the wounds, we also had to contend with brutal winters. Frostbite was a terrible thing. Sometimes you would pull their socks off and the skin would come right off with them. It's something you can't get out of your mind, those things are always going to be in your mind.

I know there are now a lot of treatment centers for things that stay in your mind like that and I know there are war veterans who have terrible memories that haunt them. In fact, I have a friend in the senior residence where I now live, who was a sniper in Korea. Every time we start talking about the war he starts crying. I was fortunate enough to have some good treatment, but nevertheless, you still think of those things and privately you say a prayer. That's just the way it is.

Something else that really struck me, the Korean people. We saw the bombed-out cities. We saw the little huts they lived in with dirt floors and filthy living conditions.

And now, to see South Korea today as beautiful as it is, that feels wonderful. Their ships sailing around the world, Americans driving their cars, our young are people using electronic toys that were made over there. They have athletes who perform so well in golf, baseball, tennis, table tennis, all sorts of sports. Seeing all those things makes it a lot easier to appreciate being over there and defending, which at the time, was a hapless, powerless country that could have easily been overrun by the Communists. I just can't say enough about the South Korean people. How they fought back from poverty and rallied to rebuild the country to what it is today.

Another thing that will never leave me is the thought of the orphans we saw while we were there. Every Christmas I think about them. There was an orphanage run by some Catholic nuns. One Christmas we were sitting around with our Christmas packages that we received from home and decided we would help the kids instead. I wrote an article about that experience for the newspaper I worked at for forty-four years, the *EagleHerald* (Marinette, Wisconsin), which was also printed in *Chicken Soup for the Veterans Soul*.

Larry Ebsch covers one of the thousands of high school sporting events during his 70-year career as a journalist with the EagleHerald newspaper in Marinette, Wisconsin.

Editor's note: Original article

Winters in Korea were brutally cold but as Christmas approached in 1952 we were warmed by the care packages from home that began to arrive. They weren't much: home-baked bread and cookies, candy, chewing gum, reading materials, a few personal items, anything that could survive a trip of a few thousand miles. But just being able to open a package from home and read the letter inside lifted our spirits immensely.

Determined not to let the holiday pass feeling sorry for ourselves, the guys in my small unit made a makeshift Christmas tree out of a winter coat. We decorated the conceptual tree with some treats from home, a few knitted hats and gloves, and even some old socks with holes in them. It looked pitiful but at least it was something we thought.

Christmas Day arrived and after our somewhat half-hearted celebration, my thoughts turned to the children in the local orphanage. They had no family or gifts and, though I knew they were in good hands with the Apostolic Sisters who ran the orphanage, I kept thinking, *Everyone, deserves a Christmas no matter where they live.*

"Let's go visit those kids at the orphanage," I suggested to my buddies. Surely we could scrounge up something to give them. They agreed and the four of us rounded up some SPAM and crackers from our supplies, and wrapped the cookies, candy gum we'd been sent from home in old newspapers we found around our hut. We jumped into one of our ambulances and drove to the orphanage, a converted school building somewhere near Conju. We really didn't know what we were getting ourselves into and hadn't really thought much about it beyond the fact we just wanted some kids to be happy at Christmas.

We couldn't call ahead to tell the nuns we were coming but we hoped they would approve of our surprise visit. Of course, they did. When we finally arrived at the orphanage they took one look at us with our arms

A Korean girl cries outside of a house.

Three boys from the orphanage that Larry Ebsch and other members of his unit visited while in Korea. (Larry Ebsch collection)

full of presents and began hugging us and crying. Pulling us along, they led us to a large room where the boys and girls of various ages, from toddlers to kids about eight years old, were eating a meager meal.

When the children saw us, their faces lit up. "Visitors! GI! GI!" they squealed. They surrounded us and, as we handed out the crudely wrapped parcels, the room filled with their cries of excited delight. Then the nuns asked us to sit down so the children could give us something. The sisters had apparently taught the orphans a few simple Christmas carols, for they began singing with enthusiasm. We sat spellbound, tears running down our faces as we listened to their sweet singing.

Their voices carried us home, far away from the discomfort and hardship that surrounded all of us.

Then it was time to leave, and as we stood, the children crowded around us again, tugging on our pants, hugging our legs, and crying, "Thank you GI! Thank you GI!" over and over. We were so overwhelmed that we choked back more tears. Gently we untangled ourselves from the children and made our way to the door.

As we climbed back into the ambulance, I thought that by all accounts, this holiday should have been miserable, offering nothing but loneliness, bitter cold, some ragtag gifts, a few carols. But as we bounced along the road back to our barracks on the cold, long drive, the night seemed warm and full of promise. It seemed like Christmas.

***

After the war, I came home, settled down, and got married. I told my wife how every year around Christmas I can't get those orphans out of my mind and she said, "Well let's do something about that." So for many Christmases, we would go to the orphanage in Marquette, Michigan, and bring some of the kids home with us to spend the holidays. We would also do that in the summer, take them on two-week vacations. She knew how touched I was from seeing those orphans in Korea and it was just great that she wanted to do something. Obviously not like what we did in Korea, but still, to do something to help them out.

You know, I was actually only supposed to spend one Christmas in Korea. That was kind of a rule they had with our outfit, but I spent two because they lost my paperwork. My original orders had me reporting to a base in California right before Christmas.

The worst part about that is my old classmate from Menominee High School, Billy Wells, was a star football player for Michigan State and they were heading to the Rose Bowl. He was going to get me tickets and we were going to get together in Pasadena. I never made it. I stayed in Korea while the Spartans beat UCLA and Billy was the MVP.

To this day, around Christmas, I make sure I go to the Angel Tree we have here and fill it out to help somebody at Christmas. It all goes back to that Christmas in Korea seventy years ago.

If I have any lasting thoughts of my time in Korea it would be twofold. One would be the absolute privilege of caring for the American soldier and knowing you did your best to treat and take care of these incredibly courageous young men. The other of course would be the experience with the Korean orphanage. I will carry those two memories with me to my grave.

JEROME SCRAY

196th Field Artillery Battalion
8th Army
US Army
Korean War

Life in an artillery unit could make for an impersonal war. There are artillerymen who say they seldom, if ever, saw their targets even through the high-powered 'scopes designed specifically to keep an eye on enemy movement.

But that doesn't mean the enemy wasn't there. In fact, they not only found ways to watch every move the Americans made, but as Jerome Scray of Green Bay relates, could surreptitiously wreak havoc inside their lines as well.

My boss at the lumber mill I was working at told me he could keep me out of the Army. He didn't want me to leave. But I told him everyone

I knew had been drafted. I didn't want to be the one guy left behind. They sent to the Dixie Division in Fort Jackson, South Carolina.

After getting trained on 105mm and 155mm howitzers they sent me over to Korea. We landed at Pusan in May of 1952. They didn't tell us anything. We didn't know where we were going, didn't know a thing. You didn't ask questions; you just went where they told you to go. It would turn out to be that way the entire time. We had one guy in our unit whose wife would send him newspaper articles. That's the only way we got any news on what was going on in the war. I made one friend on the trip over. We said as soon as we got squared away with our outfits, we would get together. He was in Battery A and I was in Battery B. After a couple of days, I went over to say hello. I couldn't find him. So I asked somebody if they knew where he was. The guy said, "Oh yeah, that's the new guy who got killed on the way up."

Jerome Scray collection

We got hit with artillery the very first day I was there. As soon as I heard that shell I ran for a bunker. The guy showing me around said, "Well I guess I don't have to tell you what to do when you hear incoming." When you heard those things whistling through the air, you didn't wait around. We got hit with at least a couple of shells every day. The enemy was just a little ways away. We would go out on missions and report back on how many trucks they had in the area, how many guns we could see, things like that. They were so close that one day one of our guys was walking to the latrine and stepped on a mine that had been planted by them the night before.

You could never really relax and it seemed like you never really got a good night's sleep. Our bunkers were basically holes in the ground with logs over the top, but nothing kept the rats out. Those things were the size of cats I swear and they would tear into anything you had.

You never knew when you were going to get hit. It got to the point that they started serving food at the mess hall at all different hours because a sniper would show up as soon as our guys started lining up for chow. Finally, a couple of our guys went out and took care of that guy.

Another time they were going to show us a movie. As soon as the screen lit up, "Incoming!" The first three rows were practically wiped out.

One Sunday we were heading to church at a different base when we started taking fire. We all jumped out of the truck and dove into a ditch. A shell came in and hit that truck dead center, blew the whole thing apart.

Our job was fire support for the infantry. We were set up on top of a hill and had to be ready twenty-four hours a day. I'll tell you what, sitting out there in the pitch dark in the middle of the night on guard duty, that can be pretty damn spooky. A mouse running around can sound like somebody is walking around out in front of you.

A forward observer with the infantry would call in the signals. You would have to determine how big of a charge you needed. It started with seven. So if they figured it would need five, you would just take a couple off and then the projectile would go on top of it. They would give us four shots to zero in, but you always tried to do it with just two. Then they would say, "Commence fire" and you would fire five or six shots. When they said they saw arms and legs and bodies flying we knew we had hit the bullseye. We actually got some unit citations for our accuracy in helping out the infantry.

I would never have wanted to be one of those forward observers. They lived in no man's land. That's the honest truth. There was a rumor that if you lasted thirty days, you got a free ticket home. A lot of them went out and never came back, just disappeared. No one knew what happened to them. We pretty much figured they were captured and then never heard from again. The thing is, they were all volunteers. I wouldn't have volunteered for that job for anything.

All I remember about the day I got hurt is that one minute I was walking on patrol, and the next thing I knew I was in a lot of pain and a medic was working on me. The guys told me later that I had stepped on a mine. But here's the crazy part, there were six of us on the patrol and I was the last man in line. They always said that was the safest place to be. Every guy walked right past it or stepped over it but me. They carried me down off the hill to an ambulance; that was around 3:00 p.m. I didn't get to a MASH unit until around 10:00 that night. It definitely wasn't anything like they showed on TV. I just laid there listening to more and more ambulances coming and going. They had been giving me pain meds every four hours, but after about two hours I was begging for more.

I remember they gave me a shot and started working on my foot. I didn't have any idea what they were doing, but they gave me a shot of penicillin and put my leg in a cast. I'm allergic to penicillin. So my leg started swelling and they had to cut the damn cast off.

All the bones were shattered in my foot and my ankle. If I didn't have a brand new pair of combat boots on, I think it would have blown my foot right off. I heard the doctors talking about taking my foot off.

I didn't know how bad it was; they wouldn't let me see it. There wasn't much I could do about it, but I just asked if they could wait until I got back to the States and let a doctor back there take a look at it.

They sent me to Japan and things started healing pretty good. In fact one day a doctor came by and asked if I would like to return to active duty. I said yes, absolutely I would. But then after a while, they said no. The wound was too bad. They would have to send me home. As crazy as it sounds, I took that as bad news. I felt like I was really doing good over there. The guys I was with were great. I hated to leave them. Here I should have been happy to have survived and was going home, but I still felt really disappointed. I can't quite explain it.

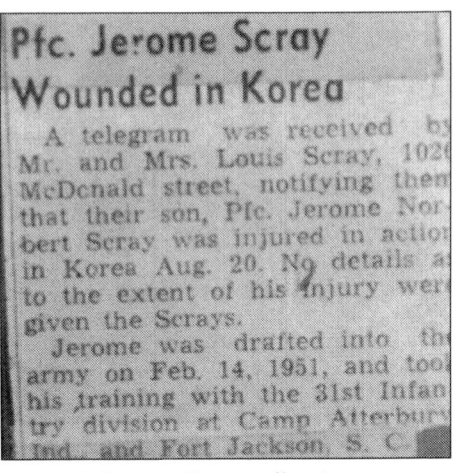

Jerome Scray collection

After I was home for a while, I heard from one of my friends who said that not long after I was wounded, the unit got attacked and overrun. Many of the guys I had been with were killed or captured. I never heard from anyone from the unit ever again.

When I came home half the people I knew didn't even know I had been gone. I think that's the way it was for a lot of Korean War vets. We just filtered back into society. There wasn't any celebration or anything. Nobody asked you about the war or what you did. You just got a job and that was that.

I ended up having six more surgeries on my foot over the years, but I got a job driving a forklift so it didn't bother me too much. The whole thing about Korea bugs me sometimes. My wife used to have to wake me because of things that were going on while I was sleeping. I guess I had what they now call PTSD. It lasted quite a few years. I'm not saying it's as bad as some guys have it, but it's there.

You know, if they told me I could go back with those same guys I was with, I would go back again right now. But thinking about it over the years, I'm not sure we should have even been in that war. A lot of great guys died ... A LOT of guys. I don't think it was ever reported back here how bad it was at the time.

VIETNAM WAR
1964 - 1975

More than a handful of Vietnam vets have admitted that the first time they ever heard the word Vietnam was in high school civics class. Others have said they had to find it on a globe in the school library. Once found, another question, in one form or another, was sure to pop up, "Why exactly are we learning about this place again?"

At the time, there were two phrases that often went along with any conversation regarding Vietnam, whether in a classroom or on the floor of the US Senate, "Communist expansion" and "Domino Theory."

Allowing the Communists from the north to freely overtake a peaceful South Vietnam, proponents of intervention in Vietnam argued, could lead to all of Indochina falling under Communist control like dominos on a game board. Furthermore, some politicians reasoned, "Isn't it better to fight communism in the jungles of Vietnam than on the streets of America?"

President Lyndon B. Johnson was hoping to avoid large-scale fighting in those jungles. His plan to stop the spread of communism was from the air. North Vietnam's bustling ports, harbors, and industrial centers were ripe targets for a bombing campaign that, (it was assumed) would cripple the enemy's war effort. US airpower, a combination of Air Force, Navy, and Marines, had the potential to bring any foe to its knees or, at the very least they reasoned, to the bargaining table.

Over the course of thirty-seven months between 1965 and 1968, Operation Rolling Thunder attempted to do just that. By December of 1967, over twice as many tons of bombs had been dropped on North Vietnam than during the entire bombing campaign in the South Pacific during WWII. During every pause in the attacks, such as the Christmas truce, Washington looked towards Hanoi for signs of wavering or possibly a willingness to discuss a prolonged truce. No such signs appeared.

Time and time again, incredibly courageous, well-trained pilots flying the most sophisticated aircraft known to man, would venture into exceedingly hostile air over North Vietnam and drop their ordnance with deadly precision. Targets were hit, and damage was inflicted. And yet, after the bombers and fighters left, soldiers and citizens alike would climb out of bunkers and go to work sweeping up rubble, repairing bridges, laying new tracks, and stoically moving forward.

Losses from Soviet-made fighter planes (MiGs), surface-to-air missiles (SAMs), and mobile anti-aircraft batteries led to alarming losses of aircraft and crews. In 1967, the most dangerous year of any to fly over North Vietnam, 655 aircraft were shot down with 584 deaths and another 163 pilots and crew members taken prisoner.

In America, there were several different opinions regarding this air campaign. Opponents generally went along the lines that it was barbaric and inhumane to bomb areas that would lead to civilian casualties. The opposing argument belonged to those who complained that the air war was not aggressive enough; that, for political reasons, certain vital targets such as the Ho Chi Minh trail in neighboring countries were being ignored. A sustained bombing campaign hitting all critical areas despite their proximity to dense civilian areas, they argued, was the way to go.

Throughout the entirety of this campaign, a determined peasant supply train utilizing trucks, bicycles and stout human backs trekked onward. Each mode of transportation laden with the essentials of war – rockets, ammunition, mines, machine guns, grenades, food, and medicine – traveled from jungle supply depots in Cambodia and Laos to clandestine jungle bases in South Vietnam. Many of the drop-off points were either underground or invisible from above because of the triple-canopy jungle. Once the supplies were delivered, this human train turned around and started all over again. This covert supply line kept a lean, shadowy enemy – one that was hard to find and even harder to pin down – in business.

There was one absolute certainty that even the most hawkish American military and political personnel had to concede; what this enemy lacked in modern technology was more than compensated with human resolve.

Although some NATO countries did send troops, including South Korea with their extremely efficient and sometimes ruthless Republic of Korea soldiers (ROKs), the majority of the jungle fighting would be left to young Americans - enlistees and draftees alike. Their mission was to go into the enemy's backyard, adapt to the exceedingly fetid, inhospitable conditions, and take him on at his own game. It was an enemy that still included hard-edge, battle-scarred veterans of the Viet Minh. In the previous decade, this group had humiliated the French

Colonial Army. Driving them bloody and bowed back to Europe. Thus ending an occupation that had lasted for nearly 100 years.

Some Americans sent to fight in this war benefited from one unique perk; the most comfortable rides into war any American servicemen had ever received. Phased out were the overflowing troop transport ships jammed to the bulkheads with seasick GIs and Marines on a voyage that could take up to three weeks. Instead, many flew on commercial airliners complete with reclining seats, stewardesses in short skirts, and all the hotdogs they could eat. These comforts were savored right up until the captain announced, "Welcome to Vietnam" and the stewardess swung open the cabin door. In an instant, the heat and smell of this forbidding country slammed into them like a right hook from a heavyweight contender.

The first question many soldiers asked once they were in-country was a basic one, "Where's the enemy?" In this war zone, the enemy might be the polite middle-aged gentleman who came on base to give shaves and haircuts. Maybe it was the farmer with the silver goatee who never looked up from his work while they patrolled along the dikes of his rice paddy. Perhaps it was the personable young guy who dealt "numba one marijuana" in the shadows just outside the gate or maybe even the teenaged girl who sold Coca-Cola from the basket on her bike. Could she be one of the locals who were planting mines in the roads at night? Mines that were killing and maiming GIs and Marines during early morning patrols? While not armed or in uniform, were these people any less dangerous than a North Vietnamese Army regular with an AK-47? There were many issues for these wide-eyed "new guys" to ponder.

For the grunts, the next year would often revolve around leeches, two-stepper snakes, rats, booby traps, wait-a-minute vines, bamboo cuts, malaria, elephant grass, rice paddies, AK-47s, Chi-Coms, short rounds, C-rations, iodine pills, claymores, ponchos, mail-call, monsoons, Dear John letters, jungle rot, medevacs, listening posts, napalm, shit-burning details, mosquitos, ambushes, Agent Orange, hot LZs, punji sticks, dysentery, lifers, warm beer, and body bags.

Prior to 1970, certain rules of engagement proved to be extremely frustrating for those fighting along the western border of South Vietnam.

The enemy crisscrossed the borders of neighboring countries, Laos and Cambodia, with impunity to conduct missions against the American and South Vietnamese forces. However, pursuit of the enemy, once they had crossed back over to their jungle sanctuaries, had to come to an abrupt end. As one veteran put it, "Once we saw that they weren't going to let us go after NVA that were literally right in our sights, you had a feeling they weren't serious about actually winning the war. That's when we started feeling like our best bet was to cover our own asses and get the hell out of there."

For some, the battle cry soon turned into a personal mantra, *"364 and a wake-up."*

The trip home was usually a quiet, personal one. There were no mass evacuations, no ticker-tape parades, no grand scale welcome-home celebrations. Similar to Korean War veterans, most Vietnam vets returned one by one to a land that did not seem to have missed them while they were gone or appreciate their sacrifice now that they were home.

Maybe a sympathetic citizen had offered to buy them lunch or a beer during an airport layover. Or, perhaps the most perplexing conversation of all, when someone would quietly suggest that maybe they should slip out of uniform for the rest of the trip, that it might just be easier that way.

Where was the disconnect? How was it that they answered their nation's highest call to serve in the same fashion as their grandfathers in WWI, their fathers in WWII, and their cousins in Korea, but were now ostracized by their own generation for doing just that? They had lived up to the credo of "What you can do for your country." And now, being advised to not wear their uniform in public was their reward? What the hell had happened?

Over 58,000 Americans were killed during the war. More than 300,000 were wounded. Many have attributed plain luck as the main reason they survived. Others have said they actually feel more *guilty* for surviving than *lucky*.

What none of them could predict was that for many, new unforeseen personal battles, ones that in some cases would last for decades and in other cases would never truly end, loomed on the horizon.

GERALD GERNDT

F-4 Fighter Pilot
555th Tactical Fighter Squadron
8th Tactical Fighter Wing
US Air Force
Vietnam War

    No matter the war, being held and surviving as a POW is incredibly challenging both physically and mentally. Torture, starvation, and lack of medical care can break even the strongest of men.
    In August of 1967, a farm-raised young airman from a small Wisconsin town was shot down over Hanoi. It would take every bit of inner strength to survive five-and-a-half brutal years in North Vietnam's notorious prison system.

You have to remember, when I was going to the University of Wisconsin it was still a land-grant school, so the guys had to take ROTC for their first two years.

When I went to sign up, the Navy, which gave scholarships, was full. So for me it was between the Army and Air Force. I thought it might be a lot of fun to learn how to fly airplanes so that's what I did. I chose the Air Force.

After those two years, you had a choice, either stay in ROTC and go on to get your commission or get out. The big incentive for staying was that now you would be paid. I believe it was $30.00 a month; which for a poor farm boy from Suring was a lot of money.

They gave everyone a test and I qualified to be a pilot so after graduation from Wisconsin. I was commissioned and sent to pilot training in Texas. This was April of 1965.

By the time we graduated in '66, the war was really going strong. We were getting juiced-up knowing we would be going. Just about everybody I knew wanted to be a fighter pilot and get into it.

In early 1967 the Air Force needed more pilots. They had upped the use of F-4s, which was a two-pilot aircraft, so they came down to our class in Texas to talk to us. The top two guys in the class had their pick of what they wanted to fly and where they wanted to go. The next fifteen or twenty guys, the group I was in, became F-4 pilots.

They would send you to one of three areas: the United States, Europe, or Vietnam. But really, no matter where you went first, maybe even for six months, you would eventually end up in Vietnam. I was sent to Ubon, Thailand. My first combat mission was in March '67. From the start, the goal was to complete 100 missions over North Vietnam.

The different areas of North Vietnam were split up into different regions. This first mission was in what was called "Pac-1." The worst would be Pac-6 which was over Hanoi. Haiphong Harbor was also a tough area. That was Pac-5, but the Navy handled missions there.

On my first mission, I was flying backseat in the fourth ship. They put the new guys in the second and fourth positions. I remember watching the guy ahead of us. We had dropped our bombs and were headed back to Ubon. Suddenly, white puffs of 37mm anti-aircraft fire began tracking that plane ahead of us. We called for him to break right and we broke left to throw off the gunner's aim.

You knew you were in a war that first day and that was kind of interesting.

I probably had fifteen missions over Laos but those didn't officially count on your record. I mean, you know...we didn't fly over Laos. That was one place you did not want to be shot down because you knew they wouldn't take you as a prisoner. They would just kill you. These were mainly interdiction missions against troops coming down from the North. I remember going to a place called "the plain of jars" because we heard there was a Communist training camp up there. Other times we would be looking for trucks on the edge of Laos and Vietnam. But again, they didn't count, only the missions over North Vietnam counted towards your 100. Instead, they gave us an air medal for every twenty such missions.

A lot of times we would have a really good target, like a steel mill or a bridge that had value. But there were some horseshit missions too. Weather played a huge role. You would get heavy clouds and rain which would cancel that target so you would be given a secondary target. They didn't want you bringing back ordnance. That was too dangerous.

We might be told about a bamboo bridge that had been built the night before, or to look for trucks. If you were really lucky you would find a truck-park. There were times when you would have massive secondary explosions after hitting a target. I would say it was close to half the time we ended up dropping on secondary targets because of the weather.

They did have MiGs, but in January of '67 Col. Robin Olds designed a strike aimed just for them. The F-4s pretended they were 105s. (*105-Thunderchiefs, used extensively in Vietnam on bombing missions.*) They used the same frequency, the same route, mimicked everything the 105s would do. The 105s were very fast but not very maneuverable. Which is why we often flew cover for them.

The MiGs went up to get what they assumed were 105s, but F-4s were waiting for them. They shot down seven MiGs, which really reduced their total. From then on it seemed like the MiGs would make a pass and run away. They also had SAMs. You would see lots of them along with lots of flak when you went up north. It was tough sledding up there.

Col. Olds probably had 100 Pac-6 missions. He only flew on the most dangerous missions. He was a great leader. Guys would volunteer to be on his wing because A, he was a great pilot who really knew what he was doing. And B, if MiGs came around, the other pilots knew they would all go after him. But no matter, Pac-6 was always a pucker-factor mission.

On August 12th, 1967, we bombed the railyards in downtown Hanoi. These were big yards, very protected targets. So now the railroad cars, the engines, a lot of rolling stock were sitting on this island, trapped there. The next thing was to go in and destroy what was left.

We took off on August 23rd. It was Major Sawhill and myself. This would be my 76th mission over North Vietnam. We were running a little late because of refueling. We really pushed hard to get to the China border before making our turn for Hanoi. We would fly down along a ridge that had very few anti-aircraft guns. Now, once you got closer to Hanoi, they would fill the sky with lead and you would have to fly through it, but it was better to fly through that stuff for twenty minutes than forty minutes.

We had gotten a call that bandits were heading north, meaning MiGs. We made the turn south and as soon as we did the MiGs jumped us and hit two of our planes.

Captain Carrigon and Lt. Lane were flying together, and Capt. Chuck Tyler and Capt. Ron Sittner were the lead plane. All of those guys were in my squadron, the "Triple Nickel." This was the first flight up to the Pac-6 for the 435th Tac Fighter squadron so they assigned two guys from my squadron to be one and three in formation. The squadron commander was flying as number two that day. You had to be escorted on a couple of missions before they would let you fly or lead missions into North Vietnam.

After getting hit, Tyler and Carrigon bailed out. They were captured and ended up in the camps with me. My good buddy Lane couldn't get out of the plane. He told Carrigon, "My seat won't work!" I think the missile from the MiG had jammed it. I saw the planes in flames, tumbling end over end and then crashing. People have said they saw three parachutes but Sittner never showed up at any of the camps.

The MiGs turned back towards China. We couldn't catch them. They were at supersonic speed so we pressed on to our target.

This was a bad start to the day. Earlier, one of our guys, "Captain Frank Midnight," got shot down in Pac-1. Then we lost the two on my wing. That made three. Then a 105 got shot down over the target. That made it four already. We were number five and two others didn't make it back to Ubon because of battle damage.

We flew into Hanoi carrying six 750-pound bombs. We were flying cover for a major gaggle of 105s heading towards the railyard. We pressed on down to the target. The MiGs didn't pay any attention to us because they were going after the 105s. The 105s dropped their bombs and headed home.

We were number three in line. We rolled into our target and dropped our bombs. There was a huge amount of flak in the air. You were looking for SAMs coming at you. There are MiGs in the air. It was the heaviest firepower I'd ever seen.

Right over the middle of Hanoi, we started losing control of the plane.

There was a really bad smell in our cockpit. It might have been hydraulic fluid. We went on 100 percent oxygen. A MiG was chasing us but he couldn't hit us because we were going all over the place. You'd step on the rudder and it would go down. You push forward on the throttle and it would go straight up. Then it stalled out. We were heading for the ridge. We wanted to get as far away from our target area as possible. We were going down and we both knew we weren't going to be able to get it back up. At least if we got to the ridge there was a chance you could escape and evade for a while and the other big thing is that they didn't have many guns around there.

I stopped the engine. Without controls, the airplane acted like a falling leaf. Like I said before, you did not want to be shot down over angry people. We got about twenty miles outside of Hanoi.

I lowered my seat, took off all my gear, put myself in perfect position, sat back, braced against the rudder pedals, and ejected. I did everything right and I still broke my back.

We jumped at probably 1,000 feet but I'm not sure of that. I saw the plane go off a quarter, maybe a half-mile away, and crash. I remember the big orange fireball and the big black smoke cloud. While coming down I kept hearing this zipping sort of noise and realized it was bullets going through my canopy. People on the ground were shooting at me, but were terrible shots and kept hitting the canopy instead of me.

I dropped down into about a foot of water and mud. Sawhill landed in a different paddy and was captured. When I landed, I pulled my gun out and saw about 100 of them coming at me with guns, yelling and screaming but nobody was shooting at me. They started yelling, "Oyooo. Oyooo," which meant, "Put your hands up." I threw my gun in the mud and put my hands up. They grabbed me and cut off my G-suit. Then they took my uniform and boots, so now I was down to my T-shirt and skivvies. They marched me out of the rice paddy to a little village and put me in a granary.

Every half-hour or so they would come in, get me up, and take me outside.

There would be a group of people screaming and yelling at me, throwing stones and mud balls. There were a couple of guards to keep the people off me, but one little old lady came up and socked me. She dropped me right to my knees. Then they would put me back in the granary until the next round.

About dusk, I felt like I was dying of thirst. They brought me some warm tea. I drank that right away and kept asking for more, more, more. Before it got dark they walked me out to the big wall that had bullet holes in it. I thought, *Well this is it. Here's how it ends.* I figured they were going to shoot me.

Instead, they had me go through this little hole in the wall. We went through there and started walking. We walked for hours. I was barefoot. When we were nearing a village you would hear a bong go off. It was an old used artillery shell casing. They would punch a hole in them, hang them up and pound on them with a metal bar.

We were blindfolded most of the time but sometimes they would take them off of us. We just kept walking from village to village. People would come out and throw things at us. That's just the way it went. Once, when they had the blindfolds off, I saw Sawhill. His T-shirt was all bloody. Somebody had hit him hard in the nose.

Back at the granary, the commissar had asked us all kinds of questions. We would only give name, rank, and serial number. The same thing happened on this march. Every place we stopped they would ask questions and we would give them the same answers. They would always say, "You're going to be sorry."

At about 5:00 a.m. they put us in a jeep and we started for Hanoi. Sawhill was in the backseat. He had landed in a different rice paddy, but they put us together right away. We walked together but they wouldn't let us talk to each other.

When we got to Hanoi they separated us. They put me under a sink and put Sawhill in a shower down the hall.

They would take you out and ask questions. We would give them the Geneva Convention response, which they would not accept. That's when the torture started.

The interrogator sat on this big chair behind a table. I sat on a little stool. He sat there and asked me questions. On the table was a big blue tablecloth. When he left I wrapped up in that thing. I was still in just my T-shirt and shorts and the mosquitos were eating me alive.

The worst thing was being thrown in the ropes. They would take straps about an inch wide; our "let-down straps" that we would use if we landed in a tree. They would wrap them around your upper arms behind your back. Then they would stand on you and pull them tight. You would try to resist, but the thing I discovered on the first day was that the butt of a Vietnamese rifle is a lot stronger than your ribs. He racked me with the butt of his gun and cracked a couple of my ribs.

With the way they have these straps on you, they can pull your shoulders out of their sockets very easily. The first time they do this you're like, *Oh my God! I can't believe this pain!*

"OK, I'll talk!"

You start giving them some kind of information. He would be like, "Who was in your squadron? So, I would tell him, "There was Bart Starr, Jim Taylor, Paul Hornung." They would write all this crap down. I know I went through every Packers player I could think of. If you gave them something, they would leave you alone at night.

The next time they came back they interrogated me with more specific questions. I refused to answer. This time they put a rope around my foot and pulled my hands over my head. It was simply excruciating pain. You would agree to talk. So they would let you out and you would talk. They would bring you some soup, which was really just some sort of greens in water, some rice and a bowl of tea.

In the afternoon they came back and asked more questions, and I screwed up. He said, "Who was the commander of the 497th and

This was one of a series of sketches done by one of Gerald Gerndt's cellmates, Lt. Commander Mike McGrath (USN), depicting a torture technique known as "the ropes," which was used on both men. It led to incredible pain and misery as it generally led to their shoulders being pulled out of their sockets. (Reprinted, by permission, from John M. McGrath, Prisoner of War: Six Years in Hanoi *(Annapolis, Md: Naval Institute Press, © 1975)*

I said, "The 479th Commander was Vince Lombardi." When I said 479th instead of 497th he just stopped. He had all the BS I had been giving him before, written down. He looked at me and his eyeballs started quivering, he knew I had been lying to him.

This time they put a bar across my legs. Then they tied my hands on a bar over my head. My hips rolled out of joint, my shoulders rolled out of their sockets, and when you screamed they would put this iron bar with a gag in your mouth. If you didn't open your mouth, they would knock your teeth out.

So I had a chipped tooth, my shoulders and hips were out of joint, and they just let me lay there. I said, "OK, I'll talk. I'll talk!" But they ignored me. They just let me lay there.

Finally, they came in and undid the ropes. At this point, you will talk to them. They wanted me to write something. Well, when they put you in those straps it damages the ulnar nerve. I told them I couldn't write. My arms hung limp. They were like that for over six weeks, which made it very hard for me to write confessions or whatever it was they wanted me to write.

They never called it torture. They said they were only punishing us. Not being able to use my arms was my excuse for not having to write anything for them.

You never totally gave in. You never gave them exactly what they wanted. You held back, figuring, *Well they're going to torture me again tomorrow anyway.* You would answer the questions they asked, but you would always throw in as much bullshit as you could.

There was this bridge that was a huge deal in Hanoi, the Doumer Bridge. The French built it many years before. It was solid, very resistant to bombs. I would always be asked, "When are you going to bomb the Doumer Bridge?" I finally made up a date, "September 14th." He jumped up and started slapping me. "Major Sawhill said it was going to be on September 10th!" I said, "Hey, he's a major, he's smarter than I am, I'm only a lieutenant. If he said September 10th, then September 10th it is." They accepted that.

All they wanted to do was to break you. After the first go-around, they knew the information they were getting was garbage. But they just wanted total control so if they said jump, you said, "How high?"

We were line pilots. We didn't know anything. The people who put together the flight missions were the only ones who knew where we were going ahead of time. What does a lieutenant know about strategic plans? Nothing. We lied. We stalled. We resisted up to a certain point. Then you had to tell them something. But we told them nothing of value because we knew nothing of value.

When I was captured they asked me what happened to my plane. I said we were probably hit with flak and they said "No! No! You were shot down by a MiG!" I told them there's no way we got shot down by a MiG. So they kicked the crap out of me until they finally convinced me, "Yeah, yeah, that's right. I forgot, I got shot down by a MiG."

But yeah, we resisted as much as we could. The really bad torture was the ropes. I was in them four or five times. That was enough. Some guys went more. A couple of guys went insane from them. There were others that died.

Later on, they switched from using straps to a fan belt sort of thing because it didn't leave marks. With the ropes, you would end up with scars. They didn't like that. They also used those fan belts to beat guys with. Guys would get beaten until they passed out.

Once we had an escape in camp, so they put us on our knees in iron bars for several months. You would be locked up, just lying there. You could barely breathe. You were incredibly hot. Your body was full of sores. You were festering.

Our goal was to return with honor. People who say they didn't give up anything, they're lying. But the idea was to hang on for that day. Make them try to break you tomorrow. Resist every day the best you can. Everybody's level of resistance varies. No two people are the same. Just try your hardest to do the best you can. Those were the rules of the camp. Do the best you can, resist on.

If they caught you doing something they didn't like, they would put you in the hot box. A concrete box, three-and-a-half by seven feet by five feet high. It happened to me. I crossed swords with one of the guards. He said to bow to him, so I bowed. He said to do it again. I said something back to him, using a word I probably shouldn't have. He threw me in the box. It was a nasty little thing. It was about five feet high, so you couldn't stand and the sun was beating on it. It was incredibly hot. You would just roast in there and sweat twenty-four hours a day. It wasn't very pleasant. The only good thing was that the door wasn't built very good. I could see through a crack into another building and flash to the guys in there to communicate with them.

Every afternoon they would bang on a gong to signal that it was time to take a nap.

Well, I'm just lying there in my sweat and I see this snake crawl in through the inch-and-a-half opening under the door. I start yelling and hollering, the guards come in to tell me to shut up. I was pointing and yelling, "Snake! Snake!" It went out and I heard them pounding on it. The guard came back and said it was a viper. He said, "Very, very bad snake. If he bites, you die." So I guess I'm glad I called them.

The best thing was when you got a roommate and you weren't in isolation anymore. That was very important. You needed someone. I couldn't move my arms and I had broken bones in my back. My first roommate was Mike McGrath. His shoulder was crushed and he had a dislocated leg. We had to take care of each other. When a guy would come back from torture, if he didn't have a roommate, it was his neighbor's job to get him on that wall and tell him to hang in there. Try and convince him that tomorrow would be a better day. Guys died from getting caught communicating, but we wouldn't stop. It was too important.

I recently talked to one of the guys who was in one of the rooms. He's from Wisconsin. He was really shot apart. They left him to die, but he refused to. He is a great guy, a great guy. The flak blew a hole in his arm, blew a hole in his hip, and he busted his leg when he ejected. They let him just lay there, but he wouldn't die on them. They finally gave him a roommate. He said this guys arm and leg were just covered with maggots. But as it turned out, that may have saved his life because that allowed blood to flow to his wounds.

During a bombing attack, we had to get under our bunks. They were about one meter by two meters. It was really just two planks made of teak about a foot-and-a-half off the ground. I got underneath the bunk and looked through the crack at the bottom of the door. I could see another room across the hall with three guys in there. We started exchanging information: name, rank, where you were shot down, all those sorts of things.

There were so many guys getting shot down that they started putting four guys in a room, which was great. So now you were able to pass the tap code onto other people. It worked out pretty well.

In one place it took us four months to establish contact with the guys next to us. We were being held in a former French film storage area. They called it the "Zoo annex." For us, it was like heaven. We went from four guys in a seven-by-nine-foot room to four guys in a twenty-by-twenty-foot room.

The walls were four feet thick. Actually, they were three walls with space in between them to keep the film dry. We couldn't tap on the walls because the sound wouldn't go through. The way we eventually learned to communicate was through the floor. It was solid. We would tap on the floor and the sound would carry to the other room.

One of the guys there became an admiral. He told everyone, "You've got three choices. One, you can feel sorry for yourself and accept dying. Two, you can sit here and say, 'OK I'm here, I accept it, and do nothing. Or three, you can say, "What can I learn today? What can I learn from somebody else? How can I better myself?" For the majority of guys that's the approach they took, try to learn something every day.

My roommate, Mike, had been a member of the French Club at the Naval Academy. So he taught me French. Other guys learned poetry. Whatever it took to keep your mind active and stay away from self-pity. There really wasn't much of that. Maybe around the holidays guys would think about their families and stuff, but there just wasn't a lot of "woe is me." If you did feel that way, you might as well crawl into a corner and die.

We didn't have pencils or paper, it was just talking to guys. One of my other roommates went to RPI (Rensselaer Polytechnic Institute) as a math major. A piece of tile had broken off the roof during a storm. He used it as chalk and taught calculus on the floor.

If you were in solitary confinement you talked by tapping on the walls. One of my best friends there, Darryl, had ridden a horse across Argentina. It took him six months of tapping to tell the entire story. He would tap for about ten minutes. Then the guy who received it would tap it to the guy in the cell next to him, and so on. Everybody learned about Darryl riding a horse across the pampas of Argentina. For us, it was a six-month adventure.

There were different types of guards. We weren't supposed to have contact with them other than following their orders. A few were complete assholes. Others were actually sadistic. You could see in their eyes that they wanted to be just as cruel as possible to us.

One of the guards who would bring us our water and things was just a normal guy. It was right around Christmas and he asked a group of us if we were married and had kids. There were four of us. Our senior guy had two kids. McGrath had two kids. Hess had five kids. I wasn't married. We asked the guard the same question and he started crying. He said he had a wife and child but they were both killed in a bombing attack.

In the summer of 1972, they moved us to a camp up near China. It took us two weeks to get there. If I remember correctly, there were 119 guys in the camp. In January of 1973, one of the guys said he had seen a bunch of trucks under a canopy. Another guy, who was on the edge of the camp, said he could see a bunch from where he was too. We started thinking that maybe they were going to bring us back. This is the first time we had ever heard of the Paris Peace Talks. Actually what we heard was that the US government had backed out of them.

Later that month there were over a dozen trucks lined up in a convoy. They were for us. It took two weeks to get up there but within two days we were back in Hanoi. We knew something was up. They were being fairly nice to us.

About a week later they marched us in formation and the camp commander had someone read the Paris Accords, which said we were going home sometime between the next two weeks to two months.

The word throughout camp was, "Don't do a thing. Just stand there." We just stood in formation. There was a political commissar who was a real ass. He started yelling, "Don't you understand the war is over? Are you not happy?" Yup, we were happy but we had talked about this, about not showing any emotion. They had cameras filming us, they wanted to film us jumping for joy. We wouldn't do it for them. Once we got back in our cells, then we jumped for joy.

Down the stretch, we kept telling one another to not do anything to antagonize them. Now we were allowed to go out in the mornings. We could talk to other guys. There was a water reservoir where we could kind of take showers.

They put us in the order we were shot down. That's how we would be released. (Future US Senator) John McCain was four cells down from me. I got shot down in August. He was shot down in October.

They came in and started measuring us. On the morning of March 14th, 1973, they came in with new clothes and a duffle bag. I stuffed my prison garb and anything I had in that bag. They took us out on buses. We weren't blindfolded, so we got to see Hanoi as we drove to the airport.

There was an Air Force officer at the airport to meet us. He escorted us to the plane. We were totally quiet. We sat down. Even while taxiing we didn't say a word. Once the wheels left the ground, the plane probably lifted up another fifty feet from our shouts. We were ecstatic. Every guy had a chair and a bunk and there were two nurses on there for us. They flew us to the Philippines.

The big thing was going to be that first meal. They were worried that we were starving, malnourished, in rough shape. So they came in with all this food that was finely chopped up. The first guy who saw it said, "This is bullshit. Give me a steak!" It went on from there. "I want some ice cream! I want some pie!" I said, "I want a dozen eggs!" They said, "OK, give him a dozen eggs."

After the Philippines, we spent some time being evaluated at Wright-Patterson Air Force Base (Dayton, Ohio). When I came home there was a big gathering to greet me at the airport in Green Bay. The County Sheriff escorted me to Suring, where they had a parade for me. Then I got to go home, which was very nice.

You look at what became of the POWs after coming home: there's a four-star general, a four-star admiral, governors, congressmen, one ran for president, one for vice president, senators. I don't know how many lawyers, but a lot. There were doctors, veterinarians, several ministers, and many, very successful businessmen.

I became an airline pilot for Eastern Airlines for almost ten years, then went back to school, graduated, and was a controller for General Mills. After that, I opened my own financial company and then became a financial advisor.

Over 300 guys were held up North. I think most came back with an incredible curiosity which led to their success. The overwhelming majority made good lives for themselves. I guess that's the best way of putting it.

LINDA GOMLICKER LT. COL. USAFR

Flight Nurse
10th AES
US Air Force
Vietnam War

On February 12, 1973, the first flight of Operation Homecoming took off from Hanoi with a contingent of released American POWs. Over the next two months, 591 former POWs were flown first to Clark Field in the Philippines and then to America. Flight nurse Linda Gomlicker recalls the thrill of flying those missions.

The flight nurses knew Operation Homecoming was going to start probably a month before they announced it. We just didn't know the exact date. There were a lot of different military service people arriving out at Clark AFB who wouldn't normally have been there. We just knew something big was about to happen. One thing that really ticked us off was when the administrative nurses were chosen to go into Hanoi first. Those of us who flew the line weren't really happy about that deal. But I guess in looking back on it, they also had a job to do.

I went to Hanoi on the third day of flights. It was really kind of surreal. I wasn't afraid. No I wouldn't call it fear. I guess a little nervous might be the best word. All of us were confident in our people because they had planned this out so much. But really, anybody with any sense would feel a little wary.

We flew C-141s on those missions because they could stay in the air the longest if there were any problems on the ground. Those planes could circle for twelve-fourteen hours as best as I remember.

As we landed, I thought, "I hope this goes like it's supposed to go and we get them the heck out of there quick." One unusual note was that the aircrew opened the tail of the plane before we came to a complete stop. That was something they wouldn't normally ever do.

There was a table set up out on the tarmac where the North Vietnamese would bring our guys to be exchanged and handed off to our side. I could see some of the North Vietnamese soldiers out the back of the plane, but to be honest, without their guns, they didn't look so terrifying in their little black uniforms. It's not like we were surrounded or that they came near us. There were some foreign newsmen at the tail of the airplane. At least, I thought they were newsmen from North Vietnam.

We had a manifest with the names of each POW that we were picking up. Each of them had been deemed physically able to make the flight. We were told they shouldn't need check-ups or physical care on the flight. Our main job was to observe them and make sure they didn't feel faint or have any unexpected problems.

Flight nurses had gotten new uniforms since most of the POWs had been captured. We used to wear navy blue slacks, navy blue lace-up shoes, and a blue button-down top. Well, the Air Force had completely changed all flight nursing uniforms. Now we wore navy blue double-knit slacks. They looked good, but they were so thick that they were hotter than a firecracker! We also had a blue top with a Peter Pan collar and a vest over it that was just as hot. Everything was double knit. That uniform was supposed to match the current fashion of the times. To someone who hadn't seen us in years, it didn't look like what they remembered. I even told each POW as they came onto the aircraft, "I'm Captain Baker and I'm a flight nurse."

After the POWs got on board, they wanted to know all kinds of stuff: where we were from, what was going on in the country, and many other things. One of our major jobs was just to get them to sit down for takeoff. A few of them were very quiet, didn't talk, and went right to their seats. It's almost like they were in a daze. But then as soon as we had wheels-up most everybody was moving around, talking and just thrilled! They just wanted to make sure we were out of there before they could totally relax. They were just tickled to be with us and going home.

Some of them were very open and talked about what they went through, but most of them wanted to talk about what movies were popular back home, another one wanted to know about the TV shows, and someone else wanted to know about pro football. I told him that he had the wrong girl to talk about football. I got one of the tech guys to fill him in on that subject.

One guy whispered in my ear, "Do you have a bra on?" I said, "Of course I do." The reason he asked that was because of what happened in December of 1972. Our side had bombed the crap out of Hanoi. At least one of the planes was shot down and the crew ended up in the camp with the rest of these guys. Well, one of the bits of information that was passed on throughout the camp from the new guys was that women back home didn't wear bras anymore.

We had water for them and a liquid drink, the type they give people who can't eat solid foods. I'm sure it would have tasted like crap to us, but they drank it down like it was a Frappuccino. Physically, they actually looked a lot better than we had expected. We found out later that their guards had started feeding them better at least a month before they were released.

Not on my plane, but later we learned some of the guys had some poorly performed surgery repair work done by their capturers. I'm not saying it was on purpose, but their surgeries, for want of a better word, screwed them up. You could see that later in photos of a few of the guys.

Our flights were from Hanoi to Clark AFB in the Philippines where they stayed at least overnight to be checked out and debriefed. When they were ready, we flew them on a different flight to the States with a stop at Hickam AFB, Hawaii. From Hawaii, they were flown to their final destination. I had former Senator John McCain on one of those flights. We picked him up in Hawaii and flew him somewhere in the South. I don't remember the exact base. The one thing I remember was that his hair had turned almost white. I also recall that he was young, tall, and drop-dead gorgeous! (Laughing) That's what I remember about John McCain. In fact, it wasn't until I was living in Arizona and he was in the news running for office that I thought, *Well, that name is familiar*. So I dug out my manifest and he was on it.

For those guys on that first flight out of Hanoi, it had to be the most wonderful plane ride of their lives. They were enjoying it. One of the guys said to me, "Meet me at the O Club (Officers Club) tonight for dinner. I said, "Well, I will be at the O Club, but I don't think you will be there." He said, "I've been locked up for six years, and I'm telling you, if I want to go to the O Club tonight, I'm going to be there!" I told him, "Sorry, but I really don't think you will be going to the O Club tonight."

On my flight, there were three or four guys in the back that we were told to keep an eye on. The word was that they had collaborated with the North Vietnamese. There was concern that some of the other guys might jump them once we were in the air. But honestly, the other guys couldn't have cared less. They were a lot more interested in talking to us about what was going on in the world. I'm sure they also knew that because those guys were all young enlisted guys, they didn't have any information their captors could use. They were in no position to have any big-time knowledge.

We had been instructed not to get off the plane until all the POWs had disembarked. That was to be their special time of celebration. Well, I had a returning POW who brought a Hawaiian lei onboard. I don't remember the stop, but when we landed he insisted that I disembark with him. He didn't care what the orders were or who gave them. So, I finally said okay and walked off with him. I thought, "What are they going to do, shoot me? All of a sudden he said to me, "Hold this lei." I said, "Okay," wondering why, because I assumed he had planned to give it to his mother or girlfriend." He said, "I want you to put it around my neck." When I did that, he reached over and kissed me. I thought, *Oh my, they are going to court-martial me and then shoot me!* Needless to say, the press was there and took about 100 pictures.

Less than twenty-four hours later, my mom gets a phone call from a reporter back at her home in Arkansas. "Did you know you daughter, blah blah…?" And my mom said, "Oh, okay." And then the reporter said, "What do you think about that?" And my mother said, "She deserved it!" (Laughing) The next time I talked to my mom she told me she had no idea why she said that. To my surprise, my commander never said anything to me about it.

Several girls did develop friendships with the guys, and some even had romantic relationships. But I felt like the guys needed time to assimilate back into their lives. I didn't think it was a good idea to date them. They needed to get many things settled in their lives. There were two guys who corresponded with me. Just thank you's for bringing them back and telling me that they were doing well. Another returning POW and I corresponded maybe two or three times a year for several years until we both were married. But there was never anything more than friendships.

I remember when I joined the Air National Guard, I was just twenty-two years old. My dad couldn't believe I didn't talk it over with him first. Many people warned me that the pilots especially, would try to take advantage of young girls. But the whole flight crew including the pilots treated us like we were their younger sisters. If we were going out to eat, they made sure they told us the places to go to and what places to avoid. I mean, they would even tell us the different kinds of wine we should have with the different meals. They were great to us and treated us like we were their sisters until we were well-oriented.

I stayed in the Guard for five-plus years and then went on active duty for just shy of four years. I always say, "Being in the Air Force was the best thing to happen in my life other than having two baby boys." As for the POW flights, they were the trips of a lifetime. I am honored to have been lucky enough to have flown those soldiers home. It was exciting as well as historic. There are a lot of people that don't even remember or care that it happened, but for those of us who have some military background, it's one of the biggest events of our lives. When asked about my time during Operation Homecoming, I always say I am proud to have helped bring home some of the finest soldiers our nation has ever had stand for them!

If I wrote my own obituary, I think I would say, "She had a great time in the military and saw the world...accidentally."

JIM BARLAMENT

Corpsman
1st Marine Division
US Navy
Vietnam War

It's not uncommon for sons of military fathers to dream of adding to the family's legacy of service to our country. What is uncommon, is for a father to dissuade his son from following directly in his footsteps.

For Jim Barlament's father, who spent time in both the hostile, malarial swamps of New Guinea and the arctic-like cold of Korea, there had to be a, let's just say, more comfortable way for his son to do his duty to God and country. At least he could always say he tried.

I was an Army brat. My dad spent twenty-three years in the Army, retiring as a sergeant major. We had thirty-one different addresses and I went to seventeen different schools. My dad's last post was Hawaii. We were actually there when it became a state. Then in 1962 my dad and some other senior noncoms and officers went on an advisory tour of Southeast Asia. He came back and said he was retiring. He had been in World War II, he had been in Korea, he knew Southeast Asia would be the next war. He told my mom he'd had enough.

I wanted to be just like him; the green beanie, Army all the way. He said, "No son, you need to join the Navy. You will have a warm bed and three hot meals a day." So I took his advice and joined the Navy.

The day we graduated from boot camp at Great Lakes Naval Station is one I will never forget. We were all standing there in formation when an officer came out and said, "President Kennedy has been shot. Everyone is on standby."

I had an aunt and uncle who lived in the area so I went and stayed with them for a few days. I still remember sitting on their couch watching TV when Jack Ruby shot Oswald.

After basic, I went to a twenty-four-week school to become a fire control technician working on guidance systems for Polaris missiles. When we graduated they said, "We're sorry but we miscalculated; we don't have enough submarines for all of you."

With my high scores and everything, they said I could probably get any other job I wanted. I was thinking and thinking and I thought, *"You know, I really miss my girlfriend in De Pere, how about Hospital Corps school back at Great Lakes?"* That way I could ride the train home to visit her on weekends. Ironically, I really liked the schooling. It was just a good fit. I enjoyed what I was doing.

My first duty was at the Naval Hospital in Philadelphia. Most of us new guys started in a ward. I went from that to the recovery room and then anesthesiology. I loved it, but the Navy had a policy, if you had fifteen-and-a-half months or less, you would not be sent to Vietnam. Every week they would call us all down to the auditorium. I had fifteen months, two weeks, and two days to go. They went through the list of those who were going to be shipped out and my name was on the list.

There were eight other guys I worked with who got orders to ship out to Camp Lejeune, North Carolina. It was kind of a mini Marine boot camp. One funny thing, our drill instructor had just come back from a sixty-day leave after a year in Vietnam. The first thing we had to do was run around the football field to warm up. We were running and he was leaning against the goal post throwing up. He had put on a little potbelly, which was definitely gone by the time we graduated.

It was interesting going through all that training. I had grown up with it so it was never a big thing for me. In Hawaii, I used to go to the rifle range all the time with my dad and shoot the M-14s. I had never fired an M-16 before, but I'm on the range one day and the instructor comes over and says, "Damn Doc, where did you learn to shoot like that?" I said, "My dad is Sergeant Major Howard Barlament." He just said, "OK then," and walked away.

This was in the spring of 1966. I had ten days' leave and the first thing my dad does is haul me to the range and has me shooting a .45. Disassembling it and everything until I could basically do it in my sleep. He knew that was what most corpsmen and medics carried in combat.

We had no idea where we were going once we got to Vietnam. We loaded up on a C-47 and ended up landing at Chu Lai. I remember looking out the window just before we landed and seeing all these sand dunes, and thinking, *"What the hell? I thought Vietnam was all jungle?"* As we're taxiing there's a hull of a tank sitting there all blown to hell and smoking. And I'm thinking, *OK I'm in a war zone. I don't have a gun and I don't know what's going on.*

I ended up getting attached to a medical unit, but they didn't know what to do with me. They had everybody they needed so they assigned me to MEDCAP (Medical Civic Action Programs) missions. You would load up a jeep with a couple of corpsmen, a Marine for security, and go into the villages to treat people.

Honestly, I treated quite a few bullet wounds on people who were probably wearing black pajamas (VC) the night before. But you took care of them just the same. The ones you really wanted to help were the kids. You felt so bad for those little kids. You tried to do anything you could for them. You would talk to one of the elders and give him extra bandages or whatever for the kids and he would shake his head, "No. No." They didn't want the Viet Cong to see that they were accepting our help. That was one of the sadder parts of being there for me.

Other than that, my main job was filling in for units if their corpsman rotated, was wounded or killed. So I would hook up with a unit for a week, two weeks maybe, something like that.

This was good duty actually because some of the corpsmen would get assigned to units and be out for weeks and weeks at a time. Most of my missions were a few days at the most.

My first patrol, wow, here I am with a bunch of Marines walking along the dike on a rice paddy. For most of the patrols my position was right by the radioman and platoon or squad leader. They were telling me all about spider holes and booby traps and I'm thinking, *OK, well this is a really delicious situation I'm in.*

We were going along and all of a sudden, about thirty feet away, a spider hole pops open. A VC jumps up, throws a grenade, and opens fire. I froze. The grenade rolls on the ground in front of me and doesn't go off. Meanwhile, the Marines basically cut him in half with rifle fire. They came around and looked and said, "Doc, you just used up all of your nine lives." I'm looking at it and just saying to myself, *"Holy shit."* Needless to say, every time after that, I took cover immediately.

But yeah, the shooting, the shock, the grenade, it's like I was stunned by all that happening so quick. I just didn't move.

I remember the first time I had to go out under fire. A guy was out in the open and he got hit in the stomach and went down. Someone yelled, "Corpsman up!" I started to go and Gunny grabbed me and slammed me down and said, "Doc you don't move until I tell you to." Then once the guys were throwing out enough heavy fire, he said, "OK, go!"

I ran out to the guy and I'm trying to get a dressing on him across his stomach, his intestines were popping out a little bit. He starts pulling on my shirt. Now, in training, you're taught to shield the patient with your body. But the Marines are taught that if you are wounded, your body should go between enemy fire and the corpsman. I go, "Quit pulling on me!" And he goes, "Doc, Doc, you're on the wrong side!"

Once I got him dressed I put him over my shoulder and made it back to cover. I remember telling Gunny about what the guy said. I told him I was just so impressed that he was more worried about me than himself (choking up). That has just really stuck with me. It was a bond that started then and continues to this day.

The first thing you do when you get to the guy is ask, "Where are you hit?" It was kind of a running joke with them because a guy will be yelling, "I'm hit! I'm hit!" And I would say, "Well tell me where! I don't have time to look all over! I've got three other people down around you!"

Jim Barlament collection

No matter how many times you told them, they were notorious for leaving their flak jackets open. So, you would get a lot of chest wounds. When you got to a guy, you had to look for entrance wounds and exit wounds. Is he breathing OK? Is he bleeding a lot? Does he need a tourniquet or a dressing to stop the bleeding? Then you want to stabilize them and prevent them from going into shock. Because if they go into shock, everything goes downhill in a hurry. Surprisingly, some guys wouldn't really feel the pain at first. But the longer it goes, the pain will eventually kick in and that's why you hit them with a shot of morphine, to help stabilize them and keep them calm. If the pain is really bad and they are bleeding really bad, then the blood pressure drops and everything starts shutting down. Shock was a very serious thing we dealt with.

Once you get them, what we called rough stabilized, you'd pick them up and haul them to cover. You might have to drag them or you might have to carry them over your back. I had one that I had treated and was carrying back when he got hit by three more rounds. I didn't realize until I laid him down that he had three fresh holes. He shielded me from those rounds.

You also have to make the tough decision of triage. If you have multiple wounded, you have to make a quick decision on which ones can be saved and which ones have the smallest chance. Once you were done with the lesser wounded you would go back to the ones who were extremely critical, that's the only way you could do it.

There was no one way they would act when you got to them. Some were totally quiet, some would talk a lot, some honestly would cry for their mamas. That's when the corpsman would try to be as cool as possible, "You're OK. You're OK. We're going to get you back." So it's always trying to be as calm for them as possible. People told me I had a stone face. That was on purpose. You can't let emotions show on your face whether it's a minor wound or a really bad one. You had to just deal with the reality of what you have laying there in front of you.

Stomach wounds and amputations were the hardest, the ones you hated to see the most. We had one guy whose leg was blown off so high near his hip that there was no way to get a tourniquet on the femoral artery. I tried everything to stop the bleeding, tried putting clamps on it but nothing would work. He bled out on me.

As a corpsman, you had to deal with mutilation, dismemberment, just some very difficult things. There was one time we brought this poor kid in and there was hardly anything left of him, but he just wouldn't die, wouldn't quit. There was a large part of his head missing and we just stood around and there was nothing we could do. He kept hanging on for at least twenty minutes and it just tore everybody up watching him. Just such a helpless feeling.

Wounds were one thing, mutilation as I said, was another. That happened more than people would realize. We had a sweep down south of Chu Lai one time in conjunction with a South Korean unit. Those were some bad-ass dudes, wow.

There had been another unit out on point and a couple of guys were missing. We found two Marines that had been captured and horribly tortured. You can only imagine what they had gone through because the villagers said they could hear them screaming. We bagged them and medivacked them out.

As gruesome as it could be at times, it was actually an interesting job because one week I might be with a line company, another week with artillery, maybe a mortar unit. I moved around like that for almost six months, including one two-week tour with swift boats. Their corpsman got wounded so I filled in. I have to be honest, those guys were crazy.

I'm telling you, the tension when you would pull up to search a sampan - wow. I mean, everybody is locked and loaded, and you're thinking, *What if somebody makes a wrong move, does everybody start shooting?* They would say, "Doc, just stand back we'll take care of it." But boy, just thick tension.

At night they would go looking for trouble. South of Chu Lai, there was a cliff with a cave in it. Charlie had an old 75mm recoilless rifle stashed up there. It was probably captured from the French. They would roll that thing out, shoot and roll it back in. Well, these guys on the boat would practically drive onto the surf. They weren't supposed to go any closer than, I believe 1,500 yards. But they would get as close as they could and wave battle lanterns at them trying to draw fire. On the front of the boat was a set of twin .50-cals. On the back was an 81mm mortar. The guys would be sitting there doing anything they could to get them to come out with that 75 so they could open up on them.

I believe it was late November when I got moved up to Da Nang. Army units were coming in to take over in Chu Lai. I remember going in and thinking, *OK, now what am I going to do here?* I mean this was a full-fledged field hospital. I went in and started talking to one of the guys and he said. "Hey, I need somebody to help me with air evac." (Air evacuation) I thought that sounded good. You get to ride in helicopters, pick up wounded and bring them back in. Jim Moore was his name. He was one pay-grade above me and was basically running the air evac operation. I got to work with him for four months until he rotated stateside. We stayed lifelong friends.

There were some crazy days, I will tell you that. I survived three helicopter crashes. Although the pilots will tell you it was just an auto-rotation maneuver. Which is BS. (Laughing) Because auto rotation is nothing more than a controlled crash.

We had one where we were coming back with two really severely wounded guys. One of them had his lower jaw blown away. He was still conscious and looking at me while I was working on him. The pilot flipped the chopper up to clear some power lines and then slammed it down hard on the pad. One thing I want to say, almost all of the guys I worked on, I never heard from again. But this guy, years later, got ahold of me. They rebuilt his jaw out of cadaver ribs and did extensive plastic surgery. He said he was doing well.

When I was walking out of the room, one of the guys said, "Doc there's something sticking out of your back." I said, "What?" One of the rounds had hit the metal frame on the chopper door and sent a piece of the frame into my back. I wasn't wearing a flak jacket but I had no idea it had even happened. That's how focused you get on the job you had to do. And no, I did not put in for a Purple Heart.

But now, here's why I didn't know I got hit, and it goes back to that very first wounded Marine that I treated. The entire time I was out there working on him, or on other guys, I did not hear the firing all around me - nothing. That's how focused you become in a situation like that.

There was one mission that was different from the rest. One night somebody comes over and says, "Doc we need you." I said, "For what?"

The First Force Recon compound was next to the medical unit and they said they needed a corpsman for a mission. I'm like, "Okay, sure, whatever."

So I grab my gear and go over there and these guys are standing around with their faces all painted up looking like death. One of the guys looks me over and says, "You don't need that, you don't need this, but grab your weapon." I said, "What's going on?" They said, "We're doing a night drop from a helicopter and you're coming along." It was going to be a four-day mission, hunting bad guys. Gunny comes over and says, "Doc you're going out with me." I said, "I've never jumped out of a plane or a helicopter with a parachute!" He said, "Don't worry, we'll be buckled together. When we hit the ground, don't move, don't do anything or say anything."

I'm an adventurous guy, but when you can't see what's below you, when you don't know how high off the ground you were jumping from, it was terrifying. I think I got more scared later when they told me how risky it was jumping out of a helicopter. They hadn't told me that before. The only thing I could think of was that there had to be a large piece of bamboo down there that was going to go right up my ass when I hit the ground.

That was the scariest time of my entire time over there. We spent four days crawling around. Charlie would sometimes walk right by us. We would lay there quiet as could be, trying to not make a sound, not make panting noises as something slithers across you. Those Recon guys were like Navy SEALS. I don't think I said three words the entire time I was with them.

While laying out there I remembered that there were thirty-seven different varieties of snakes in Vietnam. The snakes I saw ranged in size from a six-inch venomous snake to a snake that was about thirty feet long. We were on patrol, walking through elephant grass one day and the point man signaled that something was going on. We went up there and it looked like a big pipe laying there. So we start tracing it down, and this pipe has a big lump in it. And then we heard a shot. The point man had shot the snake in the head. They cut it open, it had swallowed a baby water buffalo. Once again, I just thought to myself, *Okayyyyy*....

I was supposed to carry a .45, but back when I got there, there was a shortage of sidearms. So they handed me an M-14 and I laughed. I said, "I'm not carrying that thing." There was a chief corpsman back in one of the units and he somehow got ahold of an old Thompson submachine gun for me. I'm thinking. *Alright, this is good.* I took it on one patrol and said, "Forget it, I'm not carrying this thing with me either."

We had a bunch of wounded and dead ARVN brought in one night and I see a pile of weapons sitting there. I saw a nice M-2 carbine, so I kicked it in the ditch and went back after dark to pick it up. I was excited, that was a great weapon. Well, the first time I fired it I almost got my ass kicked back to Camp Lejeune. The platoon leader said. "Doc, the VC uses them too. If my guys hear that sound they're going to shoot at it!"

I had to go back to ordnance again. The guy cut most of the barrel off, which changed the sound, now it didn't sound like a VC weapon anymore. Then he cut the stock off and brazed two 30-round clips together. I remember at least once or twice when we had to lay down a lot of fire and I would hold it outside the hole and fire off one clip and then flip it over and fire the other. I loved that thing. I thought about sneaking it back to the states in a big tape recorder case, but I figured I'd better not.

I enjoyed doing air evacs. We would go out and get the wounded, bring them in and also shuttle them to the USS *Repose* or the USS *Sanctuary*, a couple of World War II hospital ships that were both on station out there. That kept us busy. We went through so many supplies that we were running out of everything. It always seemed to be that way for the Marines.

Jim and I decided to go on R&R to Japan together. A lot of our time, not all - but we don't need to talk about what else we did – was spent going to dispensaries and hospitals asking if they could donate surgical tools, supplies, just about anything they could spare. They were great. They said, whatever we needed, to just let them know. But even with their generosity, Jim and I were also known to, shall we say, appropriate over and above.

We were walking down the hall of this one hospital and there's a brand new mimeograph machine still in the box. I go, "Ours is shot. We could really use one of these." He goes, "Keep an eye out." So we loaded it up on our cart, put it on one of the three skids we had been packing, and walked right out. We got back to base and the commander said, "I don't want to know how you got all of this. I don't know where you got all of this, but from now on you have the titles of Relocation Specialists." To this day we still talk and laugh about that trip.

After one of our missions, I was walking back to the LZ where two choppers were waiting for us. One was empty and the other was set up with all the gear from the field hospital. As we were walking toward them the crew chief of the empty one swung his head out and said, "Hey Doc, come on this one." So we climbed on that one because it wasn't packed so tight. Ten minutes after we took off the first chopper swung over the water, went down, and blew up. All we found was the top half of the crew chief. They were having trouble with those choppers because they had dual rotors and the shaft in the middle had a tendency to break.

Do you want to hear something ironic? Years later I was applying for a ham radio license and had to take the code test. A guy I knew said

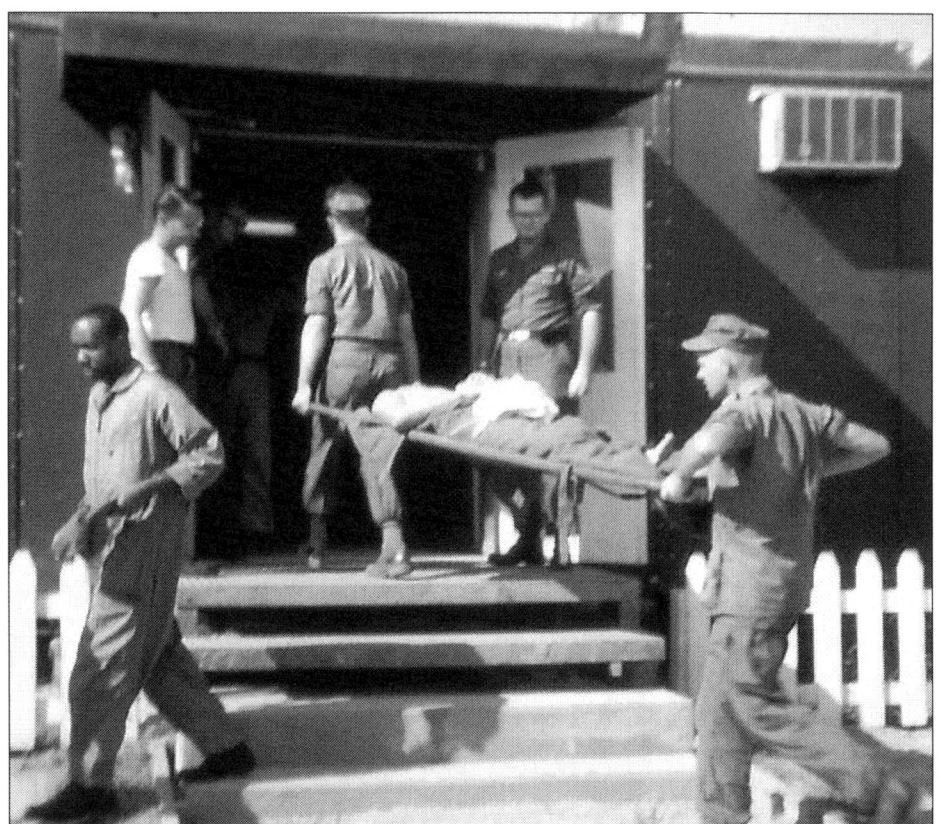
Jim Barlament (right) helps carry a casualty into a treatment facility. (Jim Barlament collection)

his son could monitor the test for me. So I go and talk to him, and he goes, "Oh you're my dad's friend, Doc, cool." After the test, we chatted a little bit and he said, "Yeah I got shot down in Cambodia, and it took me six weeks to make it back through the jungle to our lines." And I started relating the story that happened to me. He stopped, got real quiet, and said, "That was you?" He was the crew chief that waved me aboard his chopper.

There were three different times when we took ground fire that damaged the chopper and they had to basically pancake down. One time we were high enough that the pilot disengaged the blades and just let them free-wheel down. Believe me, that is ... that is something. You want to stand up a little bit to get out of there in a hurry, but you're also trying to hang on because you don't know when it hits if it's going to roll to one side or the other and that rotor is still swinging. We came in and hit hard. Luckily we were able to jump out and run away.

There were times when they would take us out to a hot LZ on medevacs. That way if they had guys badly wounded, we could give in-flight care to them especially if they need air passages opened or things like that. That twenty-minute flight could be very critical. It's what they call the golden hour.

I think I had the right approach when I went over there. My attitude was, "OK, I'm going to be here for fourteen months. I am going to work hard right up until I am exhausted and will go right to sleep." That way, I wouldn't dwell on some of the things I was seeing and doing. I will admit that what I experienced on my first patrol stayed in my mind for quite some time. But after that, I just said to myself, *"I'm learning what I need to do and what not to do. Just focus on stuff like that."*

I think what really helped me was the MEDCAP missions. You could just be the real you. You could relax. You were helping people who otherwise wouldn't be getting any help whatsoever. The people loved to see you. The average grunt didn't have a chance to do that. They didn't have any release so to speak. You would pull up and the villagers would start saying, "Oh Bác sĩ, Oh Bác sĩ!" meaning doctor. The kids would come running over, all happy to see you. Those were good days. These people were trying to do the same thing a family in the United States would be doing: raise a family, provide for that family, and not bother anybody. But they were being torn in two different ways.

We had a corpsman who had done four tours and could speak the language. He would talk to the elders and they would tell about how they had to move their entire villages two or three times because Charlie kept coming in at night and killing the elders and doing their whole indoctrination thing. It was horrible. I still feel terrible for those people.

There were a few occasions when I worked on NVA. In one instance there was a wounded guy and the South Vietnamese wanted to interrogate him. So I patched him up, got the bleeding stopped, nothing too vital, he was going to make it. But then the South Vietnamese interrogators took over and they're not gentle. They were beating the snot out of him. We got the prisoner on the UH-34 chopper and they're still screaming and hollering and beating on him. Let's just say he didn't make it back safely. And I'm like, "Whattttt? OK, how do I put that in my report?"

There were ARVN units who would fight just as hard as we did. But then other ones who would slip away at night and go home, or might even be sympathetic to the VC. You just knew to not depend on them if you hadn't worked with them before.

The ones I felt worse for, and I only got to meet them a couple of times when I went far enough up into the hills, were the Montagnards. Those people were ferocious fighters, just dedicated to our people. They were just amazing.

There's another group that was very loyal to us, Hmongs. When people complained about them coming to America I would tell them, "You don't understand. They fought for us and we abandoned them." I have many Hmong friends to this day.

The young Marines I was around were probably as scared and uncertain of what was going on as anyone. But they also would put on false bravado, talking tough all the time. When we were out and the shit hit the fan, they did what they had to do. Even though you knew deep down inside they were just as scared as anyone else.

After my buddy Jim rotated out, I got put on the worst job of my tour, Decedent Affairs with Graves Registration. Anytime they brought a body in I had to open up the bag and identify the remains. I don't want to go into detail about what I found in some of those bags. Then I would make out the death certificate. I can still see those pink forms where it said "parts missing" and sometimes there just wasn't much there.

Early on when I was out in the field, I would see guys carrying plastic bags and I asked someone, "What's that for?" He said, "If somebody steps on a landmine, we always make sure we gather up everything to put in a bag." After having to fill out reports on what was in the body bag when I had to register them with Graves Registration, I could see why.

That was a bad job. That one still bothers me.

At the end of fourteen months, of the eight guys I went over there with, five of them, including one on his very first patrol, had been killed. Strangely all the ones who died were married; the ones who survived were single.

I always had to laugh when I thought about my dad's advice as to why joining the Navy would be better than the Army. There was a time halfway through my tour that I wrote him a letter. "Dear Dad, It's been raining for six weeks. I'm cold and wet all the time. I'm eating C-rations from 1945. Where the hell is the warm bed and three hot meals you said I would have if I joined the Navy instead of the Army? Love, your waterlogged son."

The part I dream about on a regular basis, and I'm sure it's the same for nurses, and corpsmen, and medics; sitting there telling a guy he's going to be okay when you know he's not going to make it.

I've been asked many times, "Would you do it all over again?" I always say yes, because then maybe I could save one more guy.

It really hit home when I watched the movie *Hacksaw Ridge*, and Desmond Doss is saying, "Please God, just let me save one more." That stands so true for all of us.

RON UMENTUM

4th Battalion
25th Infantry
US Army
Vietnam War

Ron Umentum was a 1967 graduate of Green Bay Premontre High School who wasn't content to wait for the draft board to call his name. In December of 1968, he said goodbye to his parents along with his eight brothers and sisters and headed to Fort Campbell, Kentucky, as a new enlistee in the United States Army.

I was a shy nineteen-year-old kid when I got to Fort Campbell. I was so scared of those drill instructors. You would be out on one of those runs and the drill instructor would order you to yell out your service number. I was so nervous about getting it wrong that every night I would sit in the barracks and make sure I had that thing memorized. But thinking back on it you probably could have yelled out any numbers and he wouldn't have known. I mean there's no way he knew everybody's number. But nobody wanted to take that chance. That's how much power they held over you. I can rattle it off right now like it was fifty-two years ago.

I was only there for a few days when the sergeant came up and asked me where I learned to march the way I did. I told him I had ROTC back in high school. Just like that, he made me the acting platoon sergeant. So here I am a quiet 152-pound-kid from Bellevue, Wisconsin, in charge of forty-some guys from all over the country. But you know, that was actually a pretty big moment in my life; that really turned me around. It was the first time someone in authority had ever shown confidence in me.

Another big day was right before graduation when the drill sergeant called me into his office and said he was impressed with how serious I took the training. He said, "If anyone from this platoon is coming back, I would put my money on you." That made me feel more confident too. But then the other platoon sergeant came over to talk to us a little bit about what it was like over there. He had recently gotten back from Vietnam. He lifted up his shirt; I can still see it plain as day. He had two holes in his back. They were from a machine gun. He told a story about a bad day at Hoc Mon Bridge in early 1968.

He told us how everybody was nervous about crossing that bridge because it was too quiet. They didn't see any kids playing, no civilians walking around, which was a bad sign. The captain wanted to prep the other side with artillery from the bridge, but the major turned him down. The VC waited until one company, Charlie Company, was going across before springing the ambush. They wanted to separate the three companies and then blow the bridge. Within eight minutes, seventy-eight of the ninety-two guys were hit, forty-nine would end up dying.

Ron Umentum collection

He said, "I don't care where you get sent. I just hope you don't go to a place called Tay Ninh (Rocket City) with Charlie Company, 4th of the 9th with the 25th Infantry. They got a name for that unit. They call it "Suicide Charlie."

I arrived in Nam in May of 1969. We were about to land at Bien Hoa Air Base, which was near Saigon, but they said the runway had just been mortared and they were still fixing it so we had to circle until the holes were patched. That got our attention. When we landed they got us all on one side so the guys leaving could get on the plane on the other side. They wanted to get back in the air as quickly as possible. They opened that back hatch and the heat and smell of Vietnam just hit you in the face. Before we started off I saw a line of what looked like old men coming towards us. Some were limping, one guy was using a cane. They were all wearing old faded clothes. None of them would look at us in our fresh new uniforms and shined boots. Finally, one of the last guys coming in looked at me, looked me right in the eye, and really quietly said, "Good luck." I thought to myself, *What in the hell did he mean by that?*

We were loaded on buses and sent to the 90th Replacement Center. You didn't have any idea where you would end up. You're just standing there in a line and it was like, "You-101st. You-82nd." Then it was my turn, "You-25th Infantry."

So they sent me to Cu Chi, which was west of Saigon and the 25th Infantry base camp. When I got there they told me which unit I was going to be attached to, Charlie Company, 25th Division, 4th of the 9th, the very unit that had all those guys killed on that bridge, "Suicide Charlie." As if I wasn't nervous enough already ... I mean what are the odds of that?

I had to meet my new captain, Captain Paulson. I remember walking into his tent, hot as hell in there. I went to salute him and he goes, "Wait a minute. That's one thing we don't do here. You never salute officers." It got to the point where they weren't wearing any insignia at all. The officers didn't want to become targets any more than anybody else did. I was scared as hell just being there and then I saw a pile of AK-47s and SKSs. They had blood and hair and everything stuck on them. He saw me looking at them and said, "Yeah, yesterday was a rough day. We lost five men. Today becomes the hardest day, writing letters to their families."

A lieutenant came in to take me to the mortar squad. Seeing that blood and everything made it all real. I realized right there that this shy little farm boy from Wisconsin was heading into a new life. It seemed scary already.

About a week after I got there we were sent to an area that was really active. It was a place called Mole City. We would have regular fire missions with the 81 mortar. If we weren't doing that, we would be pulling bunker guard duty, going out on four to six-man night patrols, manning listening posts, things like that. There are a lot of boring days and nights. You would go from bored to death to the highest adrenaline high you can ever imagine. The highest of highs and the lowest of lows. You can't compare it to anything back here. You would lose track of what day of the week it was. Guys would actually have arguments over what day it was. The only thing that we knew down to the minute was when we were going home. We all had our calendars with the last day strategically placed.

After about a month we were sent to a place called French Fort, the real name was Firebase Santa Barbara. This place was loaded, 175s, 155s, 105s, quad-50s, four-deuce mortars and 81s. With all that firepower sitting there the enemy tried to make things rough on us. They didn't want us around. We were a target. We were hit almost every night for sixty days straight. In a lot of areas we would go out on patrol for four to five days at a time, but in this area, they were just one-day patrols, and then we'd come back to the fort.

Being in one place so long you had to find ways to amuse yourselves. Me and a good friend, Bill from Manistique, Michigan, used to have fun trapping rats. During the rainy season rats would come into our bunker to get out of the rain. Well, we would take cracker wrappers, leave one cracker in the back and blow out the candle. Then we would sit there in the dark, one with a machete the other manning the candle. It wouldn't take long before you would hear that rat rustling around trying to get to that cracker. Whack! One would nail him with the machete; the other would relight the candle to check out our kill. The next day we would take them down to a place we called The Barter Point. We would trade our rats to the Vietnamese for black market whiskey. Then on the nights that we didn't have guard duty one of the guys would pull out his guitar. We would drink some whiskey and we would all sing. Our favorite song was, *"You Are My Sunshine."* That song still hits me when I hear it today.

One day we were going to be going on a patrol through this little hamlet and another good friend, Mike from Boston, said, "Hey when you go through you have to try the sandwiches this mama-san sells there; they're really good." I said sure. I would try anything other than those damn C-rations. I was so sick of them. Everybody was. So I go up to this lady slicing bread. Of course, it had crushed bugs in it. That was their protein. I was fine with that. Then she puts on these nice strips of what looks like beef on the bread, then some hot sauce, then some sort of lettuce. She hands it to me. I take a bite. It was delicious. I said, "Mama-san, very good, number one. What kind of sandwich?" She goes, "No bic, no bic," Meaning she didn't understand. The lady behind me taps me on the shoulder and makes these running motions with her fingers and goes, "Same-same, eek-eek." I said, "Rats?" She started laughing. I handed it to my friend. He didn't care. He ate it. It actually was pretty good, but that's how we found out we were buying back the same rats we had traded for our whiskey.

You know, you get so close to guys being in a situation like that, that when one leaves it's almost like he died. He's just gone. That was quite a sight when you would see them jump on that chopper or the back of a truck and wave goodbye. You got so close to these guys, sitting around playing cards, talking about home, stuff like that. We always said we would look each other up back in the world, but that didn't happen for a long time. On the other hand, as happy as the guy was to be leaving, a lot of times he felt like he was leaving his job, was leaving his buddies who needed him. I know that's the way I felt. The whole time you're there all you think about is getting out. When you actually do leave, you feel guilty about leaving your guys.

I think that's what happened with one of our platoon sergeants. He was on his last day and said his goodbyes to everybody. He was just a nice guy. We watched him walk down to the helicopter pad, watched the helicopter take off, and then here he comes walking back. We had been told to expect a ground attack that night. He said, "What's one more day before going home?"

We did get hit that night. The first bunker blown up was his. He was killed along with four others.

The fort we were in was built by the French and the NVA hated it. We were harassed on a regular basis. We had three rows of concertina wire but sappers would try to come through all the time. Sometimes when we killed them before they got in, we would have to leave them out there. We had so many mines of our own placed out there that we didn't know exactly where they all were. Those bodies would just lie out there in the sun and decay. There is nothing that smells like a body rotting in the sun. It's unbelievable. It's indescribable. We would be sitting on our bunkers at night and it's like, wow, if a skunk sprayed us we would think it was perfume. Then during the day sometimes you would see a dog walking through dragging a leg or an arm. Other times we would blow an ambush and then later on you would have to walk through that same area to check it out. One time we had eight NVA laying there dead, all bloated out, worms crawling in their eyes. We weren't going to pick them up. If their own people wanted to risk it, fine with us.

I remember one sapper who was caught in the wire. He looked like he was about fifteen years old. He had been stitched from top to bottom with an M-16. It sounds crazy but I almost felt sorry for him. Some guys were throwing rocks at him and stuff. I thought, *Come on guys. He's already dead. Let him be.*

During one of their attacks, I was the ammo-bearer for the mortar pit. Because I was the green-horn I had to crawl back maybe 100 feet, get more mortar rounds, and bring them back to the gun while at the same time we were getting mortared. I got hit in the knee with some pieces of shrapnel. Then I could hear AK-47 fire from close by. I looked up and there's a gook firing from on top of one of the bunkers and the guy next to him has an RPG. (Rocket-propelled grenade) I was crawling with two mortar rounds in my arms and I could see my M-16 laying up against the sandbags around the mortar pit. There's no way I could get to it. The thing is, everything was lit up with illumination rounds. It was bright as day. They were concentrating on the 105 ammo bunker over the top of me. That has to be the only reason they didn't see me. The guy with the RPG fires. It goes right over our mortar crew and hits the 105 bunker, blows it apart, killing all five guys in there.

Do you remember the scene in *Saving Private Ryan* when he's on the beach under all that fire, but he doesn't hear it? He sees everything going on around him, but there's no sound until he snaps out of it. That happened. I could hear small-arms fire all around me, but not the big explosions. I didn't think that ever happened to anyone else until I saw that movie. I'm sure it's based on what happened to someone on Omaha Beach. It's all quiet for a while and then it comes back into focus. I crawled back to the pit with the rounds, totally exhausted.

When morning came I saw the first dead sapper. He had made it right up to one of the big bunkers. This bunker had a door over the firing pit. The guy on top of the bunker didn't see the sapper. That's how amazing they were at times. But a guy in the bunker heard talking in Vietnamese outside the door. He saw the door starting to open and a Bangalore torpedo coming in. He fires right through the door and kills both sappers. But they were that close to killing everyone in the bunker. He was one of those guys that no matter where he was, that spot seemed to get hit. He was always nervous as hell, always shaky, and could never sit still. But I don't think he was ever the same after that night.

I remember the next morning the captain came around and told us all to go get something to eat. As I was walking to the mess hall I could see chunks of scalp and stuff lying on the ground. I told the other guys, "Forget it, you go. I can't eat."

Another time we were told to expect a ground attack that night and even though I was with a mortar squad, they needed men to fill the bunker line. So me being the newest guy was sent out to the bunkers. I was sitting on top of the bunker with two layers of sandbags around me. The sergeant came around to check on everybody. He asks me, "You got enough ammo, enough grenades?" I said, "Yup, I'm all set." Then he asks me, "You scared?" I don't remember what I said, but he said, "You don't know what scared is until you taste metal in your mouth," and he walked away.

Mortars started coming in. The first one landed right in front of me. The bags in front of me were shredded from the shrapnel. I'm thinking, *Please God don't let them walk them in on me.*

Others hit behind me but didn't go off. I'm waiting for the ground attack ... flares are going up. When the parachute flares come down they swing back and forth. It makes it look like everything in the bush is moving and coming towards you. I'm scared as hell, have never been this scared. Then I hear a sound I had never heard before, kind of a "whoo, whoo, whoo." What the hell is that noise? I kept sitting there and waiting, listening to that sound with a bad taste in my mouth.

The ground attack never came. When it was over I found out what that noise was. It was from the arteries in my neck pumping blood so hard that it was fracturing the membranes in the back of my mouth. Blood tastes like metal. Now I understood what the sergeant meant when he said I wouldn't know what fear was until I have the taste of metal in my mouth. That's when you realize there are different levels of fear.

There was a time before I became a squad leader, so it had to have been within the first four months of my tour, that they came around and asked for volunteers to go on a mission with some Navy SEALS. I was told that whoever volunteered would get a really great breakfast from the Navy when they got back. Well, you always hear, "Don't volunteer for anything!" But I was so sick and tired of those C-rations that I thought it was worth it.

So we climbed on this PBR (Patrol Boat, River) that would take us upriver. There were nine of us, but I didn't know any of them. It had twin .50-cals in front, a .60-cal in back, and an automatic grenade launcher. The SEAL leader starts telling us the mission. They were going to insert us in an area to watch a certain trail. He said they were expecting a battalion to try and move through there that night. I'm thinking, *A battalion? Holy crap! All this for a breakfast?* He said it was all zeroed in with artillery, Phantoms were on stand-by, and we would be covered from the rear by the boats.

Ron Umentum collection

So they drop us off. It was very dark. We moved inland about 500 feet and set up next to the only cover there was, one big downed tree and a stump. I asked him where he wanted me to go. He said he wanted me right in the middle of the trail facing downriver. I said what if they come up the trail from the other direction? He said intelligence said they would only come from the front. *Okay, right...*

We set up in an L-shaped ambush. We had eighteen claymores set out in front of us, and a .60-caliber machine gun next to the stump. Now it was just a matter of getting through the night. I pulled the first guard. It was really quiet, that kind of quiet where you could hear your heart beating. After an hour I woke up the next guy, double-checked to make sure he knew where the claymore clackers were, that he had grenades, that he was ready to go. I laid down, dead tired. We had already gone on a patrol that day and now we were trying to do an overnight ambush. I'm lying there for about fifteen minutes, but couldn't fall asleep because when I had pulled my camo blanket over my head I had trapped some mosquitos in there and they were going after my face. So okay you little bastards, the only way to get rid of you is by sitting up and taking the blanket off. So I sat up. The guy who was supposed to be on watch was sound asleep. I looked down the trail and there, about fifteen meters away, were four NVA walking towards us. The first one had an RPG over his shoulder. He looked straight at me sitting up in the middle of the trail, dropped the RPG, and took off. The second guy ran into the third guy. The fourth guy just stood there for a short time then turned and ran. This all happened in a split second.

I grabbed my M-16 and went after the first one like he was a deer running away. I started there and swept back, knocking all four down. Now everybody was up and trying to squeeze behind that downed tree. One of our main objectives of the mission was to grab a prisoner. We could tell one of them was still alive and crawling away. We were worried there might be a lot more waiting for him. One of the guys says, "I can get him!" He grabs a grenade and throws it. Nothing happens. He goes, "Aw shit, I forgot to pull the pin!" I'm thinking, *Who in the hell did they send me out here with?* Then he threw a second one and killed the wounded VC. Now the artillery opens up and the jets are overhead. The boats come in and one of the SEALS, his face all blackened, wearing tennis shoes and carrying a .45, runs out, grabs the dead VC, and says, "Let's get the hell out of here!"

We get to the boats. I'm struggling to get on, bullets are flying around, the noise was crazy. I finally pull myself up on the bow and sit there as the boat takes off fast. Being in front I'm getting just soaked from the spray. It's miserable, but at least we were heading back and I was going to get that breakfast. That's all I kept thinking about.

Then the SEAL leader says, "Instead of going back to camp we are going to insert you from behind to see if we can intercept them." *Oh my God. We're going after the rest of their battalion in the dark?*

So they fly down the river, pull up to the bank, we scramble off, and the boats leave. We walk in no more than 300 feet and our machine-gunner opens up. He yells out, "They're all around us, get back to the river!" So we scramble down to the bank, call for the boats and artillery, and they answer back, "We don't know exactly where we dropped you off. We don't have a read on your location. Hold your position until morning." *Are you kidding me?*

So we get to the bank and just lay there. The tide comes in and pretty soon the only things sticking out of the water are our heads and weapons. That was the longest night of my life. We could have called in jets but we would have had to send up a flare and that would have given away our position. As long as we weren't being hit we were going to just sit tight. I'm actually shaking just telling this story. In the morning the boats came back and picked us up. We were soaked to the bone, freezing, covered in leeches, and still nervous. We got on the boat, and again I started thinking about that breakfast, how I was going to get a great

Christmas 1969 for Ron Umentum featured a Christmas tree sent by his mother, set up in a bunker that had been a culvert. (Ron Umentum collection)

hot breakfast. The boat takes off, heads straight for our camp, drops us off, and takes off. Not a word about taking us for breakfast. That's why when I see someone from the Navy I still tell them, "You owe me a frickin' breakfast."

We pulled a lot of night ambushes. They were scary too, but sometimes you almost felt better being out in the bush instead of sitting back and waiting for them to attack. Crazy things could happen though.

The routine was to find your ambush spot, set out your claymores around you, get everybody in position and then wait. Your senses get fine-tuned: sight, sound, smell ... oh yeah smell was one of the big senses. The worst part and I guess the best part, was that your sense of hearing was so sharp that the littlest noises out in the jungle in front of you were magnified, but you really had no way of knowing if it was some animal making the noise or a squad of NVA. You could send up a flare but then your ambush is compromised; you're done and you don't want to be walking back to the base in the dark.

One night we had six men, two of them were new guys so I put them next to me, one on each side. I said, "OK guys, one-hour shifts, when yours is done, wake the guy next to you to take over." I pulled the second shift. When it was done I woke the guy next to me. I was just falling asleep when he's grabbing my leg and whispering in my ear, "There's

Ron Umentum (center, with camera) and his team during a lighter moment in Vietnam. (Ron Umentum collection)

movement out front, sounds like they are all around us!" I hear noises. I put my hand on the claymore clacker . . . waiting, waiting, looking, listening . . . everybody's alert. I'm thinking, *Oh God, there's only six of us; I hope it's not a big patrol out there*. We waited about an hour; nothing happened. I relax, put the other new guy on watch, and try to go back to sleep. About 2:00 in the morning, he touches my leg to wake me. He's whispering in my ear, "I can hear them. I can hear them!" I'm like, "Christ you guys are jumpy, calm down, it's just your nerves, just relax, there's nothing out there." The third time they woke me it was a guy who had been on night ambushes before, he was experienced, he whispered to me, "Something just ran through our lines!" I said, "You sure it wasn't some kind of animal. He says, "No I don't think it was!" He was sure it was a human. Nobody went back to sleep that night, but we never found out who or what it was. That's just how scary it was lying out in the middle of the jungle in pitch black not knowing what could be around you.

On one occasion the captain came with us. We had about twenty guys on this one. We started moving out to our position. It was kind of hazy and getting dark. It wasn't long before we got a report, "Movement out front!" Well, the other ambush was supposed to go parallel to us and we were to move straight ahead. What happened was the other patrol kind of lost direction and was drifting in front of us, but we didn't know that. So the captain calls for some M-79 rounds. Pretty soon we hear over the radio, "Friendlies! Friendlies!" The medic that ran up was hit bad. I helped load him on the chopper. It didn't look like he was going to make it. We assumed he died. The captain felt so bad, but it wasn't his fault. It was an inexperienced NCO who led his squad in front of our lines. We called them "shake and bakes." These were guys who went to school to become NCOs. Those guys weren't all bad. If they listened to advice from the guys who had experience, they became good, but some just didn't want to listen. That wasn't the first or last time there were casualties from friendly fire.

We didn't know what happened to the guys wounded that day. They would leave and you would never hear from them again. We looked for the medic's name on the Vietnam Wall in Washington, but couldn't find it. As it turned out, he survived. One of our guys tracked him down in 2018. He had spent two years in rehab, but then got out and ran a bar in California.

Like I said, crazy things could happen on ambushes. One night we laid out there and absolutely nothing happened. We had set out claymores with tripwires. In the morning, the sergeant sent out, I think four guys to bring in the claymores. Pretty soon we hear, "BOOM!" We thought, *Son of a bitch! Either one of our guys walked into our own claymore or an NVA tripped it!* We waited. Pretty soon they come walking back. We asked, "What the hell happened?" One of the guys said, "Just before we got there, a big bird came flying in, landed on the tripwire, and set off the claymore.

We would set up our ambushes in a different area every night. This one day, they sent a few of us out to scout for the next night's ambush position. We were walking back to our original position when we sensed someone was watching us. This was the dry season. It was dusty as hell. We were covered in dust, but I saw something on the trail; a pair of Ho Chi Minh sandals that weren't dusty at all. I said, "Guys we might be walking into the middle of an ambush. Get low and radio ahead." The captain said, "Walk right past our position." After we did he called us and said, "There are five of them right on your tail." He moved the sniper into position. He got two of them. Then he called in gunships and called for eyes in the sky to see what else was out there.

The choppers are overhead firing rockets, mini-guns, everything they had. Then a call comes over the radio, "Do not advance any further! There are about a thousand of them crossing the border!" I will never forget those words, "A thousand of them crossing the border!" Our choppers had to pull up. The NVA infiltrated back into Cambodia. Our guns could have almost wiped them out, but they had to turn back. That pissed us off. They could shoot at you, but you couldn't shoot at them. The government wanted to keep the faith with Cambodia and Laos. That was bullshit. As soon as they made that decision they made the war unwinnable as far as I'm concerned.

We started our reunions in 2010 at the big event called LZ Lambeau, in Green Bay. That was forty-one years after we got back. I invited five guys up here. That's when we decided to start having reunions on a more regular basis. After our 2013 reunion, one of the guys asked me if I wanted to go back to Vietnam. In 2014 I made the trip. It's the best thing I ever did.

We had a guide who had been a 2nd lieutenant in the South Vietnamese Army. His dad was a colonel. He would only talk about the old days if we were the only ones in the car, never around other Vietnamese. I asked him what in the hell it was it like after the war. He said the people who were in support of the North Vietnamese Army came out with red armbands on. Many of them carried .45s. They were going around with loudspeakers like in World War II films, telling anyone who served with the military or helped the Americans that they had ten days to turn themselves in." He said it was on the radio, in the newspapers, all over. I said, "What did you do?" He said, "We had no choice." I asked why. He said, "Well if you didn't turn yourself in and someone knew you had helped the other side, then one of those guys with the .45s and armbands would knock on your door and shoot everyone in the house, kill the entire family. So my dad and I turned ourselves in."

He said they were separated and put in camps. I said, "Reunification camps?" He said, "Hell no! They were concentration camps. We were forced to work sixteen hours a day, living on rice and water. Most of the older guys died. They couldn't take it. We knew we needed protein to survive, but they wouldn't give us any."

He said that for every three prisoners there were two guards, that's how many people they had around now. They were cutting the jungle down to make more rice paddies and farm fields. Anytime he would see a bug he would grab it for the protein, but if the guards saw you, they shot you right away. He said they had it worked out that if one guy saw a bug the other two would do something to distract the guards. One time he saw a frog, he grabbed it and threw it in his mouth. But as soon as he did the guard looked at him. He said he was so scared the frog would make a noise while it was in his mouth. I said, "What did you do then?" He said, "I swallowed the son of a bitch!"

After four years in the labor camp he was let go, but he wasn't allowed to have a job or own any property. He said he really struggled to survive but that now things were a lot better. It was a great trip back; we went to Mole City. I said to one of my buddies, "Hey Chet, remember the shower was outside the wire and we had to stand there naked in front of all the people?"

It was an emotional trip, with so many memories, good memories, bad memories. The people were very, very nice. I would encourage anyone who spent time there to go back. It was the best trip I ever took. But if you go, be prepared for the heat.

Steve and Marge Aznoe

STEVE AZNOE

River Boat Section 511
US Navy, Vietnam War

"My grandmother made me a great deal; she said she would give me $500.00 if I joined the Navy instead of the Army. She said it was worth it to keep me out of Vietnam. I took the money. Little did she know." – Steve Aznoe

In 1965 I was in boot camp at Great Lakes Naval Station in Illinois. Then they sent me to NAS (Naval Air Station) Corpus Christi, Texas, for a year. Our job was retrieving P5M's, they were big seaborne, floating aircraft. We would pull them up to the beach with big cables with an oversized bulldozer. I put in a year there and then I got orders to report back to Great Lakes for BPE, Basic Propulsion and Engineering school. When I finished that I was sent to Coronado, California, for training on gunboats. Before they sent you to Vietnam they made you go through Escape and Evasion school. That was something else. You'd try to escape the guys playing the part of the VC. When they caught you they would put you in this concentration camp kind of thing. They'd kick you around, put you in a dark hole, then take you out and beat the hell out of you. That wasn't too cool.

For exercise, they would have you pick up these big rocks on one side of the compound and carry them to the other side. When that was done, you picked them up and brought them back. They had us do that for three days straight with hardly any sleep. But you know what, you join the Navy, you get the hand you're dealt. It wasn't fun, but it was good training. I don't have any bad feelings about it.

If you graduated from that you went to the Philippines for another school. This time it was Jungle Escape and Survival School. We went into the jungle and learned how to eat off the land and things like that. One thing I remember the most; if you get the runs, take burnt wood, like charcoal, and eat it. It will stop you right up.

Steve Aznoe collection

If you survived all those schools, you were promoted to Vietnam.

I was assigned to a PBR (Patrol Boat, River) in River Boat Section 511 at a place called Binh Thuy. It's right where the Mekong River empties into the South China Sea. There was a small Air Force base right by it. I was the old guy, twenty-one years old, so I could go to the bar, the Acey Deucy Club. Most of the other guys were eighteen or nineteen. Our living quarters were sort of like an old Motel 6. There was a pier where we kept our boats. We stayed there for a while then went out to one of our supply LSTs (Landing Ship, Tank) was moored at the mouth of the river and we stayed there. We would switch off with another unit every other month. That was nice too, clean sheets, good chow, twelve hours on twelve hours off.

I started as an engineman. My job was to take care of the two engines and man the aft (rear) .50-caliber machine gun. I eventually moved up to Third Class, then acting Boat Captain. They would send out two boats on every patrol. They were both a little over thirty feet long, with twin .50-caliber machine guns in front and the one aft.

Our main job was to stop the VC from bringing down supplies. That's why we were there. I was OK with where we were. Some of the guys around Cambodia had it rougher than us I believe. Around noon or one o'clock, we would sometimes stop at one of the little villages along the way. We always brought a chest full of ice with us. We would buy beers and have a few before heading out again.

During the day our main job was to check the boat traffic, check their ID cards, make sure they didn't have any guns, make sure nothing was hidden under the floorboards. At night there was a curfew. They weren't allowed on the water from dark to light. If we spotted something on radar or if we spotted them after dark, they were pretty much fair game. That southern part of Vietnam was loaded with rivers intersecting the entire area. You couldn't watch all of them. They could just pick a path and find a way to the Mekong River.

One time when we were staying at the ARVN base there were about ten of our boats lining up to get back to it. You had to go slow through this channel which had a little island on the mouth of the river. We were always getting shot at from there. On this day we were all going through, and the VC had claymores set up in the trees. The first boat in line tripped the claymore, killing four of the five guys on the boat, good friends of mine. Then they opened fire on the other boats lined up behind it.

One of the Patrol Boat River (PBRs) in River Boat Section 511. (Steve Aznoe collection)

They called for a Huey. It came in and sprayed the entire area. You can spray all you want but you're probably not going to hit anything, because they had little caverns to hide in. We opened up and sprayed the jungle all around us as they brought a medevac in.

When I got back to the States, I went and visited the parents of one of my good friends who died that day.

There were other times we would go in canals and it was just crazy. We would take B-40 rocket fire. They would be devastating if they worked properly, but there were a lot of duds. There were other times they would go straight through the fiberglass hulls of boats and out the other side. If they hit the engine, then there was trouble because that would turn into shrapnel flying all over the place.

Some of those canals were only fifty yards wide in some spots. You'd have VC firing on both sides. Well if they didn't hit us, they had to be hitting their buddies on the other side. I mean that's where the fire was going, both ways.

We had a big piece of armor in front of the .50, but if they ambushed you from both sides you knew you were only protected on one side. So the odds were pretty good you were going to get hit in the back. If you were young like I was, or like the guys younger than me, you took your chances and didn't think too much about it.

I made water skis over there. Made them out of rocket boxes. I cut them out of the box and then covered them with fiberglass. I would water ski behind my PBR. The Vietnamese would use long sampans as taxis. There would be a bunch of people in there. I would go toward them and spray the boat. I wasn't trying to be mean. I was just trying to be friendly with the people. They must have thought I was crazy, skiing out there like that.

We also had a Boston Whaler available that we could use anytime we wanted to. I had a buddy who was a Vietnamese interpreter. He was probably VC by night, but whatever. I would have him drive the Whaler up these creeks while I skied behind it. I got shot at one time doing that and I thought, *Whoa, turn this thing around!*

Steve Aznoe waterskis behind a PBR in Vietnam. (Steve Aznoe collection)

Steve Aznoe mans the .50-caliber machine gun on the aft section of a PBR. (Steve Aznoe collection)

and we headed back the other way. That was a dumb move on my part.

My twins were born when I was over there. That's when I thought, *I'd better not be so footloose and fancy-free over here anymore. I haven't seen my kids yet.* That's when I thought twice about doing dumb shit.

There was a guy from *Look* magazine who came over and said he wanted to see some action. He was in the lead boat, recording everything he saw onto a tape recorder. Pretty soon they came under fire. A B-40 rocket hit them. I've got a copy of the tape someplace, it made the rounds with us. You could hear him saying, "The boat is sinking! We're sinking!" He was OK, but some guys were wounded and had to be sent back to the states.

We would give the South Vietnamese Briggs and Stratton engines. That's what a lot of the sampans were powered by, two big engines. They were as fast as a PBR. The VC would find a way to get ahold of them. This one was running from us, which is nothing to brag about, but we got the guy driving it in the back of the head. It was only a small hole in the back, but it almost took his whole face off. I had never seen anything like that.

If someone was hit, the survival of the crew was priority one. The first thing we needed to know was if someone was in danger of dying - if they needed to be airlifted out. If not and the boat wasn't sinking, we would stay there and give the river banks hell for a while.

In some parts of the country, it looked like something out of a horror movie, with all the dead trees from Agent Orange; which was kind of OK because then they didn't have as much protection to hide behind. You would see where their tracers were coming from. My aft gun had a grenade launcher. You'd fire, see where it landed, fire again and see where it landed. If they fired back, you would just follow the tracers, walk them in on them, and then start cranking them out, "Bop, bop bop." That was a pretty cool deal.

Steve Aznoe collection

It was the same thing with the .50. You don't really aim, it's not like there was a person you were aiming at. You just walk the rounds in from where the fire was coming from and totally spray it down.

Sometimes we felt like ducks on a pond. If you were going through a known VC area, you would put your helmet and flak jacket on. Otherwise, you didn't, even though you were supposed to.

You'd hear rounds go by, but you didn't really have time to think about it. It's not like you'd say, "Whoops there goes one right by me. Maybe I'd better move over a little to the other side." You didn't have much protection anyway, plus you always knew that a rocket could go right through the boat like a hot knife. They shoot at you, you fire back. If you get hit, you get hit. It all comes with the package of being on a patrol boat. I'm not saying you got used to it, but I guess in a certain way you just accepted it as part of your job.

It seems like guys either loved them, (PBRs) or hated them. We always said, "They either make you or break you, nothing in between." Personally, I had some sort of sense of adventure. There were quite a few of us who were like that. There were times, if we were bored, we would go to certain spots where we figured we would attract attention just to stir it up a little bit. Some guys loved contact, some guys hated it. I was fortunate, very fortunate. We took rounds and maintenance would patch them up and we would go out again the next day. I hate to say it, but at times I actually really enjoyed it. That's just the way it was.

We had one guy, Terry, my forward gunner, he came in halfway through my tour I had left when this happened, but I heard he and three other guys got tired of always getting sniped at from this little island and from watching planes get shot at from inside there. So they decided to do a night mission, pick a fight with the VC. Well, the planes going over saw the fire and opened up, not realizing there were friendlies on the island.

Steve Aznoe (back center with beret) poses with crews that teamed up on missions. (Steve Aznoe collection)

The commander found out about it and shipped them out the next day. He said they were "too aggressive." Too aggressive? You'd think they would have gotten an "atta boy" instead of being shipped out.

But we had one guy, who my wife and I went and visited after the war, and I brought all my pictures and videos and everything to show him and he said, "You know what Steve, I never had any love for those boats and I would rather not see the films or the pictures." I had no idea. He never acted that way while on the boats at all. Usually, people are really proud of being on the boats. They have a great heritage and most guys are proud of serving on them. But then there are guys like that friend of mine. I never had any idea he hated it that bad until he told me that day.

I've asked guys how many firefights they were in. I'm documented for nineteen. I don't know if that would be considered a lot or not. Everybody saw a different part of the war.

Editor's note: *Marge Aznoe, Steve's wife, grew up on the east side of Green Bay, and then attended UW-Oshkosh in the early 1970s. She was a strong opponent of the war.*

Marge: I started college in 1971. There were protests going on, absolutely. I took part in some of them. I will be honest, I hated the war. I just thought it was a dumb war and we never should have been there.

Boys that I went to high school and hung out with had come back changed. I remember talking to them and they would tell me about some of the things they had seen. Horrible things. One of the guys said there were times when young boys would walk straight up to them and you didn't know if you should shoot them or if you could trust them. He said things like that happened all the time. He talked about some of the atrocities he had seen. It was just crazy.

Vietnam didn't only affect the guys themselves, but lots of times it affected their entire family. Even when I started going to Steve's events with the Vietnam Vets group, it was incredible how many guys had developed drinking problems when they came back, which then led to divorce. Drinking, anger issues, all sorts of things that went along with it.

I kind of wonder if, because they had seen humanity at its worst, that they came out of there with a lack of respect for authority. Does that make sense?

I told the vets I had hung out with that I protested the war. They were like, "What, you protested against us?" And I said, "No, absolutely not. I have all the respect in the world that you went to war because your country told you to go to war. But I was sure as heck going to fight to save your lives and the lives of guys who would have to follow behind you."

Our protests aren't anything like you saw on the national news from Chicago or New York, places like that. No one ever had a mean thing to say about the troops themselves.

I'll tell you how bad it was. I remember playing the Woodstock album and the song, *"One-two-three what are we fighting for"* came on and my older brother came into the room and told me to turn it off. I said, "Why?" He had a new girlfriend there and her brother had been killed in Vietnam.

When my sister's stepson was killed in Iraq those same feelings came right back. "Why? What did he give his life for?"

Here's how I put it. I hated the war. But, I respect every single one of them who, when the country asked them to do something, they put their lives on the line and went and did it. No matter how stupid it was for our country to send them there in the first place.

CHUCK WELLENS

26th Marine Regiment
3rd Marine Division
Vietnam War

Khe Sanh is a name etched in Marine lore. A muddy outpost surrounded by towering hills, it was for a time, a relatively quiet, secure area in the northwest corner of South Vietnam. Its geographical isolation generally kept it out of range from the ubiquitous eyes of military brass.

That all changed in January of 1968, both for the troops assigned to the firebase itself and the isolated men clinging to the tops of barren, vulnerable hills in the surrounding area. A seventy-seven-day battle of incessant rocket, mortar, machine gun, small arms, and frontal attacks led by determined North Vietnamese troops would leave many survivors with memories impossible to erase.

Chuck Wellens, of Stiles, Wisconsin, went from being a two-way starter for the Cadets of the Green Bay Premontre High School football team to a member of that beleaguered contingent.

"When I enlisted in the Marines in 1967, I had a 121-day delay. Mainly that meant I had three months to party and have a good time.

"When we graduated from boot camp I did well enough to be chosen to go to communications school. They told us to write down everything that we have on your record right down to parking tickets because we would be getting a top-level security clearance if we were selected.

One day I got called in and was told that they found a ticket I had gotten for underage drinking. I had no idea it was still on my record, but they found it and said, "Sorry, but we can't accept you into communications." From that moment on I was in the infantry.

I didn't realize at the time that, for lack of a better word, how violent the life of an infantryman would be.

After my leave at home, I had to report back to San Diego on the day before Thanksgiving. We did a few more weeks of training at Camp Pendleton and then boarded buses for LA airport right before Christmas. That was a pretty quiet bus ride, looking at all the lights and realizing it would be the first Christmas away from home for a lot of us. Of course, we were also thinking about what this next year would be like. Now it was real. We were going to war.

When we got to Okinawa my first sight there was of some guys going home on emergency leave. I looked at them and thought, *Oh my God they look horrible*. They had red mud all over them and just looked beat. We boarded the plane alphabetically from back to front. So naturally, I was one of the last ones to board. I was seated up front between two lifers and they acted like I didn't exist. It was like I wasn't even a speck of something sitting next to them.

The ride was, I believe, only a couple of hours at most, but it really gave you time to think. I mean, when you come out of boot camp you feel like you can take on fifty guys. That's how confident they make you feel. At first, they break you down to nothing and insult you and call you every name in the book, but then you keep training and by the time you graduate you feel invincible. But sitting on that plane that night, a lot of other thoughts were going through my mind and I remember this vividly. I just kept thinking that now it's not make-believe; it's not practicing for war. There was no more pretending. It's the real thing.

I remember having two major concerns. One was, how would I react in real combat to Marine standards? To be under fire? Would I react the way I had been trained or would I curl up in a ball? The other was that I really didn't want to go home severely wounded. I just thought about what it would be like going home to my family having lost my legs or arms or being blinded or something like that. I knew that was happening to a lot of guys fighting over there and that just really scared me. I just had a lot of anxiety over those two things.

I think a lot of guys had similar thoughts about personal fears. It was a very quiet plane ride to Vietnam.

When we landed at around 10:00 at night and the plane was taxiing, I looked out the window and saw a big forklift loading caskets onto the back of a cargo plane. The caskets all had flags on them. This is something I mention when I talk to students in schools. I know the flag is just a piece of cloth with different colors, but to me, it represents the sacrifice of veterans. That's why I and so many veterans find it sacred. That image has stayed with me to this day.

That night they told us to find a place to sleep and that they would take us to our units the next morning. There was this guy who was getting ready to leave, to go back home, and he looked at me with what we would call the thousand-yard stare. He asked me where I was going, I told him with the 3rd Division. He said, "You will never make it." And he walked away. That's all he said. Well, that scared the crap out of me. I thought, *Why did he have to say that?* But evidently, he knew that there was a big build-up in that area and was just being honest.

The next morning we flew out on what we called gooney birds (C-47s) to a place called Phu Bai. I went to check-in and the guy behind the counter just pulled an M-16 out of a barrel of oil and hands it to me. Then he grabs a handful of grenades and hands them to me. I was thinking what the hell? In boot camp, the Marines prided themselves on being really rigid with equipment. Well, I'm in a different world now.

They told us we would be convoy security. So they loaded us up in the back of some trucks and we took off. I had no idea where we were going. I do remember going through the city of Hue and thinking about how beautiful of a city that was. I was just struck by the difference in culture, from where I came from to where I was now, just a different world. I'm not sure what we were supposed to do security-wise. I guess if somebody shot at us, we were supposed to shoot back, but I don't know. They didn't give us a lot of instruction.

My assignment was Khe Sanh. They flew us there in C-130s. As we were flying in I could see that it was in a valley with mountains surrounding it. I must have had a scared look on my face because a Navy Seabee sitting next to me said, "Don't worry, they haven't been hit there in eight months." I wanted to believe him. This was in December of 1967.

The unit I was assigned to was out on a mission, so I had a couple of days to get situated. But the one thing you learn right away is that if you don't take care of yourself, no one else is going to do it for you. It was raining hard; so me and another new guy put our ponchos together and that was our shelter and home for a few days.

I spent Christmas there. We got a nice meal, nice at least for Vietnam. I remember there were three or four helicopters flying around playing Christmas carols. They had a big Santa painted on the front of one of them. It was a lonesome time but you looked around and everybody was in the same boat. I was a nineteen-year-old kid. I'm sure for almost all of us it was the first Christmas away from home; so you kind of leaned on one another and talked about your home and family, things like that.

The day after Christmas we packed up and walked to Hill 861. I was in a 60mm mortar squad. About halfway up that hill, I started to appreciate the advanced training we had at Camp Pendleton right before we shipped out. We were constantly climbing those hills during training missions. I don't know if I would have made it, if it hadn't been for that. One of the new guys in my squad who had trained in the swamps of Parris Island just couldn't take it. He almost died from the heat and exhaustion.

I really didn't have time to meet many of the guys. To be honest, the guys who had been there for a while really didn't pay too much attention to us new guys. Most of them were very distant to us. I was told to expect that. Guys didn't want to get close to new guys. There was one exception. He was a Black gentleman, who became a tremendous friend of mine. From then on whenever we were in a fight, he would always check to see if I was okay and I would do the same for him.

On maps, they named all the hills based on elevation. This was during the monsoon season, and being so high up, we were socked in when it came to being resupplied. We had to go down the side of the hill to a stream to get water. Being one of the new guys my job was to carry the five-gallon cans. On one of the details we started hearing shots nearby. I stood there looking around when all of a sudden I was absolutely jerked to the ground by this huge hand of the man behind me. He turned me around and said some extremely nasty things to me. Basically saying, he didn't really care if I got killed, but I was drawing fire to the rest of them by being a standing target. I never forgot that lesson. From then on no one ever had to tell me twice to get down when bullets were flying.

Chuck Wellens collection

That was also the first time I saw a casualty. Our machine-gunner was spraying the area from where the shots came from, but then when he stopped firing a cook-off round went off. It hit a Marine right in the back and went right through him. They called in a medevac. I'm sure I was just standing there with my mouth wide open. I mean, this is stuff you couldn't prepare for.

The machine-gunner went berserk. They had to hold him down. He was so distraught about that happening they had to get him out of there.

The amazing thing is that the guy wasn't hurt that bad. It was a clean shot, straight through without hitting anything vital. He was back in a few weeks. I remember when we had our shirts off filling sandbags or whatever and he would show everybody his scars.

There had been reports that something might be brewing in our area. But to be honest with you, I was so naive that I didn't think it was possible to successfully attack our position on top of that hill. We had a perimeter with a trench line and fortified positions all the way around. We had a 106mm recoilless rifle, which was a tremendous weapon. We had 81mm and 60mm mortars. We had a four-deuce, which was basically four .50-caliber machine guns together. I believe we had somewhere in the neighborhood of 250 men. The command post was in a bunker in the middle of the perimeter. When I would look around at these fortifications and the men we had there I thought there's no way anybody could knock us off this hill.

My greatest day there was the day of the Ice Bowl. (NFL Championship - December 31, 1967) I was in my little bunker with two other guys and I had the radio watch duty that night. We would get calls for fire missions and things like that for our 60mm mortar.

Well, that night I was listening to the *Armed Forces Radio Network*. It was the only entertainment we had. They would play music and they had this girl on there with a very sultry voice. So I'm listening and I hear, *"And now let's go live to Green Bay, Wisconsin."* Oh my goodness, I couldn't believe it. They were broadcasting the Packers vs Cowboys championship game! I sat and listened to that all night. Right near the end of the game, the signal started fading out. I had my ear right to the radio and I faintly heard, *"Starr, touchdown!"* I let out such a yell, both of the other guys in the bunker jumped up wondering what in the hell was going on. They weren't too happy with me. But boy, that was really something to be sitting in a little bunker on a hill in one of the most godforsaken places on earth and to listen to that game.

We went out on patrols regularly. One of our patrols found a cave with a huge cache of weapons in it. Three other new guys and myself were given the job of cleaning it out and bringing everything back to our area. We didn't know any better, we were talking and laughing and everything, you know the way guys do. We never even stopped to think that there had to be NVA watching our every move. We hauled all that crap up the hill, making noise and everything. I'm sure they could have killed us in a heartbeat, but they didn't want to tip their hand. We found out later that they were crawling all over that area.

About the middle of January '68, we started getting probed at night. They sent out scouts to see where our machine guns, our mortars, where all of our crew-served weapons were. Nothing major, but obviously they were looking for possible weak spots. We would send up illumination mortars on a regular basis. I still wasn't scared. It really didn't seem like anything too serious, but again, that's because I was so naive.

On January 21st, we were on Red Alert. They must have received some intelligence or something that the NVA were going to make a move. Our guys in the perimeter trenches had been throwing grenades down the hill. One of the guys said they could hear people moaning down below, but they wouldn't shoot back.

I had so much respect for those guys manning the trenches that again, I figured whatever they threw at us, we could handle it.

The bunker where we lived was just a few feet from the mortar pit. That night we were dropping illumination rounds. I was in the bunker making a cup of cocoa with a little heat tab. One of the other mortarmen yelled for one of us to come help break out more ammo. My friend said for me to finish what I was doing, that he would take care of it. I'm sitting there with my cocoa and I hear this explosion. I remember thinking that it certainly didn't sound like any outgoing rounds that I had ever heard before. I knew the 106mm recoilless had been firing and the backblast is really something, but this explosion just sounded a lot different.

The next thing I knew, I was waking up to a room full of dust and dirt. They hit our bunker with an RPG or a mortar round. A direct hit. It blew all the sandbags apart and knocked me out cold. The first thing I thought of when I came to was, *OK I'm alive, now what?* I started searching for my rifle and helmet. I couldn't find them. Then I heard the scariest sound I had ever heard in my life, Vietnamese voices outside my bunker. We didn't have any ARVN troops on our base which only meant one thing; NVA were inside our wire. I could hear them yelling commands to each other.

I was so scared that I physically started shaking. Then I realized I had to settle down and do my job. It was dusty and dark, and I'm fumbling around looking for my helmet, looking for my M-16. I was not prepared the way I should have been. Once I found everything I pointed the rifle at the doorway and just told myself that I'm going down with a fight. If anyone with a different looking hat comes through that doorway they're gone; they're dead. But in my mind I was thinking, this is probably the end for me too. I started praying, saying *Our Fathers* so fast you wouldn't believe it.

All of a sudden I heard my squad leader. He was calling for a corpsman because one of the guys from the squad had been hit real bad. I hollered out to him and he yelled back, "Wellens? You're alive?" I'm sure he saw that my bunker was blown apart. We were still getting mortared, small arms fire, they were giving us everything they had. Then he said, "Get your ass over here!"

By now everything was getting blown apart and on fire...I mean it was sheer hell. I said "OK, but don't shoot me!" I went running out to him, yelling, "Don't shoot! Don't shoot!"

I started running toward him. I was fine with going over there. I wanted to be with someone on our side in the worst way. You don't want to be alone in a situation like that. I ran toward the trench line but it was so smoky and everything that I fell right into it and on top of the guy who was wounded.

I started patching him up as best I could. His leg was torn up really bad. He was a big huge guy. We used to call him Hillbilly. So we got him up and brought him to the aid station. It's amazing how strong you can be in a time like that when you absolutely have to be.

After dropping him off, I ran back to the trench, but they said everybody was falling back to a secondary position. I was fortunate to get teamed up with a guy who had been there for five or six months. He was pretty well combat-seasoned.

It was so crazy, thick smoke, flashes, explosions, people running around, you didn't know if they were NVA or Marines. The first thing that happens to me in that foxhole is that my M-16 jams. That's how it started, taking my ramrod and clearing my rifle.

You just had to be careful before you pulled the trigger. You never knew who was going to appear in front of you. You tried to see the outline of their helmets. These were NVA regulars. They weren't Viet Cong. They were well-equipped, full uniforms, the whole bit. These guys knew what they were doing. And I have to give them credit for their ability to fight. For many of them, I'm sure they knew it was suicide.

We weren't there long before I was waking up again. The NVA had gotten through and tossed a satchel charge into the ammo bunker right behind us and blew it sky-high. Just a tremendous explosion. The concussion knocked us both out cold. Debris fell from the sky for a long time.

It's possible they had run right by us and we didn't even see them. Everything was just such a blur; it was happening so fast you just couldn't comprehend it all. They were all over the inside of the perimeter, blowing stuff up. You would see flashes and someone running, but you didn't know if it was one of them or one of ours. You sure as hell didn't want to shoot one of your own people. Our mortar was just obliterated. I started thinking again, *OK, no way you're getting out of this one. It all ends here tonight.* It was sheer hell. It really was.

Mercifully the sun started coming up. By now the guys on the front lines were almost out of ammo so the platoon commander, a lieutenant, told me to deliver some to the trenches. I grabbed a couple of cans and started heading down. Once again, I yelled out, "Don't shoot! Don't shoot!" Those guys were so nervous and jumpy after what they had gone through, that it's still a wonder I didn't get shot.

Usually, the NVA tactics were to hit you, cause all sorts of problems, and then hit you with another wave. If they had done that it would have been horrendous. Khe Sanh couldn't help us with artillery because they were under attack. So we called on Lima and India companies on Hill

881 South. They started dumping rounds just below our area. They hit an area where the NVA were staging for another assault and just wiped them out. That may have saved us. Our guys were really low on ammo. We had numerous wounded. It would not have been good if they had attacked again.

That morning was like something out of a movie. Smoke coming up from everywhere. The NVA were still sniping at us. You would hear the cracking of AK-47s. You had to be careful with every step you took. Helicopters were coming and going with the wounded and dead. We had to go around and pick up the pieces and everything. It's like you were in a bad dream and now you were seeing the result of it.

Our gunnery sergeant was killed. I just totally respected that man. Just a pure Marine. The kind you had total confidence in to follow to hell and back. He's lying there. He was the first dead person I had ever seen. One of the guys said to give him a hand to put him in a body bag. He had his feet and I went to grab for his hands and kind of pulled back. I had never touched a dead person before. It was just a natural reaction. The other guy saw my face and looked at me with the coldest eyes I had ever seen and said, "He won't hurt you, he's frickin dead." I couldn't believe how cold that sounded and what an unbelievably cold look he had in his eyes. Unfortunately, that would be only the first of many I would help load into body bags.

Picking up bodies that day was very devastating. When somebody you truly admire like Gunny gets killed, the reality of death hits you really strong. You see all the body bags lined up on the LZ and you start thinking, *Wow, I'm just starting my tour. How can I possibly survive a year of this?*

You wanted to process everything but you couldn't. You didn't have time. There was no let-up. Maybe that's best. Maybe it was best that we didn't have time to dwell on the reality of what a bad situation we were in. Maybe your mind would go crazy if you tried to handle all of the thoughts and emotions and the reality of what was happening around you. The only reality I understood from that day on was that I had to do my part to stay alive.

One thing I remember vividly was the smell of death. I was on a detail to burn the NVA bodies with JP-4, (jet fuel) and that was horrible. I mean, we had to do it for sanitary reasons, but I mean, to just drag them over in a pile and pour fuel on them and light them, and then the smell of the burning bodies. I will never forget that smell. It was just terrible.

One of the other vivid memories I have of that morning was of one of our guys, who we nicknamed Big Brown. He was built like an NFL defensive tackle. He had a friend who was much smaller who we nicknamed, Little Brown. They were best of friends. Well, Little Brown got killed that night. And I will never forget the sight of Big Brown, dragging an NVA prisoner across the base by the nape of his neck, dragging him around like he was a little toy. The look on the face of that NVA was pure shock and terror. The look on the face of Big Brown was very scary to anyone, absolutely anyone. I don't know what happened to that NVA soldier.

We had thought that maybe with how hard we had been hit that we would be taken out or something, but nope, just dig a new hole and get ready. We had been told that we were totally surrounded. Hills 881 South and the hill we were on, 861, were two of the primary quadrants toward the Khe Sanh base. So it was a high priority for them to knock us out.

I will say this, the nights from then on were pretty scary. The night belonged to them. I don't want to say we were paranoid, but the sun coming up was a beautiful sight. We were on high alert all across the base all night long every night.

We had lost a lot of machine-gunners during that first attack. It's such a dangerous position because every fifth round is a tracer. It makes you such a target and there's no hiding from it.

The lieutenant hopped in the mortar pit I was in and asked, "Are you Wellens?" I said, "Yes sir." He said, "We're going to train you as a machine-gunner." Oh boy, well the word was that the lifespan of a machine-gunner was about ten seconds in a firefight. It was just so easy for the NVA to follow those tracers in, but I helped man the machine guns for the rest of the time I was there.

I was also given a meritorious promotion from PFC to lance corporal. I wasn't sure what it was for. He said for my role in delivering ammo under fire to the guys in the trenches.

It was pretty rough up there for the rest of the time on 861. We lived on C-rations. They couldn't resupply us because of the weather. There also seemed to be even more rats than before. They would crawl over you at night in your bunker. You couldn't get away from them. Every day we were mortared and sniped at.

There had been a time when we would throw away the C-rats that no one wanted, like lima beans and ham. We would toss them in a big bomb crater, but once we stopped getting resupplied, we were literally starving, and we would go into that bunker and dig out anything we could find.

We weren't being supplied with water either. So we would rig up our ponchos to catch rainwater. I remember one time my bunker mate and I found a box of dehydrated soup. We had to mix it with rainwater that had rat crap in it. We didn't care, we spooned out the crap and ate the rest. That's the way we had become.

But even through all this you still kept a sense of humor. You would still find something to laugh at once in a while. That was really important. That's where being around great guys makes a difference.

Another thing that might be surprising is that much of Vietnam is actually a beautiful country. Since we were high above the valley there were many days when the clouds were actually below us. But if you got up early and crawled up on top of your bunker, which I would do, you could look out at the clouds below you and the mountains around you as the sun was coming up and it was just beautiful. It was just a peaceful serenity. You could only stay out about twenty minutes because once the clouds burned off you were exposed to sniper fire again and you would have to find a hole to jump into. But in that short period of time it was nice to just enjoy the beauty even though we were in such a terrible place and terrible situation.

We continued living like that. They tried to overrun us at least three times. I believe the thing that saved us was the B-52 strikes. They would strike right between the Khe Sanh base and us on the hill. You couldn't even see them. There was about a three-mile gap between us and the base. You would look up in the sky on a clear blue day and then you would hear them screaming down and the entire valley would be lit up. Everything would shake and you would be certain that nothing could survive that devastation. And then a few hours after the bombing, we would get sniped at again. It was like, "What do you have to do to kill these people?"

There was a different company of Marines that set up on a plateau of a hill down below us. We could see them plainly and you could tell it wasn't a good position to be in. There was vegetation and elephant grass all around them. Sure enough, one night the NVA hit them. They were on them so fast, the guys didn't have a chance. It turned into hand-to-hand combat. We kept pumping out illumination rounds for them. It was just a very chaotic night. The next day we had to go down and help with the wounded and the dead. It was just very, very sad.

It was like that for seventy-seven days from January through April of 1968. Then we received word that we were going on the offensive. We teamed up with Lima and Mike companies. We were going to try and overtake Hill 881 North.

We prepared hard for our attack. We even practiced the attack at night, how we were going to maneuver through our concertina wire and move into position as quietly as possible. We were confident we were ready.

It was right around 1:00 or 2:00 in the morning when we got the word to saddle up and roll. And believe me, our guys were ready. They wanted revenge.

We wound our way through the perimeter in single file. I was near the colonel and could hear him talking on the radio. I heard him say, "Well we expect about forty percent casualties." I started thinking,

Chuck Wellens collection

That's me he's talking about. Oh my goodness...

So, we moved out of our perimeter, got into position, and as soon as daybreak hit, we made our assault. You could not believe our guys in that fight. They were so mad about the friends we had lost. Once they started going, you couldn't stop them. They fought with revenge on their minds; there's no question about that. They didn't plan on showing any mercy or anything. That's the way they fought. We were very successful that day. We literally caught them with their pants down. They were sitting around, eating, playing cards, things like that and our guys just unleashed all the anger and frustration that had been built up while on that hill.

When it was over we set up in a defensive night position. The following day was Easter Sunday. They told us to fill in our holes, that we were moving out from our position and that choppers would be coming in to take us all out. So, okay, we're sitting there waiting and all of a sudden mortars started coming in. They had us pinpointed. They nailed us, just nailed us. We lost a lot of guys. One of our lieutenants was dead, other bodies were laying there.

One of the wounded was a good friend of mine. His last name began with the letter V so we were always in line together. He was a machine-gunner. I used to loan him my wristwatch when he would be on night watch. We would rotate, two hours on two hours off. He must have been on duty that night when we got hit. I helped carry him to the chopper. His whole arm was pretty much blown off, just barely hanging there. He looked at me and said, "I'm sorry about your watch." And he was being sincere. I can still see the look in his eyes. I've always wondered what happened to him. I hope he survived and had a good life.

One of the dead was one of the original nine I had come in with. We put him in a bag and got ready to leave. There were only seven of us left to be picked up. Then word came over the radio that it was getting too dark, the choppers won't be coming back. They told us to dig in for the night and they would pick us up in the morning.

So I started digging a hole and thinking to myself, again, *Well I'm pretty much digging my own grave because there are seven of us and probably 150 of them out there and they know exactly where we are so the odds don't look very good.* We didn't have a chance. I even said to someone, "Let's be honest, we don't have a prayer of getting off this hill alive." If the choppers didn't come back, and we had to spend the night there, we were dead. You always wanted to be optimistic, but when you know the sheer numbers, you have to be realistic.

I'm going to say this; I always had the utmost respect for chopper pilots. They were incredibly courageous on so many occasions. But in my mind, never more so than that night. When I heard the "thump, thump, thump" at first from a distance and then becoming louder and louder I realized we were saved. Those pilots knew what they were facing and I'm sure they weren't ordered to come back for us, but they knew Marines were trapped on that hill and they were going to do whatever they could to get us out.

It was almost totally dark when the first one landed. My friend and I carried the body of our mutual friend aboard. When we landed at Khe Sanh, we tried finding Graves Registration. We must have walked around for over an hour with our buddy's body until we found it.

Someone told us that we were going to be flown out on C-130s the next day. I turned to my buddy and I said, "They've got to be kidding us." There were C-130s all blown up laying around the runways. There was only one runway and every time one of the planes came in for a landing, the NVA targeted it with artillery.

They changed their plans the next day and took us out on helicopters, alternating their landing sites the entire time so the NVA couldn't zero in on any one area.

We flew to Quang Tri for a little rest. I remember when we climbed aboard the helicopters we were like, "Go! Go! Get off the ground!" We were so happy to leave Khe Sanh. When we were on Hill 861 we had a clear view of the base getting hit on a regular basis. Not just mortars, but heavy artillery, just pounding them. On one of those days, a C-130 got hit and blown up. We were watching through binoculars. You just felt so bad for those Marines who had no place left to go. They just had to absorb the shelling and try to stay alive somehow. I was only there for three days and it was terrifying. Many of them were there for a couple of months at least, if they survived that long.

I'll never forget getting off that helicopter at Quang Tri and starting to run. An Air Force guy in a baseball-type cap told us to relax. He's like, "Don't worry, don't worry we're secure here, relax."

There was a big tanker truck that was rigged up for showers. They told us to take off our old clothes, that they would give us new ones. We took long showers and then afterward they treated us to a steak dinner. It was wonderful, but after months of eating C-rations and drinking rainwater we all got dysentery so bad...it was just horrible.

We slept in big tents. They didn't have cots, but we slept on soft white sand. You just laid in there and it felt so good. I couldn't believe it. I was clean. I had a new uniform that didn't smell. I had a full stomach. Life was good.

In the middle of the night, the NVA sent some 122mm rockets into the base. I'm sure they weren't aiming, just taking pot shots while trying to hit the airstrip. The rockets overshot the airfield and hit one of the tents near us. Everyone inside, eleven or twelve guys were killed while they slept.

You just couldn't stop thinking to yourself, *How in the hell do you get away from this? How do you survive for a full year?* There was no safe place. There was no place you could be truly safe.

We got sent to an area near Da Nang. It felt like we were back in civilization, but we spent most of our time out in the field on operations. We were called a "bastard unit." They would send us wherever they needed us. Much of the time was spent in what was called Dodge City. We were usually used as a blocking force or a pushing force.

The strategy was for one company to set up an LZ and perimeter then the next company would go ahead and set up another one further ahead. We had engineers that would blow down the trees and everything. The units would basically leapfrog each other.

One terrible day we were watching a company clearing the jungle when we received word that there were incoming choppers and we had to get to the LZ and help with, what they said were, external loaded bodies. What happened was that one of our jets had mistakenly attacked a platoon of Marines. But because it was a triple canopy jungle the chopper had to lower a big cargo net and the surviving Marines had to load the dead on it. It was our job to take them out and reload them on other choppers.

That is a sight I can't get out of my mind. In many cases, it was just arms and legs. Those poor guys had been blown apart. Just completely blown to hell. It was horrible, just horrible.

As we were doing that my thoughts were on their poor families back home. They had no idea what just happened to their sons, husbands, brothers. You knew that just before this happened they had been talking about all the same things we all did: going home, buying a car, just picking your life up again from where you left it.

That's the way life was over there. You just never knew from day to day. You would be talking with a guy about how they only had a month left and maybe the next day you were zipping him up. You had to accept the fact that you could be next; that you might not be walking on that plane for the trip home.

One thing that really changed me was when I became acting platoon leader. I was E-4, but we had lost so many guys ahead of me that I was next in line. Up until then, my main focus was on finding ways to stay alive. Just stay alive for one day after the next. But then you realize you've been put in a position of authority. You feel responsible for your men under you. You realize if you make a mistake, they might not be going home. You don't realize the weight of that responsibility until you have it given to you.

The Dodge City area was an NVA stronghold. It wasn't uncommon to come upon fortified bunkers, which was surprising seeing how close we were to Da Nang and all the firepower we had there. This is the only place I ever disobeyed an order. This would have been in December of '68. We were walking from Hill 1055 just south of the city. The fighting was very intense. I remember wondering how they were able to build such fortified positions this close to one of our bases. On this day my squad was in a bomb crater, pinned down from an NVA machine gun inside one of those bunkers. We had artillery, air support, and helicopters at our disposal. We could have called any of them in to take care of it. But this young lieutenant wanted the squad to attack the bunker head-on. I told the guys, "Stay down. Just stay down. Don't move." I had been around long enough now to know the difference between being brave and being an idiot. I thought to myself, *Don't you try making a name for yourself with my squad's lives.*

I did see one act of courage that absolutely blew my mind. There was this one really skinny, sort of nerdy guy with thick glasses in the platoon. Well, we were in a position and getting sprayed hard by small arms and machine gunfire. One of our guys out in the open got hit and went down. We didn't know if he was dead or alive. All of a sudden, there goes our nerdy guy running out through the gunfire, gets to the wounded guy, and drags him to safety. We were like, "What the hell just happened?" Later I asked him, "What the hell were you thinking doing something like that?" And he was like, "I don't know, I thought the guy needed help." It was just remarkable. Believe me, we showed him all the respect in the world after that.

When I first got there, I thought very little of the enemy. Many of us were that way. We didn't think they were as well-equipped as us, didn't have our training and so on. But man, when they hit us the way they did on the 21st of January in '68 and I saw their ability to fight... wow. As horrible as it was, afterward you had to respect the way they fought. They had a lot of drive. They were fighting for a cause in their own country.

The hard part for us is that you would be so miserable on patrol. You would be loaded down like a mule. You're in the hot jungle, there's leeches, mosquitos, everything there combined to make it just tortuous. So you would think of home. That was your diversion to keep your mind off how miserable you were. Then all of a sudden they would ambush you. So you go from boredom to being scared as hell. And then you would hear screaming and someone yells, "Corpsman up!" Now you knew one of your guys was hit. Then all your emotions turn to anger. You had incredible swings of emotion in a matter of seconds.

To me, the people who deserved the most respect were the corpsmen. Boy, when somebody hollered, "Corpsman up!" I never saw one hesitate. We would be hugging the earth trying to crawl inside our helmets. But they would grab their bag, bullets would be flying and they would go out to try to save someone's life. I think every one of them should have gotten some sort of special commendation for what they did in combat. They were just super.

We did quite a few killer-team missions. We did a lot of them around Quang Tri because there had been a lot of Viet Cong activity. Those were terrible too. You would lie there all night in the dark, mosquitos eating you alive. On this one particular night, some VC walked into our area and we sprang the attack on them. When it was light enough to see, we saw that there were women in the group. That was horrible, VC or not I still felt horrible about killing women. I mean you are just brought up a certain way. If you hadn't been hardened or whatever you wanted to call it, something like that will bother you tremendously.

One of the officers was a strict body count guy, so he wanted to see them. We had to tie them up on poles in between two guys and carry them back. I thought that was sick. I thought, *You bastard, believe us, they're dead.*

I was about halfway through my tour when I really started asking myself, *Why are we here? We can't win this war.* You could just see that it was going nowhere and guys were getting killed and maimed every day. It was a no-win situation. For America, it was fought too politically. The South Vietnamese government was full of corruption and the regular people were poor farmers caught in the middle. We were trying to force our way of life on them, but all they wanted to do was grow their rice and be left alone.

I got discharged in August of 1969. I didn't want anything to do with the war when I got home. I got married in 1970 and when my wife and I would sit down to supper and the news would come on if there was something from Vietnam on I would ask her to turn it off. I knew what those guys were going through, I didn't have to watch it. I was trying to forget it.

The one thing I did watch, and it hurt so much, was the evacuation of Saigon in 1975. To see us leaving the country like that, all I could think of was holding a guy in my arms that was wounded badly. He looked me in the eye and said, "I don't want to die, I don't want to die." I lied to him and told him he was going to be OK, that a medevac was on the way. I could tell by his breathing that he was fading. Then his chest stopped rising and his eyes were frozen open. The only thing I could do was to close his eyes and respectfully zip him up. And then to see everyone running to get out of the country. You just sit there and think, "What did those guys die for?"

I was very tight-lipped about Vietnam for a lot of years. I think I was resentful in a certain way that I lost my youth over there. Before I left home I was a happy guy, had lots of friends, and liked having a good time with everybody. When I came back I was different. I had changed. It took me a while to realize it. I just felt like my old friends were immature, at least that's how I perceived it. Suddenly I had a real bad attitude. It gradually went away, but I just had a hard time going from what I had gone through over there to jumping right back into my old life. That's what I mean when I say I lost my youth. I would never be that happy-go-lucky kid again.

It was only after I started talking to classes at the local schools that I started realizing that it was okay to open up and talk about what happened. Now I'm on four or five different Facebook sites talking with other veterans.

When I do talk to students, I never, ever glorify war in any way because there is nothing glorious about it. It's terrible. It's absolutely terrible. I don't care how macho or whatever you think you are. If you've actually been there, experienced it, lived with it, it's not possible to glorify it. It's just not.

HUBERT "HUB" JOSKI

26th Marine Regiment
3rd Marine Division
Vietnam War

For those of us who grew up during the 1960s, watching the national news with legendary anchormen such as Walter Cronkite or Chet Brinkley was a nightly staple. This was our daily, and in many ways, only window into what was happening around the country and the world.

Filmed reports of organized protests against the war and scenes of young men burning draft cards were common-place.

Hubert "Hub" Joski of Green Bay also hoped to foil his local draft board. Not because he didn't want to serve his country, but because he wanted to beat them to it.

For some reason, I didn't want to be drafted. I wanted to be known as someone who volunteered. That it was my choice, it was my decision to go and serve my country and I wanted to serve it as a Marine.

Somebody, somewhere got it in my head that the Marines never left a man behind. That was a difference-maker for me. I didn't want to be in a situation where you get overrun and all the guys weren't brought back, guys who were still alive much less dead ones.

I went in with a really great friend, Joe Van De Hei. They said, "Oh sure you guys will stay together all the way through." Well, that was

Hub Joski points out the name of his friend, Cpl. Joseph R. Van De Hei, on the Vietnam Veterans Memorial. (Hub Joski collection)

a crock. We went in the front gate together and out the back gate together and that was about it. Maybe they did that on purpose; maybe they didn't want good friends together in combat in case things happened. We both got sent to Nam; Joe didn't make it back.

I was trained as 0300, a grunt basically; then they gave me specialized training. They had these little tanks called Ontos. They had six 106mm recoilless rifles mounted on them. Those things were pretty cool. Then I got trained on mortars, machine guns, you name it, just enough to get me in trouble.

I was shipped out to Vietnam in January of 1968. You hear about some guys getting a thirty-day leave just before heading over...we got one night in Tijuana.

Once we landed in Nam they didn't waste any time. They

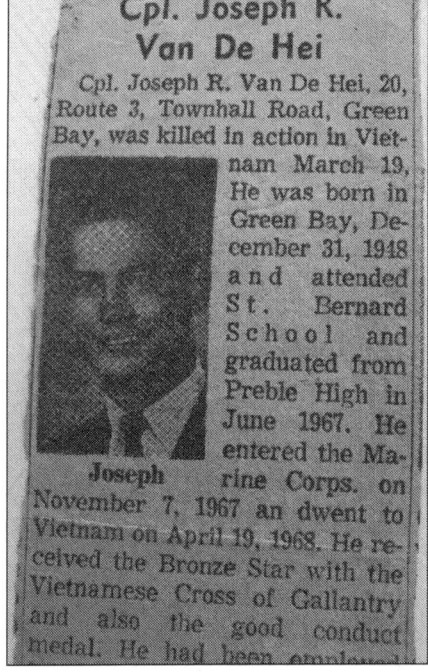

Cpl. Joseph R. Van De Hei

Cpl. Joseph R. Van De Hei, 20, Route 3, Townhall Road, Green Bay, was killed in action in Vietnam March 19. He was born in Green Bay, December 31, 1948 and attended St. Bernard School and graduated from Preble High in June 1967. He entered the Marine Corps. on November 7, 1967 an dwent to Vietnam on April 19, 1968. He received the Bronze Star with the Vietnamese Cross of Gallantry and also the good conduct medal. He had been shipped us right to Khe Sanh. They were convinced a big attack was coming and they shanghaied every new guy they could find. General Westmoreland was convinced it was going to be the biggest attack of the war and he didn't want another Dien Bien Phu where the North Vietnamese slaughtered the French. Later on, we heard that they had a big sand model of Khe Sanh in the White House and the president checked it every day. That's how worried they were.

They brought us to the LZ on Chinooks, but they didn't really slow down a whole hell of a lot. We got off on a dead run. They were starting to mortar and drop artillery on the runways. About the third day, they started hitting it pretty hard. They were eyeballing everything we did. We dug in deeper. It seemed like the deeper we dug in the more they would hit us.

On the second night of taking heavy fire we didn't know if we would see the next morning. When I saw that sun coming up through a real smoky haze, I just remember taking a real deep breath and thinking to myself, *Wow... made it. I made it through that unbelievable night.* I didn't realize at the time that this was just day one. We had a long way to go. I just sat there and looked around at all the stuff blown up around me. On the side of a bunker, about six feet from me, was a B-40 rocket sticking in the sand. I'm like, "Hey guys. I think we had better get the hell out of here in case this thing decides to blow!" That was quite the eye-opener to see how close you could come to getting killed. That's the way it was a lot of times. If it goes off, guys get killed; it doesn't go off, you stay alive. It was out of your control.

During the day they would send us down to the airstrip to do repairs and stuff like that. You knew they were watching us, watching us walk around. Wherever you would be walking you always kept your eye out for shell craters. You'd think to yourself, *OK there's one right here.... here's another one.* You had to do that because when you would hear, "Boom! Boom! Boom!" you'd better find a crater pretty damn quick. We figured we had between ten and twelve seconds before it all hit the fan. You never knew when it was going to happen. No idea. You just figured it was going to happen every day. Day or night pretty much from the word go. More toward the middle and end of the battle, they came in hard every day...every day. There was no place to go except deeper. I built my own bunker, dug down about seven to eight feet, put extra sandbags on top, and made a little bunk in there. We would get together with four to five guys and you felt pretty safe.

We had fifteen guys who all came in together and they didn't really know what to do with us. So they just had us fill sandbags, build trenches, work on repairing the runway, stuff like that. Then after a while, they put us on the lines. I used to work in construction, working on excavating water and sewer lines. Sometimes we used augers to install laterals under roadways. You could hear those augering sounds through the ground from a long way off. Well, one day I'm in the front trench and I kept hearing, "chuk, chuk, chuk" coming toward us. I told the guys on the machine gun, "Hey, I think you've got somebody digging right between your legs." I told them I was going to be pointing my M-16 toward that sound instead of outside the wire. They were joking. "Joski, get your damned rifle out of here!" I said, "No, somebody is trying to get into our trenches I'm telling you!"

The sound of digging stopped about twenty to twenty-five feet from the bunker. All of a sudden one of them stood up in his little diaper as we called them. That's what the sappers wore. That way they wouldn't get their clothes caught on the concertina wire, and they loaded them down with grenades. He was going to frag the bunker. Well, that machine gun let loose and just tore him up, eliminating the problem. The next day they put smoke grenades down the tunnel to see where it would come out. The smoke came out of the other end about 200 yards from our bunker and outside of the wire. They must have been digging that tunnel for weeks. It was just insane what they could do. That was just one tunnel. They had tunnels all along the outside of the lines.

You had your good days and you had your bad days. I remember the day the ammo dump got hit. It was like ninety percent of our ammo: mortar rounds, machine gun ammo, 105 shells. It blew a big hole in the ground like you can't believe. You started thinking, *What in the hell is going on here? Did they come up with some new kind of powerful artillery or was it one perfect shot?* We didn't know what to think anymore.

You never volunteered for anything, but that didn't get you out of work. Loading and unloading on the landing strip was a tough job. One day I was helping load a wounded Marine and I started talking to him a little bit and asked him where he was from. He said, "Manitowoc, Wisconsin." I told him I was from Green Bay. I said, "I think you got a million-dollar wound there, you're going home." But he had it pretty rough. I saw him about four to five years after I got back. The poor guy was pretty messed up.

Those choppers would come in, at first they were coming in slow then after they started getting hit they started coming in faster. It got to the point where they would just shove the pallets off. Then they started putting parachutes on the loads and shoving them out the back of the planes and Chinooks at higher elevations. Then it became too dangerous to land at all. They had to drop stuff that way because there were so many burning hulks of aircraft sitting around the runway.

I know one thing, the best view to see what was going on was on top of Hill 881 North; the enemy watched us from there all day long.

It was really important to have a good group of guys around you.

We would have old-fashioned BS sessions hunkered down in our bunkers almost every night. You really needed that when things were really hot and heavy. You had to support each other, keep an eye on each other. I had a feeling I was going to get out of there. I don't know why, but I really did. Maybe it was because we all encouraged each other.

It didn't matter how well trained you were, sometimes, hell, most of the time you just had to be lucky. There were a lot of different times I could have gotten hit. One time I jumped in a crater and a rocket sails right over it and hits the bank behind me. Another time me and another guy tried diving into a crater at the same time. He got hit in midair, but I was a split-second ahead of him and didn't get hit. This other one I can laugh at now. I jumped into a trench where there was a big fifty-five-gallon drum. There was shrapnel flying all over the place. A good-sized chunk hit right above my head. Once the shelling stopped I thought, *Well I dodged another one.* Then I looked close, that fifty-five-gallon drum was full of gasoline. I couldn't have picked a worse hole in all of Vietnam to be in. One tiny piece of hot shrapnel, just one of the thousands upon thousands flying around, and I wouldn't be here today.

For as much as they pounded us, our B-52s gave it right back. They did airstrikes pretty much every night for a while. Normally they weren't supposed to drop bombs within three miles of friendly troops, but they started bombing within one mile. They would run strings of

Hub Joski shows off the Vietnam-era truck he restored.

500 pounders along the enemy lines or where they thought the lines might be. You could never tell. We used to say the B-52s rocked us to sleep; the ground would just tremble. We had the 81mm and 60mm mortars and the 105s for closer work.

We went out on patrols into the hills, trying to flush them out. The first time, we had to back out. They had us surrounded in a V-shaped ambush. The way we found out was from one of the scout dogs. They were the most fantastic animals you would ever want to see. They would lift their nose up and that would tell the handler that there was an enemy in the area. I was probably 100 feet from that dog and that nose was just bobbing up and down. We didn't even turn around. We just backed out of there totally alert because we knew we were right on the edge of the kill zone.

The next time we went up on Hill 881 North we went in with a reinforced battalion. We had Army and Marine units. We cleaned it out. They weren't as strong as they had been; the bombings had done a lot of damage. From what we heard it was the most amount of desertions the NVA ever had. I'm sure it was to get away from the B-52s. I was lucky. I was an assistant gunner for the M-60, carrying two boxes of ammo. After taking the hill we went down to the base and we were like, *Where in the hell did everybody go?* They had already evacuated a bunch of guys out. Everybody had Easter candy in their bunkers. I don't remember where it all came from, but we raided everybody's bunkers and took all of it.

When we left I looked around and everything was brown. This area had been a coffee plantation, a big lush plantation, all green, beautiful. I thought, *Wow, we sure bombed the hell out of that place* not knowing that a lot of the dead brown area was from Agent Orange. We were soaked in it. That's where I believe I got a lot of my physical problems from - stomach problems, diabetes, lung issues.

It was a great feeling to leave that place, but I still had ten months left. We went to Phu Bai after that. It got to be a routine of running patrols. I was still an assistant gunner and worked with the mortar units. It could get pretty interesting on some of those missions. One time our machine gun needed ammo, but a .51-caliber North Vietnamese machine gun had spotted me behind this big teak tree. They hammered that thing so hard...splinters were flying everywhere. That thing started snapping and rolling on top of me, I didn't have any choice. I remember thinking, *Well this is like World War I where you just have to go over the top.* My job was to get ammo to our machine gun. It didn't matter how scared you were, just had to bear it and do your job. You just do what you got to do.

One thing you learned to do was notice anything that looked out of the ordinary, even little things. One time we were helping some kids rounding up their water buffalos and I saw these sticks stuck in the ground behind some bushes. I thought to myself, *That looks like a mortar emplacement.* So we got the coordinates and wrote them down in our book for future reference. It wasn't a week later that we took some rounds from that area. We dialed up those coordinates, put ten rounds in the air, and knocked that thing out.

There were some odd things that would happen. There was this really hot day that we put a bunch of wounded under some trees. When the chopper came in it of course blew the branches to the side. That's when I saw this red and yellow striped snake on a branch right over the head of one of the guys that I had put there. Son of a gun I felt so bad!! I took a machete and chopped it in half and carried the guy away from there. I kept apologizing for not seeing it. But that's what I mean about keeping your eyes open all the time.

Another night we were out on an ambush and we had the command center right in the middle like we always did with everyone else set up around it. This was in the middle of the night and all of a sudden we hear someone yell out - which is the worst thing someone could possibly do. When you give away your position you're putting everyone's lives at stake. Anyway, one of the guys had been telling the guy next to him to get his leg off the back of his. Another guy said the same. As it turned out it was a huge python snake that was crawling across the backs of their legs. The one guy never got over it. He could never really handle lying in the jungle again.

The worst thing that I was a part of was when a forward scout squad had gotten too far ahead of the rest of the platoon. By the time we got close to them, they had been captured and hung in trees but they weren't dead. Our guys tried getting close, but they had an ambush set up around them. We lost a couple of guys trying to get to them or to even put them out of their misery. That's not a day you want to remember.

When I got home I hung out with guys who had also been in the service. So that helped, but I developed a bit of a drinking problem. I think it would have helped to have talked to others about some of the things a lot of us were dealing with, but it seemed like nobody wanted to hear about it. I remember my dad, who was a vet saying, "You were in combat; you were in battles; you're done with that now. We don't talk about it anymore." I'm sure he was trying to help me, but in the long run, maybe it would have been better to talk to people instead of letting it all stay bottled up inside.

You did what you had to do to adapt to civilian life again. I was troubled in a way. I used to go to a bar called Speeds. There was a motorcycle club that liked to hang out there. I was sitting at the bar and one guy said, "Move over." That happened about four times until I was at the end of the bar against the wall. I said, "That's it, it's as far as I can go." So the guy says, "Well then get the hell out of here." I said, "I ain't going anywhere." I said, "If anything, you're going somewhere." He says, "What do you mean?" I said, "Well for one thing I will pull your eyeballs out of your head and stick them up your ass!" I was, how do I put it, not afraid of confrontation or of anybody. Then the head of the Chapter came over and said to his guy, "Hey, this guy just got back from Vietnam, leave him alone." Then he invited me to sit at his table.

It took a lot of years, but once I started talking to guys from the Vietnam Vets Association, things got better. My wife was mad. She said, "We tried to help you forget and now you're bringing this all back up." Again, she was just doing what she thought was best for me. But one of the guys said to her, "You have to let him talk. If he doesn't, it will be worse for him." It made a big difference to talk to other vets who had been there. I mean, how do you talk to someone else about survivor's guilt and things like that? Or how much you dreaded the 4th of July because of firecrackers? It got to the point where I would set them off myself just to overcome it. It was the vets themselves who made you feel like you were okay. I owe a lot to them.

Ken Vanden Heuvel displays a North Vietnamese rifle and binoculars he brought home as souveniers.

KEN VANDEN HEUVEL

4th Marine Regiment
3rd Marine Division
Vietnam War

There are numerous stories about the cold-shoulder treatment replacements from stateside training camps received upon arriving in Vietnam. Ken Vanden Heuvel of Green Bay, Wisconsin, had heard those very same stories, which is why he was surprised at the friendly welcome he received from his new unit in the Quang Tri region of central Vietnam in 1967.

The shocking part for him was how short some of those newfound friendships would last.

We used to hang out at a place in Bellevue, Wisconsin, called the Bluestone Bar. We were regulars there. Some guys who had graduated ahead of me from Preble High School had joined the Marines and were home on leave. My buddies and I had been thinking about joining ourselves. So one day three of us: Randy, Denny, and myself all went down and signed up on the buddy plan. We all ended up in Vietnam, in fact not too far from one another. We all made it home. Although Randy got shot right through the neck over there, but survived.

I graduated from boot camp in San Diego on my nineteenth birthday. I thought that was the best birthday present ever. In those days, once you graduated, you pretty much knew what was coming next.

When I arrived in Da Nang I was given orders to report to Dong Ha. I was standing there with my "willy peter" bag as we used to call them. Everything I had fit into that bag. I threw the bag on the C-53, the old bumblebee they called them and climbed in. A couple of minutes later they had everybody get off. They said Dong Ha was taking heavy fire and we would have to wait.

The next day we climbed in again, we're all set to go, and had to get off again because Dong Ha was getting hit again. I started to wonder what the hell kind of a place they were sending us to. Finally, a few hours later they told us to get on board again. This time we were going.

Ken Vanden Heuvel heads to the airplane on the tarmac at Austin Straubel Airport in Green Bay on his way to Vietnam in 1967. (Ken Vanden Heuvel collection)

We get there, we land, and I see my willy peter bag sitting there alongside the helipad. I was going over to pick it up when somebody yelled, "Incoming!" I just stood there. Somebody grabbed me and pulled me into a deep muddy trench. It was the first of many, many, many times I would be under a mortar attack before I left the country.

The attack stops, we climb out and someone asks where I'm going. I told him, First Battalion, Fourth Marines. He said, "OK, just go over there, a truck will be coming by to pick you up. I'm standing there, everything is red clay and mud and I'm thinking to myself, "*What in the hell have I gotten myself into?*"

They took me to A Company. There were tents set up and everything. I didn't know what to expect but they were the greatest guys you could ever ask for. They did everything they could to make you feel welcome.

A guy came in, great guy, he was from Costa Rica. He took me to a bunk to get squared away. They were all so happy to have a new face around. He introduced me to some of the guys. He also introduced me to marijuana. That was a first for me.

My first job was to work with the choppers taking supplies out to the guys in the field. I asked one of the pilots where we were going. He said, "Son, we are going to the DMZ." If my memory serves me right, that was the end of the line, as far north as you could go.

When we were going in to land, I saw the guys who had been out on an operation. Two of the guys had their bags packed, they were heading home. One of them was a guy they all called, "Sergeant Rock." He was the friendliest guy of the bunch, just a hell of a nice guy. Everyone introduced themselves to me, asked where I was from and stuff, told me they would teach me everything I needed to know to make it out of there. They really made me feel welcomed to be joining their unit.

It was kind of crazy, I mean just six or seven days before I was in California and now I'm out in the bush, on the DMZ. If you didn't know there was a war going on and North Vietnam was just on the other side of that border, you would almost think you were on a camping trip with a bunch of your buddies.

Sergeant Rock was one of the guys who was supposed to leave on that chopper, but he decided he would stay one more day with his men and then go out.

Everything was great until that night. That's when we got hit with artillery. They had me in a four foot hole. The artillery was very, very accurate. Eight of the guys I had just met were killed. One of them was Sergeant Rock. That was so devastating to everyone that I can't even describe it. He had been with them for thirteen months. You could just see the respect everyone had for him. He could have left for good, but stayed for one more night.

That was my first night in the bush of Vietnam.

The next day they sent me out on an OP (Observation Post) with a guy named Stewart. He was halfway through his second tour. They said he would be a good guy to learn from. We went about 300 meters to the west and just sat there waiting to see if there was any movement, any activity around the area. It was late in the afternoon when we heard, Thump! Thump! Thump! *What the hell?* "Get down!" He yells. All of a sudden, "Sheeeeeee bang!" We were getting mortared. He was the first one to tell me that it took eleven seconds from the time it detonates, until the time it lands and you had better find a hole in that time.

He says, "Grab your rifle, follow me!" We took off running, I had no idea where we were going. We go about 100 yards and all of a sudden we come face-to-face with four NVA. We open up on full automatic, "Bruuuuuuup, bruuuuuuup!" We killed all four guys, then we grabbed the mortar tubes. There were shells they still hadn't fired. Grabbing those was probably better than killing the NVA because maybe we saved some of our guys.

On February 2nd, 1968, we were making a push when we started getting mortared. I was told to stay back and help the wounded until the choppers got there, but we were taking so much fire that the choppers wouldn't come in. Stewart was laying there with a chest wound. The corpsman comes up to me and says, "Do you have a pack of cigarettes?" I gave it to him. He took the cellophane off, pressed it on Stewart's chest, and said, "Keep this on him, keep the pressure on it!"

As I'm doing that, we start taking sniper fire, "Zing, zing, zing," all around us. Stewart started pointing out where the snipers were and told everybody to open up on them. After one would quiet down, another would start from someplace else. Stewart was turning blue, but still pointing out the snipers. I figured that was the end of him, but the choppers came in and he was the first one out. I heard later that he survived.

There was a time when he was on patrol with other guys and they were taking fire. They all hit the ground and started shooting back and throwing grenades. They said he took off and ran right up to the trench and blasted three guys that had pinned them down.

I have no greater respect for anyone in the entire military than the combat corpsman. When you needed them, I never saw a single one shirk their duty. They were right there administering aid. They would go from guy to guy as he did with me and Stewart. They would tell you exactly what to do, try to ease the guy's pain, and then move on to the next one.

We were given a special assignment to move to a hill about five miles from Dong Ha and set up a series of ambushes along the way. We were setting up an ambush when the point guy comes back and says he

Ken Vanden Heuvel (second from right in sunglasses) enjoys a pastry treat in the Vietnam jungle. (Ken Vanden Heuvel collection)

lost contact with the rest of the company. Nobody knew exactly what to do other than to sit tight and hope they sent somebody back to find us. Nobody did.

Now it's daylight. We still don't know what to do. So I said, "Well according to the topo (topography) map, there's a ravine here and a hill here…" and so forth. They said, "How in the hell do you know that?" I said, "Because I had seen the map. I used to spend a lot of time wandering around the north woods in Wisconsin and the U.P. (Upper Peninsula of Michigan) looking for deer-hunting land. I know how to read a map and terrain and everything like that." Somebody said, "This guy knows his shit."

So they "rewarded" me by making me point man from then on.

No problem, I was OK with it. It brought me back to deer hunting. You sit in the stand for a few hours in the morning and then go out sneaking around trying to find one. Walking point in Vietnam wasn't a lot different.

I told the guys not to come any closer than fifty feet from me unless I was breaking in a new guy. I didn't want to hear any sound coming from my guys. If I heard a little noise like metal-on-metal or something like that, I didn't have time to try and figure out if it was from one of ours or one of them. You listened to every sound and you constantly smelled the air because if they were nearby you could smell them. That's not even a question. That's the honest truth.

When I switched to walking point I started carrying an M-79 instead of an M-16. I was now a grenadier. I carried ten flechette rounds with me. It's funny, but you never really shot at a target. You're going along and bullets are coming from someplace so you just turn and fire and move and fire some more. But you don't really see anyone, you don't know if you ever hit someone.

After Cam Lo we got shipped to Con Thien and back to those dreaded mortar attacks.

The captain came up to me and said, "You went through Recon school right?" I told him I had. He said, "I want you to go out on a killer squad." He told me where he wanted us to set up. So we went out that night and set up in an old rundown temple. We were quite a ways out. We stayed there all night. Later on, we found a cache of stuff: ammunition, mortars, more than we could carry so they sent out engineers to blow it all up.

They asked if we wanted to keep doing that. We said sure. That's when we started coming up with kills. We would get three or four in one place, maybe four or five in another. We had a five-man team. It worked out pretty good.

Editor's note: *In 1966 construction started on a land barrier roughly forty-five miles wide by 650 yards deep. It began just south of the Demilitarized Zone and extended from the western border of South Vietnam eastward across the peninsula. The zone was laced with landmines, observation posts and highly classified, electronic sensors which conceptually would alert US personnel of enemy movement through the zone. It was quickly dubbed the McNamara Line, named after the man behind its conception, Defense Secretary Robert McNamara.*

At Con Thien, there was a big buffer zone that had been created to separate us from them. One moonlit night we had an ambush set up and all of a sudden one of the guys says, "Somebody's out there. Do we have anybody out there?" We didn't. So we opened up. I started blasting with the M-79. Guys were throwing grenades. We gave them everything we had.

The next day we went out there and figured out what they were doing. They were going through the minefield, taking out the mines, and using tree bark, a type that would shine in the moonlight, to mark a trail.

One of our guys, Sergeant Rodriguez, had a starlight scope so he would set up at night and pick them off one by one when they would go in there to take out our mines.

We were getting mortared all the time. They never quit. We got the word, "OK guys go out there and find that mortar!" We were going through the area we figured it was in when all of a sudden our point man disappears, just disappeared. Then we hear, "bruuuuup, bruuuuup!" He had fallen right into their mortar pit. The NVA were sitting there eating breakfast. One of the NVA guys climbed out and started running. I got him before he got too far. As it turns out, he was their forward observer. I still have his binoculars.

There were lots of stories of guys getting hit when they were short. (Close to the end of their tour.) We had one guy who was getting down to his last couple of days, so he built himself a bunker. He dug deep and covered it with everything he could find: sandbags, logs, you name it.

Sure enough on one of his very last nights, we get hit. A mortar hit his bunker straight on, but he survived. I kind of have to laugh when I think of that. I mean I've seen guys walking around in a daze before, but this was an entirely different level. We were like, "Hey man are you OK?" He just looked right through us. He did make it out of there and went home. That man-made bunker saved his life. But wow was he stunned.

In spring of '68, we got sent to Khe Sanh. They took us in Hueys and dropped us off on the downslope of Hill 881 North. We climbed to the top and looked around. It was covered in NVA garbage and stuff. You could see the entire base of Khe Sanh from up there. You would watch their artillery hit and everybody down below would disappear. All you would see were flashes and dust. When it stopped everybody would climb out and start walking around again.

After Khe Sanh, they sent us to someplace in the middle of nowhere. All we knew is that it was near Laos. This was a battalion operation. There were a series of grassy hills. We set up our perimeter and then waited until dark. As soon as it was pitch black, we saddled up and moved out to a new spot nice and quiet. That night the shit hit the fan, but not where we were - where we had been. They hit exactly where we had our first perimeter. They had eyes on us the whole time.

There was a road going through there, probably coming right from Laos, that wasn't even on any of the maps. The NVA needed that road to move supplies down south. That's why they wanted to get us out of there so bad.

For the next three nights, we got hit hard with artillery and mortars. At one time we counted eleven mortars coming in together. We had a spotter plane above the hill. He would fire a phosphorus round to where the mortars were coming from and the next thing you knew a jet would be there blasting the area.

At Con Thien, if we were taking artillery fire, they would call in rounds from the USS *New Jersey*. Once those guys got a good read on the location, you never got artillery fire from that spot again.

Ken Vanden Heuvel (left) near Con Thien in 1968. (Ken Vanden Heuvel collection)

This was my first introduction to satchel charges. You couldn't throw those things very far so you knew they were that close to us. We were on two hills, the size of about a half-square block. By the end of that third day, we were all huddled up together because we had lost so many guys.

Earlier that day I was helping get bodies out when mortars started coming in. I was running to jump in a hole, but my helmet fell off and, before I had a chance to get in the hole, a piece of shrapnel about an inch long and half-an-inch wide hit me in the top of my head. I was knocked out. I remember waking up. My head was splitting. There was blood all over the place. Then I found out that most of the blood wasn't from me. It was from a guy next to me who had gotten hit worse. I pulled the shrapnel out of my head myself. I don't know why I didn't save it.

One of the guys hit was a good friend of mine by the name of Patrick. He goes, "Vance, (that was my nickname) I think I got hit in the back with something. What do you think I should do?" I told him if it was bad enough to get him out of the bush for a while, then go. I helped get him on a medevac. To make a long story short, he ended up being paralyzed from the waist down. A piece of shrapnel had hit him, but it hadn't done all its damage yet. Those are the kinds of things that happened.

My best friend over there was from Oregon. Carlson was his name. He lived on a ranch. He would say, "When we get out of here, you're coming to visit me. I'm going to show you the mountains. You're going to stay on the ranch. You're going to love it out there."

One morning after an attack another good buddy and I were picking up bodies and stuff from our area. Mortars started coming in again.

I had my helmet on this time, but no shirt or flak vest. We laid down right where we were. He says, "Hey I've got one cigarette left, you want to share it?" So we're passing it back and forth and he would be like, "I wonder if this is the one that gets us?" I'm like, "I don't know, maybe." And then you would hear the bang and be thankful it missed you. I remember just lying there, sharing that cigarette, maybe the last one we would ever have, while hot shrapnel was falling on my bare back.

When the shelling stopped he said, "Come on, I will help you carry him up the hill." He meant my buddy Carlson. He had been killed by one of those satchel charges the night before. It was very, very hard to see what that did to him. We carried my buddy to the top of the hill.

Whenever I hear *Taps* being played on Memorial Day, I always think of him and that ranch he hoped to go home to.

That was my worst time over there. I believe out of the 1,500 guys who spent time in that area around Laos, by the end of the summer, there were less than 300 who weren't killed or wounded.

One day one of our guys came walking up to me and said, "Hey Vance, there's a guy here who says he knows you from back home." Here comes Joe Van De Hei from Green Bay. Oh, man was that the greatest thing to see him. I believe he was in B Company, I was in A Company. We talked about everything back home. We had gotten together at the Bluestone when I was home on leave and he was getting set to join the Marines. I knew his entire family. It was just so great to catch up with a friend from back home. The only bad thing is that I broke the news to him that I had gotten a newspaper clipping from my mom that some mutual friends of ours had gotten killed in a car accident in Green Bay. He took that hard. He said, "Oh man I was just partying with them when I was home on leave after boot camp."

Seeing him and catching up was one of the rare good days over there. It wasn't long after I got home that we got the news. Joe had been killed in action from a grenade while working with a CAG (Combined Action Group) unit.

That war just wasn't going to let you rest. It's like you never had a chance to get away from it. To take a break from it. You just stay in it all the time.

I got hit a couple more times. We were chasing NVA troops toward some trees. We actually had some tanks with us this time. We get on the tanks and catch about 200 NVA in the open, but once again here come the blessed mortars. Me and another guy jumped off the tanks and "Bam," we got hit. This time I got four or five pieces of shrapnel in my hands, the other guy had seventeen holes in him but lived. That was one time we hit them hard. The grass had been sprayed with Agent Orange so it was only two-three feet high. The tanks and everybody just poured it on them. Somebody saw a reflection coming from on top of a hill so we opened fire on that too. It was probably their forward observer who had been calling in fire on us. We caught them in the open, but we paid a price too. Whoever decided this was a good spot for us to set up was nuts. We had hardly any protection from their mortars and artillery. We could see exactly where their artillery was coming from. We wanted to go over there and knock it out, but they wouldn't let us because it was over the Laotian border. Which was so frustrating it's unbelievable. We could have ended that war and saved so many thousands of lives if they had let us fight it to win, it's unbelievable.

We went about as far north and west as we could go. On this one day, I was breaking in a new point guy. Everybody else was way back, the way I liked it. We came down a hill and saw a grass hut. We get a little closer and there's a bunker. I went back to LT and told him what we found. He told me to fire a couple of rounds into it and see what happens. I said, no, that I would go up and check it out first. So I go in and the thing is just full of weapons and ammunition. It had so much ammunition in there that if I had thrown a grenade in it would have blown us all to bits.

I took my squad to secure the area, walked across a nice cool creek, and saw another bunker. Me and four or five other guys check it out and the same exact thing: stacks of rifles, mortars, ammo. We thought, *Wow, is this cool!*

I look around and there's another one, this one full of rice, just loaded to the top. You have to know, we were past the DMZ. This might have been as far as any American troops had been. They had to feel pretty secure using this as their main supply area where they would load up before hitting us at Con Thien.

It took us a day to pile everything up and get out of there. When the engineers set that thing off it blew a mile high. The next day we went back and there were fresh tracks all around. The NVA had to be wondering who in the hell blew up all their stuff.

The next day I got hit.

We were going up a trail that took us to an area that was more like normal woods than jungle. I'm standing there and all of a sudden, "Zing! Zing! Zing!" Rounds start hitting all around us. I'm firing with my M-79. There are rifle flashes all over as my guys move up, explosions all around. Every damn thing is happening.

I just keep moving and firing, moving and firing. It slacked off a little, I went to take another step and I fell right to the ground. A piece of shrapnel had gone deep into my thigh.

It didn't really hurt. The guys are like, "We can dig that out." That didn't work. So they called in a chopper, but there's no place for it to land so they lowered a harness to pull me up. Here I'm going up, spinning in the air, just hanging there waiting for somebody to shoot me.

Ken Vanden Heuvel sits atop a tank near the DMZ in Vietnam. (Ken Vanden Heuvel collection)

They got me up and dragged me into the chopper. That's when it started hurting. Oh did that thing hurt now...wow.

They got me out of there and got me to a medical aid station. I'm lying there and they start cutting, I'm watching them, which was pretty cool until they started cutting off chunks of meat from my leg and throwing them away. That's when I couldn't watch anymore.

Some of my guys came to see me. One of them said, "We saved something for you." It was one of the SKS Russian-made NVA rifles from the first bunker we had found. I didn't know they had saved anything. He said, "You earned this," and handed it to me with the bayonet still attached. I carried that with me, with the bayonet off, on the plane all the way home. I still have it.

I was laid up in the hospital for a while and then sent to a two-week school in Da Nang to learn about working in a CAG (Combined Action Group).

We trained the South Vietnamese Army troops and worked with what they called the "Combos" which were village police. They were kind of like part police and part military. I was with two-three of our guys training them. We lived in an old church near Phu Bai.

I did that for the last two months of my tour over there. It was really interesting. You got to find out what these people were really like. Exactly how talented they were, how ambitious they were. They were very determined to take care of the people in their villages. They wanted to go on every ambush with us; they wanted to take their turns walking point.

I was with them every day, all day, and I learned to admire them very much, the Combos that is. We had about fifteen of them and they were with us all the time. They paid close attention to what we taught them. They took it seriously, whereas the others, the typical South Vietnamese soldiers we had with us, didn't at all. We would go out on patrols and the regular Army guys would be shooting at birds and things like that. It was like taking a bunch of kids on a hike. But the Combos didn't screw around, were professionals. They were determined that the North wasn't going to take over their country, but they just didn't have enough help from their own military.

Ken Vanden Heuvel collection

In fact, here's an example. We were on a patrol one day near the Perfume River and started taking fire from across the river, small-arms fire mainly. Luckily there were some old buildings next to us that we were able to take cover in. I remember at least two of the Combos were hit. But when things calmed down and we looked around, there wasn't a single ARVN to be seen. Every one of them had taken off. That's why when I was asked, what I thought of the South Vietnamese military taking over once the Americans pulled out, I said, "The day the South Vietnamese Army takes over is the day South Vietnam falls. I will give it two weeks." There's no way they would be able to defeat the NVA on their own.

I got to be pretty good friends with some of the local villagers. They would invite us into their homes for meals all the time. They became our friends. They treated us with great respect and we did the same toward them. And that is why it really tore me up when the war ended the way it did. I just keep thinking about what happened to all those friends who defended us. You knew they weren't going to make it and that hurt. Oh, that hurt. I remember hearing about it on the radio, the day Saigon fell. If I could, I would have gone right back over to help those people.

Another group I had a lot of admiration for was the Hmongs. I was all for them coming to the US because I knew what they did for us over there and how bad it was going to be for them in their own country.

When I was sent home we landed at El Toro Airbase. They told us to walk straight to the buses and not respond to anything around us. People were yelling things at us. I sure would have loved to have heard the order, "Marines, right face, attack!"

I was still wounded when I got back and that's the welcome I received. It took me a long time to forget that. From then on when anybody gave me a hard time I didn't hold back. I didn't hold back at all.

One thing that has really bothered me since then is fireworks. I have a very hard time with fireworks being shot off randomly. I have to get away from them if they are bad. I have a place up north and I used to go up there and just roam the woods. Just roam the woods to get away from everything. I've done that countless times, just get out of town for the whole 4th of July weekend.

The worst part is when I have to get up to use the bathroom in the middle of the night and then I can't get back to sleep without thinking about something from Vietnam. I think of talking to guys who were wounded, asking them about where they were from or about their families while waiting for a medevac. Or I think about Carlson and all the things he told me we were going to do when I visited him out in Oregon.

Vietnam doesn't go away. I'm sure it never will.

Rich Karki and his wife, Karen

RICH KARKI

5th Marine Regiment
1st Marine Division
Vietnam War

    Negaunee, Michigan's Rich Karki, Washington state's Terry Quick, and Illinois native John Wheeler reconnected for this special interview to offer insights into their shared experiences in Vietnam.
    A photo of them following a mission in Vietnam is on the cover of this book.

Rich Karki (from left), Norman Calcote, John Wheeler, and Terry Quick pose for a photo in Vietnam while smoke rises behind them. (Rich Karki collection)

RICH: I remember right near the end of Marine boot camp when they were going to be giving us our orders, I was so worried that I was going to get an office job or something. We all wanted to be 0311's which is a grunt. When they called out my name my first thought was, "Thank God." I was going to the bush and get to do what they had trained us to do.

So I get my orders to Vietnam, the first stop is Da Nang, this would be February of 1969. They told me I was going to a place called An Hoa. I had never heard of it. So they fly me out there, but not to the base camp, to the area where the platoon I've been assigned to is…out in the bush. I'm looking down as we're going to land and there's a firefight taking place. I'm thinking, *Well we can't land here. There's shooting going on down there. What the hell, we're landing in the middle of this? Where in the hell did they send me?* That woke me up in a hurry. I didn't know it at the time but this was an area they called Arizona Territory. I'm not sure I could have been sent anyplace worse during that time. From that moment of jumping out of that chopper my life has never really been the same."

Editor's note: *The Arizona Territory was an area in Quang Nam Province, southwest of Da Nang nicknamed by the Marines for its free-fire zones and consistent enemy contact. An Hoa was the main* *base camp with individual units stretched out to and including Liberty Bridge which was a vital transportation link to Da Nang.*

They put me with a four-man fire team. Those guys taught me the real stuff I needed to know. You just kept your mouth shut, watched, and listened. Some of them hadn't been there but a few weeks before I got there, but it didn't matter. What they said could mean the difference between me going home alive or not.

Terry Quick had arrived in the An Hoa region just prior to Rich's arrival. They became squadmates and remain close friends to this day.

RICH: When I got off the chopper they lined me up with you guys right off the bat. We got tossed in together right from the minute I got there.

TERRY: There's an old saying in the Marines, "A bitching Marine is a happy Marine." Well, I thought to myself, *This is going to be one happy Marine we got joining us.* (Both laugh)

John Wheeler had been a member of the platoon for approximately six months before Rich and Terry arrived.

JOHN: In March of '69 we were on a company patrol. The 2nd Platoon was the point platoon. We were walking through an area we had been in many times before and evidently, the VC expected us to return because this time the area was mined.
As we were walking into that area, the point man stepped on a mine and went down. The corpsman starts running to take care of him. He steps on a mine and gets his legs blown off. A medevac chopper came in to take out the wounded and it landed on a mine. More guys were killed and wounded. In that one day, we had five dead and eighteen wounded.
We actually had no platoon left. Not after losing that many guys. That's when they started bringing in replacements such as Rich and other guys to fill our platoon back up to strength.

TERRY: That was my first patrol. I was in 3rd Platoon. I was like third or fourth from the rear in the column. We had 100 plus Marines out there and I was like 98th in line. We were moving along and I heard an explosion from the front, then a second. A few minutes later a chopper came in. Then there was a third explosion. Nobody knew what in the hell was going on so we just sat there. At some point, we started to dig in. The squad leader came up to my team leader and said we had KT that night. I asked him what the hell KT was. He looked at me like I was an idiot and said it was a Killer Team. "It's when four guys go out about a click, sit out there all night, and kill anything that comes by." I said. "You've got to be shitting me. People go out there all by themselves at night…all night?" He said, "Yeah, we do it all the time." I had trained to be on a recoilless rifle team, you know, just stay in a fire support base and man that thing. I stood there thinking, *Boy am I in the wrong goddamn outfit.* The next morning they moved me to 2nd Platoon to fill in for the guys they lost the day before.

RICH: You know, you have all that training and everything and they drill it into you about being a gung ho Marine. And you get there, right into the shit and the only thing you can think of is, *How in the hell do I survive?* And not even for the long haul, I mean you would think, *What do I have to do to survive this patrol, or this ambush, or this attack?* It was just a day-to-day grind of wondering if this was the day it was your turn to get hit. I mean you break it down to minutes and hours. There were so many guys getting hit by booby traps you figured sooner or later it would be your turn. I've tried hard to forget some stuff, or my mind blocked it out, but there are some things that just stay with you clear as can be. I remember an early patrol and there was this young kid from Louisiana, nice kid, he talked in that slow southern accent. We went out in a platoon-sized patrol, with four guys on each side to keep from getting ambushed from the flanks. Well we're walking along and there's an explosion and the young guy from Louisiana got his leg blown off from a booby trap. We never knew if he made it or what happened to him. That's the way it was, good friends one day and then they disappeared.

After a while, you get more comfortable about what's going on out there. I spent a lot of time walking point. I was proud of that. I felt comfortable doing that. It's funny because even though I said there are a lot of things that I seem to have pushed out of my mind, there are patrols from 1969 that I can recall absolutely in the smallest detail. I can see it in my mind almost every step of the way on a patrol. But then when I'm talking with guys about certain firefights or whatever I'm like, "Really? That happened? I don't remember that."

One day they told me I was going out on an eight-man night ambush. I had come down with a bad case of dysentery. I was crapping the entire day. Dysentery is the worst thing you can imagine. I told the lieutenant, "I can't go out into the bush. Hell, they will smell me." He was like, "You're going, end of story." I didn't even have a different pair of pants I could put on. God, that pissed me off. I had walked point on a regular basis, lots of times when I didn't have to. I went on…I don't know how many ambushes, and yet he wouldn't give me one night off because of dysentery.

TERRY: If you remember, we were late getting out there. I seem to remember we made a lot of noise, going through dry leaves, knee-high bushes, things like that. We didn't set up any claymores, just got down and stayed real quiet. The geography of it was rice paddy in front of us, then a tree line, a little creek, and the foothills behind us. About 9:30 at night two NVA appeared about fifty yards in front of us. I leaned over and said to the squad leader, "You want us to get those two?" And he said, "No, let's wait, there might be more." About thirty-forty minutes later there were so many in the paddy, we couldn't count them all.

RICH: We had split up, four on each side. We had one of those green infrared scopes with us. Sometimes those things didn't work all that well, but this time, it was pretty clear. There had to be at least 100 NVA passing by us. Somebody said they counted at least 125.

TERRY: They got to within about twenty yards of us, I heard something that sounded like pots and pans bumping against each other. I raised up a little bit. There were four of them standing there whispering, it seemed like for a long time. One of them pushed the other on the shoulder and they headed out.

RICH: All of a sudden a "willie peter" round comes in to mark for artillery. So I crawled over to the other side. I said, "What the hell is going on? Is our artillery going to blow us right off this hill?" They were right there in front of us, but the odds were at least 100 to 8. So this is one thing that stuck with me, has been stuck with me since that night. We didn't open up on them because we would have been annihilated. I guess being a trained warrior, I still wish we would have. I still debate it in my mind. Dead or not doesn't matter. I still have that argument with myself. Is that weird or what?

That was a very, very scary night. We called in Spooky, the gunship and he flew around us for hours but he couldn't spot them. Very, very long night. We waited until morning and decided to "didi mau" out of there.

We got chewed out a little bit when we got back. The captain told the guy in charge of the mission, "I could get you court-martialed for not opening up on them!" I'm glad he didn't go off on me. After being forced to sit out there with dysentery all night I was wired a little tight when we got back. That might not have been too good.

TERRY: We could have opened up and gotten a few, but there's not a chance in the world our names wouldn't be on the Wall in Washington if we had. No one would believe we were right in the middle of that many NVA.

RICH: I'll tell you what, nobody fell asleep on that ambush. I don't know if the NVA had any idea we were there or not, but they were pretty goddamned good soldiers. So I don't know, maybe they knew something was up. Maybe they were waiting for us to make the first move. You know you have to give those bastards credit, they were tough. Think about it, they traveled all the way from North Vietnam just walking the whole way.

Ambushes are almost like deer hunting up north. You're sitting there and listening to every little sound in the woods, your mind wondering what it was. Same thing in the jungle. We used to have two-hour watches. Everybody takes their turn. Well, one night the guy who was supposed to wake me fell asleep. I opened my eyes and the sun was shining. Everybody was sleeping. I just started chewing ass. Pretty soon I calmed down and started thinking about it. I figured if someone snuck up on us, I would be the first guy to get my throat slit because I talk in my sleep. I would be the easiest to find. They didn't know what in the hell was going on back at headquarters because they weren't getting any response to the radio checks.

I wasn't going to let that happen again. One night we were set up on a perimeter with guys on watch. I decided to sneak around to make sure everybody was alert. I get up to this one foxhole and the guy is sitting on top of it just staring into the jungle. I'm thinking, *What in the hell is wrong with you?* So I snuck up behind him, grabbed him, put my knife up to his throat, and said, "I should slit your throat!" Well, he was stoned out of his mind and goes, "Rich, don't do it! Please Rich, don't do it!"

Heading into Vietnam I always wondered what it would be like when I saw my first dead person. But then you get there and you saw so many that you got used to it pretty quick. You would see VC that had been dead for days and the body was moving like they were still alive because of all the maggots and stuff in them. That freaked me out the first time I saw something like that. That shows how young and naive we were. We were kids, just absolute kids.

But that's just how it was in that area back then. You had to get hardened pretty quick.

That area had been bad for a long time before we even got there. You had NVA traveling back and forth through that area, plus you had Viet Cong all over the place which meant booby traps up the ass.

Some guys, as you know, Terry, just lost it out there, just couldn't handle it anymore and snapped. I know I came close one time. It was the day I got back from R&R in Sydney, Australia. As soon as I got back they told me I was going right out on an ambush that night. Don't ask me why, but that was the most nervous I had ever been to go on an ambush.

TERRY: I remember that night. We found a good hiding spot and sent two new guys out to set up claymores on the trail, one on the south end, one on the north end. They went out there and as soon as they got to the trail, which was really only about five-ten yards away from where we were setting up, one of the other new guys opened up with his M-16, "Brrrrrrp." And I'm thinking, *That damn new guy, what the hell is he doing?* He comes crawling back and goes, "I got one, I got one!" I said, "You got one what dammit?" I figured a big rat had walked across the trail or something. And he goes, "I got a gook!" By that time the company on the hill had sent up some illumination rounds so we could see what in the hell was going on. So I crawled out and looked down the trail and sure enough, there was a body lying there. So we sent two guys to check it out. All we knew was that there was one dead guy on the trail. So we thought we better frag the area in case there are others around there. So that's what we did. Everybody threw grenades. Well, it got quiet. Then we heard the sound of a spoon flying off a grenade and landing in the bushes near us. It didn't go off, but we didn't throw it. So somebody else was out there.

RICH: I remember throwing grenades like a mad-man. In my mind, we were getting attacked by a big unit. I was throwing grenades like there was no tomorrow. Other guys were wondering what in the hell was wrong with me. I didn't totally lose it, but that's as close as I had ever come. You would think a week away, having a good time would have relaxed me, but I came back more nervous than when I had left. It's a little weird. I had to keep telling myself to settle down and work my way back into the groove of being in Vietnam.

TERRY: I sent Franklin and Garrett out there, one to check the body, the other to watch the trail. They get out there and Franklin just freezes. He doesn't do anything. He's just frozen on his knees looking at that body. Finally, Garrett hits him with his elbow and says, "Grab that shit and let's go!" So they grabbed the stuff and we all gathered at the bomb crater where the commander was. We all start looking over the stuff they had brought back, including a belt with Chi-Com grenades still attached to it. The captain said to the new guy, Bendiz; "You got the kill, do you want the belt?" And Bendiz, being new, said he didn't want it. I said, "Hell I'll take it." So the captain called this engineer, said, "Take the belt, get rid of the Chi-Coms, and give the belt to Quick." So the engineer grabs the belt with the Chi-Coms still attached and picks it up. Well, the captain got all over him, "Don't you know those damn things have been known to go off just by picking them up!" And we hear this sound, "Ooooohhhhh." It was Franklin, he fainted.

The captain said since we got that kill we could go back to our holes and we didn't have to stand any watches during the night. So we go back to our holes. I'm lying on the ground, Garrett is laying right next to me and he starts talking about how scared he was out there. He kept saying it all over again. Finally, I said, "Hey, we're back, everything is okay, let it go. Go to sleep." But then we got hit and we were up all night anyway.

RICH: One of the saddest days over there was the morning we went on a patrol along some dikes and there's this old Vietnamese guy sitting there with one of those low straw hats on. One of the guys who was pretty salty goes up to the guy and knocks his hat off. I said, "Hey don't be screwing with him, let's just move on, leave him alone. Let's not provoke anything." I know some of the guys in my squad wanted to shoot him right on the spot.

But anyway, we moved on and got into a situation where we had to cross a river. It was raining hard and nasty and it was just a miserable day. I had to swim across to bring a rope to the other side to help everybody get across. We were in a bad situation all around so we got the hell out of there and headed back towards Liberty Bridge.

When we got back to that dike I could see that the guy was gone but his hat was there along with an ammo can. In fact, the hat was sitting on the can. My explosives guy said he would go check it out. I said, "Hell with that. Let's just shoot the can and see what happens." He said, "Nah, don't worry. I will check it out, no big deal." Well, he got close to it and that's as far as he got. He was blown to smithereens.

We called in a medevac to get him out and started picking up whatever we could to put in the poncho liner. Two guys who got off the chopper came over to carry him back when all of a sudden another booby trap goes off and one of the guys from the chopper starts running around, screaming, "I can't see, I can't see. My eyes, my eyes!" I'm yelling to my guys, "Don't anybody move! Stay exactly where you are!" Then another booby trap went off and another guy from the chopper went down.

I think there were four that got hit. The bird took off with the wounded, and our dead guy. I said. "Everybody step in the tracks you think you came in on, don't step off that trail!" You didn't know what else they had planted there so we had to try and walk back in our footprints. Oh God! You want to know what being scared is, that's truly what being scared is.

The guy who died was just one of the good guys. Just a good-looking young guy with his whole life ahead of him. He shouldn't have been out there. He had seven days left in the bush. When you're that short they usually keep you in the rear.

I mean, I hate to say it, but a lot of times you're out there and you're walking and you're seeing shit and you know stuff happens and you think to yourself, *I hope it's not me today.* There were so many guys who got hit from booby traps, just lots and lots. Afterward, you play the whole thing over and over, you know? You keep thinking about what you could have done or should have done. In this case, I kept thinking that if we had killed the son of a bitch on the dike, my buddy would still be alive.

There's no question that guy was working for the Viet Cong. That's when the hatred starts coming in. So you mix that with the fear you have every day in the bush and you put those together and if you don't control it, that's when the really bad shit happens to guys. I mean I hated them, but I never wanted to hurt anyone on purpose who didn't have it coming. Does that make sense? I mean I think most of the people there just wanted to live their lives as they had for the past thousand years. Just grow their rice and sit around their hooches. But here we are and here's the VC and there's the NVA and they're caught right in the middle of everything while their lives get destroyed.

I ended up capturing five enemy soldiers including one officer during my time there. We were on patrol and I was going up to these hootches. I could see something moving and the guy to my side said I think I saw three VC run to one of the hootches. I let out a burst and they stopped. So I went up and captured those three.

Then there was another time, and this ahh ... this is getting into a rough part of my service over there. I was walking point on a platoon-sized patrol. It was getting dark and it was in the same area as where those 100 or so NVA had come through that one night. I came around a corner and stepped up on a dike and a gook came running at me. I told him in Vietnamese, *"dừng lại"* which meant stop. He didn't stop. He kept coming so I shot him, but as it turned out, didn't kill him. He was wounded, went down off the side of the dike and we figured he was going to try and sneak around us. It was late in the afternoon so we set up a perimeter. Now it was getting real dark and we could hear him moaning and groaning, making lots of noise. We knew we were in a bad spot. We had been told there were two companies of NVA around us. During the night some guys went down and made sure he didn't make any more noise and give away our position.

So now you're sitting there, and this is the really weird thing, you start thinking about how he's never going to have a family and this and that. You're like, *Where in the hell did those feelings come from?* It really takes its toll on you. That was a very, very hard time for me in Vietnam. I wish I could have left it there, but there have been a lot of nights since that I can't get that one out of my mind. Even after fifty years it still wears on me.

There were some points just lower than others and will never leave you. We were on a company march at night, I wasn't on point, I was back in the middle. There was a unit to one side of us. We were going in straight, they were kind of at an angle, sort of an L-shaped thing. All of a sudden there was a shot. The guy right in front of me drops right over into the rice paddy. I go down with him and I'm thinking, *What in the hell is going on here?* I called the corpsman and we both worked on getting a trach in the guy, but he didn't make it. He was just a real young guy. I didn't even know who he was. You see, that's the part of war that just kills you. You don't know his name. So you couldn't tell his family or whomever that you did everything you could to save him but he died in your arms. That at least he was with somebody who was trying to help him when he died. That has stuck with me for a long time too.

We had another day, I was on point going through this tall grass. I sensed something wasn't right. So now I'm really on high alert. I'm going through as quietly as I can, but I thought I saw something hiding in the grass. So I put the barrel of my M-16 down there and yelled

Rich Karki displays the pistol he took from a captured NVA officer.
(Rich Karki collection)

for him to come out. He came crawling out of there. It was an NVA officer. He had all sorts of paperwork and everything on him. He was a top gun. I got him out of there, took his pistol. In fact, I've got a picture of the pistol, but later on someone stole it from me. Anyway I got him out of there and he's lying there and I turn to these two guys who were sort of loose cannons. I said, "I'm going to get the lieutenant and bring him over here, keep an eye on him." I turned, took two steps, and "balooom." They killed him. All the information we could have gotten off this guy and they killed him, blew his brains out. Later on, I heard from somebody that one of the guys said he just wanted to make sure he killed somebody before he left Vietnam.

9 June, 1969
Quang Nam Province

TERRY: I remember that day. It was a really hot day, even hotter than normal it seemed. We walked and walked and walked. There was a grove of tall bamboo we were heading towards. The LT was screaming at us to double time. I took point, the LT is still screaming at us. We lined up at the edge of a tree line. The bushes were like a hedgerow. We got down on one knee and dropped our packs and started sweeping the tree line.

RICH: I was behind kind of a dike and we were shooting and the next thing I know Sergeant Jones says, "Ok let's go, let's go!" We get up and start going and all of a sudden, "Boom!" He gets hit and goes down right next to me. I remember grabbing him and starting to drag him back.

JOHN: I was the radio operator, so I wasn't as much in the assault as I was with the squad leader directing the assault. When Jones went down I went up to get him and help pull him back too. The corpsman came running over to help. As we're pulling Jones back he gets shot again. This time in the throat. Then the corpsman gets hit through the right forearm. Then I got shot. It went in my left shoulder and out the back. It didn't hit any bone, so I wasn't incapacitated.

The medevac comes in. We climb on. The chopper takes off in the spiral fashion that they do. It was about halfway through the second spiral, maybe ten feet off the ground when it goes down. The hydraulics were all shot up. So we climb out of that chopper. The firefight is still taking place, with rounds hitting all over. We get down behind that little depression which was maybe three feet at the most and wait for the next chopper. When that came in, we ran and climbed aboard and got out of there.

RICH: We were online with our machine-gunner and a couple of other guys. All of a sudden they started shooting a 122mm recoilless rifle at us and there were gooks running all over the place.

TERRY: We got up inside that tree line, the NVA were shooting at us. Jackson, our machine-gunner, was yelling at us to shoot some guys that he could see. But from where we were, we couldn't see them. He finally yelled, "I will get them myself!" He opened up on them and that's when all hell broke loose around us. But the three NVA he was yelling about were dead.

RICH: That's when you and I ran over to a hootch and came upon two or three other guys. One of them looked at me like, *Where in the hell have you been?* I wanted to kill him. I said, "Don't you ask me where I've been buddy!" So those guys took off and it was just us left there.

TERRY: The thing I remember next was one of our planes coming over and shooting rockets in the same area we were in. They couldn't tell who was who. Rich, I believe that's when we jumped into that big hole.

RICH: Yup, that's what I remember too because all of a sudden here comes this Phantom jet, just screaming at us. He's coming in, I swear it seemed like I could have touched him with my hand. The biggest worry was him dropping napalm. We jumped down into that hole that was about ten feet deep. So we're down there in the hole and I told you to get down so I could get on your shoulders. So I climb up and the first thing I see is a gook running straight at me. I got my rifle strapped to my side and can't get the damned thing off to shoot him. He looks me straight in the eye and keeps running with a pistol in his hand. All of a sudden I hear, "Bang! Bang! Bang!" The guys down below us killed him.

So we get up and go to a bomb crater. We're getting shot at. You can hear the rounds coming in hitting all over the place and now it's getting dark. In comes a helicopter to pick up the dead, and they shoot it right out of the sky. It was a mess. I don't think we knew where they were, where our guys were. It was a mess.

When it got dark it got scary. We took Jones and wrapped him in a poncho liner. There were four of us that carried him out. So now we have to go and grab the machine gun and everything out of the downed chopper. Then another one comes in and they are getting shot at like crazy. It lands and picks up the other two pilots and our dead.

Editor's note: *Rich Karki was awarded a Bronze Star with V for Valor for his actions that day.*

Excerpts from the citation:

"As the Marines proceeded through a village they came under a heavy volume of mortar, small arms and automatic weapons fire from a large North Vietnamese Army force occupying well-concealed emplacements. Reacting instantly, Private First Class Karki skillfully deployed his fire team and led his men on an assault of the enemy positions. Fearlessly moving throughout the fire-swept terrain, he shouted instructions to his men and effectively directed their fire at the North Vietnamese Army unit, thereby killing eleven of the enemy and capturing several weapons.

Suddenly the platoon came under fire from an estimated platoon-sized North Vietnamese Army force occupying another hamlet. With complete disregard for his own safety, Private First Class Karki led two assaults on the enemy positions and on each occasion was driven back by the intense hostile automatic weapons fire. He organized and led a third assault which completely annihilated the North Vietnamese Army force."

RICH: I will say this, you can take a lot of the medals they hand out and shove them. As far as being a good Marine, I was. Because it doesn't matter if you were in a big fight like that one or not. It's what you did the whole time. That's what they should hand out medals for. It's not for that one thing. It should be for all the ambushes, all the patrols, nobody getting hurt when you walk point. Those are the things that I feel proud of.

I always thought one of the worst jobs was doing mine sweeps on the road from Liberty Bridge to about halfway to An Hoa. Those were pretty scary.

JOHN: That's where I had my very first firefight. November 1, 1968. We had been doing it for three days. On the third day, we got hit. The three guys in front of me all got hit. I had two canteens busted from rounds and shrapnel had holes in my shirt but somehow didn't get hit.

RICH: We had four-man teams on each side of the road. One day I was on the left flank, our good friend Mitchell was on the right. All of a sudden we heard this explosion where our buddy was walking.

TERRY: Yeah, that was March of 1969. I was walking point that day. On the road, we had a fireteam of Marines. You had the point man, three guys behind him, then you had the combat engineers with metal detectors behind them. So you had at least four Marines ahead of the engineer; which was crazy. At the end of the squad was a tank bringing up the rear. When we got to Outpost-8, at the end of the sweep we would hop on the tank and ride back.

    I had been walking flank for a week. So when we were staging that day, I remembered that we were supposed to swap. My group on the road, the other group on the flank, which was about fifteen-twenty meters from the road. We switched spots, moved out, and did our sweep. Well, right near the end of our route, near OP-8, the engineer spotted something that he wanted to check out. So they held us up. Over to the left on the side of the road were a group of Delta Company Marines, three of them. I was going to walk over and shoot the shit with them, but when I got close one of them yelled and told me to stop and pointed to a boot. He said, "You see that?" I said, "Yeah." He said, "Well, our buddy was in it earlier this morning." So I turned and walked right back to where I had been.

    We got word to move out again. Everybody took about three steps and we heard an explosion. I looked over to my right, but because of the smoke and everything I couldn't see much. I could make out the point man standing up, then the third man in the column, then I realized that one of our guys, Mitchell, wasn't getting up and I felt sick. I thought, *Oh God not him,* you know?

    The corpsman got there right away. I dropped my gear and ran over; which was stupid as hell really. I could have hit another booby trap. They were everywhere. I got to him. The corpsman and another guy were working on him. They had managed to slide a poncho under him. One leg was completely gone. His left leg was still attached by a piece of skin about an inch and a half wide. That's all it was…just skin. The corpsman picked it up and laid it up near his head. He said that it wasn't going to do any good, but he wanted to send it with him anyway.

    A Huey had just left An Hoa and was heading to Da Nang when we made the call so he came in and landed right there. They shoved some ammo off the floor and we put Mitchell on that chopper and it left. The squad leader came around later that day and told us that Mitchell had died on the hospital ship.

    Tough, tough day, but that's just the way that area was down there.

RICH: It's just like when you're going out on ambushes and stuff and walking point. I was very, very careful. I never lost anybody on patrol, but there were lots of people blown up around you, lots and lots.

    I was getting set to leave on my in-country R&R. That was my reward for the guys I had captured. I was at An Hoa getting on the truck to go and we started getting rocketed. I could see them coming, dropping down, one after another. I jumped out of the truck and jumped into a ditch. What are you going to do if one lands where you are? Well, you know what's going to happen and there isn't a damn thing you can do about it. We were lucky nobody got hit. But that's all it takes, wrong place, wrong time, and you were done. Happened all the time.

TERRY: I remember when they took us off the line for the first time. They took us back to the base, let us shower, get some clean clothes. It was the first time we were able to do that for ninety days.

You just knew that some guys were going to drink beer and raise a little hell. That was to be expected. If I remember right, after that first night, five guys ended up in the hospital. One was cut up real bad trying to sneak through the concertina wire so he could find himself a woman in the village. I do remember another one having his head smashed in with a liquor bottle.

The next day the base commander told our captain. "You get your animals out of this camp immediately!" We had to walk back. They wouldn't even give us a ride. (Both laugh)

You know, when I was first sent to An Hoa, they had a little indoctrination and things like that. The only thing that stuck with me was that in one of the classes they had a big map that showed all of Vietnam and it had all these little colored pins sticking in it. The instructor pointed to the pins on our location and said, "Right now you will be working in the second hottest area of Vietnam." Later on, I thought, *Well that was BS. He didn't want to tell us the truth that we were going into THE hottest area.* He didn't tell us that because he wanted us to keep our shit together.

I also remember going out on a squad-sized ambush, not a KT, (killer team) a whole squad of ten. We got out there and set up and it was pitch dark. I knew the other Marines were there, but I didn't know exactly where they were. At some point during the night, grenades were being tossed around. I remember lying on the ground. I had a grenade in my hand with the pin straightened and my finger in the ring. I don't know how many explosions there had been by then, but then there was a moment of silence and my heart was pounding in my chest so hard that in my head I was screaming at myself, *Goddammit they're going to hear you and know where you are!* I know that was the most scared I have ever been in my life. That's when I started thinking that I didn't want to die in Vietnam. I wanted to make it home. I remember looking up to God or whatever and saying, *I don't care if you have a truck hit me as soon as my feet hit the ground when I get home, that will be OK, but just please don't let me die in this jungle.*

RICH: I know, but after a while, we didn't feel that way did we? It got to the point where you didn't give a shit if you died or not actually. It was like, *Let's just get it over with. I don't care if I live or die anymore. I just want this shit to end.* How freaky is that?

TERRY: That's right. It was a process. Because as scared as I was during that first ambush and after Mitchell died, that's when it all really hit me. You lose a friend like that and realize there wasn't a damn thing you could do about it. Then it became, OK, if I die, I die, don't mean nothing. But then later on you start getting short and things change a little bit because you saw guys who maybe only had a week left get killed. At some point it turned into a job, you punch a clock, you do this, you do that. If you have to shoot somebody, you shoot them, if you don't, you don't.

You change a lot during the time you're there. One of the first few days I was there things happened that I didn't know could happen. I didn't know a lot of the crap that was going on. We had swept a little ville (village) and an old woman had gotten hit. The bullet must have come out her knee because it was just blown wide open. She's laying on the ground and I'm standing like ten feet from her. She, of course, is moaning and groaning and all that and there's a Marine just across from me and he's yelling, "Hey we got one that needs killing over here." And I'm thinking, *What in the hell is he talking about? She needs a medevac. She needs someone to help her.* He said it one more time I believe and here comes this other guy from my right and he walked right up to the woman and stood over her and put three rounds in her. Killed her, right there. I thought *My God ... what?* I never imagined anything like that could happen. They weren't going to call in a chopper for her. It's like, *How could someone do shit like that?*

But here's the ironic part, one day we got ambushed and everybody is down and firing back, and I look to my left for some reason and there's the guy who had shot that woman, laying on the ground, face down with his rifle lying beside him, not in his hand, not hurt, but not firing.

RICH: There's a lot of stuff. I don't know if it's from PTSD or what it is, but I think I've blacked out stuff that I know I was part of but maybe my mind doesn't want me to remember. I know it's there but it's kind of scary at the same time. Because you want to know everything that happened, but then again, in some ways, you don't. Does that make sense?

TERRY: I know what you mean. I have a lot of those same feelings and regrets.

RICH: The lieutenant and I just didn't get along. I think he was pissed because one day the colonel came in and wanted some advice on how to patrol a certain area and they called me into the command tent and asked for my advice instead of the lieutenants. That really pissed him off.

There was a guy, I think his name was Sanchez and he got wounded. And before they took him out he told the LT, "Karki should be your squad leader. He knows more than anybody here." So they made me the squad leader.

Not long after that, we were on patrol, heading into this little village that had two huts on the side. I wasn't walking point. There was a new guy on point and I'm behind him telling him things, pointing out things. I remember telling guys on my flank to frag a couple of hootches that were empty. Just when I was turning back to say something, I felt something tug at my shoe and I said to somebody behind me, "I think I tripped a ..." And "Booooooom!" I went flying backward through the air.

My M-16 went flying. I got hit everywhere except my head. Flak went underneath my flak jacket into my armpit, my ass, both legs, ankles, and my arm was broken. I thought, *Well this is it.*

I asked the corpsman to check and make sure my important parts were still there. I was throbbing, just the most painful throbbing all over. The corpsman gave me a shot of morphine and got me ready to load on a chopper.

The lieutenant came over and said, "Calm down you will be back in a couple of weeks." I said, "To hell with you, I will never come back to this country again. I'm done!"

I feel like I'm dying on the ground and he looks at me and says, "Well what are we going to do now?" He was worried about his ass because he didn't know jack shit about where he was. I said, "I don't know what you're going to do, but you're going to have to figure it out on your own!" He couldn't even say, "Hey I'm sorry about you getting hit Rich." All he was worried about was himself.

TERRY: All I can see is you lying there bitching. (Laughs) We called in the medevac. I was busy with that and seeing what else was going on around us. I also remember you and the LT having some words about you ever coming back. That conversation was pretty heated, too. (Laughing again)

The chopper came in and we loaded you up. You know, when you put somebody on a medevac, it flies away and the chances are you will never see that person again. I didn't know you were hurt as bad as you were. I thought it was just your elbow. So I was leaning in, tapping you on the foot, telling you to stay in touch or let us know how you are doing, things like that. And you just raised up from the stretcher and looked right past me like I'm not even there and go, "Hey Doc can I get another hit of that shit (morphine) before I go?" (Both laughing)

After you were gone, the corpsman walked up to the LT and told

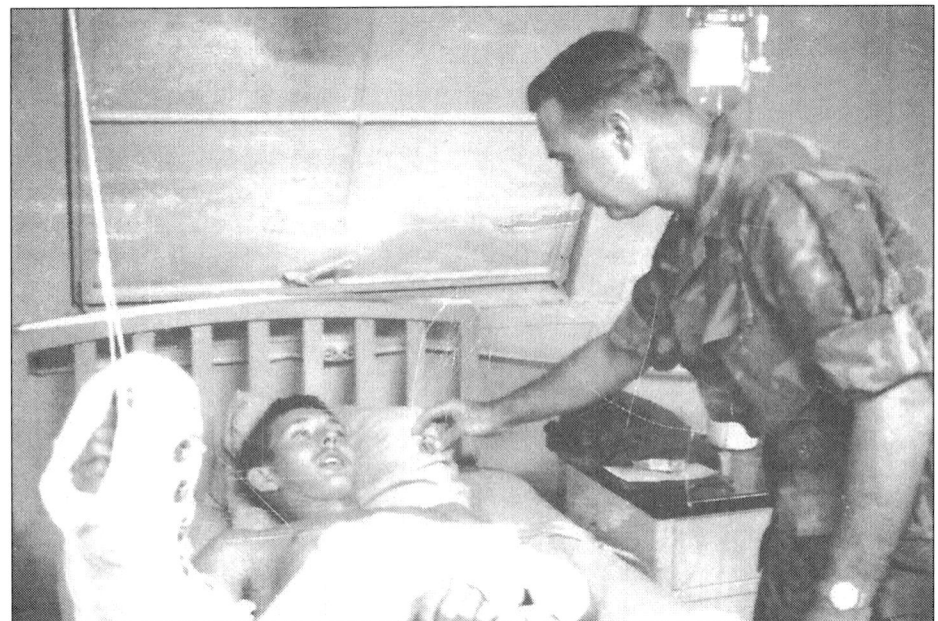

Rich Karki receives his Purple Heart while recovering from his wounds. (Rich Karki collection)

him that he was out of battle dressings and morphine. He said, "Look if this continues you are responsible for any casualties from this point on." That was it, the patrol ended and we went back. I don't remember the exact number of booby traps we hit before yours, but that was the first time I knew of the corpsman running out of everything from one patrol. That's how many casualties we had.

RICH: Here's something that I keep thinking about. I remember getting ambushed a few weeks before, pretty bad in that same area. It seems I hit the ground about ten feet from where I ended up getting wounded. We were pinned down and then I got up and ran to another position. When I got there I looked down and I was missing two grenades. Here I am second-guessing myself again, but is it possible that the booby trap I got hit with was from the grenades that I had lost? That's another one that has been rolling around in my mind for a long time.

Anyway, I remember pretty much everything from the time I was wounded. I was flying in the chopper and thinking, *I hope to hell we don't get shot down because if we do, I'm not going to make it*. They fly me into Da Nang and bring me into a hospital. I remember seeing a whole shit load of wounded people in there. Then there's a friend of mine from boot camp, Al Dobroy, and he sees me and says, "Rich what the hell happened to you?"

The first thing they did was cut all my clothes off and shaved me all over, right over the cuts from the shrapnel and everything. Then they rolled me into a room and left me there. I was looking at the floor and I saw this big puddle of blood forming. I realized it was mine and I started thinking, *Holy shit, I'm going to die.* They just left me there, for I don't know how long, and that's all I remember until I woke up.

When I woke up my arms were in a sling over my head and I had bandages all over me. It was two days later I guess, that General Bowman gave me my Purple Heart in the hospital. Then they flew me to Okinawa.

I remember them coming in to change the bandages. They had been on for like four or five days. Well, they came around and ripped them off. They didn't put any solution on them or anything to soften them up, just ripped them right off. Christ did that hurt.

After I fell semi-asleep I heard a guy come in and say, "Oh shit, we have to get the doctor!" So they ripped the bandages off my arm again. The main artery was leaking. They were going to do emergency surgery right there. They told me to take a deep breath of whatever they put in my mouth. So I take that puff, and all of a sudden I'm walking in downtown Negaunee.

I was like, "What the hell, this can't be right, when did I get back from Vietnam?" I was having conversations with people that I knew as plain as day. I don't know what they gave me, but in my mind I was back home.

They sewed me up with something like 140-150 stitches in my arm. Then they sent me to a hospital in Guam. There were a lot of guys there bandaged from head to foot. It was gruesome, but with so many guys getting wounded and blown up where I had been that you almost accepted it as normal. You hate to say you were hardened to it, but I think maybe I was. I hate to admit that.

After a while, they sent me to a hospital in Chicago for therapy and rehab. Therapy was a joke. They didn't seem to care. They just wanted to move you along with everyone else.

They gave me a job, escorting prisoners from the brig to different places. So here I am. I couldn't even use one arm and I'm doing security. I remember this one guy, big guy, he had to be 6'6. I was escorting him someplace and I told him, "Hey if you want to make a break, just go for it. I'm not going to do anything to try and stop you." And he was like, "Nah man, you're cool."

So one of my doctors sees me and he goes, "What the hell are you doing?" I told him they had me working with these prisoners. And he goes, "No! You're not going to do that. I'm getting you out of here!"

So anyway, and this is a little cloudy because I was still out of it mentally, just numb to the world. But I wanted to get back home. So

Rich and Karen Karki about the time of their marriage in 1971.

here I am, no bus ticket or anything, standing out on the highway in my dress uniform hitchhiking. This was either November or December. It's freezing cold. I couldn't even use my right arm to hitchhike with. I had to use my left arm. A guy in a van stops. He says, "What in the hell are you doing? You do know that there are a lot of people around here who don't like you right?" I remember telling him, "I don't care. I thought I was dead once so what can they do? I just want to get home."

He took me to the north side of Milwaukee and dropped me off. Before I got out he grabbed a quilt, gave it to me, and said, "I wish you well brother."

So here I am standing alongside the highway, freezing, a quilt wrapped around me, cars whizzing by. I had to look like a hitchhiking fool. Then a car stopped and asked me where I was going. I told them Negaunee. They said they could take me to Iron Mountain. I said, "Thank you, Lord." I honestly don't remember much after that.

It kills me to think about that time in my life. You put your life on the line and believe in everything that is good about serving your country and doing the right thing and you come back and nobody cares. There were so many young guys who got killed or maybe had a leg blown off and you get back and it's like, "We don't want to hear about it." And you're like, "What the hell, the sacrifice those guys made...was it worth it?"

Once I got out of the Marines and moved back home I was nuts. There's no better way to put it. I wasn't thinking right. I remember one time when I was bartending and a guy gave me a hard time about his drink or something and made a remark, something like, "You Vietnam vets are all a bunch of losers." I told the guy to come outside. I beat him to a pulp. I'm ashamed of it today. A guy came around and grabbed me, lifted me right in the air to stop me. I think I might have killed him if he didn't grab me. That's how messed up I was.

It (Vietnam) changed me, Oh yeah. If it wasn't for my wife Karen, I probably wouldn't be here today. You know how God gives you something? It's hard to explain, but it's like it was a gift because he was looking out for me. She put up with a lot, a lot of my anger and dark days. People would be like, "What the hell is the matter with him?" They didn't know my story.

We got married in July of 1971. I never admitted this for lots and lots of years, but I always felt a lot of guilt right from the beginning. I was almost afraid to share a lot of things with her because I was afraid that if I told her everything, that she might back away. But then I felt guilty because I wasn't being honest with her either. In looking back I should have opened up more and let her decide if I was worthy to have her as my wife. It's weird. I just couldn't let that stuff go, but I couldn't talk about it either. I remember I would get up and my pillow would be covered with hair. All night long I had been back in Vietnam.

KAREN KARKI: It was awful. He would be thrashing, sweating, and yelling during the night. I had no clue what was going on, but I couldn't make the bed until I rolled up a handful of hair every morning. He just wouldn't talk about it.

RICH: I would walk point in my mind every day from the time I got home until into the '90s. I could take you everywhere I had been over there. It was like a video running in my mind. I was going to walk point for the rest of my life whether I was over there or here at home. When you're on point, if you miss one detail, it could mean the difference between your survival and the guys that are counting on you. That's why I always wanted to walk it. I didn't want to leave that in someone else's hands.

KAREN: To be honest with you, for a long time, I still didn't know it was from the war. I just thought, *Well that's his demeanor and I have to work with it.*

RICH: I didn't want to be that way. It's like my nerves were shot. I would come home from a softball game and I would replay every single pitch, every strike, every ball, every hit, every out and tell myself, *Well why didn't you do this? Why didn't you do that?* The same thing I would do after missions. And then I would go to bed, throw hand grenades in my sleep all night and wake up with a pillow full of hair.

KAREN: There was a time when he would sit and not move. I would be vacuuming the living room and have to lift his legs so I could vacuum under him. He just wasn't there.

RICH: Yup there was a time when I realized I was losing my marbles. I figured it was the end. All that stuff kept coming back and I couldn't get rid of it. Karen would tell me I had to do something, but I froze. I physically couldn't leave the house. But then I got a call from a Vietnam vet, Donnie Harju, he asked me to come to a meeting with other vets. So we were all sitting around on overturned buckets talking and he says, "You're all screwed up in the head, you know that right?" And I said, "screw you." And he goes, "No seriously, you have really bad PTSD." I didn't even know what he was talking about.
Pretty soon I started thinking about it and it kind of hit me, *Holy shit, maybe I am messed up. Maybe I do have some problems.* Isn't it crazy that I had to have somebody who had been in 'Nam tell me that before I would believe it? I started going to meetings and started seeing a shrink. It would take a while to see progress, but at least it was a start.

KAREN: There was a time that you thought asking for help was a sign of weakness. All you guys were like that. But I think talking about it and getting it out helped a lot. You don't walk point in your sleep anymore.

RICH: One thing that I hadn't told anybody about before talking to the doctor was that I always blamed myself for getting wounded. I had a lot of guilt over that. He asked me why I would blame myself. I told him I didn't know.

KAREN: I know. It's because you have so much pride that you have to do everything perfectly. You were watching out for your guys ahead of you and maybe you feel like you let your guard down for a second and that's what happened.

RICH: I wish I could go back and start over. I'm not saying I wouldn't go to Vietnam, because I'm proud of what I did over there. They can never take that away from me, never. I never wanted to leave the Marines. I wanted to be a lifer, but because of my wounds, they wouldn't let me. They said I was forty-five percent disabled.

KAREN: You have always been a proud Marine. I've known that through all the years of our marriage. The Memorial Day parades when you would put on your dress blues and carry the flag. Everybody had better be in step because you would get so mad if they weren't in step. And they never were. (Laughing.)

RICH: For the young veterans, I would tell them this, be honest and don't be afraid to talk to your wife or anybody else about what's bothering you. Let it out.

KAREN: That's exactly right. We can handle it. What's hard is when we don't know what's bothering you. It's okay to talk, it's not a weakness.
You know, it's funny I was just talking to someone about this recently. They asked, "What attracted you to him?" I said, "Now remember, I was an impressionable seventeen-year-old, but I loved how he stood so tall and proud and had an air of confidence about him." I thought he could be my knight in shining armor and you know what, he has been. We have three married kids and eleven beautiful grandchildren who are the love of our lives.
Another thing about first getting to know him, my life was pretty dull and sheltered at the time and I remember thinking, *Here's somebody who might bring a little excitement into it.*
Oh, he brought a little excitement into it all right. (Both laugh.)

RICHARD KONITZER

515 River Division
US Navy
Vietnam War

A peacetime hitch in the Navy can mean months on the wide-open seas visiting one faraway port after another. For those with adventure and wanderlust in their blood, it can be a great way to ride out a military commitment. During the Vietnam War a hitch in the Navy could still mean a year spent on the water, but in some cases with jungle and enemy eyes little more than an arm's length away.

After graduating from Mishicot (Wisconsin) High School in 1965 I figured it wouldn't be long before I got drafted into the Army and sent to Vietnam like everybody else. In '66 I got my notice, but I thought I would take my chances with the Navy. I signed up for four years. I was assigned to San Diego. It was beautiful. You couldn't have asked for a better place to be. I was an engineman. I went on a couple of cruises. For three years it was fantastic. Then in late 1968 I got new orders, Vietnam.

The Navy played a major role in Vietnam. I don't know if everyone realizes that. The main means of transportation throughout much of the country were the waterways. There was an incredible number of rivers and canals connected to one another. It was the Navy's job to patrol those waterways and basically keep the NVA and VC from using them as supply routes.

I never thought I would be sent there.

But they needed enginemen for the riverboats, PBRs (Patrol Boat, River). The Navy always labels their stuff kind of backward. The next thing I knew I was in language school and then survival school and then on my way. I was assigned to River Division 515 out of Nhe Ba which was in the Delta Region near Saigon.

There were ten boats in a River Boat Division. We would go out on two-boat patrols, a lead boat and a cover boat. The boats themselves were made of fiberglass, thirty-one feet long, eleven feet wide. They had two diesel engines and running wide-open could get up to thirty-five miles per hour.

We had a four-man crew: the coxswain, one gunner on the twin .50s on the bow, one on the mid .60, and I manned the aft (back) .50. I was also the engineman.

We would go out on seven-day missions. We'd start up the Mekong River then patrol the small canals along the way. There were small stations set up along the river. We would stay at those places during the day. They had messes where we could eat. We would sleep most of the day, usually right on top of the canopy of our boat. Then at dusk we would head out again.

Anything that was on the water after dark was fair game. The Vietnamese knew it. Everybody knew it. It was a very strict order. We usually ran dark, no lights, no sound, oftentimes just coasting, sometimes not moving at all. Most of the time the sampans came to us, not even knowing we were there. We would hear them coming with their little motors, "Putt, putt, putt…"

We had starlight scopes so we could see what was on the water. You'd see a sampan and maybe three-four guys on there, sometimes you would see the weapons. We would radio in to command, tell them what we had coming toward us, and, usually, we would get the command to open fire. They knew they weren't supposed to be there, but evidently took the chance anyway, hoping they wouldn't be spotted. We had to shoot first and ask questions later. It was a different sort of war.

On my first night-patrol, my very first one, we were floating down the river at about 3:00 in the morning. A sampan started coming our way, right toward us. It got between us and the lead boat. We both opened fire on it. As soon as we started firing, we started taking fire from the shore. We must have been right in front of the drop-off point for the sampan. So I'm opening up on the sampan and taking fire from the beach. I'm wearing shorts, it was so hot over there that's what we wore. I'm firing away and it felt like I was getting hit in the legs by hot shrapnel. I even yelled out, "I'm getting hit back here!" One of the guys yelled back, "It's just your hot casings hitting you, keep firing!"

Once we concentrated on the shore, the firing subsided. There were three guys on the sampan; they were all dead. Everything quieted down. But that was definitely a crazy night. Everybody wants to talk macho about things they would do in a situation like that, but let me tell you when you realize it would only take one bullet in the right spot to kill you, and you've got, who knows how many coming your way, it's scary.

Even during the day we'd be out in the middle of a river someplace, everything quiet, and all of a sudden you'd hear, "Whizzzzz," go right over your head and you'd realize there was a sniper out there. Some person is just sitting there in the tall grass and weeds trying to kill you. You could never relax, never let your guard down. You just never knew where they could be.

Some of the canals we went down were so narrow that we couldn't turn around. They were about the size of a city street at the most. You would just pray VC wasn't sitting and watching because you definitely couldn't see them through the growth. You were a total sitting duck in those situations. They could fire point-blank; they could toss grenades at you. In fact, we had heard reports of sappers in the water tossing satchel charges into the boats. Many times we would go to the end of the canal and then have to back our way out and hope we weren't going through a kill zone.

Some nights we wouldn't have any contact at all and then on another night we might have several contacts. A lot of times, if we were taking fire, we would call in airstrikes. If there seemed to be a major crossing area we would back off because we knew we would be out-gunned. We always had two PBRs which means six .50-caliber machine guns and two .60-calibers which sounds like a lot of firepower, but if you can't maneuver the right way and couldn't get into the most effective firing position it didn't matter what you had. That's when the Cobras and maybe even a Spooky gunship would show up.

In thinking about it later, I believe the VC may have used regular villagers as human bait. It just seemed like too much of a coincidence that when the sampans came close to us and we started firing on them, that we got opened up on from the shore. It seemed like a set-up.

The thing we had to remember was that we were fighting in their backyard. They knew every inch of the place. They knew where they were going and we didn't. It would be like them coming to our area around here and starting a fight. They just had an incredible advantage when it came to the terrain and the landscape.

They also knew exactly where we were all the time. It's like they always had one eye on you. They could be working out in the rice patties, but you still felt like they were watching. We used to joke that they would plow their fields by day and shoot at us by night.

You never felt like you could trust anyone. When we would go into the small hamlets I always wore a sidearm, a .38 pistol. I just felt that carrying my M-16 was too conspicuous.

Obviously, we would only go into the villages during our day patrols. But we would bring in food, medical supplies, sometimes we would bring in doctors. There were certain villages that we did stay away from. The ones where we suspected there were VC sympathizers. But the regular Vietnamese citizens in the villages were great people. You know, Vietnam is actually a very beautiful country. The land was extremely fertile all through the delta. There were palm trees along the river. There were times when you would wonder why we were destroying such a beautiful country. But then again, the VC would use everything they could as cover to fire on us. That's why they started dropping Agent Orange all along the river banks. We were right in the middle of that, you couldn't get away from it.

There were times we would take fire from hamlets that had kids running around and the VC knew damned well we weren't going to fire back because we didn't want to hit the villagers. It was frustrating, very, very frustrating. They used the locals as cover many times.

We would stop sampans during the day missions if something didn't seem right. If there were young guys on there, you'd wonder what they were doing on the river instead of being in the South Vietnamese Army. We would ask for their papers, but to be honest, even though we all went through language school, we really didn't know what we were looking at. It was more of a feeling in the pit of your stomach at times. You would just sense if something wasn't right. A lot of times we would take them to the local police and let them handle it.

There's no question the VC forced innocent civilians to do some of the work for them, to maybe transport food to a VC unit hiding out somewhere. Maybe not so much weapons, but definitely food which they needed to survive in order to keep fighting.

Even if you were searching the most innocent-looking sampan, you had to be careful. We had heard stories of guys who would be searching a sampan, see a weapon, pick it up and "Boom!" It had been booby-trapped. Again, maybe the people on the sampan didn't even know it was there, especially if they were being forced to transport the contraband.

I think one of the reasons I started off in the Delta was because it was supposedly much more pacified than other parts of Vietnam. It was a way to break in the new guys.

But it wasn't completely pacified.

My worst day in Vietnam took place south of Saigon. We were on a typical two-boat day patrol. Somebody spotted a VC flag just inside the shoreline. The lieutenant, who was on the lead boat, turned toward shore and beached his boat. He and two other guys jumped off the boat and went after it. It was a trap. They were waiting. We heard firing. He got hit first in both legs and then his torso. I believe he was hit in at least six places. The other two guys were both hit, one in the lung, but they both came running out of there.

The gunner's mate, a guy named Lennie grabbed his M-16 and yelled, "Konitzer, grab the .60!" So I grabbed two bandoliers of ammo, pulled the .60 off its mount and went in with him. I was wearing shorts and flip-flops, that's all I had on.

We ran right through a hootch and into the backyard where the flag was. The lieutenant was lying on the ground. We couldn't take him out, he was about 6-6, 250 pounds. Lennie said, "Konitzer, stay here. I'm going back to get another guy and a stretcher!"

So I stood over the lieutenant with the .60. I can hear people in the bush moving around and talking. Lennie was only gone a couple of minutes, but it seemed like hours. He and another guy came back. As soon as we started moving I opened up with the .60 spraying everything in front of me just to keep them down.

I kept shooting and walking backward, I got through the hootch, and as soon as I took another step my foot dropped down into a hole. It was about a foot deep and about a foot around with a punji stick in the middle of it. Those were razor-sharp pieces of bamboo with all sorts of poison covering them. Somehow my foot went down along the side of it instead of it going straight through my foot. I fell back and the .60 rounds went straight up in the air. I still can't believe how fortunate I was to have missed the stick. With how deep it would have gone, especially with flip-flops on, and the amount of poison on it, I could have easily lost my foot.

We put the lieutenant on the boat, laid him out, and tended to him. We called for a medevac. It came in and hovered above, dropped a cable from a winch. We hooked him up and they took him out of there. He died on his way to the hospital. He had just come back from R&R in Hawaii visiting his wife and kids.

As soon as he was gone we called in an airstrike. Cobras showed up and peppered the entire area, just hammered the hell out of it. They knew we had lost a lieutenant. They made sure if there were any VC around they would pay.

My adrenaline was so high, so incredibly high, that I barely thought about what I was doing. In fact, I didn't know what I was doing. How do you prepare for something like that when you're twenty years old?

I didn't start shaking until the next day. That's when it hit me. *What in the hell did I just do?* I mean, I could have been wiped out while standing there. I just kept thinking about it, the lieutenant dying while

I'm standing over him, VC in the bush moving around in front of me. All they had to do was open up and I was dead. Or throw a grenade, or worse yet, attack me from the side or something and capture me; which would have been the worst thing in the world. But they didn't. Why? I've wondered that so many times. Boy, I had nightmares about that for a long time. That was 1969, but I had them for a lot of years after.

Editor's note: *Dick Konitzer was awarded a Bronze Star for his actions that day. One of two he would earn during his tour of duty, along with a Purple Heart.*

After leaving the Delta we went to an area near the Cambodian border. They actually airlifted our boats in with big Chinook helicopters. They took our entire river division, ten boats and dropped us there.

This was a very scary area. I'm sure there were times when we were actually in Cambodia. You really had to be on your toes here. There were times we could see them on the Cambodian side loading up supplies at night and there wasn't a thing we could do about it until they started to cross. Our job was to intercept them.

The majority of our patrols here were in the middle of the night. If we saw a sampan coming through, we knew it wasn't friendly, but we would call to get clearance and then open fire with our .50s. The next morning we would recon the area, looking for bodies. But they were very, very good at getting rid of their dead.

One bad night was on the Vin Tae canal. We were beached, waiting for sampans to go by. We were watching through the starlight scope. Two-three guys at a time were going across the canal down below us. These were not VC; these were NVA regulars. They were tough. They were just like our Army. These were the best of their best. I was in the lead boat; we radioed back to our cover boat that we were going to move. We started our engines and backed off the beach. As soon as we had all the guns ready we hit it hard. We caught them just as they were crossing the river. We ran over a sampan, opened up on them, and then started getting hammered from both sides. We cleared the kill zone and called in the other boats. They came flying in and it became a major, major firefight. You want to talk about fireworks...wow. What they would do is set up two machine guns a little ways apart from each other. One would open up on you; when you returned fire the other one would see your tracers and open up on you. It was tough...oh my God. The NVA knew what the hell they were doing.

We had two Vietnamese soldiers on the boat with us that night. They were both killed. We got shot up pretty bad. I was wounded in the arm.

If you've ever seen the movie *Apocalypse Now*, which I have about ten times, there are some very factually correct scenes.

One is where the helicopters are coming in to drop off troops. That is very realistic. Another is when the boat gets in a firefight and there are tracer rounds coming in on them from the jungle. That scene is also very, very realistic. As a matter of fact, our local Vietnam Vets chapter used to go to Manitowoc Lincoln High School when they were studying the Vietnam War. I would take that clip and play it for the students to show them what a firefight, while you are on a riverboat, was really like. You could hear a pin drop during that scene. I tried to explain to them that war was very scary and it was hell to be in it.

Coming home from the war was very strange. You'd think, *"OK what do I do today? Do I look for a job? What am I supposed to do?"*

I mean, one day you're on a river in Vietnam fighting for your life, the next day you're walking the streets of your hometown looking for a job which, as it turned out, was very difficult. You would hear about a place that was hiring and you would go in and talk to them and then it got around to the fact that you just came back from Vietnam and it was like, "Thanks, but we don't need anybody right now."

I don't know how many places I looked and it was always the same reply. It was tough. I'm not sure the story has been told about how the Vietnam vets were discriminated against when it came to finding jobs when we came home. It's like we were being blamed for all the things that went wrong over there. They had this idea that had been portrayed in the media that we were all baby killers; which was the furthest thing from the truth. I'm sure there were a few bad apples that the media got a hold of and ran with. But then we were all put into the same boat. In reality, the only thing we wanted to do while we were there was to do the job we were trained to do, stay alive, and go home. It got to the point where we realized the only way you could get a job was by not saying you had been in Vietnam.

You didn't realize you were still wired a certain way when you got back. Like if someone dropped a book on the floor or something I would jump out of my chair. It's still that way. Or in a restaurant, I always want to have my back against the wall. It's a trust thing. It's hard to trust anybody. It's weird, but it really does stick with you, even after fifty years.

I'm fifty percent PTSD. I still think of it now and then, even after all this time. I think a lot of it has to do with the age we were when we were going through some really difficult scary times. We were so young that those things make such an impression and they just stay with you.

I had to fight for everything I got when I came back. Yes I was resentful with many things, but how far do you take it, how far do you go before you move on? I got a job at the JC Penney Auto Center for $2.00 an hour. I knew I had to make my own way, nothing would be handed to me on a silver platter.

My dad, who was a WWII veteran, told me when I went in, keep your nose clean and do what they tell you to do. I followed that advice as best I could. I rose to the rank of E-5 before I got out, which is the highest level I could attain. I'm very proud of my Navy service. But mostly I'm appreciative of the fact that I made it home.

There are over 58,000 names on a wall of others who weren't as lucky. It was an expensive war for our generation.

JIM JAKLIN

12th Infantry Regiment
1st Air Cavalry
US Army
Vietnam War

"I remember during an interview at one of the camps I had been at and they would ask questions like, 'You like fishing? Do you like hunting? You like shooting guns?' I'm like, 'Sure, you bet.' Maybe that led them to believe I would like walking around the jungle with Lurps. I didn't have a clue as to what that was going to be like, not a clue." – Jim Jaklin

I was on my way to a biology degree from UW-Whitewater when I ran out of money. Okay, no problem, I had a job lined up. I thought I would work for a bit, save some money and get right back into school before anyone even noticed. Well, I don't know who in the hell turned me in, it had to be someone from admissions, because it wasn't two weeks later that I got the letter, "Greetings from Uncle Sam."

I went through all the normal training for 11-Bravo, Fort Knox, Fort Jackson, Advanced Infantry Training. They offered me a spot in OCS (Officer Candidate School) but I turned it down. Once I did that they whisked me right to Vietnam.

As soon as I got there they put me right in a LRRP group (long-range reconnaissance patrol, commonly referred to as Lurps). I often wondered how I got picked for something like that. They must have pulled my name out of somewhere. A heavy Lurp group is maybe ten guys, a light Lurp group would be four or five. We moved around to wherever they needed us. If there was something going on, no matter what unit was involved, we might get sent there. Or if they needed information from an area, we would go. If a bird (chopper) went down, we would get the call to go to it. Our main base was An Khe but we didn't stay there very long. They would send us out to some other firebase where we would go out on missions.

One of our first missions was to secure a perimeter at a place called Albany that was right after the famous battle of the Ia Drang valley.

Editor's note: *The battle of the Ia Drang is chronicled in the book and movie 'We Were Soldiers Once...and Young.' From November 14th - 17th in 1965, the book's author, Lt. Gen. Hal Moore, led his troops against a numerically superior NVA force in the first large-scale battle between US Army and North Vietnamese troops of the Vietnam War. The battleground, in the Central Highlands, was known as LZ X-Ray. Following the three-day battle, which led to large numbers of casualties on both sides, the remaining American troops were ordered to move to LZ Albany, approximately two miles northeast, in order to clear the kill-zone for a B-52 bombing mission over the mountains around X-Ray. En route to their destination, they were ambushed by NVA forces and again suffered extremely high casualties.*

Our job was to secure the far perimeter. We got there and hunkered down. It was a real rocky area. We couldn't dig foxholes. As the guys got closer to us the fighting picked up more. We thought we would be sent in, we were all set to go, but they said no. They said to stay in our position because they didn't know how many NVA there were around us or even where they all were. We were told to keep our perimeter secure because a full battalion was coming in the next day to sweep the entire area.

It was very hard to just sit there. We wanted to go in and do whatever we could to help those guys. But we were told to stay where we were. As it turned out, the NVA went around at night killing our wounded. They just butchered them. That was a horrible situation.

Our normal missions were a lot of what we called "sneaking and peaking." We'd go out with six-seven guys and our main goal was to not be seen. Make it like we were never there. I remember the guys telling me that there was absolutely no smoking allowed on our missions. I was a three-pack-a-day smoker at the time, but had zero in the field. You didn't question what they told you.

Another thing I remember is the day they handed me my new shoes. They were a pair of sandals just like Charlie wore, made out of old tires. Ho Chi Minh sandals they called them. We weren't about to leave footprints from GI boots out there. We got our uniforms, I believe from the South Vietnamese Army, because we couldn't get camo uniforms from our Army supply people and we needed them out in the jungle.

The M-16s didn't have a good reputation. We heard lots of stories about guys being found dead with the ramrod in their hands. What we heard was that the steel barrel jammed up, but once they switched over to a chrome barrel there weren't as many problems. I carried everything from M-16 to M-.60 to AK-47s. That damn AK, it didn't matter what you did to it, it didn't jam up. They were crudely made. There was nothing fancy about them, but they shot. They were reliable.

When a regular unit went on a mission they would pick an LZ and go in there with up to twenty choppers. When we went in they would take us to maybe four different drop zones. That was so Charlie wouldn't know exactly where we were. They might know there were GIs in the area, but they wouldn't know exactly where to go look.

There were times when the chopper couldn't land, so we would rappel down. We did that under fire a couple of times. You would be halfway down the damn rope and snipers would open up. Well, you couldn't go back up so you just dropped to the ground. Meanwhile, Charlie thinks he had you nailed down so you would have to run to get ahead of him.

We could move pretty well, but so could Charlie. They didn't carry much stuff. Depending on how long we planned on being out in the bush we might have sixty-seventy pounds of gear on our backs. But you talk about being in shape, I went over there at 130 pounds. When I came home I weighed 105 pounds, but I could pick a guy up and carry him to town. We were in incredible shape. It scared the hell out of everybody when I got home.

The worst part about being smaller is when we would find tunnels and you would hear, "James get your ass up here!" That's something I dreaded. No one else could fit so I would go in. I would take all my gear off. They gave me a flashlight and a .45. They told me to watch the ground in front of me because there might be punji stick traps, but also to keep an eye up above. I said, "Why's that?" They said, "Charlie has been known to take poisonous snakes and hang them in there by their tail and that really pisses them off."

These were really tight tunnels, built for the VC-sized people. You go crawling in, you'd come to a corner, wondering what in the hell is around the corner, stick the flashlight around it and fire a couple of shots, just in case somebody was there waiting for you. I personally

Jim Jaklin collection

didn't encounter any live persons, but one of our other guys did and killed him. I never liked that job, being a tunnel rat totally sucked.

You never knew what you would come across on missions. One day we were on patrol in the middle of the jungle and stumbled right into a field hospital. We were like, "What the hell?" Fortunately, Charlie had taken out all of his able-bodied troops and left all the sick and wounded behind. It didn't take much to mop them up. They left behind a lot of first-aid type stuff so we gave it to all the Vietnamese villagers.

But yeah, that was a coup for us because there weren't many people guarding it. So once we took care of them we called in a platoon, got everything worthwhile out of there, and blew up the rest.

One of our best days was the time we got orders to take out a VC tax collector. He was just a horrible person. He would go into a village with a couple of bodyguards and just terrorize the place. They would rape the women, take the young boys and make them join the VC. We had heard that in one village his guys had bayoneted the village elder's baby granddaughter in front of him. We got information on where he would be. We got to them while they were coming out of a village. They didn't make it home.

It was a no-win situation for the villagers. We would go in and help them and they treated us like we were the greatest thing since sliced bread. As soon as we left the VC would go right back in and terrorize them for being friendly to us. There was one village where we were real friendly with the villagers, but one day I went into one of the hootches and there was mama-san whittling punji sticks. Her hootch was full of them.

Our missions would be anywhere from three days to three weeks. When we ran out of food we would go to a village, fill up an empty sock with rice and move on. We were a unique group. Sometimes we had Montagnard guides who would find us something to eat. We were out of food one time and the guide goes, "Today we eat number one!" We were like, "Okay, what's on the menu?" It was a big old lizard with its tail cut off. We ate it. Hell yes we did. It was meat. It was either that or more stale rice. When you run out of food you will eat whatever nature has to offer.

We also would start out with what they called Lurp rations. They were freeze-dried and all you would do is warm up some water in a canteen cup and then pour it into this pouch and mix it up and you'd be eating whatever it said it was supposed to be on the package.

There were times when they would tell us, "Where you are going, you have to get your wounded and dead out. Period. And oh, by the way, leave anything that would identify you back at camp." We would ask where we were going and they would say, "We'll tell you once you get there."

I know damn well we were in Cambodia and Laos more than once. They put us in and said, "All you have to do is set up on this bluff and watch the trail down below."

So we would watch it and if there was enough activity we'd call in artillery or an airstrike. Then we'd get the hell out of there as fast as we could. Charlie knew somebody had called that in and it would not be a good thing if we hung around.

The pilots we had were first-generation Air Cav pilots. They were from the 11th Air Assault back in the States. They trained and trained and trained. These guys were unbelievable. We made contact one time and were trying like hell to get out of an area. Charlie was right on our ass and the pilot said, pick-up point is such and such. We ran there, shooting our way over and when we got there we were like, "Oh Christ, it's the side of a mountain!" It was just a big rock outcropping on the side of a mountain. We were like, "You don't think he meant for us to go here, do you?" Then we heard him coming in. He radios to us, "How many you got?" We had eight guys. The pilot goes, "Eight, I thought you were a Lurp team?" Our guy goes, "Yeah we're heavy this time." The pilot goes, "Oh shit, all right, get ready, you're going to have to dive into the chopper."

So he comes down, his rotors are so close to the side of the mountain you can't believe it. He lands with one skid on the rock, the other hanging over the cliff. We piled in that thing, but because we were so heavy he slid the one skid off the rock and we just plunged down the hill until he could get enough bite in the air and slowly pull it up before we hit bottom. Boy, there was some hootin' and hollerin' when he lifted that bird out of there.

We told that guy and his copilot, "You know where our EM (enlisted men's) club is right?" They said "Yeah." We said, "Be there tonight and you won't buy a drink." We got them drunker than two snakes. There was definitely a love affair between them and us.

When choppers got shot down it was usually a Lurp team that got the call. First we would get an alert to be on stand-by. If they said there was no rush, well, that wasn't good. If it was like, "Load up now and get out there," we figured there were survivors. It never took us long to load up. Our weapons never left our side.

We never knew what we were getting into. We would just jump on a bird and go. On the way there we would find out a little more about what we were getting into. It might be a fiery crash with not much hope for survivors. Other times maybe the guys had a chance to radio back that they were still alive. Or it might be a couple of pilots trying to hold off Charlie.

We always knew going in that it might be body retrieval. The bad thing is that there was so damned much magnesium in the choppers that they burned incredibly hot. It was a nasty thing to see. I can close my eyes and still smell that. The burning chopper, the bodies, the whole thing. It was just really bad. In a lot of crashes if they were still alive, they were wounded: broken bones, gunshot wounds. They weren't going anywhere on their own. Their only hope was us getting to them before Charlie did.

If they were able to fly for a while after being hit there was a chance we could get to them before Charlie. But if they went down right after they got hit it was tough. Some of the missions were really good and we felt great about it. And then the next time we would be all bummed out because we couldn't do anything.

It was the greatest feeling in the world if we got to a downed chopper and everyone was still alive. We would have fought like twenty monkeys to get them out of there. On those good nights, we got drunk. We got really drunk.

We hated the thought of those guys being captured. We all feared that. We didn't talk about it much but we all understood one thing, save one round for yourself. Save it for a time when you might have to say, "*OK boys this is it...*"

The only thing we feared more than getting captured was our napalm. That would be a hell of a way to die. I know it was for them. I remember one time we were pinned down lying on our backs. We had NVA infantry out ahead of us and we were trying to get back through a rice paddy to our extraction point. We got the word, "Big Bird is coming in, get your asses down!" They didn't have to tell us twice. I'm lying there on my back in this rice paddy, half-covered in water and I'm watching this Skyraider plane come in. They were prop jobs, had this whiney, "Eeeeeee, eeeeeee" sound to them. I'm watching and he's coming in straight and low toward me. I'm thinking, *This ain't good. This ain't good.* Well, it got worse. "Clink," he released a napalm canister, *Oh shit, is that thing coming right on top of us?"*

We knew that the pilot knew what he was doing, but it was still scary as hell. We watched that thing go right over the top of us. You could feel the heat sweep over you and you could hear lots of hollering and screaming from Charlie. After a few of those canisters, we were able to get out of there without any problem.

Once our buddies in the sky showed up Charlie didn't hang around. The Air Force served us well. Sometimes we had F-4s supporting us. At the time we mainly had Huey gunships for support. We didn't have the Cobras yet. We didn't get those until damned near when I was leaving the Lurps. When we first saw them we were like, "Holy shit, those things are nasty!"

When we set up our ambushes they were either L-shaped or V-shaped. We set up all the claymores we had because we might only have six to ten guns at the most. We only sprung them if it was a small group like us walking through. If there were like fifty guys coming through, we let them go. What the hell are you going to do? I mean we could have knocked off the point man and maybe three or four behind him, but that wasn't our main job. In those situations, we just had to hunker down and shut up.

There were times when we would get spotted or whatever. If we knew it was a bigger force than us and we would just have to run and gun as we tried to get to an extraction point. Just fire behind you as you go.

We captured a couple of NVA. We took turns guarding them. This

A bayonet that Jim Jaklin found hidden on an NVA prisoner.

one guy was acting kind of strange towards me. I said, "Did they check this guy out before they brought him in? And they said, "Oh yeah." I said, "Well something isn't right." So I got right in his face and looked him over. He's still acting kind of hinky to me. In the meantime, he's got his hands behind his head and starts bringing a hand up. So I butt-stroked him in the face and knocked him out. He goes down. I reached behind his neck and pulled out a home-made knife. The blade was cut from a French bayonet. The handle was made out of a piece of napalm canister. He had hidden it right between his shoulder blades and the guys checking him out missed it. He wouldn't have missed me with it, that bastard. I still have the knife.

Charlie kept a close eye on what went on around the villages. That's where you would find the most booby traps. There was one that was made out of a couple of two by fours with spikes in them. When you stepped on it they would slap together on your ankles like a bear trap. Those were nasty. We had one guy who stepped on one of them. I went over to check him out while they were working on him and he was hurting. Oh, he was hurting.

They would watch us. Watch how we would react to things. If we were crossing a dike and started taking rounds, they knew we would dive in the water. That's how I got wounded.

We started taking fire so I dove off the dike into the water like we always did. They planned it perfectly. A punji stick went right through my kneecap and out the back of my leg. Normally when a punji stick would go in you could pull it out or pull it right through. But the stick that got me had a barb cut into the end of it so you couldn't pull it out. What they did was cut it off the front end and then pull the rest out the back. They couldn't get a chopper in to get me out; so I hung in there until the next day. It hurt like hell, but I knew the worst part would be the infection. You are told right away about the poison they would cover them with. Within a day or two, if it wasn't taken care of, you would have a raging infection. I mean big time.

After being sent back and treated and everything I wanted to go back to my unit in the field, but they wouldn't let me. They saw that I wouldn't be able to keep up. They gave me a job as the colonel's driver. I didn't like it. I missed my buddies in the Lurps. I had been with them for around eight months.

I had kind of a hard time getting home. I had malaria so bad that when I got on the plane I was shaking like a leaf. They said they weren't going to let me fly in that condition. There were some Airborne guys with me who were going to fight for my right to fly home. They had to send MPs out to the plane to try and calm everyone down. I said, "Forget it guys. Thanks, but it's not worth it."

They stuck me in the hospital until they got my fever under control.

There were good days and bad days over there. The worst day was when we lost two guys from our squad. The best day was when we got that tax collector and his bodyguards.

Actually, there was one other really good day. We came back from a mission and there were these guys standing around. We were like, "What the hell do you guys want?" One of them said, "Division sent down this CONEX container. We don't know what it is. It just says it's for the Lurp team here. So we went and opened it up. It was from a guy from San Francisco who owned Lucky Lager Ale beer. He was a Korean War vet. He had read about us and wanted to send us a little thank you. The CONEX was full of his beer. All he asked in return was a picture of us enjoying it. They got pictures of us from later that night. It looked like there were eight or nine corpses lying on the ground covered in beer cans. We enjoyed it all right.

When I got home my mother said she wanted the Army to take me back. She said, "That's not my son." I had a lot of issues that a lot of Vietnam vets had, or maybe still have to this very day. I keep weapons handy around me. I don't like anyone getting behind me in a restaurant or anyplace else. There were anger issues. PTSD is pretty rough stuff to get rid of. I'm still working on it. We have a really great group of vets who meet regularly. We really help each other. I've had guys tell me I've calmed down and seem more relaxed. I tell them it's because of the group.

I always try to help vets who don't have a support group. I try to do what I can to help them with VA issues and everything. Some guys are like, "No, I don't want anything to do with them. I still remember the way the government treated me when I came home." I tell them, "That was fifty years ago. Things have changed. Get the help and benefits you deserve. You earned it. We all did."

CLETUS NINHAM

1st Battalion
101st Airborne
Division
US Army
Vietnam War

Suffer a physical wound in battle and you are forever recognized as a Purple Heart recipient. But some wounds aren't physical, don't come with a medal, and don't surface until the veteran is years and miles removed from the battlefield.

A hard-nosed paratrooper from the Oneida Nation Reservation in Northeast Wisconsin battled through the pain of enemy shrapnel and nightmarish demons at home before triumphing over both.

People talk about having it rough. We had thirteen kids in my family and no electricity or running water. But I never say I had it rough because I know how much rougher my family and my Oneida people had it before me. My people fought for George Washington back at Valley Forge. They honored us by giving us land. A lot of our people couldn't speak English and were later told by non-Indians that they were just leasing the land, that they didn't really own it. That's how a lot of them ended up losing it.

When my mom started school at five years old the teachers used to beat her because she couldn't speak English. My parents had it rough, my grandparents had it rougher. I didn't have it so bad.

In 1965 I got a draft notice. I ignored it. I hoped they would go away. Then I got another one and they said you'd better come in or else.

I didn't want to go. I was living in Milwaukee and had a good job. For the first time in my life, I was making good money. I was a car nut. I had a 1932 Ford, a flat-head V-8 Oldsmobile with three-quarter-inch racing cams, a '58 Bonneville convertible, and a '39 Chevrolet. After that second notice, I sold them all except the Ford just in case I made it back from Vietnam.

I went to basic training at Fort Knox, Kentucky, and then advanced training at Fort Gordon, Georgia. I got trained on all sorts of weapons, it seemed like every weapon the Army had. I think the main thing they wanted to teach us was how to hate and how to kill. That's what they talked about more than anything.

After that, I decided to sign up for Airborne school. It was interesting. I didn't mind it. There was a lot of running and things like that. At first, I didn't like jumping. I don't think anyone does. But after you're up there and the parachute opens and you're coming down it's kind of nice. I just never wanted to be the first one out the door. I ended up making seven jumps in training and two in Vietnam. The two in Vietnam were so we could keep our jump status. Those jumps must have scared the VC because later on, we found fields where they had six-foot-high punji sticks planted all over.

After we graduated from Jump School we were made members of the 173rd Airborne Division. We were expecting to get passes before getting our assignments, but they canceled them and told us we were going directly to Vietnam. Every one of us was sent to Vietnam, every person in the company.

When we got to Vietnam they had busses lined up for us and took us to where we were going to be assigned to units. The thing I remember most was watching women going to the bathroom right alongside the road. I was like, *Oh man, I'm in a different world now.*

They took us to our headquarters, told us to stand in formation and count one through four. I told my best friend to get away from me. I knew if he didn't, that we would be separated. He didn't listen. I was sent to the 101st Division. He was sent to a different unit. He ended up getting shot up pretty badly. He was handicapped for the rest of his life.

I remember my brother, who fought in the Korean War, telling me to not make close friends because it would hurt bad if they got killed. He was right. It hurt badly. But it's hard not to make friends. I was an outgoing person. I wanted to have friends.

The outfit I was put in had one mission, search and destroy. Just find the enemy and kill them. That was our main purpose. We went six months straight out in the field living in the jungle. No hot food or showers. We'd be walking through rice paddies, where you would get all wet, and then you would dry off in the sun and then get wet again. You would walk through bamboo groves and get all cut up with sores that wouldn't heal. You would get jungle rot. Your shorts and socks would rot right off of you. The mosquitoes would drive you nuts. The repellent didn't do much good. Guys were getting malaria. It was miserable.

My number one fear was snakes. They had what they called a two-stepper. Two-steps after getting bit you were dead they used to say. They also had cobras. There was one incident; we were crossing this village on a path with water on the side and a cobra came out with its head full-blown puffed up. The lieutenant grabbed his pistol and I was like, "Wait, wait for the shotgun man!" He didn't wait. He took three shots, missed every time, and the snake went back underwater.

Before that, we were walking on a dike and we started taking fire. You could see the bullets hitting between us. We were probably about ten feet apart. It was one of our choppers firing at us. I could see the gunner. I was going to shoot him. My sergeant said, "Don't do it Chief, don't do it!"

The only guy hit was hit in his backpack. He went down and reached around and could feel it all wet and everything and he started yelling, "I'm hit. I'm hit!" We all ran over to check him out. The round had gone through his big pile of C-rations. I think it was beef stew that had spilled all over. We laughed so hard. I think that's the hardest I ever laughed in Vietnam.

The worst times were at night. It was so dark you couldn't see your hand in front of you. When we pulled guard duty you would have two guys, one on, one off. We did that for six months. On ambushes we just laid out there in the dark, listening for any sound, trying hard to not fall asleep even though you were so tired you could barely keep your eyes open.

We got supplies from choppers but I ran out of food lots of times because I carried extra ammo instead of food. I carried as much ammo as I could, usually around twenty magazines. I knew how to survive without food. I could find stuff out in the boonies to eat, but I never wanted to run out of ammo for my M-16, which was a piece of junk.

It malfunctioned on me in the middle of two firefights. I would pull the trigger and nothing. One of the times was when we came into a hot LZ. We were under heavy fire. When you're coming in on a chopper you can hear the bullets go by you and you could see the trail of rockets being fired at you. When we would get just below the treetops they would start hollering and screaming, "Out, out, get out!"

When we got on the ground my M-16 wasn't working. My squad leader said, "Come on Chief, (which they always called me) pull out your Bowie knife and let's charge. So I pulled out my Bowie knife and attacked with that.

Cletus Ninham (center) in full gear in Vietnam. (Cletus Ninham collection)

In another firefight, we were at the base of a mountain. We were in a straight line and taking heavy fire. You would hear bullets going by your head, "Peweeee. Peweeee." This wasn't a rice paddy, it was kind of a dry area. The bullets were hitting all around. I had picked up a new M-16 and again, it didn't work. The sergeant said to me, "Just pretend you're firing. Keep your rifle up, it will keep their heads down." Those were bad, bad rifles.

I remember one time when one of our outfits was getting hit bad. They choppered us in. The first thing I saw was forty or fifty body bags laying there. That's how many of our guys had been killed. I looked to my left side, just before we landed, and I saw another big line of bodies. It looked like something out of the Holocaust. Bodies upon bodies piled high of Viet Cong. They were all naked and maggots were coming out of their mouths, their ears, their nose. I had been hungry before that. Now I couldn't eat. I had to force down some peaches just so I didn't get sick.

I don't think a young guy is supposed to see something like that. All that horrible tragedy, I don't think we're made for that. Sooner or later something has to give.

After a few days there we had to hit this other mountain. We went in a straight line. I had a gut feeling that something didn't feel right. Sure enough, we got hit by machine-gun fire, rifles, snipers. Guys were falling all over the place, getting killed, getting wounded. The lieutenant got hit right through the stomach and it came out close to his spine. He survived and then went on to become a priest.

I remember him laying out there and my fire-team leader, a good friend, said, "Come on Chief let's go get him." Bullets were flying all around us, but we ran out there. You can't think about it at a time like that because you might not do it. You might be brave for that moment and do what you have to do. But your brain might be saying, *Let's run the other way!* But what are you going to do? Sit there and let a guy bleed to death? My sergeant took the head and I took the feet. We didn't get too far before the sergeant got shot in the knee and went down. So I pulled him over to the side and bandaged him up. Then I went back and pulled our wounded guy about 200 yards to where the medevacs were. I headed back to the fighting and passed some guys carrying out another lieutenant. His intestines were hanging out and it looked like he was dead, but I helped carry him back. By the time I got back to the firefight, everything was dying down.

I just kept thinking, *How come I didn't get killed?* Bullets were hitting all over. They were going past my head, between my legs but none of them hit me. How did they miss my big back and somehow hit him in the knee? Why, why didn't I get killed? I was haunted by that for a long time. Years later somebody told me it was something called "survivor's guilt." I used to have that. I'm sure of it. Later on, I just tried telling myself that maybe it was God's will and that he had a purpose for me.

After seeing lots of killing and stuff, guys got a hard attitude. They used to tell me, "Hey Chief why don't you scalp some of the VC?" They were serious. I said, "No, no I can't do that." But some of them really wanted me to.

I was a point man. I used to play cowboys and Indians when I was a kid but you know what? I always wanted to be the cowboy because the cowboys always won. Years later that helped me when I walked point in Vietnam. I'm not kidding. We used to hide in trees and everything. That was a good lesson on how to spot them. You can tell when something is out of place in the woods. You can just tell if something isn't natural. If branches are turned a certain way and things like that. I started hunting with shotguns when I was nine years old; so I was good for that job.

I always carried my rifle on a long strap so it was by my hip. I would have the selector switch on full automatic all the time and then just open up right from the hip. You never aimed. You just sprayed what you were shooting at. I will admit that I was scared lots of times, but you didn't let anyone else know that. We were at a reunion one time and someone told my wife that as long as Cletus was on point we felt safe. You couldn't let it show that you were as nervous as anyone else, but I had a job to do and that was to keep everyone else alive.

You couldn't feel good walking point because you knew if there was a booby trap, you would be the one to hit it. You would see some of those booby traps and wonder how men could be so cruel and so wicked to come up with such terrible ways to kill people. They would have a hole with a cover over it and in the pit there would be three-foot-high punji sticks. If you stepped on the cover over the top of the hole, you would go down and get impaled all through your body. There was another one that they attached to a branch that had sharp stakes on it. If you tripped it, it would come back and hit you in the chest. They had a mine they called a Bouncing Betty. It would fly up to about your waist before it went off.

Many times the people in villages must have heard we were coming because there wouldn't be anyone there. If we were told it was one-hundred percent a VC village, we burned it down. That's just what we were told to do. Sometimes when you went into a village, their food was still hot. We ate it. It's a wonder they didn't poison it. We went through one village that was like that and were on our way out when I saw a big wicker basket. I was going to shoot it but something told me not to. I wouldn't usually open up lids or doors because of booby traps, but this one I opened. Inside was a young woman with a very young baby and an old papa-san. They put their hands up and started saying something in Vietnamese. I just put my finger to my lips and said, "Shhhhhhh, be quiet, nobody is going to hurt you," and closed the lid. Nobody messed with them and we took off.

We went into this one VC village and their leader had just died. He was all dressed in black and was up on a platform like a Sioux burial ground. I was still going to shoot him, but then I thought, *Nah, I'm not going to shoot him. I'm going to set him on fire. I'm going to make sure he's dead."* That's the way you think when you're over there.

You just become so hard. You see your friends die and the terrible ways they died that you build up hatred, just bad anger and you want to do something, anything to get even.

We had one prisoner that was wounded. He was about three feet away from me. He was out of commission. He wasn't going to do anything. Some of the guys were like, "Shoot him Chief, shoot him." I wasn't going to do it. The prisoner was looking at me right in the eyes. Somebody came walking up and shot him in the head. I thought, "Why, why did he have to do that?" But I know why. It was the hatred that was built up and the feeling of revenge. It turned you into a different type of person. The memory of him looking right at me, hoping I wasn't going to kill him haunted me for a very long time.

I remember how I felt when a good friend of mine got wounded badly. He was a guy I had gone through airborne training with. He was a cowboy from out west. We were still in the same squad. On one mission he opened a gate. He should have known better. It exploded in his face. It didn't kill him, but he was taken away and I never heard anything about him again.

There was another village we went into with woods on one side and

(Cletus Ninham collection)

a clean dirt path going through it. Some guys went ahead of everybody else to clear it out. Big mistake, you were always supposed to stay in a line with everyone else. It's kind of like deer hunting when you're making a drive. So this one guy had gotten way ahead and went into one of the hootches. Another one of our guys, who was in line with the rest of us, went up to that place and was about to go inside. At the same time, the guy who went up ahead of us started coming out. As soon as the guy on the outside saw the door open and the barrel of a gun sticking out he opened fire. He shot the guy across the chest and killed him.

Sometimes guys would do dumb things that could get them killed.

John Maino

One night we were on an ambush and it was pitch black. We heard some noise around us. Some of the guys wanted to open up. I was the fire-team leader and said, "Do not open up! Do not shoot, do not shoot!" One of the guys was whispering, "We're going to be overrun! We're going to be overrun!" I didn't know what it was, but there's no way it could be VC. They wouldn't be making that much noise.

Whatever it was kept walking right toward our lines. Our guys were so trigger-happy; it's a miracle they didn't open up. Turns out it was one of our guys who had taken his entrenching tool and went outside the lines to go to the bathroom without telling anyone. He didn't have a helmet on, no weapon, nothing. It's incredible he wasn't shot. I told him he needed to thank me for saving his life.

Nobody was bullet-proof. We had a platoon sergeant, a big guy who thought he was invincible. One day he was walking back and forth while the firing was going on and got shot right through the head.

We were sent on one mission to try and rescue an American soldier that had been captured. We had to chop our way through some really dense jungle. My hands were so cut up and sore I could hardly move them. A guy said he would take over for a while, but he lasted

Cletus Ninham collection

about three minutes and said he was done. I had to take over again. I was so tired and worn out that I could barely move. We had to go up the side of a mountain to where we heard the American was being held. When we got near the top, they sent five of us to go on up ahead and see if we could spot him. We were in a line side-by-side. We were on our way when there was a big explosion. I went flying back. I felt like it was slow motion. I hit the ground and looked myself over. I was bleeding bad. My legs were getting covered with blood. The stock of my rifle was destroyed. I believe if my rifle hadn't been there, the shrapnel would have gone right into my hip. I called out to the other guys to see how they were. The first guy had a leg blown off. The next one was mangled real bad. The third guy had his shoulder almost completely torn off. I was laying there and telling a young guy to do something, to start bandaging us but he just froze. He wouldn't move. He was the only guy who wasn't hit but he was just frozen. He was shaking and looking but wouldn't move a finger to help.

The medic came up and started working on us. He bandaged me up and gave me a shot of morphine. They called in a chopper but there was no place for it to land. It hovered above, but it was really windy and rainy. They put me in a harness and started pulling me up, but the chopper was so unsteady that I felt like Tarzan crashing through the jungle hitting all the bamboo trees and branches. I thought I was going to get crushed to death. So they dropped me down and unstrapped me. The medic put me under two ponchos. The medic kept slapping me and saying, "Chief you have to stay awake, you can't fall asleep!" He told me that the choppers would be back in the morning once we cleared out a landing zone. I told the medic, "Enough with the slapping, do it again and I'm going to punch you!"

The medic ran out of morphine. The guys were screaming in pain all night long.

They got me out the next morning and flew me to a field hospital. When they checked me out they found that I had been hit in seven different places. I shouldn't be here today, but again I really think God had a plan for me.

I had just gotten a new pair of jungle boots. I loved those boots. When they started cutting them off I begged them, "Please don't cut them up! I don't want to lose my boots!" Something like a good pair of boots was really important. The guy cutting them off said, "Don't worry we will get you another pair." They never did.

I found out later that the guy who lost his leg ended up dying on the operating table but the other guys survived.

I spent a month in the hospital. My time was running short so instead of sending me back to the bush, they gave me a job as a mail clerk. That was one of the saddest things to do. I had to send the letters back to the families of the guys who had died. That was hard. I forget exactly what I had to write on them, but it was really sad. When they sent food packages I gave them to other guys. I wanted the families to think that at least the guys got the food that they sent to them.

My legs were hurting so bad that I couldn't do anything else. One of the officers told me I still had to do PT (physical training). I said no. Then the sergeant said, "You're going to do it." I told him the same thing, "No I'm not!" The doctor stepped in and said, "No way does he do any PT, no guard duty, nothing like that!" I don't know why they didn't just give me a medical discharge and send me home.

One day we all got orders, wounded guys, and everybody to load up. They were sending us to a place called Dak To. This was in 1966. The 101st was getting hit hard and they needed all the help they could get. It didn't matter if you were still recovering from being wounded or not.

I was assigned to the 2/502 Regiment. By the time we got there things had pretty much calmed down. But we heard the story of the captain of the unit who had called in napalm on his own position to try and keep his unit from getting wiped out. That's a pretty hard thing to do, call in napalm on your own guys. That was pretty controversial at the time, but they say it worked.

Editor's note: *There were several battles that generally go under the heading of "Dak To." The major ones were the battle led by the 101st Airborne in 1966, the vicious battle in November of 1967 on Hill 875 which resulted in over 1,800 US casualties, and the NVA efforts to wreck as much havoc as possible on the Dak To base camp in 1969. Dak To was situated near the Laotian and Cambodian borders and was a vital transportation and supply region for Communist forces.*

I don't remember anything about going home except landing someplace in California. I had a thirty-day leave. When I got home I could barely hold anything. I was shaking all the time. It was probably from lack of sleep and my nerves.

One night at home in bed I started shaking and running a high temperature. My legs had gotten infected from the wounds. My mom and dad had to take me to the VA hospital in Milwaukee.

When I was in the hospital I got a notice from the Army that I was in trouble because I was AWOL. My doctor had to call them and tell them I was going to be there for a while. So they extended my leave.

I met my wife in 1968 and we got married in '69. I was having a hard time getting a job or keeping a job. Every time I got a new job, every time, I ended up in the hospital with another infection in my legs. I had to work because I had to support my family. I was 100 percent disabled but I couldn't support them on that. Once the VA found out I was working they knocked me down to thirty percent.

We moved around trying to find a job that I could do that wouldn't put me in the hospital.

We had a daughter that was born with cerebral palsy. Then we had another daughter and she died at four months old. I was told that Agent Orange could cause things like that. We used to walk through areas that had just been sprayed. When you walked the stuff would come right up from the ground and into your lungs. It was so bad you would lose your breath and wonder what in the hell was going on.

I blamed myself. I was angry at everyone including God. I kept saying *"Why didn't you do something to me instead of them?"*

We later had another child who turned out to be a really good son. But this was during a time when things turned dark for me. I started pulling away from my wife, from everybody. At the same time Vietnam came crashing down on me. I was having nightmares and terrible sweats. I kept having the same dream that I was falling down a hole. Just falling straight down a volcano and before I hit I would wake up just covered in sweat.

Things got worse when the Communists took over Vietnam. I knew how many of the people who had helped us were going to be tortured and killed. I believe we could have won that war if we really wanted to. I felt like we let those people down.

But then on the other side, I was seeing Vietnamese people coming to this country and being given jobs, free houses, all kinds of things like that, and here I was barely able to take care of my family. I hated them for being given all those things.

I was hurting so bad on the inside. I was filled with anger, with hatred, just fits of rage is the only way to describe it. If someone was tailgating me, I would go after them. I would throw things at them, do whatever I could do to them.

We were living in San Jose, California. I had a job hauling cars, but I was still in a bad place. I had become a person I didn't want to be. A person that I never thought I would be.

We lived in an apartment complex and I got into an argument with a guy over a parking place. He said I was in his spot. The next day my tires were missing. When I saw him he said, "Now you've got a permanent spot."

He lived upstairs of us. I went into our apartment, loaded my .44, and pointed it up to where he was walking. My wife said, "What are you doing, are you nuts? Don't you know he has kids up there?" I said I didn't care. That's how far over the edge I had gone. That's where I was. My anger and hatred were that strong.

I put the gun down, but I did take a razor blade and cut all his tires. I thought, *Well okay, now we're even.* That's how I looked at things; that's just the way I thought.

Not long after that incident, my wife left me. She moved back to Wisconsin. I was going to commit suicide. I felt sorry for myself. I was tired of being angry all the time. I just wanted to end it all and get away from everything. But in my mind something was saying, *You're a coward if you do that.* Nobody likes to be called a coward, even if it's just in your mind. I opened the gun and let the bullet fall out.

Before all this happened my wife wanted me to go to a church with her. I said, "OK fine, I'll go to church with you." Well, there were no crosses or anything, none of the things you would normally see in a church. When we left I told her that place seems more like a cult than a church. I told her I wasn't going back.

One day out of the blue a lady walked up to my wife in a restaurant and said that somebody loves her and his name is Jesus. My wife felt unloved at the time because of the way I was. Something told that lady to do that.

There was also a neighbor lady who lived in our apartment complex who told my wife she wanted to talk to me for a long time about her church, but was afraid to because of the way I looked with my long hair and the way I acted.

After my wife divorced me that lady came up to me, handed me a religious card, and asked me to read it. Then she asked if I would go to church with her and her husband. I said sure, why not. I didn't have anything to lose. So I go and it's the same place that my wife had taken me to, the place I called a cult. But things started getting a little bit better. I started reading the Bible and decided I didn't need to carry all this guilt and junk inside me.

I prayed and prayed for my family to get back together. My family members used to ask, "Have you become one of those Jesus freaks?" I just told them, "Call it what you want, but the Lord changed me and he changed me for the better." They said I had freaked out. I didn't care. I just know that I prayed hard for two years and got back with my family. My wife and I got remarried.

I used to pray to just become the person I was before Vietnam, my mind and my body. I knew that couldn't happen. Too much damage had been done to my body, but at least my mind cleared up.

I accepted Christ in my life and eventually became an Evangelist minister. There's a verse in the Bible that says the truth will set you free and the hatred and prejudice will leave. I truly believe that. Sometimes a person needs to open a wound when it's infected to let all the poison out. That's what I had to do. I had to let it out to get forgiveness and give forgiveness. It changed my life and it saved my life.

LEE PIECHOCKI

1st Air Cavalry
US Army
Vietnam War

For some families, service in the military wasn't looked at as much of a sacrifice, but as part of their family tradition and obligation. It's the philosophy Lee Piechocki grew up with.

But one thing this 1963 graduate of Shiocton (Wisconsin) High School would discover once he was in uniform, one decision by someone of higher rank could change your entire destiny.

"My family has always been patriotic. Whatever came up we answered the call. When it was my turn, I was going to do it as well. I wasn't going to go running to Canada or anything. Something like that didn't even cross my mind."

We started at Fort Polk, Louisiana, in WWII barracks. The floorboards had cracks between them. You could look down and see the ground underneath. They were heated by wood stoves. Someone had to be on fire watch all night. Seeing as how I was the biggest of the group

I was put in charge of getting everyone up by 5:00 a.m. and at the mess hall by 5:30.

We got all of our equipment and everything and then bused to Fort Hood, Texas. When we pulled up there were three of the biggest guys I had ever seen in my life standing there waiting for us. Three sergeants: S-2, 1st sergeant, and sergeant major. Each had to be over 6'5. I'm 6'3 but with them, on the curb, I felt like a midget. These guys were huge. This is where all our training would be for a full year. We were 2nd Armored Division, 1st of the 50th Infantry Battalion. When it was over I was promoted to PFC and given my MOS of 11-Bravo, Infantry.

One of the armorers in our company came back from Vietnam and said he was leaving the service. He took care of all the weapons and stuff. I told the XO (executive officer) I would like to apply for that position. He said, "OK, we will put you there and see how you work out." My second day on the job was a big day on the shooting range. It was crazy. I had to get two guys to help me, I was so overwhelmed. Guys would have to give you a card before you gave them a weapon. We ended up missing one weapon, a .45. They ended up finding it in a guy's locker. He wanted to keep it for himself. I was so mad I was hoping they would send him to prison for that.

In July of 1967, we had been told that we were going to Germany, but by the first of August things had changed. They sent a different battalion to Germany and we got orders for Vietnam.

When we were about to get shipped out my job was to load everything on railroad cars: weapons, APCs (armored personnel carriers), everything. We packed all of our luggage in the APCs. That way we didn't have to worry about it getting lost on the way to Vietnam.

We set sail on an old WWII troop carrier, the USS *General John Pope*. A guy who had traveled on these types of ships before told me the first thing I should do is to volunteer for a good job; otherwise I'd be in the mess hall with guys puking all over. It wasn't a good place to be. So I volunteered to be the ship's movie projectionist. They had said it was going to be a seventeen-day trip; so we had seventeen movies. My job was to show the same move twice during the day and then go to the officers' lounge and show it to them at night. That's all I had to do. I got to eat with the officers. That was pretty good duty. The officers were Merchant Marines, the best people in the world. I don't know if they get the recognition they deserve. Technically civilians, but paid by the government.

We skirted two typhoons going from Okinawa to Vietnam. When we were off-loading a detachment of Marines at Vong Tao, I looked over the side and there was an incredible amount of debris floating in the water. It looked like that for every piece of debris there was at least one snake on it. I'm not a snake person. So I see all these big snakes that I assumed were poisonous. In the back of my mind, I'm thinking, *This is where I'm going to be for the next year?*

The port we landed at was Qui Nhon. After getting shots and everything we drove up Highway 1 to An Khe. At this time I was assigned to Company C, 1st of the 50th Battalion, 1st Cavalry Division.

The first night there we were sent to check on a couple of MPs that hadn't arrived when they were supposed to. We took one squad in my APC and traveled south along Highway 1 for about a mile and found the jeep had been hit with a B-40 rocket and both of the MPs were dead.

Our location was LZ Uplift. I enjoyed being an armorer for the company, but I also had to take care of all of the other supplies. When the company went out on patrol, which they did about two or three times in the first week, I stayed back and took care of my other jobs which included laundry. On one of the days I went to the local laundry at about 10:00 a.m. to pick it up. It wasn't done yet. They told me to come back around noon. In the meantime, the company had come back from patrol. I explained to the 1st sergeant the situation and that I would be picking it up around noon. That was too late for him. He says, "That's it, you're not taking care of supplies anymore. You are now out in the field!" Then he handed me an M-.60 machine gun.

So in that one moment, I went from a job I really liked to the infantry as an M-.60 machine gunner; which is a job almost nobody wants. And it was all because I didn't get the 1st Sergeant's laundry done in time.

When we flew into an LZ I was the last man off the chopper and would then walk point. Because the chopper was so much lighter with everybody out I could be ten feet off the ground when I jumped.

On Halloween day, October 31st, 1967 we jumped out of the chopper at an LZ near Bong Son. I twisted my ankle when I landed. I had hurt it in high school and now I screwed it up again. I tied my bootlaces as tight as I could and went up to the point position.

We were walking on a nice path down the hill. On the sides of the path, you could see places where it looked like grass had been tied in a knot. Whenever we saw that we looked for booby traps. The knots were from where they tied their fish line (tripwires) across the path. So you would spot one and then point it out to everybody. We got down to a flat landing at the bottom of the hill without any problems.

The Marines had left us a circle of foxholes, one inside the other, making a fall-back ring. If the first got hit hard, you could always fall back to the second hole. In the center was the command post.

There were three of us in the foxhole. Each one of us had two hours on and four hours off. PFC Kraig, PFC Harold, and I manned a foxhole to the southeast of the circle. Kraig and I were going to sleep first. I was laying outside the foxhole. I couldn't sleep with my boots on so

I took them off. Around 11:00 p.m. the NVA attacked. The first thing they did was throw a grenade into a foxhole to our left. That foxhole was overrun. Another one further to my left was also overrun. Harold decided he was going to throw all ten grenades that we had. That also blew out the electrical lines to the claymores we had set up out front. Now they were of no use anymore. When the first foxhole got overrun, a guy came running right over me hollering, "I can't see! I can't see!" I rolled over and just as I did a grenade went off about six or eight feet from me. I didn't know that it had hurt me at all because in that sand the explosion goes straight up. I grabbed my boots, the M-.60, and sort of squirmed into the foxhole. When I slid in Harold jumped out. He didn't like the spot we were in. Then Kraig slid in with his M-16 and we started doing our thing. I was on the .60 all night. That's one gun that you respect and will always do the job. I don't think I had any real feeling. It was just something you were trained to do and the role you are expected to do.

At about 1:00 a.m. I was down to about fifty rounds of ammunition. I had started with 400. One of us had to go for more. The area was still lit up somewhat from tracers and flares so we did the old rock, paper, scissors to decide who would be going. Kraig lost. So he slid out of the foxhole and that's the last I saw of him. I had no idea what happened to him. By morning I had ten rounds left.

During the night I saw a muzzle flash from about 150 feet away. There was a rock about an inch-and-a-half in diameter on the top edge of the foxhole I had been looking over. After I looked up again the rock had disappeared. I figured I must have had a half-dozen angels looking over me. When it got light enough and I could see what was going on around me, I started to crawl out of the foxhole. There was a five-gallon water can, the type you carry on a jeep, sitting up behind my head. It had five bullet holes in it.

I found out later that Kraig, the guy who went to get ammo, had gotten shot in the buttocks. It severed the sciatic nerve to his leg and he was medevacked out. Harold was found shot in the head about two feet from that water can behind me. He had barely gotten out of the foxhole. There was an NVA soldier about twenty feet from my foxhole. He had taken many M-16 and M-.60 rounds. He was laying on top of his rifle. You weren't supposed to move the bodies because they could be booby-trapped. Well somebody came running in right away and grabbed his SKS Russian rifle. I wasn't in any mood to collect souvenirs. I was still looking out of my foxhole trying to figure out where the round came from that hit the rock in front of me. We lost four guys that night. They lost twelve.

When we got back to LZ Uplift I went to see the medic because there was sloshing in my boot. It was blood from the grenade that landed by us. My foot was full of embedded metal and sand. He handed me a handful of Band-Aids and said, "Here you go. Take care of it."

After that firefight our job was mostly guarding bridges and things like that. Mainly we did that at night. During the day we worked on the LZ making sure everything was in good shape. We even got to swim in the South China Sea; which was nice.

One day I was helping clean up around the LZ, burning brush and garbage. Some beehive 90mm rounds were lying there that had gotten wet. The casing is about a foot-and-a-half long with the propellant and three rows of small nails with wings inside. Seeing as how it was wet we had to dispose of it so the VC couldn't find a way to use it against us. The propellant was in a bag about eight inches long. I took that and threw it in the bonfire. It hit a branch from the brush we were burning and came back at me. It landed by my foot. It still seemed fine to pick up and toss back. But a lump of small hot coal must have gotten inside and when I bent over to pick it up it went off. I didn't have a shirt on. When it went off it burnt my arm and my entire side. The arm received second-degree burns and my entire side had third-degree. Half of my face was black with all the hair burnt off.

When it went off it burned so hot and so fast that the nerves must have been shot. All I remember saying was something like, "Aweeeee!"

My APC was just a little ways away. I went over, crawled on top, and told the guys to grab the five-gallon water can and dump it all over me. That cold water on my burnt skin was something else. Just a really cold feeling all over.

I bet it wasn't five minutes before a medevac came in. They brought me over there and the first thing the medic did was give me a shot of morphine. Just jammed it in my leg and we took off. They took me to LZ English to spend the night. The first night I slept on a bench. The next morning they gave me another shot of morphine. Then it was off to Quy Nhon Hospital. They cut off all my clothes, put me in a bed, and rigged up one of those IV stands with a strap on it to hold my arm up. They said it was so my arm didn't stick to my side.

On one of the days, Major General Tolson came through the ward with two of his adjuncts. He stopped at my bed. The first thing he noticed was my boots under the bed. They were so beat up that I had staples holding the soles together. But I loved those boots. I have flat feet so I had them specially made for me in Ft. Hood. He told the adjunct to get rid of those boots and get me a brand new pair. They did and they were at least a size too small.

Then he asked, "Soldier what can I do for you?" and I said, "Get me out of the infantry sir." He said, "Let's see what we can do." Five days later I got orders to report to the 228th Aviation Battalion as a draftsman. Mainly they wanted me to make new signs for their area.

It wasn't long after that, they came and told me they were going to make me an air traffic controller. So I did that for the rest of my tour. I would be assigning sorties for CH-47s. There are times I would volunteer to be the door gunner with the M-.60. I usually went on the commander's aircraft which was a Huey.

On one of the missions we were escorting helicopters that were hauling howitzers and caterpillars to clear an LZ in the A Shau Valley. One of the flying cranes got hit by 37mm anti-aircraft fire. They have two engines up on top and the right engine started on fire. I don't know if it was the fuel line or what. There were three men on board: the aircraft commander, the pilot, and the load commander. They dropped the cat they were hauling as soon as they got hit, but slammed into the side of the mountain. Everybody was killed.

We did some firing from the commander's copter. Before we got out of the A Shau a round came up through the floor and could have done some real damage to my butt, but I was pretty well protected. Somebody had told me that when you're a door gunner you should sit on two flak jackets. The round went through the first but not the second. It still would have knocked me out of the aircraft if I wasn't strapped in. All I got out of it was a huge bruise.

Door-gunning was sort of fun. You had the best view of the entire territory. When you did have to use the gun, it was hard sometimes to see exactly what you were shooting at. You wanted to make sure you didn't hit your people. And at times it was very close combat. You had to make certain of your decision when you pulled that trigger.

There was one week of my time over there that I've blacked out. It was on a mission to visit with the local people around An Khe. Again, I simply cannot remember exactly what happened that week except for one incident. Something happened years later that triggered this memory. It's the most gruesome thing a person can imagine. But it gives an idea of how barbaric things could be over there.

The VC had gone into this village to get reports on what we were doing. They took the leaders of the village, the mama-san, and papa-san, and tried to force them into telling them about where we were, what we were up to. They didn't know. They didn't know anything. There was nothing they could tell them.

In one of the most horrific things imaginable, the VC took their little girl and skinned her alive in front of them and put her on a fence post around the chicken and pig pens. Her body was still there when we got to the village. We saw it.

To think people would do that to other people. It's beyond belief. But that's what they did.

I think God makes people in a way that if they can't handle something in their mind, it can be blacked out. I can't tell you anything else that happened that week. It was years later when I saw a dead animal that that horrible memory was triggered.

On one mission we followed the Ho Chi Minh Trail into Laos. They had that trail so well camouflaged it was incredible. They had tied the tops of trees together to form an archway so they couldn't be seen from the air. We didn't know we were in Laos at the time. We figured that out later on.

Before I went into the service I had a job with the Corps of Engineers as a surveyor. I could judge distance and direction pretty well. One day I was called in and asked if I wanted to go on a trip. I thought sure, any kind of a trip out of there would be great. I was thinking it might be some sort of R&R.

It wasn't.

This was in 1968. I was chosen to go on a classified four-day mission to North Vietnam. One SEAL team member and a few of us Army guys. We didn't know each other's names. I was told that another one of the other reasons I was selected is because I didn't snore. That was important.

The Navy took us up off the coast of North Vietnam. We had black fatigues and sandals that were made out of tires, with the sole being the same in front as in back so you couldn't tell what direction someone was walking.

We went in on a horseshoe-shaped raft. It had a tube about the size of a coffee can. When it hit the saltwater the propeller would start. It would go about four-five miles an hour. Once you got on land and took it out of the water it would quit. We buried it on the shore.

The SEAL was in charge. Our mission was to recon a POW camp. We found the camp, got to around 1,500 yards of it, and had to find places to hide. Each guy found their own place. I found a pig pen with some bamboo leaning up against a shed. The pigs didn't care that I was there, but I was afraid the chickens were going to give me away. I don't think I slept for four days.

We could see the fence, the gate, the barracks, the whole thing. My job was to get direction and distances of different things. That was before GPS. I also wasn't allowed to carry a notebook or a map. I had to take the tip of my knife and scratch out distances on my fingernails so if I was caught they wouldn't find anything.

When we left we used the same rafts to go out and were then picked up by the Navy. They came in with rubber boats that had tremendous horsepower, two guys in each one. One operated the boat, the other grabbed your arm.

I was given R&R when we got back and I went right to Japan. I was never a drinker, but I got hooked on soda. I started drinking an eight-pack a day.

For the trip back home I started at Cam Ranh Bay. We got more shots and they checked all of our paperwork and everything. While I was doing that someone went into the barracks and stole my suitcase. I had it chained to my bed, they broke the bed to get it. All I had left were the clothes I had on.

We were told to wait near the runway for the aircraft to come in. Here comes this pink Braniff 707, pink like the color of Pepto Bismol. It gets near the runway and the left engine falls off the wing and starts rolling down the runway. The engine fell off! The plane still landed fine.

They told us they didn't have any barracks for us so we had to spend the rest of the day and the night on the runway. It was 117 degrees.

The next day the same plane comes in, but with one engine that wasn't painted pink. They did a good job because it got us to the Aleutian Islands.

I made it home to Shiocton on August 28th, 1968.

I was going to take a month off before going back to my job with the Corps of Engineers. My dad had plowed some fields around our farm so I thought it would be fun to take the Farmall with a spring tooth and work the field. At the same time one of the neighbors had decided to blow some duck ponds. When the first explosion went off I found myself on the ground with my hands over my head. I started looking around. Did anybody see me? I had to tell myself, *I'm home. It's okay.*

When I had come home for leave right before leaving for Vietnam, I went on one date with a girl named Barbara I had known all my life. I was four years older than her. I remember that one date because her parents told her to be home by 11:00 and we talked so much that I brought her home at 1:30. That wasn't a great start. But she was great at writing to me when I was in Vietnam even though she would write three to my one. Long story short, in 2020 we celebrated our 51st wedding anniversary.

I always believed we could have won that war if it weren't for two things: journalists and politicians. They let the journalists travel along with the soldiers, but they got so many things screwed up. They would write their stories and the politicians would read that stuff and it was like, "Oh you can't do this and you can't do that." They hamstrung us and we couldn't do anything about it.

I don't know about other units, but with the 1st Cav we went through areas where we completely changed the attitude of the people because of the way we helped them. The people in South Vietnam basically wanted American money, but the people in the northern areas were very good to us because we took care of them the best we could.

Mentally I didn't have issues until many years later. Then I started having dreams. Not always horrific, just dreams about what I could have done. One of the dreams is of a hand sticking out of a bush and someone saying, "Help me!" and I grab the arm and pull it out and it's just an arm that comes out. Another one is about the time I picked up a guy and was running and slipped on his intestines. Those are some of the dreams I would have.

I talk with other vets regularly. I've gone to Family Services and still go to a Vets Center. For twelve years now a group of us vets get together every Tuesday for breakfast.

Vets do a good job of looking out for one another.

JOE RESOP

513 Signal Detachment
US Army
Vietnam War

Anyone who has ever seen the movie "Full Metal Jacket" has, at the very least, a Hollywood glimpse of what the Battle of Hue looked like. In just over three weeks over forty percent of this scenic, historic city was destroyed.

For American forces it would be the longest and bloodiest battle of the war. Official reports list 147 US Marines and 74 American soldiers killed along with more than 1,300 wounded. It's estimated that over 8,000 NVA and Viet Cong took part in the siege. A soldier from Berlin, Wisconsin, would be face-to-face with some of those Communist fighters from the opening salvo.

I was working full-time at the Ripon cookie factory when I got my draft notice. I had graduated from Berlin High School in 1964. I had to go to Oshkosh and meet in front of a draft board and explain why I blew off the first draft notice they had sent me. I was honest, said I just didn't pay any attention to it. They said no problem, here's a ticket, go down and get your medical work taken care of. So I go down, get my physical, and I flunk it. I was 4-F because of a heart murmur. So I went back home and told my dad. He was happier than hell. He had fought on Okinawa during WWII. He knew what war was like.

At first, I felt OK about it, but then I got to thinking, *Do I really want to make cookies for the rest of my life?* I was kind of curious as to what the Army would bring to my life. So I went down and talked to a recruiter. He told me about the different types of jobs I could get in the Army. One was in communications. I thought that sounded pretty good. This time I passed my physical. My dad wasn't too happy with me.

After basic training, I was sent to Monmouth, New Jersey, for a twenty-eight-week communications course for what they used to call Microwave School. This was in 1967. After that, I was sent to another school. This one was Tropo school where you learn about sending signals 500 miles into the sky. They were working on that because of all the mountains in Vietnam. This unit was under the direction of the Pentagon.

From there they sent us to Fort Huachuca, Arizona. A corporal said, "This unit needs to know how to fight once they get to Vietnam." So what do they do, but put us with a bunch of Green Berets. They had us do war games up in the Huachuca Mountains. Here's the thing, as we were leaving our base the Green Beret guy says, "Drop all your C-rations. We live off the land." We did. We ate snakes, rats. They shot a mountain lion. Those guys were something else. They were truly badass. I think we went over the mountains into Mexico. I don't know if that was in the rules or not, but that other group never found us.

When all that was over they trucked us up to Tucson and put us on a commercial plane. Here we were with our M-16s, flak jackets, helmets, sitting right there like other passengers.

We got to Vietnam in October of '67. We were in Long Binh until the middle of December and then got orders for Hue. We were happier than hell. That's all we kept hearing was what a beautiful city it was. So we went there and set up communications. We were the main line of communications for Hue and Khe Sanh. The communications group at Khe Sanh would shoot a signal to us and we would relay it to Da Nang.

The first month or so went by fine. We had all the communications set up at our radio site for back and forth communication between the different bases.

We would get updates on situations around the area. They would say either condition blue, amber, or red. This one day it was blue in the afternoon, then later in the evening it was amber and then at about 2:30 in the morning we were woken up from a rocket hitting in the street just outside of the house we were living in. We were just off of Highway 1. We knew it was aimed at us, but missed and blew a hole in the highway. This was the start of the Tet Offensive.

Fifty Strong

Editor's note: *On January 31, 1968, North Vietnamese Army and Viet Cong units sprung surprise attacks throughout South Vietnam. Their coordinated efforts attacked five major cities and hit over 100 other targets including military installations, villages, and hamlets. Hue was one of the hardest-hit areas in the entire country.*

I was sleeping in an upstairs room with some other guys when it hit. We all ran down. All you felt was adrenaline, just pure adrenaline. We needed to get to our communications site which was a big CONEX container. Two ARVN soldiers had been shot outside of our house, and some of our guys carried them in and put them on cots.

We started running to our station, we were probably about fifty yards from a building that was used as a jail for political prisoners. The big wooden gates were wide open. My buddy Danny said to me, "I just saw a guy shoot another guy. What should I do?" I said, "Shoot him!"

We were in a bunker next to the CONEX where our equipment was. Danny had a .60- caliber machine gun and was firing through one window. I had an M-16. I put it on full automatic and sprayed everything in front of me. There was a pig barn and rice paddy in front of me. That's where the VC were. I would open up and then put my back against the wall and twenty to thirty rounds would answer.

Danny's firing and then I see sparks and sand flying around. Danny was hit. I was the only one who had a bandage so I gave it to my buddy Jimmy. He was holding Danny's arm up and bandaging him.

I went up on top of the bunker so I could see more of what was going on. There was an MP up there with an M-79. He didn't know what in the hell was going on either. Mortars started coming in all around us. The only protection we had was two rows of sandbags, but there

The view from the small hole through which Joe Resop fired his M-16 at Viet Cong attackers during the battle for the city of Hue during the Tet Offensive in 1968.

(Joe Resop collection)

The exterior (above) and interior (below) of the bunker from which Joe Resop and others fought off Viet Cong attackers for three days without food or water.
(Joe Resop collection)

was a .60-cal up there so I started firing that. It turned into a machine gun-versus-machine gun kind of fight.

They were in the prison yard so I could see them, but they couldn't get to me because of the high wall. They were sitting ducks for me.

The MP ran out of ammo for the M-79 so he left and went after more. In the meantime, they started firing more mortars at us. They were walking them in. I think there were four in a row. One splattered right in front of me. I got hit with shrapnel in my face and over my arms. I still have a piece in my left bicep. I don't know why they stopped. One more click on the tube and they would have had us dead center.

The MP came back with more ammo for his M-79 and the machine gun. My memory is pretty vague about the rest of the day because my adrenaline was pumping so hard it was unbelievable.

For the next three days, we had no water, no food, very little ammunition. I thought about draining the water out of the radiator of one of our trucks. It was hot as hell, humid as hell, there was tear gas in the air. I remember punching a sandbag on one of the days that was misty and foggy. A little water came out, it was mostly sand but oh was it good. It was so good.

On the second day, a Marine patrol tried coming in. Three of them were killed and a corpsman was shot trying to take care of them. On the third day, they came in with tanks. They said they found sixteen VC bodies around our area and other blood trails. In the archives of the battle, it said that there was probably a battalion of NVA around the area we were in. Their base camp was the soccer stadium which was probably half a mile from us.

On one of the days me and a buddy almost got killed by the Marines. We were upstairs of our house on a balcony watching the Marines come in on Highway 1. We didn't know that some VC snipers were firing at the tanks from a rice warehouse behind us. All of a sudden one of the tanks stops and starts spinning its turret right at us. I said, "Holy shit! Let's get out of here!" We got down the first set of stairs and got blown down the rest of the way. That tank put a shell right through our upstairs. They assumed we were doing the sniping.

After the Marines came in we still needed water, so some guys from the 327th went with a detachment of Marines to look for some. They came back with what we called a Water Buffalo, a water tanker. We had no idea where they got it from but those guys from the 327 got a citation for it.

The Marines set up a mortar pit in our area. Things were pretty scary for nine days. There was still a lot of sniper fire all over the place. We kept communications going the entire time. We never got knocked out. We were pretty much in our own little world there. We did our thing and nobody bothered us. I remember asking a Marine one time

US Marines in a tank blasted a hole (right) in the house where Joe Resop was living when they mistakenly thought they were taking fire from his location.
(Joe Resop collection)

for a couple of phosphorus grenades. I straightened the pins and put them on top of our equipment. A few weeks later a colonel was in the area and went crazy when he saw that. He said, "What in the hell are you doing!?" I said I was just making sure no one was going to steal our equipment.

The thing I remember most was the sights of that beautiful city burning and smoldering. It had been hit hard in that short time. I will also never forget the smell of dead bodies lying there.

Editor's note: *Joe's unit was awarded a valorous unit award for its actions during the enemy offensive.*

Excerpts: *The 513 signal detachment distinguished itself by extraordinary heroism while engaged in military operations during the period of 31 January to 9 February in defense of the hue troposcatter radio site. When the signal site came under rocket, mortar, and small arms fire 31 January at the outbreak of the joint North Vietnamese Viet Cong Tet offensive, the detachment's personnel immediately assumed a defensive posture and placed accurate return fire upon the hostile force which effectively blunted the enemy attack.*

On 2 February, 1968, an interrogation compound which was approximately 25 meters from the site was captured and the enemy launched a heavy concentration of small arms fire upon the site from this position. *Although without food or water and running low on M-79 ammunition, held their ground and soundly defeated the attackers.*

The men of the 513 signal detachment displayed extraordinary heroism and devotion to duty which are in keeping with the highest traditions of the military service and reflect distinct credit upon themselves and the armed forces of the United States.

Years later I made a trip back to Hue. There was a lady on the bus. She was about sixty years old. She said she was at the Citadel; which was the first main target of the VC when the battle started. Her father worked for the government. She said she remembered guys in black pajamas looking for him. He disappeared and everybody assumed they would never see him again. Then one day he reappeared and they all left the city.

She said that when the VC grabbed people, they would take them to a big ditch, tie their hands behind their backs, and bury them alive.

It's funny how you can remember the funny things that happened. The things you would laugh about even being in the middle of a war. I remember one night when it was really dark and raining hard and all the electricity was out in our area. I saw a piece of our equipment laying out so I took off running to pick it up. All of a sudden I went down hard. I was sure a sniper had shot me right in the nuts. I was in so much pain I couldn't believe it. I'm thinking, *They got me! They got me!* The guys

Shelling virtually destroyed the city of Hue during the early stages of the Tet Offensive.
(Joe Resop collection)

heard me moaning, came out, and dragged me inside to check me out. What happened was that in the dark I ran full speed into the ball hitch of the generator trailer. I was totally convinced I had been shot. The guys got a kick out of that.

I do know one thing, I owe my life to the Marines. Those "jarheads" came and saved our doggy asses. I remember going to Da Nang with a three-quarter-ton truck and filling it with as many pallets of beer and Pepsi as I could. When I got back I told the Marines to help themselves.

I stayed in 'Nam until December of '68. I moved around, first to Dong Ha then to Quang Tri. We went through some shit, but nothing like the ground pounders went through. Our main thing was keeping the communication lines open. After Hue I think they kind of forgot about us and just let us do our thing. We wore cutoffs, let our hair grow long.

Joe Resop, second from left. (Joe Resop collection)

I will say this, Vietnam made a man out of me. I grew up very, very fast. When I came home I drank beer like a son of a bitch. I did that until I was fifty-two years old and quit cold turkey.

I've got PTSD, oh yeah. Nights can be hard when it's really dark and you don't know what's around you. That's when I started thinking of the rice paddy across from our bunker and not knowing what was in there, what was going to be coming at you.

I don't know how many we actually killed. Like I said, they found sixteen NVA or VC bodies and a bunch of other blood trails. But that's another thing. Those guys were doing their job just like we were doing our job. I've got twelve grandkids. I've got great-grandkids. You sit and think about the people you killed over there, how they could have been the same as you. They could have had kids, wives, parents. It's not fun to take another person's life. Everybody says, "Oh well it was either them or you." It was, but it's still not a good thought. I don't know how other people feel about it, but that's just how I do.

JACK SHAVLIK

9th Marine Regiment
3rd Marine Division
Vietnam War

"We had a career day at Reedsville High School (Wisconsin) when I was a senior. All the different branches of the service were there including a Marine recruiter in dress blues. My buddy Kenny and I went over and talked to him. We joined that same day. We wanted to be like that guy. Patriotism was still running high then. There was a big American flag hanging on the wall in our gym. I thought it was pretty cool just looking at that. I wanted to do my part to serve my country."- Jack Shavlik

Boot camp was rough for everybody, but I had been a track star in high school. I ran the 100-yard dash and the broad jump. I was MVP of the team and held some school records. I was in the best shape I would ever be in. I could handle it. When we did our PT (physical training) test at the end of boot camp I aced the test. I thought I was going to be the Honor Recruit, but they gave it to another guy. I found out later that the guy's uncle was a major in the Marines. That might have had something to do with it. I didn't care. I was just proud I aced the test.

We had one DI, a little guy, he was a 6th-degree black belt. He would screw with everybody, some more than others. I got mine too boy. He would come up to you and grab you by the throat and just before you passed out he would wake you up.

They do take your mind and bring it to wherever they want. They would take guys who weren't sure they wanted to be Marines anymore and make them cry in their beds until they were dedicated to the Corps to the max.

There were guys who had it pretty rough. If they put you in the fat platoon or the motivation platoon...oh boy. There were these twins from Kansas City. They were too heavy. They couldn't do PT. They couldn't do anything. The DIs just ridiculed them, worked the hell out of them, and only let them have a small amount of food. I'm telling ya, they must have lost fifty-sixty pounds. They were turned into lean-mean Marines. Today if a DI did what he did, they would put him in jail.

After we graduated from boot camp the DI looked at us and said, "Your asses are still mine until tomorrow morning...to the grinder!" We had to go down there and do 100 sit-ups and 100 push-ups, and they had to be all as one in unison. Then he said, "All right, now I'm through with you."

When I went home on leave before being sent to Vietnam I married my high school girlfriend. I told her that if I didn't make it back at least she would have $10,000 in the bank. That's what they gave for life insurance to the beneficiary back then.

My bunkmate all during boot camp was Jimmy Ahrens of Green Bay. We became great buddies all during camp. He was a hell of a good guy. At the end of training, we got sent to different units. He was killed in Vietnam on May 19 of 1969. I remember my Ma sending me his obituary. That was tough to take. Great guy, a great friend.

Green Bay GI Killed In Vietnam

Another Green Bay man has been killed in action in Vietnam. Pfc. James J. Ahrens, 20, son of Mr. and Mrs. Roy Ahrens, 1961 Preble Ave., died Thursday as a result of hostile enemy fire. He was on platoon patrol in Quang Nam Province, South Vietnam when he was killed.

A graduate of East High School, in the class of 1967. Ahrens joined the Marine Corps in September 1968. He was employed by the Straubel Paper Co. before entering the service

***

We got to Da Nang in the middle of the night, or actually early morning. They took you to a big Quonset hut and told you where you were going. Just boom, boom, boom, right down the line. A guy came up to a group of us and said we were going with the 9th Marines near the DMZ because "They're getting hit like crazy and they need new blood up there."

So it was like, "Grab your stuff, choppers are on their way to take you out there!" I'll tell you what, I was one scared son of a bitch at this point. They dropped us off at LZ Stud and now it's for real. We were up near a place they called "The Rock Pile" and not far from Khe Sanh, right along Highway 9.

When you get there, they don't really say too much. They just tell you to watch and learn. There's no training or anything. You just go out on patrols and learn as you go. When you get sniped at or get into the shit, you just react like everyone else. You learn on the job.

We spent the majority of the time in the bush. Patrolling one area after another, up one hill and down the other. We got sniped so many times that we stopped using trails and hacked our own trails through the jungle and elephant grass with machetes. I don't know how this happened, but we would take fire even when we were making our own trail. They still knew where we were going. I swear it seemed like there wasn't a day that went by that we didn't at least get sniped at. We couldn't figure it out. It wasn't until later on we realized it was from all the tunnels they had right underneath us.

You could never let your guard down. Where we were was a 360-degree free-fire zone so you had to remember where other units were too or who was around you.

April 21st, 1969 is the day we got hit real bad. We were walking up and down some hills around Dong Ha. The lead platoon was on its way up one side of the hill; we were still coming down the other. They needed a radioman for one of the squads. So my buddy Griff had to go and hook up with that other squad. That's when all the shit started. This was about nine in the morning. The side of the hill seemed to open up from above. When we got there everybody was going nuts shooting up into the hill. We started blasting away. It was crazy. You just kept shooting, but you couldn't see anything.

I looked to my right where one of my buddies was on the .60 and just like that his head was gone. I don't know what caliber he got hit with but it was just gone. Then the A gunner of the gun squad grabbed it and he's going bananas with it and boom just like that he got it in the head. So another buddy, we called Duck, grabbed it and he's going nuts, and then just like that the firing stopped. I looked and he was just sitting there. I went over there and he was like out of it or something. He had been shot in the femur of his left leg and I think he was in shock. So we carried him out of there. But he died before he got medevacked out that afternoon.

Then I saw Griff and there was blood all over his head and his face.

I figured he got shot in the head too, but it wasn't too bad. It looked worse than it was.

A guy named John was walking point when we got hit. He must have been shot ten or eleven times. The sarge told me to help carry him out. He was still alive, but stuff was hanging out of him and everything, bleeding like crazy as I was carrying him out. I still can't forget that.

The choppers didn't want to come in at first because it was still so hot, but then they came in and medevacked the wounded. They dropped off a platoon on the other side of the mountain to attack from that direction. Then after that, they came in and bombed the hell out of the hill. I want to say it wasn't until 3:30-4:00 in the afternoon before everything subsided.

When it was over we went around collecting weapons and everything and there are dead NVA bodies and pieces of bodies lying all over. We had to collect everything, all the bodies and stuff, and put them in a big pile and pour fuel oil on them and burn them.

That was probably one of the worst deals I was in. A lot of that day is still foggy. You remember flashes of it. Griff was okay. He had gotten hit in his forehead, but they patched him up and he was back with us in a week, week and a half maybe.

The point guy was alive when we got him to the medevac. I don't know if he made it. Once guys left you never really heard anything about them again. I don't know what it was like in other places, but unless you were shot up to the max and almost dead you're going to be coming back and that's that.

You know, you leave the farm or whatever and then you have a short leave, and the next thing you know you're in Vietnam, and then you're in something like this, deep in the shit and you're like "Wow." You learn in a really short time.

I spent most of my time in the A Shau Valley. We spent very little time at base camps. We were up north in the hills. The only people we dealt with were the Montagnards.

I was there a couple of months before I started walking point. My squad leader, who had been the main point man, was getting ready to rotate back to the states. He was on his second tour. He had been shot in the shoulder. He was a good guy. He came walking up to me one day and said, "Hey I'm getting short. I'm not walking point anymore. We need a new point man. That's you."

I said, "Hell with that, those guys get killed up there." He took his M-16, put it up to my head, and said, "Get walking."

When you're out there on patrol, especially when you're on point, you're all cranked up. You've got a lot of emotions going through you, just a lot of things going through your head. I bet on my first patrol it took me forty-five minutes to go fifty yards. You have, like a nine-point

Jack Shavlik (left) poses with an M-60 machine gun in Vietnam. (Jack Shavlik collection)

---

reference that you're checking on every step. You look way up in the center, to the left, to the right, then down to the ground left to right. You are a scared son-of-a-bitch when you start out. When you're walking, you feel like there's a big weight on your shoulders. You would be thinking, *I got about eighty people behind me depending on me. I can't screw up.* It's the fear of the unknown that really gets to you. What's out there? What are you walking into? You couldn't see two feet in front of you sometimes. You're hacking through the brush and you're looking for booby traps, looking for snipers, the whole deal.

After a while, hell, it's what you do. The walking comes easier. You're still scared, but you're so aware of your surroundings. That's what keeps you going. I think that helped me for the rest of my life, especially with riding motorcycles. Once you've walked point you're always on your toes so to speak.

The A Shau Valley was a heavily wooded area, thick jungle, really high jungle grass. We would be out there for weeks at a time. When we needed supplies we would have to clear out an area for the chopper to land or drop supplies. We'd always get C-rats, but we never got clothes or other stuff. You wore what you had on. I wore-out two pairs of boots,

I still got one pair that I snuck home with me. There's a hole in the bottom. I walked for a long time with my utilities ripped from the knees up to the crotch. I had jungle rot. You'd walk around like that. If you had to go to the head, you got off the trail and squatted and that was that. You get up and start moving again.

Mosquitos were nuts. Leeches, every time you stopped for the night you had to check yourself for them. You'd be walking through that elephant grass and some of it is six to ten feet tall. You walk through that during the monsoon season and they would be all over. You could never keep them off you no matter how tight you tied your boots or anything.

There was a lot of water in the mountains of the A Shau. Mountain streams and stuff. Some of them were pretty big. One time we're wading through water up to about our waists and this big black snake comes swimming right through us. I have no idea what it was, but it got my willies going. We couldn't shoot it because we were supposed to be silent.

There were a few different times we got ambushed in the A Shau. I was a walking point and a good buddy of mine, we called him Bull, we were pretty close friends, was right behind me. Over there you're not

Jack Shavlik (right), with his buddy in Vietnam, Bull. (Jack Shavlik collection)

supposed to get too close to anybody but you always had a couple of guys who became good friends. We were both car nuts and stuff. We always talked about going home and checking out all the cool cars they were coming out with back then. That's what kept us going.

They would always say to keep ten feet apart or whatever, but Bull was always only about five or six feet away. We were a good team, always in sync. Then all of a sudden he says, "Hit the deck!" We hit the deck and he started firing his M-79 with beehive rounds in the trees. A gook sniper fell out.

If they only had a couple of guys, they would sometimes wait until the point man went past before they opened up. That happened one time. They were in the jungle off to the side. I didn't see them. They stayed down until I passed through, then opened fire in the middle of our column. They didn't do too much damage because our gun-squad unloaded on them. It was over just like that. But that's the kind of stuff that can happen. You had no idea where they would pop up from. That's the unknown factor I was talking about that can really mess with you.

Another one, I had been walking for I don't know how long, but we stopped to take a quick break or something, and they decided to switch squads. A different squad took point. It wasn't, I would say, fifteen minutes later when the point guy who replaced me got shot twice.

That's just one of those close calls like you had over there. It should have been me on point. It bothered me, but you see and go through so much stuff that you couldn't dwell on everything. You get numb to it. After a while all you thought about was finding a way to survive. It was later on that your mind got messed up from keeping stuff in.

You just got so tired of humping all the time. I remember saying that if I got out of there, I wasn't going to walk more than fifty feet for the rest of my life. I would drive everywhere.

One night on Dong Ha mountain it was pouring rain and we were just miserable as you can be. We were supposed to be dug in, but you were so tired you just dug a little depression or something. If you got hit, you wished you had taken the time to dig deeper. But I was sleeping in this pouring rain and when they got me up for my watch, I was about twenty-five feet below where I started from. I was so tired that I stayed asleep as I slid down the side of the hill in the mud and rain.

***

My wife had our son in June of '69. I didn't hear about it until a week or so later. The LT (lieutenant) came up to me and said, "Your wife just had a kid." That's it, no feeling in what he said or anything,

So here I was, just a young dumb farm kid in Vietnam with a wife and kid back home. I had something to live for. I always thought about what I would do when I got home: get a job, work on cars for a living, buy a house, raise my family and be happy for the rest of my life. That's the kind of stuff you thought about. That's what kept you going. Go home and be happy. It's a good thing I didn't know it didn't always work out that way.

You needed to think of home to try and not think about the goofy stuff going around your head. Like, *What does it feel like to get shot? What's it going to be like if I get blown up? Will I feel it before I die?* You think about a lot of different things, but you don't dwell on it.

I wasn't the only guy who wanted out. One really hot day we were taking a break in the jungle grass. It was in the afternoon, just really sunny and hot as hell. All of a sudden we hear a "CRACK!" I had my pack on so I couldn't jump up. I had to roll over to see what was going on. One of the guys was sitting there and his leg was shaking. He had shot himself in the foot. He had just come back from R&R, saw his wife and everything. He said he wanted to go home. That's all he kept saying since he had gotten back. They medevacked him out. When I was on my way home I was in the chow hall in Okinawa and there's a group of prisoners going through the line. He was one of them. I talked to him. He said he got a dishonorable discharge, but he didn't care. He was out of Vietnam and would eventually be going home. He didn't care how long it took.

There was another day when one of our companies was near, I believe, Cam Lo when they got hit hard. I mean hard. They were between two mountains with a river running down below. They were following the river bank; which you should never do. The NVA were dug into the hills and just started shooting the hell out of them. We were back at LZ Stud. We were told to grab our stuff and go. We went out to the choppers, but they only brought us to within around three or four clicks from the fighting. We had to hump through the jungle to get to them. We were humping in the dark and the sky was all lit up from the firing and everything. You'd hear the fire, guys yelling, guys screaming. It was all echoing off the sides of the mountain. We're hearing all this as we are trying to get to them. It was freaking nuts. By the time we got there early in the morning, it was pretty well done. We got a few licks in here and there, but for the most part, it was over. There were so many dead and wounded lying around...it was just crazy. One guy was sitting on the ground, he was out of it. He'd lost his mind right there. One guy said it smelled like dope, that the NVA were all doped up and just kept coming at them.

I don't know why they dropped us off so far away. It was nuts trying to get to them and hearing everything going on.

They told us to go around and collect stuff. Just like after that first big fight that I was in around Dong Ha. I was so wound up from everything that when I went down to pick up something from the first dead enemy soldier that I grabbed a rock and smashed his head in.

I served my entire tour out in the bush and then got sent home. We had to spend a couple of days in Okinawa. I was in the mess hall and I saw a guy I thought I recognized. It was one of my DIs from San Diego. I went over and sat with him. I thought that was pretty cool. I told him all the training and crap he put us through definitely paid off.

When I got out of Nam, I flew to Los Angeles. I was proud to have my uniform on. I didn't know why people were looking at me the way they did. I'm walking proud and people are looking at you like you're a piece of crap. Somebody else gives me the finger. What the hell is going on?

My brother-in-law, Kenny, my sister, and my wife picked me up at the airport in Green Bay. It was so good to see them. The last time I saw my wife, in fact, the first time I had seen my son was during R&R in Hawaii. I figured all I had to do now was get a job and things would be great.

A few days after I got home, I went to have a beer at the Courthouse Bar in Manitowoc. I was in my uniform, still a proud Marine who went and did his thing for his country. All I wanted to do was have a beer. A guy at the bar started pissing me off. Saying this and that about the war and Vietnam vets and he wouldn't shut up.

We got into it and started to go outside. There were four or five steps going down to the outside doors. I dragged him down those stairs, got him outside, and started in on him. I took his face and smeared it across the bay window leaving a trail of blood and left him there.

That was the start of, I don't really know how to say it, but different things, bad things that would happen in my civilian life. All I wanted to do was have a couple of beers in my hometown and that had to happen.

I found a job as a grease monkey at a car dealership. I was happy as a pig in mud. I didn't stay very long at most jobs. I didn't communicate well with people. I had a lot of different jobs and also started up a custom motorcycle painting business on the side. Then I got into motorcycles and joined a club. That was my release, that became a big part of my life.

I just never thought in a million years that even though I was home, I would still eat, sleep and think about the war. I thought therapy was in a bottle and getting into fights.

It wasn't easy on my wife. Nam very much messed up my marriage. She was pretty understanding, but things were rocky at times. One thing I didn't realize is that Vietnam had taken over my life. I had lost my innocence so to speak. People who knew me said that I had changed, but I couldn't put my finger on it. When my wife came to Hawaii for R&R she was on the bus looking for me. She said she saw a guy walking down the street that looked like me, but it couldn't be me because he was smoking. She said she never thought she would see me smoke.

She told me years later that I was different when I got home, just different. We grew up in high school together with all this lovey-dovey stuff. I do remember that it was pretty hard saying goodbye when we were in Hawaii. I was going back to Vietnam and she was going back home to Whitelaw. I wanted to get on that plane with her. It was hard on her, hard on me too.

One time in the winter of 1975 we had a party in Green Bay for one of the guys who was joining the service. I got drunk and dumb. I told my wife she had to drive. We were driving out of town by Fleet Farm. The next thing I remember was cop and ambulance lights. I was thrown out of the car. My wife was killed.

I had a hard time handling it. I wasn't good at taking care of my son by myself. Most of the time her mom would take care of him and I would just leave. Just go, California, it didn't matter...just go.

I started spending most of my time with the club. Late summer of that same year, we all went to Hurley, Wisconsin. One night a guy from Illinois got into it with some of the bikers. The next day, we're coming up this hill and a big Cadillac coming from the other way swerves into us. I was in the front of the pack on the left side. I saw him turn towards us and instinctively drove into the shoulder. It may have been from being on point that got me to move so fast. He drove right into the middle of the pack. Five were killed, three others had legs cut off. That was Labor Day weekend 1975.

Now that I look back, even before the accidents, I had issues and I was the only person who didn't see it. I used to carry a sawed-off shotgun on my bike. I just had it sitting right in front. I lived on the edge so much, wired for sound as they would say. It's like I was running on an empty gas gauge and trying to see how far I could go. I thought some of the stuff I did was normal. Like the day at my shop in Kewaunee when I was doing something and the phone kept ringing so I grabbed the shotgun and blew the phone off the wall.

There were other times when I got home at 3:00 in the morning and I would take my dog that was half-shepherd and I swear half-wolf, and go on patrol in the woods behind my house. I would crawl through the weeds and woods with my .45 checking the perimeter. I'm not kidding you. I did a lot of crazy crap man.

Things kept getting progressively worse. I was going down for the count so to speak. I had a couple of good friends from another club who were veterans. Timmy, who had lost his leg in Vietnam, and another guy, MP we used to call him. He was at the Veterans Hospital in Tomah. They were two of the only guys I felt I could talk to about Vietnam. And that was usually only after we had had a few drinks.

MP called me from Tomah one day in the mid-'80s and said, "You need to come down here." I said, "What the hell for?" He said, "Because you're wacked out." I said, "There's nothing wrong with me, I'm still good." I thought it was all the people around me that were messed up. I drank a lot but I didn't really get into any of the other drugs some of the other guys were using. I was pretty naturally stimulated from my nerves being on edge all the time.

He finally convinced me. He was there for PTSD. He knew I was going down the wrong road and wouldn't stop without some help. I said, "I'll go as long as I can leave anytime I want because I ain't staying there against my will."

So I go down and meet with a doctor. I bet we didn't talk for ten minutes before he got up and said, "I'll be right back." The first thing I did was jump out of my chair and made sure that the door didn't lock behind him.

When he came back he said, "We need to admit you." I said, "Not today, I got too much stuff to do back at my shop." He said they would put my file on a list and call me when there was an opening. They told me it would be at least three to four weeks before I would get a call.

I told MP what the deal was and went home. A couple of days later I got a call. They said there was a spot for me. As it turned out, MP and some guys got into the office one night where they kept the files and put mine up near the top.

All the guys at Tomah were in different stages. It was almost like Nam. Some guys would be short, others just FNGs, others halfway through. But we were all together in groups. At first I didn't say a word in the meetings, not a word for weeks. I didn't think I would be there long. As it turned out I stayed for over three months.

Doctor Palmer was the guy who worked with us. He was one of the leading guys in the country in treating PTSD. Our meeting room was set up just like a hootch. He wanted to bring you back to situations that were causing you problems in your head.

You would actually find out what's cooking in your mind. They connect the dots on why you might have done the things you did. It's like chasing your fears. They make you dig so deep you realize more happened than you really thought. You had put it on the back burner and tried to forget about it. Nobody wanted to know anything when you came back and you didn't feel comfortable talking about it even if they did. The first question someone would ask was, "How many people did you kill?" That's the last thing you wanted to talk about.

The big thing is that I finally found people I could trust. There were a couple of guys in the club you could talk to about some things, but mostly I kept everything that happened over there bottled up inside me. Well, at Tomah I spent a lot of time just listening, listening to some crazy stuff that these guys went through. It probably took about a month before I said anything. After hearing some of those stories, I thought, *Well maybe I can trust these guys, maybe I can let some stuff out.*

For me, the one situation I really had to get out was the night we humped all night, hearing the fighting taking place and trying to get to it and by the time we got there it was pretty much over. That's the day I lost it with the rock and the NVA soldier. I kept asking why? *Why didn't the choppers bring us closer so we could have done something?* You see all that carnage and you feel like you should have been there to help. That's what Marines do. You felt so frustrated. You just lose it. You want to kill them all over again. There were so many times you felt that way. You just started to get numb to everything. You had to.

I remember he had me talk about the day at Dong Ha. He had a blackboard set up and everything I mentioned he would have me draw it on the board. It didn't matter if it was stick people, or whatever, anything to bring out every detail. Stuff like what time of day it was, how hot was it, where were your buddies? Every detail. It got to the point where you were so focused on remembering everything and bringing it out that you didn't even realize there were other guys in the room anymore. You didn't even see them. You were just back to that day. It's like you could actually see it as it was happening. Just vivid. That's when I started getting it all out. You can't believe the stuff guys talk about. But it helped, at least it did for me.

When I got remarried, my wife Chris had two boys and I had my son. I told Chris I didn't want to have kids because we had started to hear about Agent Orange and I didn't want to pass anything on. Well, she said we were having a kid. That turned out to be our son, Bob. He has some health problems, which we believe are Agent Orange-related. But we are super close and he is such a super dad to his daughter, Abby. I didn't do a lot of things with the kids like I should have. He takes care of his kids like I wish I would have taken care of mine.

Growing up in my house was crazy at times, to say the least. But I will say this, my family learned a lot about respect, honor, love of country and to never forget all those who died in war, and also to never forget your family and friends. Those are the people who count.

I lost my first son, Steve, in 1996. It was the same date, June 19th, that my good Marine buddy, Jim Ahrens, died in Vietnam. I'm just so thankful for Chris, for dealing with all the stuff I did and doing what needed to be done to keep us going. We get along so good it makes my head swim. I'm just so lucky and happy that she is in my life.

I still work on street rods and custom painting bikes. One cool thing was that in 1995 a chopper (motorcycle) was built to donate to the Vietnam Veterans Wall in Washington, D.C. I went to a meeting and asked

Jack and Chris Shavlik pose with the motorcycle he custom-painted and was displayed at the Vietnam Veterans Memorial Wall in Washington, D.C. (Jack Shavlik collection)

Jack Shavlik details a motorcycle that is now property of the National Archives of the Smithsonian Institute and National Parks Service. (Jack Shavlik collection)

if they had picked somebody to custom paint it. They said they were still looking at bids. Some people were looking to get paid to work on it. I said, "Bids hell, I'd be proud to paint it for free." It meant a lot to me personally.

They shipped it up to my shop in Oconto in a specialized truck. They had something like a one-million-dollar insurance policy on it. After I finished, it was put on display at the Wall to honor Vietnam Vets who were killed. It's now the property of the National Archives of the Smithsonian Institute and National Parks Service. It's kind of a cool deal that my family has seen it there.

Mike Berzinsky with a Montegnard crossbow

MIKE BERZINSKY

299th Battalion, 18th Engineer Brigade
US Army, Vietnam War

"It was the summer of 1967 and I knew I was going to get drafted sooner or later. So I thought if I signed up I would have a better chance of beating them to the punch. I was a big fan of the old TV show called Sea Hunt when I was growing up and I wanted to be in underwater demolitions. My recruiter said, 'Absolutely, no problem. Just sign right here. There will be a class starting the day you finish basic.' Blah, blah, blah. He lied from the minute I walked through the door, but you didn't know any different. – Mike Berzinsky

When I signed up I was working at the Mirro plant in Manitowoc, (Wisconsin). I went to Milwaukee and took my physical. I wore big, Coke-bottle type glasses at the time. That immediately eliminated me from any chance of getting into any type of underwater program. The recruiter must have forgot to mention that to me. So here I am, eighteen years old and my head is spinning. What do I do now? Somebody mentioned combat engineer. I always wanted to learn how to operate heavy equipment and all that stuff; so I thought that sounded cool.

Most people probably would have killed for my first job, stationed in Germany. I loved it there. Who would ever want to leave that beautiful country, right? But after a few months I thought, "Well crap, I want something more to do." So I signed a 1049 for a transfer and within a month I was on my way to Vietnam.

They let me come home on a thirty-day leave and I wasn't even concerned that in a few weeks I would actually be in Vietnam. I really didn't even know what Vietnam was all about to be honest with you. I mean, I know a couple of people from the class a year behind me had been killed, but I didn't really comprehend the whole picture. I was a young kid. When you're that age, nothing phases you. In fact, I think I was actually excited, like, "Hey I'm going to Vietnam. I'm going to fight a war!"

That didn't last long.

Mike Berzinsky mans a guard tower in Vietnam. (Mike Berzinsky collection)

I started in Cam Ranh Bay. There was a big reception center, and every morning all the guys who had just come in would attend formation where they would call your name and tell you where you're going. All I really remember was hearing my name and the word, "Pleiku." Somebody said it was up in the mountains. It didn't really mean anything to me, never heard of it.

I get to Pleiku and the same thing - reception center, wait for your name to be called. I hear my name and the guy says, "You're going to Dak To with the 299th Engineer Battalion." There were a couple of short-timers there, and they kind of laughed and rolled their eyes and said, "Nice knowing you."

By then I was starting to get scared. I'll be honest with you, I started getting nervous right when I got off the plane at Cam Ranh Bay. That's where I first saw caskets being loaded onto a plane. All that excitement and big talk back in Manitowoc on my leave was gone. Now I'm worried.

They loaded about fifteen of us in the back of a deuce-and-a-half truck to drive us from Pleiku to Dak To. We had no weapons, no equipment, no helmets, no armament, nothing. It's about a three-hour drive through the mountains and jungle. Now I was scared shitless. The driver and the guy sitting next to him had weapons, but nobody else did. I just kept thinking, *If we get attacked, we don't have a chance. They will take us out like nothing. That will be it, all over.* I was a happy guy when we pulled into Dak To. I thought, *Well, OK. We made it. Things should be OK now.* This was January of 1969.

The first couple months were actually really nice. I worked in the motor pool, ran convoys once in a while, went out on minesweeper missions, things like that. It stayed that way until April. We started getting a few rockets, some mortars. Then it started getting a little worse.

We still weren't too worried. We still had infantry support from the 4th Infantry Division. Then they pulled the 4th out and replaced them with an ARVN unit (Army of the Republic of Vietnam). Now we started to get worried. The unit they sent us was completely useless. They brought their families in with them. It was just terrible.

This was in May of '69, and up until then, except for those few rockets and mortars, everything was pretty calm. Now things have changed. We started getting ground assaults. It seemed like almost every night they would probe the perimeter. They got inside, I don't know how many times. And then they started bringing the heavy stuff, 122mm rockets – six feet long and 122 millimeters in diameter.

All they did was prop them up on a tripod somewhere in the jungle and fire them like a giant bottle rocket. You would hear the "whoosh" when it was fired, then a "thump, thump." If you were on guard duty in the main tower looking out into the jungle, you could see a puff of smoke. You could see them coming in. In fact, there were times when I would get my camera ready and follow them in, hoping to get a picture just when they hit.

We had dug holes, like little foxholes, to jump into and take cover when you heard them coming. But after a few weeks, I didn't worry about it anymore. What was the point? They weren't aiming at you. They just fired the damn things. So if you were going to get hit, you were going to get hit. That was my attitude; which I realize now was really stupid. But that's just what I did. I don't know why I did it, but instead of jumping in a hole I walked around with my camera taking pictures.

There was an outdoor shower close to my hootch. I was in there one day and I heard a rocket coming in. I didn't think anything of it at first. Then I thought, *OK, that one sounds like it's heading this way.* So I wrapped a towel around myself, ran, and just as I jumped in a hole, the rocket hit the shower. That's when it finally hit me that this wasn't good. This wasn't a good situation we were in. But it gets to that point where you just don't care. It's just easier to not worry about everything going on around you. People talk about that "thousand-yard stare." We had it. We all did. Because it was every single day and it just takes a toll.

When sappers got in the perimeter, they would have explosive charges and satchel charges on them. A few were suicide attacks with everything strapped to their bodies. They tried to kill as many guys as they could. It seemed like that was their main mission. One night they blew up the mess hall. Another night they hit the motor pool and tried to blow up all the trucks. They set charges around the guard tower at least once. It didn't seem like they had one specific target, really. They just wanted to destroy and kill anybody they could.

There were a number of times they tried to probe the bunker I was in. You would just start shooting and try to keep them from coming in any closer. The ground assaults were almost always at night. They rarely hit during the day. Once in a while they would probe, but during the day we had air support from gunships. Inside, we had gun trucks with quad .50-calibers on them.

We would still call in air support at night, but it was harder for them to target the enemy troops. We would call in strikes all around our perimeter. Sometimes we would call in our favorite gunship, *Spooky*. That was cool. You would see a line of tracers that flowed to the ground. It was pretty amazing.

Depending on the night, there were always three or four of us in the guard bunker. Our front window view was Cambodia and Laos. That is where we were. You would pull a two-hour shift and then you would sleep. Believe it or not, it got to where if you weren't on duty, you could sleep through a rocket attack.

A mess hall shows the effects of a sapper attack. (Mike Berzinsky collection)

This guard tower was a frequent target of attacks by the North Vietnamese Army (NVA) and Viet Cong. (Mike Berzinsky collection)

Generally, when they would attack you would hear the shooting right away because it was a small base. You would immediately grab your weapon. We had a .60-cal on my tower most of the time. We also had M-14s. We didn't have M-16s; which I'm thankful for because they were garbage in the beginning. You would just man your weapon and start shooting because you didn't really know what was happening. You might hear it way off in the distance, but that didn't mean they weren't creeping up to your position.

They would be firing B-40 rockets and RPGs (rocket-propelled grenades). They would use those on the bunkers mostly. It got to the point where you were just comfortable pulling the trigger and shooting. You didn't really see anybody, but you figured somebody was out there. We had a couple of night vision scopes, but they didn't work that well. So you just fired off as many rounds as you could: machine guns, M-14s, M-79 grenade launchers, a bunch of different weapons. We even had some AK-47s that we used.

There was a unit of the Fifteenth Engineers who were attached to us. They had an underground command center. One night, a 122mm rocket went right down the steps into the bunker. It was a freak shot that couldn't happen again in a million years. It killed the company commander, 1st sergeant, operations sergeant, company clerk, communications guy, and a reaction force.

This was early in the siege. I know that because it was during the time when I was still scared.

There was one night we were up in the tower firing and I saw a B-40 rocket heading toward us. I could see the sparks trailing it. I was firing right in that direction and I'm thinking, *"OK I'm dead. I'm dead."* There were three of us up here firing and I expected us all to be killed. We kept firing and nothing happened. We just kept firing. The next day we did an inspection and here's that rocket embedded in the sandbags. It could have taken off the top of the bunker and killed us like nothing; they were that powerful. We were standing about fifteen feet up and that thing hit at about twelve feet. I close my eyes today and can still watch it coming towards us like it was yesterday.

There was another group of guys up there who weren't so lucky. One night a sapper came in and threw a satchel charge on top of the bunker. It killed everybody inside. We had to go up there the next day. They were blown to pieces. There were body parts everywhere.

Every single day on that base, I thought to myself, *Well okay, this could be the day. This could be it.* You just accepted that you weren't getting out of Vietnam; that it was not going to happen. You didn't know exactly when, but you were all going to die and you stopped giving a crap about it.

Even with all this going on, the road projects didn't stop. We just had to be a little more cautious. Our responsibility was to keep the road open between Dak To and Ben Het; which was about seven miles away and where a Special Forces camp was situated. This was right in the middle of the Ho Chi Minh Trail. There were bridges on that road that the enemy would destroy constantly and we would have to rebuild. They mined the roads almost every night. We ran convoys, basically a supply chain of men and supplies, between Dak To and Kontum.

It was frustrating as hell. The minesweeping team would clear the mines and the convoy would run. They would put in new mines as soon as the convoy was gone. The convoy would do their mission, turn around and head back, and "Boom!" they would get hit.

Without the 4th Division there, everybody had to do a little bit of everything. It didn't matter that your classification was Engineer. You couldn't depend on the ARVN unit we had for protection. I worked in the motor pool working on equipment. Then I would go out on minesweeping missions. That was dangerous work, but again, we just accepted it as part of our job. We had a reactionary force set up where if there was an ambush or a problem on the road, we would send out what basically amounted to a rescue team. I was on that team and there was a time where the minesweeping team got ambushed. They had some ARVNs for security, but as soon as the ambush hit the ARVNs ran and left our guys out there like sitting ducks.

Two of our guys were killed immediately and the rest were pinned down. Within fifteen minutes we were on the road. When we got to about a mile of the ambush site, there were the ARVNs huddled in a ditch. We were pissed when we saw that, really pissed. We still didn't know what was happening. We got to the sweeper team and we got pinned down. So we hit the ditch and started firing back. Air support was called in and they brought a gun truck up. After a while the firing slacked off.

We started heading back to Dak To with some wounded guys in the truck and the company commander said to stop the convoy. He said, "Where are the bodies?" The two guys killed had been left lying along the road. That can't happen. So the captain said we need some guys to go back and get them. I'm thinking, *I hope it's not me.* And he points, "Brezinsky, Sheets, come with me. We're going back to pick up the bodies." And I'm like, "Captain, what do you mean? Can't we take the truck?" And he said, "No because they would just blow it up and we can't afford to lose it."

I took my helmet and flak jacket off. I could never run in those things, although I knew one well-placed bullet could kill me, and we started running back to the bodies. We started getting shot at. So we're running and shooting and diving in the ditch, and getting up and running some more. We get to the bodies and it dawns on me, *How in*

Under attack, Vietnamese huddle as one GI fires and another (foreground) loads

This Life Magazine photo shows South Vietnamese military (ARVNs) refusing to fight.

Mike Berzinsky (front center, without helmet) is shown in this Life Magazine photo after picking up American GIs killed in an ambush.

the hell are we supposed to carry them back? The captain says, "Give me your rifles!" We each gave him our M-14s and started picking up the bodies. The one I picked up had his chest blown away. The guy my buddy picked up, his head was basically gone. So we picked them up and started carrying them back, kind of half-assed running and carrying them, scared out of our minds. They're still shooting at us. How they missed I do not know. They must have thought we were nuts. We got about a quarter mile back and somebody had decided to hell with it, "Let's go out there with the truck and pick them up."

That was a bad day. I was so scared going back there and trying to carry him back that I couldn't even think.

We didn't know it at the time, but there was a photographer from *LIFE* magazine in one of the vehicles and he wrote an article on the ARVNs hiding, cowering under fire. My picture ended up in the magazine. It was the September 19, 1969 issue.

When we got back to base, I was covered in blood. Afterward, I puked. I don't know what you call it, nerves, or being scared or what it was, but I just got sick to my stomach and then drank myself into a stupor. There were a lot of things that happened with ground attacks and rocket attacks and stuff, but that was actually the first time I had ever touched a dead body. You would see them on the roadside from mines and dead NVA all the time, but that was the first time I actually touched one. That affected me. I drank until I passed out, and then got up the next morning and went back to work. I was miserable.

By early July, things were starting to quiet down somewhat. Now, we didn't know this at the time, we found out about this years later, but we were surrounded. There had been a plan for us to leave, to move to Qui Nhon - which we eventually did, but much later - and have the ARVNs take over. Just one problem with that plan, the ARVNs weren't going to do it. They knew they would be slaughtered if they were there by themselves.

So the powers that be decided we would stay and defend the base. This is what we heard forty years later at our reunions.

Once we got word we were staying, they started bringing in more ammunition and more supplies; so we realized we were gearing up for a fight. But again, they never told us we were surrounded. We just thought it was normal day-to-day life, being rocketed and probed.

The thing we all can't figure out, and we also talk about this at the reunions, is why didn't they go ahead and try to overrun us? They could have done it anytime. We were pulling rounds out of machine-gun belts for our M-14s. We only had a few machine guns on base. We had to rotate them around. That's how scarce they were. We weren't a combat unit. We were engineers. We didn't have the weaponry of an infantry company.

Now I will say this, we had bunkers every twenty feet or so. I mean, we had bunkers between bunkers and they were manned 24/7. We also wondered if they were afraid of our air support. Those planes pounded the hills around us relentlessly. But just with the sheer manpower they could have thrown at us, there's no question they would have overrun us if they really wanted to.

There were thousands and thousands of enemy troops that passed through that area on the Ho Chi Minh Trail. One thing they really hated was the Special Forces camp at Ben Het. Those Special Forces guys were a different breed. Living out there on their own in primitive conditions, with just some Montagnards around them. The NVA wanted to knock them off, but those guys just hung on. They were like a bunch of dirty ruffians and also a little crazy. And I mean that in the best way possible. You had to be a little bit off to live the way they did.

But you know, once you've gone through a year in Vietnam with the things you had to do, it changes you. I wasn't the same person when I got back in 1970 and I'm still not the same person I was before I went there. You didn't realize this was going to happen, but Vietnam would never leave you. You try to focus on other things, but it always comes right back.

I guess I didn't expect the anger that awaited us. We had some replacements come in before we left for home and they told us to be prepared for a different country than the one we left. They told us some things and that got us mad as hell, but nothing compared to what we saw when we actually got here.

I couldn't believe it. Sitting at home, I was watching the news and these demonstrators in Madison were waving the North Vietnam flag. I got so angry. So angry. I went to sit in on a VFW meeting in 1971, and they introduced me and someone stood up and said, "We don't want any drug addicts or baby killers in here!" People think that's one of those old wives' tales, but it's true. It happened to me.

I started doing what so many Vietnam vets did to cope, drink heavily. We all thought it would help, but that just made it worse. I drank very heavily for ten years. It definitely affected my marriages. I've been married four times. When we go back to reunions, you will hear guys talking about how many times they've been married. And you will hear them, "Five, three, four." And almost everyone will admit it was drinking that caused many of their problems.

Drinking seemed like our only option. You didn't really hear about counseling or anything like that back then. Nobody wanted to hear about your problems. I worked for Budweiser beer for thirty years and I think the only people who knew I was a Vietnam vet were other Vietnam vets. You just didn't even mention it to others.

I meet with a group at the VA Center in Green Bay once a month. It's just combat vets; so you don't have to be careful about what you say or what you talk about. It's nice being in a room of guys just like yourself. We all know exactly where each other is coming from. That's helpful. I come out of there feeling good. I wish I could say I've learned to totally forgive and forget the way so many people of our generation turned on us, but I have to be honest. I just can't. I would say I'm still a work in progress, but I've also accepted the way I am.

The motto of the Vietnam Vets of America is never again will one generation of veterans abandon another. We will not allow that to happen. We will welcome them home the way they deserve to be welcomed. These kids coming home today from the Middle East ... ahhh, I shouldn't call them kids. They just seem so young, but I guess they're the same age as we were right? Hard to believe. Anyway, I know I wouldn't want to do what they've had to do. For one thing, all that gear they have to wear. I can't imagine walking around in that heat in all that sort of stuff. I can show you pictures of us, we didn't have shirts on, no helmets. That's the way we lived. But these poor guys and women with the IEDs (improvised explosive devices) and roadside bombs and stuff. To me, they have it worse than we did. But we will make damn sure they will have it better when they come home.

CLYDE "BLACKIE" ROSIN

1st Air Cavalry
Americal Division
US Army
Vietnam War

After graduating from Wrightstown (Wisconsin) High School in 1966, Clyde "Blackie" Rosin got a job working at Bellin Hospital in Green Bay as an orderly. After getting married in February of 1968, he assumed he was exempt from the draft. However, in April of 1968 he received a letter from the President of the United States. He jokes that he hoped it was a letter to Lucy Bird's wedding. He was wrong.

So I got drafted, went through boot camp, and was designated 11-Bravo, infantry. We were about halfway through Advanced Infantry Training at Fort Polk, Louisiana, when a buddy and I looked at each other and said, "This really sucks." I told him I used to work in a hospital and was going to see if that would help get me out of the infantry. I went to the 1st sergeant, he said if I could get two registered letters from the hospital I worked at, that he could get me into a new unit. So I got word to my wife, who was a nursing student at Bellin at the time and she got me the letters. Two days later the 1st sergeant pulled me out of formation and said to report to his office. He said, "I got your MOS changed; you are now 91 Alpha 10." I said, "What's that?" He said, "Combat infantry medic." I thought, *Oh boy you did it now; you just dug yourself an even deeper hole.*

So, I get reassigned, finish my schooling, get a thirty-day leave, and then head to the swamp. When the plane landed in Vietnam a lieutenant colonel came aboard. He said, "I want all the 91 Alpha 10s to stand up." There were only two of us. The other guy was 6'2. I'm 5'7 and I remember thinking to myself, *God buddy, you're going to make a pretty good target.*" As we were getting off the plane I turned to the guy and said, "Hi, I'm Claude from Wisconsin. He said, "I'm Craig from Florida." We hopped in the back of the old man's jeep. He took us to the end of the tarmac where a couple of Hueys were idling. He yelled at us at the top of his lungs, "Pick one. It doesn't matter which one. The odds are you will be dead within thirty days anyway!"

The chopper didn't even land when they took me to my unit. They just dumped me off about six feet off the ground. The first man I met wasn't wearing a shirt. He had muscles popping out all over and he was carrying a sawed-off 870 Remington pump shotgun. He had the most gravelly voice I had ever heard. He said, "Welcome to the 1st squad of the 1st Armored Cavalry, the most battle-honored unit in the United States Army." I thought, *Oh boy, here we go.* He said, "I hope you're the new Doc." I said, "Yup." He said, "Good we lost three medics in two weeks." Dumb-ass me, the new guy, trying to be funny, asks, "Are you looking for them?" He looks right at me right in my eyes and goes, "No, they're dead!"

He told me to go over to this other guy to get squared away. It was a skinny guy with a bandana around his head. He said, "Are you the new Doc?" I said, "Yea." He said, "Are you a conscientious objector?" I said, "Nope, you shoot at me and I will shoot back." He offered his hand and said, "I'm Chuck, from Texas. Welcome aboard."

That's how it began. I was now the medic for Charlie Troop, First Squad, 1st Armored Cavalry. We went out on missions in APCs and tanks. I remember heading out on the very first one. My legs were dangling off the side and Chuck said, "Don't do that Doc, you should keep your feet up. Otherwise, if we hit a mine, they will get blown off." That was my first indoctrination to Vietnam.

I was in charge of the other two medics from Bravo and Alpha companies. They were great guys; they were always volunteering to go out on missions on their own. We were in I Corps up near the DMZ. In that zone there was the 196th Light Infantry Brigade, the 11th Infantry Brigade, and bits and pieces of some Marine units. When those ground pounders got pinned down, you went. Day or night it didn't matter. But I'll tell you, going down Highway 1, there was a definite pucker factor heading out there.

I remember the first guy I ever bandaged, a soldier from Alabama named Wesley. I used every bandage I had in my medical bag, got him out of there on a dust-off. He was bleeding all over the place; his legs, his stomach, his face, he looked like a sieve. Twenty years later my son bought me a book of all the names on the Wall in Washington. I looked for his name, he wasn't there. I thought, *What the hell. How did they miss his name?* I went to our reunion next year and there he was.

Blackie Rosin collection

I remember almost all of them. George from Tennessee, I pulled him out of an APC. He got hit by an RPG that landed right behind the driver's hatch. He had shrapnel all in his neck and stuff like that.

Then there's Wally from Connecticut. He hit two mines. I could go on and on, but the reason it's hard to talk about this is that I can't remember the guys on the Wall. The guys I couldn't save. My wife always found that ironic. She'd say, "It's like you're trying to forget, but yet on the other hand you're trying hard as hell to remember." She'd say, "You want to forget because you couldn't save them, but you remember the guys you bandaged up that turned out okay." I think she was probably right.

It was different bandaging up a friend versus some kid you didn't know. Your emotions get into it more. Sometimes you're trying so hard that you think you screwed up, but you had to treat everyone the same. The bottom line was trying to keep them alive long enough to get them to the next stop.

People ask why medics got hit so often. It's because if you were a good medic, you were also a dumb-ass who, when somebody yelled for you, you got up and went running to him no matter what was going on. Guys always say, "You spent your entire war trying to save guys." But that worked both ways. There were times when you would run into the crap and find the guy who got hit, and you might not have enough supplies to take care of him. So you would have to try and carry him back. As soon as guys saw that they would jump up, run over, and help carry the guy. The guys knew I had their backs and I knew they had mine. That's what it was all about, simple as that. To hell with the President, the commanding officer...none of them mattered. We were all there for each other.

The crazy thing, as much as you tried to anticipate what might happen, it never worked out the way you expected. We had this one guy, crazy as hell. He must have gotten four or five medals for bravery. He would jump off the back of the APC and he wouldn't know if he had one round in his rifle or a full clip, but he would crawl in tunnels; he would do every damn thing. When the shit hit the fan you wanted to crawl in his back pocket. He never got so much as a scratch on him.

Then on the other hand, my buddy and I were outside of our bunker one night when a 122mm rocket came in. You could hear it coming, *Okay, no sweat.* We could tell it was going to miss us, but not by much. "BOOM!" It went off. *Holy Christ that was close!* I turned to say something to my buddy and he was on the ground. *What the hell? I wasn't hit. How could he have been?* I looked and looked and looked all over his body ... nothing. His hair was a little longer than any of us and I finally saw this little bit of blood seeping out from under his hair. It had gone right into his brain and killed him instantly. It was probably the size of a piece of lead from a number two pencil.

Guys reacted in different ways when they were hit. I've seen guys who were hit pretty good and didn't even know it. They just keep firing. The battle is over and they realize they were bleeding like a stuck pig. Other guys seemed to know as soon as they were hit that they weren't going to make it. I would always tell them, "It isn't that bad...you're going to make it home." They might have their guts hanging out, but you never ever told them anything other than they were going to be okay. They would be like, "Tell my mom I love her..." and I would be like, "You ain't gonna die ... you ain't gonna die!" But then a few minutes later he would be gone. It ran the whole gamut. There isn't a day that goes by that I don't think of it. That's why I go speak at schools. So they know about these things firsthand.

We would have to do a mine sweep of the roads every morning. I had a real character in my squad, big guy, half-Hispanic, half-Native American. He would get impatient with the Marines who were using the old-fashioned hand-held minesweepers. If it was real hot, he would tell everybody to get off his tank and onto mine. Then he would tell the Marines to get the hell out of his way because his beer was getting warm. He would gun his tank straight down the middle of the road a mile or two, turn around and come back. If he didn't hit anything, we knew the road was clean. He went through two tanks in the time he was with us.

One time we were in a place called Cigar Island. It was just off the mainland, pure white sand. One morning there he took off, probably didn't go 300-400 yards from the perimeter and he hit a buried napalm bomb. The VC would find our bombs that landed in the swamp and didn't explode. They would hump them for miles, then set up their

Blackie Rosin's unit following the discovery of Viet Cong weapons and suspects. (Blackie Rosin collection)

---

detonator with a little piece of bamboo and a 9-volt battery. When the bamboo got compressed, she lit up. Well, here he comes walking out of the tank. The tank is burning; .50-caliber rounds are cooking off. It sounded like a popcorn machine. He goes, "Hey Doc, you got your camera? Bring it here!" I'm thinking, *Now what?* He had crawled under the burning tank, found that damned detonator, and wanted me to take a picture of him holding it. Our captain told him if he did that crap again, he would be buying his own tank.

There was a time when the ARVNs got overrun so we were sent down to where they were. By the time we got there the VC were starting to retreat, but the air cover and Loch helicopters caught them and cut them off. We went in like a cavalry charge from the 1800s. Guns were blazing. You're firing the .50-cal until the barrel turns almost white. The driver reaches back with an asbestos glove, screws off the barrel and shoves a new one in, cock it, and you're ready to go again. It gets so intense that there's nothing else on your mind. You don't think of home. You don't think of dying...nothing.

The worst times were when they tried coming through the wire. On this particular night I had just walked over to have a beer with a friend of mine from Charlie Troop. All of a sudden a trip flare went up in the wire about 300 yards away. Well you hoped to hell it was some kind of animal, but you knew better, and then it started. My buddy Wilson was on the tank next to me and I crawled up on another one. I see Wilson shooting away, and everything is lit up like daylight from the flares. There was a VC running at him, couldn't have been more than twenty yards away, and that .50-cal just blew his head right off. This guy was still running and firing his AK-47, and didn't know he was already dead.

Then the flares went out and they were running all over the place. You can't see shit and you're bumping into guys. You don't know if they're your guys or not. The only way you can tell that it ain't your buddy is from the smell. Different things like that you can't forget.

All you're taught about times like this is to keep going until someone yells halt or cease-fire or something. There's a lot I can't remember about that night, whether bandaging someone up or killing somebody, my mind won't let me remember. Maybe I just don't want to.

The one thing I do remember. I asked for a cigarette, but I couldn't keep the cigarette between my fingers. Finally, somebody had a Zippo lighter. I looked down, I had so much blood on my hands that the cigarette kept sliding out. That's when I really started to shake. The 1st sergeant lost an eye that night. A lieutenant lost an arm. It gets goddamned hairy awfully quick. The Fallstaff beer wasn't strong enough anymore. Everybody went through the Jack Daniels they had stashed away.

Blackie Rosin poses with a captured rocket. (Blackie Rosin collection)

***

I honestly think my post-war problems started when the wheels left the ground on my flight home. I had a friend I had met by the name of Mickey. He was in the infantry and one time we ran into each other when rounds were coming in and he still wanted to stand and BS. Well, we went home on the same day. We left Cam Ranh Bay and landed in Guam. You could buy four to five quarts of booze for a pittance. We brought it on the plane and the stewardess said we weren't allowed to open it. Okay fine. Then a Marine with a lot of stripes got up on the intercom and said, "If you have booze, go ahead and open it. What are they going to do, send you to Vietnam?"

It was interesting when I came home. My dad's dad was still alive. We sat under a big oak tree in the yard. Grampa and I sat out there all night. He had his case of Rahr's beer and Four Roses whiskey. I had Jack Daniels and Pabst Blue Ribbon. The next morning Ma and Pa went to milk the cows and there were Grampa and me still sitting there. That's when my Ma first knew there was going to be a problem.

The first Sunday I go to church with Ma and Pa in my full uniform. We sit in the front row. Some kid drops some coins on the tile floor while putting them into the collection basket. The first thing that flashed in my mind was the sound of a spoon of a Chinese Chi-Com grenade coming off. I don't remember who I hit on the left, but I hit someone on the right...I was ready to go underneath the bench. You were so accustomed to reacting to sounds. Because over there if you stopped to think about what the sound was, you could be dead in that span of time. It's a learning experience. Like Pa always said, "You learn until they close the lid."

I got a job driving a milk truck. I picked up the milk at 5:30 in the morning, worked for twelve to fourteen hours, and didn't have to talk to anybody. The next morning I was gone again. My wife said if I didn't have something like that, I probably would have blown my brains out. But that's when the real drinking started. You'd stop at the tavern just for a little while. Then it wasn't just a little while. You stayed and stayed and stayed. When it came time to pick up the milk the next morning you were suffering. You would put your head up against the cold steel of the truck and say you would never do that again. But you did.

One night I must have had some bad dreams. Somehow my wife got me awake. But in my mind, I was fighting hand-to-hand-combat. I never really thought Vietnam led to my drinking problems, but to this day I still wake up in a cold sweat sometimes. You didn't really think about a lot of things when you were over there. It wasn't until you got home and had lots of time to think about what went on over there. When you were there the only thing you ever thought about was keeping your head out of your ass.

My wife was my crutch. I was married thirty-seven years, seven months, six days, and twelve hours. She was an RN and had worked in psych wards and stuff so she had a real good idea of some of the things I was going through. She came to the reunions, talked to the other wives, and listened to their stories. She got it. But after she died I started drinking hard again. Different people would take my friends

Blackie Rosin's armored personnel carrier (APC) burns after hitting a land mine. (Blackie Rosin collection)

aside; "Hey you've got to get this guy some help." They could see it.

One of my friends told me, "Come on, we're going to see a counselor." I ended up finding a good one, an ex-cop who had had guys killed around him. It took going to this counseling before I accepted that my drinking problems were tied to Vietnam. You see guys die. You save guys. It was what you did. But no matter how hard they try to train somebody, nothing prepares you for real war. How devastating it is, the cost of it…the mangled bodies, the burned bodies. Nobody had a cure for what you would go through when you got back. After World War II people were like, "Oh that's just battle fatigue. He'll get over it." Bullshit. Some of those old boys hit the bottle hard right up until the very end.

I had a buddy I was with over there. He visited us here at our house. We were sitting outside and my mom asked him, "What did you think of my son?" He got out of his lawn chair, stood right in front of her, saluted her, and said, "Mrs. Rosin, we didn't think the little bastard would make it out of there alive. I saw tracer rounds go between his legs." She never asked another question. Matter of fact other than my son, none of my family really asked too much about what happened over there.

I got hit a couple of times … two Purple Hearts. Both times from shrapnel. I still have some in me. Before my son got married my wife made me get some taken out of my forehead. I still have some in my head, my arm, my nose. Other pieces were taken out of my chest, my back, and my elbow.

I've never told anyone about the Silver Star I got. The only person I told vaguely was my dad. I tell them all, "When I'm dead you will find out." All I will say is that a lot of innocent people died that day, and you wonder if you did everything you could. I do think I saved a lot of lives that day, but that's all I'm going to say while I'm alive.

When I speak at high schools and kids ask me about what it was like to go to war, I look them right in the eye and tell them, "You get drafted, from the day you set foot over there you realize you are probably going to be dead within 365 days." There's no other way of putting it. One day you're a happy-go-lucky kid going to beer parties in your '66 Oldsmobile, and the next day, "Welcome to Vietnam boys." It was a rude awakening.

People have asked me what I appreciate about life after having been over there. I tell them, just life in general. I shared the ultimate experience with my buddies, death. Not sure anything will make you appreciate every day more than that.

Bill and Kathy Enz

BILL ENZ

10th Cavalry
Regiment
4th Infantry
Division
US Army
Vietnam War

It's interesting how often Vietnam veterans, whether by chance or careful selection, seemed to be assigned roles that meshed with their personalities. The criteria of a cavalry scout in Vietnam was one of being able to head out on dangerous missions into unchartered territory without hesitation and with a devil-may-care attitude.

Somehow, the Army found a young man from a small town in Manitowoc County, Wisconsin, who fit that description perfectly.

I went to a country school in Maribel, Wisconsin, that had twenty-one kids in eight grades and I was born on the same farm I live on today. I'm a country boy. I was working construction in 1968 when I got the letter telling me to come down and get my physical. The draft was going strong then. You got that letter and it was law; you'd better report. You know, most of the kids that were drafted and signed up were eighteen-nineteen years old. They were young, dumb, and patriotic as hell.

Those doctors poked and prodded every place they could. After getting checked out and cleared for everything I decided to just keep on marching. My dad and I weren't getting along so I figured it was a good time to skip town. I said, "Sign me up right now." They tried to get me for three years, but I said, no, two was enough for me.

I had friends in Vietnam at the time. My view was if I could do something to help people in this country to stop the war from coming over here, then I would go do it.

I had a '59 Ford Convertible with a 390 engine and ¾ inch racing cams. I was going to leave it to my brother, but my dad said, "You're not killing your brother with that thing. It's gone the minute you leave!"

If you were sent for Advanced Training at Fort Polk, Louisiana, you knew your next stop was Vietnam. The climate, humidity, snakes, scorpions all that stuff, they were right around you. It was a tough place. Tough, tough place.

There was brush and stuff all over. You go to kick something and there would be a scorpion with his stinger out. A couple of guys got stuck by them and got extremely sick, extremely sick. There were water moccasins, copperhead snakes, I know of one guy who got bit and we never saw him again before we shipped out.

Three days before I left for Vietnam I was back home with some buddies. We were by the old Swan Club in De Pere when I got stopped by the cops. I had tried to outrun them. The cop asked me if I knew what the speed limit was. I said, "I believe thirty-five." He said, "How fast do you think you were going?" I said at least that. He said, "I had you at 126 miles-per-hour. He said, "What's your rush?" I told him I was 11-Bravo and heading to Vietnam and things weren't looking too good over there. He said, "I'll tell you what. Here's your driver's license. Have a safe journey and I will get you when you get back."

I had a few brandies on the way over. That was an interesting time to fly. The stewardesses were all in mini-skirts. I tried talking to a few of them, but I was so tense and wound up I don't think I even comprehended that one of them was trying to be real friendly.

A Marine sergeant was sitting there. He said, "Where are you going trooper?" I told him the whole situation, where I was headed, and everything. He said, "This is my third tour. You'll be back. You'll be back." Just then there was this huge clap of thunder and it looked like lightning danced off the wings. I had about three or four more brandies.

June 10th, 1968 is the day we landed in Cam Ranh Bay. It was the dry season. There was nothing but dirt. They loaded me up in a deuce-and-a-half and dropped me off at Pleiku. Welcome to the 1st of the 10th Cavalry, 4th Division.

I never realized how a third-world country operated until I saw it myself. What we throw away here is better than their best. Any old piece of tin lying around, they will take and pound on it and make a door or something out of it. I never realized people were in that dire of a situation. They weren't all bad people. There were lots of villagers and Montagnards who would have gladly ended the war, but they didn't have a say. It was a terrible thing.

Scout Troop was nothing but a bunch of renegades. We were very undisciplined, to put it mildly. We didn't shave, no haircuts, we were just a pretty raggedy crew. The only things we took real good care of were our weapons and vehicles.

Whenever the brass came around they would kick us out of camp. The only time we were ever there at night was to pull security. Those turned out to be very interesting times. Like I said, that was a rough-rugged group.

There were some guys who were living scared every minute. There were others who said, "Hell with it, if I die, I die." My way, I looked up and thanked God every morning. I thanked him for the day I got through and said I hoped to hell I'd be thanking him again when the sun came up the next morning. You had to assume every day was going to be your last day; that your life was just in God's hands.

The new guys got all the shit duties, literally. I'm an old country bumpkin so I knew all about outdoor shitters. They had fifty-gallon cut-off barrels of diesel fuel. When they got full you pulled them out and burned them.

Well, the officers had their own special one built just for them. It had a flap in the back and everything. One of the FNGs was told to burn the officers' shitter. He did. He just didn't pull the barrels out first. He literally burnt the officers' shitter.

We usually had five APCs, two tanks, a tank with a blade on it, and what they called a track recovery vehicle. There was also a jeep, but that was for the medic. There were a lot of convoy security missions, escorting troops, and supply trucks all over.

We didn't stay long at firebases. We moved steady and went all over. I didn't know a damned thing about the Central Highlands before I got there. I never imagined Vietnam had so many different types of terrain: rivers, valleys, mountains so high you could barely climb them, everything.

A lot of times our job would be to go out and pick up choppers that were shot down, convoy trucks that had gotten hit, trucks that got hit by mines, whatever.

Usually, if a chopper got shot down, it was dark by the time you knew anything about it. So you would head out with just a grid to guide you. No light, no roads, not a goddamned clue. Those were the absolute worst missions.

Other times I would either drive the APC, or man the .50-caliber. If we had a higher ranking guy, he would man the .50, and I would man the .60. We were one of the few with two .60s on the back and a .50 in front.

Sometimes they gave us grid coordinates of places that our guys had used before. That's where we would stay. It might be about the size of a football field with some old concertina wire around it. You'd get in there, open up cans of Black Label beer that was about 110 degrees. They had so much yeast in them that if you didn't have your mouth over the can when you opened it, you would lose most of it.

That was scary shit though. You didn't know if the Viet Cong had been there and set up some booby traps. Same thing when you're riding along in the APC to one of those places. If they had an idea of how you would come in, they would string tripwires so fine, almost like real hair, across the trail and hang Bouncing Betty mines in the trees. If an APC hit that, every guy on top would be cleaned off.

The best days were when you would get to a downed chopper in time to rescue them. Those guys said there wasn't a prettier sound in the world than, "Roar, crunch, roar, crunch." That's when they knew they were going to get out of there.

For us, if we got in trouble, there wasn't a better sound than gunships coming in and then, "Brupppppp, bruppppppp…" We'd say, "Okay, now we got them on our side. Now let's see what happens."

We were a full-fledged Scout Troop. Mainly we were there to see how much VC and NVA traffic there was. We weren't supposed to confront them unless we knew exactly how many there were.

In reality, we feared the VC more than the NVA. The NVA were more professional and they had their standards to do things a certain way. But with the VC the guy selling you soda pop during the day might be trying to crawl through your wire at night. They caught one of our barbers on base doing that.

But hell, the VC would steal kids and booby trap them. Booby trap the poor little bastards. The hardcore VC had zero respect for life over there. Absolutely none. If you weren't totally with them, you were treated worse than a dog.

We had short-range and long-range reconnaissance patrols. Short-range were usually three guys: one had a machine gun, another had the radio, another had his M-16. You'd only be out there for a night and a day. Seldom were you out there for two nights.

With long-range patrols there would usually be seven in a squad. They would drop us off probably about three miles from where we had to go. We'd find our grid and head out. Usually, we set up right before dark. We'd spend our time there, call in what was happening, and then go to the next grid post. Walking in the dark scared the piss out of me every time. They owned the night. They knew the country.

You didn't want to be too far away from the rest of your guys. If you ran into a full platoon or company of NVA and it was going to take two hours for your guys to get there, you might as well kiss your ass goodbye. We didn't have enough firepower to hold off that many guys and half the time the radios didn't work anyway. If there was something big going on, our job was to mark it and call in the big boys.

If we got captured, we were dead. We knew that and chances are it wouldn't be quick. I remember when we found a Lurp (Long-range reconnaissance soldier) who had been captured. He had been castrated, his testicles were stuffed in his throat, his mouth tied shut, and was hanging upside down from a tree branch. If you were captured, nothing humane would happen to you until you died.

Guys who saw these things and spent most of their time out in the bush started justifying some of the things they did. There really would be guys with a string of ears hanging on them. You could even tell if some of the ears were matched or not. Living out there you weren't the same person as you were before.

One mission I can remember real plain was near the Cambodia River, the river that separated Vietnam from Cambodia. I mean we could read a map. We knew what was on the other side. They told us we just weren't allowed to get killed over there.

On this mission, we had a Chieu hoi with us. That's a former Viet Cong or NVA soldier who came over to fight on our side. He went back and forth between us and them three different times. After the first time with us, he went back home. His dad had been a mucky-muck in the village. The NVA had murdered him. So he came back to us again. He could go pretty much as he wanted. We didn't really have any legal right to hold him.

I didn't trust him. I believed he was getting information on us and then going back and giving it to the VC.

One of the times he went back to his village he found out that the VC had annihilated his wife and kids. Killed them all because they found out that he had come back over to us. So back he comes again. I still didn't trust him, didn't have any faith in the guy.

It wasn't long after he came back that he came on this mission with us.

We found our spot and set out claymore mines. If there weren't too many, we were looking to get some of them as they were going back from Vietnam into Cambodia. We angled them in a way that if they came down the trail, we could nail them and then get the hell out of there.

We were all set-up and laying there. He was right next to me. We had .60s on the right and left, a couple of guys with M-16s, and the radio guy. The det wire (detonation wire) for the claymores was all covered up. We were there probably about three-four hours when we started hearing banging and chatting. It kept getting louder and louder. It's like they were having a party. It sounded like a whole company and there were seven of us. All of a sudden I heard a guy fall. He must have had all kinds of stuff on his back because he really made a lot of noise. They started coming close, maybe fifty feet away, and then the Chieu hoi started getting up. I took my rifle and stuck it in his ear. He looked at me and laid back down. We stayed there all night, never firing a shot.

What happened was, the guy who fell had tripped over one of our det wires. When we went to pick the claymores up in the morning they had been turned around back towards us. If we had set them off, there wouldn't have been enough of us left to put in a thimble. They outnumbered us probably 20-1.

We knew they had found the claymores because after that one guy fell there wasn't any more noise. Not a sound. They might have been just as scared as we were. They didn't know how many we had either. We tried following them all the way to Cambodia, but we never caught up with them.

The only thing I know for sure is that I wouldn't be alive today if that Chieu hoi had fired a shot.

We used to pull Med Caps (Medical Civic Action Program) missions. We would go out with a medic to the different villages. He'd give them pills, maybe pull a tooth, do whatever he could. We really enjoyed those. That was the greatest thing. We loved coming up with ways to make the kids laugh. It just made you feel good. It broke my heart sometimes too.

There was one day I was in a hootch talking with the village chief's son. He was motioning for me to take a drink out of this thing that was like a quarter barrel of beer. It was made out of bamboo with a lining inside of it. It was rice wine that they were fermenting. They would take the lid off and drink out of little bamboo shoots. I said, "Sure, I'll take a pull." Okay, not too bad. I went down to take another big swig and as I'm down there I see the head of a frickin' snake coming up. I spit that son of a bitch out and got the hell out of there.

We loved meeting with the Montagnards. They were very honest, very hard-working people. They were altogether different from city people. The village chiefs were very proud. They took care of everything associated with their village: food gathering, buildings, everything. The chief was in charge.

They had some very pretty women. Some of the young ones were gorgeous. It almost looked like some of them were part French.

We went to one of the villages we had been to before but on this day things were different. The people weren't friendly. They didn't want anything to do with us. It was like some sickness had come over the whole village. It had never been like that before. We had to look for the

Bill Enz (with shirt off) on a Med Cap mission to a South Vietnamese village. (Bill Enz collection)

chief. He was hiding. He finally came out with his daughter in his arms. She was probably about fifteen years old. The VC had been there looking for food a few hours before we got there. They killed the pigs, the chickens, and wanted all the rice which the village had hidden. If they didn't have that, they would starve to death. If he gave it to them, they would kill him anyway.

They kept threatening the chief to tell them where it was hidden. He wouldn't do it. So they took his daughter, this beautiful girl, and did something so horrific I will never get over it. They placed a small explosive, like an M-80 firecracker, in her genitals and set it off. She didn't die right away, but it tore her up something awful. It was the most sickening thing I have ever seen in my life. How can you do something like that to a human being?

Our medic did what he could. He gave her morphine and we left. I'm sure she died, but at least maybe the morphine eased her pain. We never went back to that village.

That medic was a great guy. On one convoy security mission, he kept bugging me to let him sit behind the .60-cal for a while. He was going to be going home in a month and wanted a picture for his fiancé. I said, "No if something happens, it could be my ass."

He said, "Come on, we haven't hadn't taken fire in weeks." I said, "All right, five minutes, give me the camera." I took it and went up front to take a picture of him behind the machine gun. I bet then we didn't go fifty yards down the road and a rocket came in and blew him right off the APC.

We called in the dust-off. We got him out of there and never heard from him again. I don't know if he lived or died. I still wonder what happened. That should have been me. He was a wonderful, wonderful man.

People say you shouldn't make friends over there. I'll tell you, if you don't have a friend, you're a dead man. A good buddy over there would be tighter to you than any relative you've ever had. You needed a friend and you needed mail. It didn't matter if it was only one line. You lived for those letters, especially if they smelled nice. Everybody else wanted to read those too.

We were out in the bush so much that sometimes we had a hard time at bases. I mean we would go three to five days without any fresh water. We would find a creek that had water the color of baked beans, throw some pills in it, and hold your nose. At the same time, one of the officers at the base was getting flown into town by chopper on a regular basis to take showers. There was a lot of resentment between the guys in the bush and the officers. A lot. There was one morning when an officer woke up with a star-cluster grenade in his bunk. The pin was pulled, but there was a piece of tape holding it on. If I remember right, we started getting more fresh water after that.

I will admit we didn't always act the best when we did stay someplace. There was one camp they told us we could stay overnight and sleep in tents. That was a rarity. We had this one guy in our unit who

Bill Enz (second from right) with some of his squad.
(Bill Enz collection)

was always in trouble. He had gotten a hold of some rice wine and who knows what else and got totally drunker than a skunk. So he gets up in the middle of the night and walks to what he thought was a tree, but was actually a tent pole, leaned on it, and takes a piss right on top of a guy sleeping beneath him. He did that twice before they kicked us out of there.

You put off thinking about going home until the last thirty days. Anything else was too far off to think about. Every morning you would get up and do a little count, make sure you didn't lose anybody during the night.

When you had time to think about it, you realized that this was the wrong way to fight a war.

First of all, you don't put a limit as to how far you can go. You don't have parameters and you don't have a thousand people giving orders who have never fought in a war. We had so many guys over there we could have walked from the southern border to the top of North Vietnam holding hands. Instead, we fought on this one hill over here. We took the hill. Three days later we moved out. Six days later you're fighting for that same hill again because the VC took it over. Why in the hell would you not maintain something that you fought for? Why are you so willing to let the enemy come in and take over?

Maybe we didn't give them (the NVA and Viet Cong) enough credit early on. They were sharp. If we didn't police up (clean up) an area real good, they would come in, take what we left behind, and use it against us. They watched us. They figured out how we did things. They never came charging out if we had more power than them. And discipline, wow. If one of their soldiers said he didn't want to do something, he was dead. Once that happens the rest will follow orders a lot closer.

When I got home to Ft. Lewis, Washington, I kissed the ground. I kissed the ground. In those days there were people who would go to airports and yell at the guys, throw piss at them. They would scream that our country hated us. They could scream all they wanted. I had a lovely little lady waiting for me that I couldn't wait to see.

We had to stay at Fort Lewis for a while. While I was there I got a letter from my sister Nancy, she said, "We were planning a housewarming for you, but the house got too hot." I didn't know what she meant. It wasn't until I got home that I found out two things: my parents had gotten a divorce and our house had burned down. Both happened while I was in Vietnam.

KATHY ENZ: I didn't date Bill in high school. He graduated from Denmark High School in '66. I graduated in '69. I always told him he was too fast for me.

I had several friends who had boyfriends in Vietnam at the same time. In fact, one of the boyfriends was killed over there. He was just eighteen. His last letter said, "Mom I love you, but if you're reading this I'm not coming home."

BILL: One of the worst things was when guys would get "Dear John" letters. Some guys, after getting one of them, just didn't care what happened to them anymore. I had a friend who could get out of the Army sooner if he extended in Vietnam for thirty days. He did and on the twenty-eighth day he got a Dear John letter. Talk about sad, he went goofy as hell.

KATHY: I had a boyfriend and a brother in Vietnam at the same time. You would see all the protests against them on TV and there was nothing you could do about it. Northing. It was horrific. People didn't care. They just didn't care. Although that was really more in the big cities than around here. Here they stood behind them for the most part. But when I watched TV I just thought, *What's wrong with those people?*

When we met my brother at the train station in Green Bay he was in regular clothes. It was very, very sad in some ways. I wanted to say that if it weren't for the people who fought we wouldn't have our freedom. But we didn't talk about it, we really didn't.

Bill came back in June of 1969 and we got married in February of 1970. He seemed a little bit odd personality-wise. It took him a while to get back to normal.

BILL: Tell him what it was like when we first got married.

KATHY: I didn't know that these guys were coming back with baggage. No one really talked about it. He would have a lot of bad dreams. I would get hit in the middle of the night while he was having a nightmare. He would be back in Vietnam. He was back there. His eyes are open, but he would be asleep. He would say things like, "Get 'em! Get 'em! Watch your back! Watch your back!"

I got hit in the face, the head, pushed out of bed. He was always in a fight mode and kept a hand down on the floor like he was ready to grab a gun. It was like he could never let his guard down. That's how he slept for years.

BILL: When I fell asleep we would be hugging. When I woke up she would be out of bed standing by the wall.

KATHY: I would try to hug him when he was having those dreams, but get pushed away. I tried saying, "You're home Bill, your home! It's

OK. It's OK." I would turn on the lights, the radio, anything to get him out of it.

BILL: It started up again five years ago. We're talking forty-five years after Vietnam. Things that I had locked so deep in my head started coming out. I do think it started up at the same time I began having health problems. You start thinking about the places you had been, places that probably put you in the condition you're in today. Then you start going back through the trauma and you end up sleepless. You wake up scared. You get depressed and that's a bad spot to be.

I went to counseling, but I didn't like the way the VA did it. You went there and met a resident, not a therapist. Then you would see a different person, then someone else. You never built up a rapport with any of them.

KATHY: I told him he had to get better help than what he was getting. I went to a few meetings. They would be like, "How's your day going Bill? How are you feeling? Do you want to change meds?" And he would be like, "Oh I'm feeling really good."

They didn't ask about what was really bothering him, about his nightmares. Their only solution was to change meds. They put him on one that gave him illusions. I threw them away.

For years you just learned to deal with it. Just handle it and hope it will get better.

BILL: I thought I was going crazy. I really did. But she was always there for me. Always looking out for me, always.

KATHY: One night I took a tape recorder and taped him talking to me. I wanted to play it for the doctor. I wanted him to know he wasn't getting better no matter what he said in the meetings.

BILL: When I heard it I said, "That's not me."

KATHY: I said, "If that's not how you feel, why do you talk like that?" I told him he had to make himself better. He had to do it himself. I couldn't do it anymore. I've had it. I quit.

BILL: That's when a lightbulb went off. I wasn't mad at her. I was mad at me. I couldn't believe the way I sounded. I thought I was a carefree happy go lucky, "Give 'er hell" kind of a guy.

KATHY: One thing that helped was when he started speaking at schools. Our grandson Marcus told his history teacher, Mr. Tomashek, that his grandpa had been in Vietnam. The teacher asked if Bill would go speak to the class. At first Bill said no. He said there were things he wanted to forget, not bring up again. Then Marcus goes, "Would you please, they have no one to teach us about the war." I think that's when things started changing for you.

BILL: Yes it was. It was a great thing knowing someone finally wanted to hear the truth about it. I believe there is a lot of important history regarding the Vietnam War and if that's what it was going to take to get it out I was willing to do it. There were times when I would start talking about things and then get teary eyed and have to turn around.

KATHY: He would come home and talk about how respectful the kids were, about the great questions they would ask. He did it by himself for three years. Then I suggested he should ask a couple of friends, who I knew had struggled, to go with him. He said he didn't think they would want to go. But he asked them.

BILL: Jim and Charley. They agreed to go. They were a couple of guys I had gone to high school with and then went to Vietnam. I thought it would be good if they could spit some things out too. They've thanked me numerous times for asking.

KATHY: When those guys all came back from Vietnam no one had even heard of the term Post Traumatic Stress. People have no idea what the family of a vet goes through when they are dealing with PTSD. Not just the wife, the entire family.

I would ask him questions about what was bothering him but he didn't want to talk about it. I told him, "I will go to Hell and back with you, but I can't help fix you if I don't know what's broken."

BILL: You think you can bury it and for a while you do. But then you see reality again and you're mad at yourself and the whole world. You're mostly mad because of the misery you put your family through.

I honestly don't believe I will ever be totally normal. A lot of people will say I never was. (Laughing) But I think I'm 70-80 percent of the person I want to be.

What does a vet need? A very understanding wife, good counseling, and to pray more. At least that's how I look at it. My wife is the most supportive person in my life. Just incredible.

You also have to start accepting things for what they are. Because one thing you have to realize, you can't change the past and if you don't accept that there's no way in hell you will ever go forward.

RANDY TRUTTSCHEL

HML 367
USS Hancock
US Marines
Vietnam War

They are still some of the most impactful images of the Vietnam War, helicopters being tossed over the sides of ships and citizens clambering to get inside the US Embassy in a desperate attempt to escape certain terror at the hands of the invading Communists.

A Marine from Manitowoc, Wisconsin, was a witness and participant during those chaotic and heart-breaking final days.

Eight days after I graduated from Manitowoc Lincoln High School in June of 1973 I was in the Marines. By the middle of January 1974, I was in Vietnam.

I had wanted to join the Navy and be a diesel mechanic in the Seabees. The Navy and Marine recruiting offices were in the same building. The Marine recruiter says, "The Navy guy is gone to lunch, but you can still take the Department of the Navy test." Okay, I take the test. He gets done correcting it and says, "Randy, I'm going to tell you something right now, you would be wasting your time as a diesel mechanic. We've got great opportunities in aviation in the Marine Corps." And I'm thinking, *Well you know, this doesn't sound too bad because you watch TV and all you would see is people running around with guns in those jungles. You don't see much about anybody flying around.* OK, that sounds good.

The day before we graduated from boot camp, they told me my MOS is going to be a 6114. I said, "What's that?" He said, "You will be a Huey mechanic and you will turn into a crew chief after your training."

I got sent to NAS (Naval Air Station) Millington and a guy came walking into the room and said, "Gentlemen we won't lie to you, of the twelve in this room training for Hueys, it's more than likely three of you will be dead within the year."

It's like this, you're sitting on the side of a helicopter with nothing in front of you except a machine gun. For the six seconds that you come in and the six seconds that you take off, the enemy is training all of their firepower on you. Because if they knock off the gunners they can come at the bird from the sides. The pilot and copilot have nothing but pistols on them, what are they going to do? So yeah, everybody is going after you. It's kind of a scary thing. It wasn't uncommon to find a bird that had lots of holes in it and lots of blood in the back. Even in those days.

When I first got overseas I was on the USS *Midway* for about three weeks. Then I transferred to USS *Hancock*. It was an old wooden flat-top ship. When the war was done in Vietnam, they took that ship and reduced it to nothing but razor blades in the scrapyard.

The captain of the ship was a raving maniac. (Laughing) I can still remember this, every hour of the day from the time you got up until the time you went to bed, he was on the P.A. going, "Sweepers. Sweepers. Man your brooms. Throw all trash and garbage over the fantail. Now sweep!" Every hour on the hour. And when he went around for inspection, and you have to remember, this is an old World War II ship, he's got white gloves on inspecting above the pipes that run along the ceiling. We were like, "We're going into Vietnam; it's dirty and filthy there but we're supposed to make this thing spotless?"

This ship was so old that when we started picking up refugees, the ship's evaporation system couldn't keep up with the fresh water that was needed. So I learned a sneaky trick. On board the ship there's a thing called the "Admiral's passageway" and there was a water fountain up there. I would go there and fill canteens for the guys and hand them out. I never got caught and I did it quite a bit. Otherwise, we couldn't get fresh water and we weren't going to drink the water in Vietnam. You want to get sick, drink that water, you'll get sick.

In '74 things were pretty laid back. You would fly to the US Embassy, fly over to Cu Chi, Da Nang, Chu Lai, where there was a big hospital. We would drop off supplies. Most of the people getting wounded were South Vietnamese troops. You'd get shot at now and then but not very often. We would stay close to the treetops. When you're close to the tops they can't get a fix on you. If you go high, they could hit you with a missile. Somedays I didn't even have a mission. I would just stay on the ship.

Things changed in the spring of 1975. We knew something was coming. We knew the end was near. One week for four mornings in a row they would go, "Deep Purple. Deep Purple. Operation Deep Purple. All crew chiefs and flight personnel to the flight deck immediately!"

So people start grabbing flight suits, you run up on top, they're bringing the helicopters up, everything is going on. From the bow all the way to the fantail are helicopters, all the flight crews are up there loading ordnance. They're putting rocket pods on the Cobra helicopters. You'd be like, "Okay get set, we're going in!" And then you'd wait. And you wait. And you wait. And four hours later they would say, "Stand down." And you would put everything away. We did that four days in a row. The fifth morning, the same thing, they came on the P.A. but this time they said, "This is not a drill. This is the real thing!"

Huey helicopters have skiffs. So, they put wheels on them that were hydraulic and that way you could move them around. They got my bird up there and I was ready to pop off the wheels when I heard something flying. I look up and lo and behold here's a CH-47 South Vietnamese helicopter coming in to land. These guys have never done a carrier landing on a pitching deck, and, believe me, this ship was moving. Everybody takes off. Me? I don't know if I was struck with dumbness or I froze or whatever. But I stood there by the back end of my bird and kept watching while everybody else was running down in the catwalk.

This thing never even radioed in. It just showed up. He puts down on the deck and shuts down his engines. Five minutes later here comes another one. No call-in no nothing. I'm still standing there on the flight deck. When he landed we moved both of them back by the fantail. Those were two of the ones we threw over the side. Later that morning Hueys started showing up. The first one had the pilot, copilot, crew chief, and two motorbikes. There was nobody else on board. We just tossed that thing, motorcycles included, over the side. They could have put more people on board but these guys were running scared. So finally around 1:00 in the afternoon they said, "Okay, everybody load up and head out." That kicked the whole thing off.

It was kind of awesome that on the carrier you would land in one spot to drop off the people, then over on another spot was where Air America birds would come in. Their birds did not get thrown over the side. They had a lot of hi-tech gear on them.

The refugees would get off, go to a delousing station, then down into the hanger bay. We had over 3,000 people in there. We had some though that jumped off the ship; it was so foreign for them. These people are coming from a land where they were living in huts. A lot of the mama-sans and papa-sans had worked on the bases or they were informers for us. We had promised them we would get them out of there. Some of them worked for the bigwig officers. They took care of their houses and everything and then at the end of the day went back to their little place in the middle of nowhere. So they got on this huge ship and they didn't know what was going on.

A lot of people say we should have won in Vietnam, but my feelings are that winning in Vietnam was impossible because these people didn't give a damn about democracy. They didn't care who was in charge of their country. They didn't care what flag was up that pole. All they cared about was their rice, their chickens, and their goats. That's all they cared about. They didn't have running water or electricity; so why care about politics?

Randy Truttschel collection

If one of our birds got shot at from a village, we would go there and check it out. Sure as heck you would find a machine gun, maybe an RPG or Russian-made sniper rifles. We used to call the actual snipers, "paddy-daddies."

What always got me was our president, Richard Nixon, flew to Moscow to improve relations with the Russians. But where do you think the SAM missile batteries came from? And their radar equipment? It all came from Russia. I actually had a chance to see a SAM missile battery. All the writing was in Russian and then below it Vietnamese. They were handing that stuff out like candy to the North Vietnamese. The Russians were training the North Vietnamese pilots to fly MiGs. And now we were going to be friends with them? I saw machine guns made in Czechoslovakia, pistols made in Hungary. It was all Communist-made.

When Vietnam started to fall and everyone was making the mass exodus from the north going south to Saigon, we were still going north to try and help the South Vietnamese Army slow down the North Vietnamese. But you would see South Vietnamese soldiers walking down the road with their guns over their shoulders and in clean uniforms. They weren't doing anything to stop the Communists. They were going backward. They were leaving.

During one of the days of the air evacuation, we were supposed to pick up some South Vietnamese troops and move them from one area to another. You couldn't use the roads, they were blocked, chaotic. Everybody was running to Saigon. There were miles and miles of people.

We land at this LZ, get out, and look around. There are some dead South Vietnamese troops laying there. There are some dead VC laying there. There was no one alive.

After we got back in the bird and took off, I said to the pilot, "What about that orphanage we had been taking care of?" We had been flying corpsmen out there to tend to the children, giving them some humanitarian aid. Some of the kids were Amerasian, half-American. They were little cuties; visiting them kind of broke up the boredom of the war for us. We headed there. Another bird came in with us. There were twenty-three children and a couple of nuns at the orphanage. The priest who worked there was dead. He had gotten on his bicycle to go to Saigon and they found him down in a ditch with his throat cut. So we got everybody loaded up.

Every once in a while a stray shell would hit around that orphanage. Where could they hide? The buildings were ancient. There were no basements in them. You try putting a basement in a house in Vietnam and it would be full of water.

The nuns got in our bird. This one nun was just chattering away. I tried telling her I didn't understand what she was saying. I'm looking at her, and I look toward the front of the bird and the copilot motions for me to come up by him and he says, "She wants you to go in the church and take the cross down that's above the altar so it doesn't get desecrated." So I went into the church. There's the cross. It was kind of ornate. It had been there a long time; you could tell that. It looked like the French would have made it. I felt kind of funny ripping a cross down out of a church. This is God's house, you know? But I guess I was doing a good thing. So I jumped up there and I tore it down. I came out to the copter and handed it to her. She just grabbed it and hugged it and she stayed like that until we got to the ship. She walked toward the check-in station in the ship hugging that cross.

Nobody knew we were bringing these people back. These kids and nuns get off the bird and there's Marines with M-14 rifles pointing at them.

So anyway, these little kids get off the bird and start walking toward the ship's island. Well, there was a news crew on there taking pictures. One gets posted on UPI. It was of a sailor with a crying baby in his arms that's all bandaged up from being wounded.

One day the captain of the ship calls the pilot, the copilot, and myself in and starts screaming and yelling up and down at us. Then he throws down the newspaper and he goes, "I can't do a damned thing because of this photo!" He goes, "How's it going to look if I court-martial you for saving children and nuns? As far as I'm concerned this incident never took place!" He said, "They're here, they're checked in, and the next stop for them is the Philippines."

It was worth it. We knew that if we hadn't taken those kids out of there they would have been killed. And the nuns would have been raped and then killed.

Later that day we flew by that orphanage again. It was just before it got dark out. The church and the building they kept the children in were gone. They were both burned down. What it looked like to me was that the North Vietnamese were using a lot of tanks. They had never used tanks before. But it looked like tank treads through the cemetery. You could see the tombstones that had been knocked down in a row. They didn't care. There was nothing stopping them and they were coming quick. There was no real line of defense. At this point how could you make a line of defense?

Three days before the war ended we got called into the Ready Room on the ship. A guy from the American Embassy stepped up.

He said, "Gentlemen, we have a situation at hand. Presently we estimate the enemy strength around Saigon as 250,000 troops. And somebody goes, "Ahh great." Another guy goes, "So, we're going to have a Custer's last stand?" The guy from the Embassy said, "No, we guarantee we will get everyone out of there."

Nobody believed him. Nobody. They hadn't told us the truth since day one. The American ambassador did not want to end the war. On board the *Hancock,* back by the fantail of the ship in the hanger bay, were pallets of ammunition, pallets as high as the ceiling. And it wasn't for our machine guns on the birds. It was for M-16s. There were M-35 grenade launchers in there, boxes of hand grenades. I guess they thought we could still do it. That was crazy. No one was going to stop the North Vietnamese. Not now. But that's the type of thing that was going on.

One time they brought in a great big Pan American flight into Tan Son Nhut. The bird touched down. As it started rolling down the tarmac, masses of South Vietnamese troops converged on it trying to get out of the country. Well, they gave up on that idea. The South Vietnamese were scared. They were very, very scared. They knew the end was coming and the American ambassador could have gone ahead and started the air evac a couple of weeks earlier. He waited until the last moment. The very last moment.

So then our wonderful president, Gerald Ford, 2:30 in the morning on April 30th, calls off the air evacuation. Okay, one problem, we've got forty-some Marines still at the embassy. Who's going to go get them? So at about 6:00 the word comes back to us that we're going back to the embassy to get the Marines. Because now they're up on the roof and there's no place else for them to go. What they did was a few Marines at a time would go into the embassy, get in the elevator, and go up to the top. The last group that went up to the top blew the elevator in place. The embassy compound at this time was being completely controlled by South Vietnamese troops.

They fitted my bird with rocket pods and two M-.60 machine guns. Like I'm really going to be able to do much with those? Come on, everyone is going to be all bunched together. Who are you going to fire on?

When we came in a CH-46 had landed on the embassy roof. We were flying cover, circling it. I'm looking down on Saigon and there's a burning car here. There are some dead bodies over there. There's another bunch of stuff on this street that's all wrecked. But here's the thing that hit me. Saigon was quiet. It was deathly quiet, eerie, almost scary. I was used to seeing people all over the place going in and out of the markets and everything. The markets were empty. There was nobody running around. We didn't know it, but the Communists were already there.

They piled the Marines up and headed out. One bird is in front of them, one Huey and one bird in the back, and the two CH-46s in the center. We were covering them. We headed north first and hit a clearing. There were three or four North Vietnamese tanks sitting in this field and you could see the barrels start raising up. Our pilot shifted gears, shifted hard left. And out to sea we headed. Nobody fired a shot at us, but you saw those barrels move. We came over that clearing at tree-top levels and there they were. They had a whole bunch of dinks running around too. That's what it was like all around Saigon now.

So we get to the ship. We put down and they come running up to us, "Is everybody OK, everybody OK?" I'm like, "Yeah, we're alright." I said, "Check my guns, we didn't fire a shot." I said, "What's the big deal?" They said, "Ten minutes after you left, Vietnam fell."

It was a twenty-minute flight. We flew over an enemy-held country to get these guys out.

Why did Gerald Ford call it off when he did? I don't know. There were still people down in the compound. I imagine they all got shot and killed. We left people behind. We left 300-400 people down there. We had enough copters. We had enough room. We could have gotten them out. We left them behind.

Some of the dissension you get from the Hmongs and the South Vietnamese is that we didn't fulfill our end of the bargain. Some of the people we left behind were relatives of the people we had aboard the ship. From 2:30 a.m. until the time the country fell, we could have gotten a lot more people out of there, at least 400 more. But the president called it off. Nobody knows why.

The Communists must have watched us when we took the flag down on top of the embassy. A warrant officer pulled it down. And I'll tell you what, there were a lot of wet eyes when that happened. All the men that had been killed over the past years and we left. I saw the flag go down.

The night before, they had taken the placards off the front of the embassy that said "United States Embassy." They took them down. They weren't going to let the Communists capture that either. I'm young. I'm only, what, nineteen-twenty years old? I was like, *Wow, I'm watching a country fall.*

When we went to Vietnam we weren't expecting brass bands to be playing and everybody to be happy because we were there. There was none of that. And when we came home there was none of that either.

My mom and dad picked me up at the Manitowoc airport. We went home. My dad sat up for about ten minutes and went to bed. He had to work the next day. My mom went to bed twenty minutes later.

I've been overseas for over a year. I didn't know what to do. TV? That's fine if you know what the shows are, but we really didn't have regular TV over there. So I went down to the basement, put on my BDUs (battle dress uniform), grabbed some bottles of beer, and went down by the old breakwater on the north side beach in Manitowoc. And I sat out there. I'm sitting out there and I don't have a clue about what to do next. A cop car pulled up and shined a light on me and told me to come over. I handed him my papers. He said, "You just got back from overseas?" I said, "Yup." He said, "Did you see any action?" I said, "I was part of the air evacuation of Vietnam." We stood there and talked for over two hours. I asked him all kinds of questions about what was going on in the area because I was totally out of touch with everything.

I got a hold of a buddy that I knew since seventh. We went into the Marines on the buddy system. He was over there right until the end too. I went over to his house and we decided we were going to go out that night. My mom and I walked down to Sears and she bought me some civilian clothes that fit. I had lost a lot of weight.

We went out. Had a good time. We were talking to some girls. It was all good. I said, "I've got my dad's car, I'll give you a ride home." He said, "OK." I'm giving him a ride home and he's got this girl's phone number and he's all happy as heck. I dropped him off at his place. He went into his house, lit a cigarette, went into a closet, pulled out a rifle, and killed himself. Never gave me any indication he was going to do that.

Nobody worked with us when we came home. You just left the war and went home. Here's the thing with war and a lot of people don't get it. And a lot of these young guys from Iraq and Afghanistan are going through it now. I wish I could sit in an auditorium of people and explain this to people. You come home and they ask, "Do you have any issues from what went on overseas?" You don't know. You feel normal. You think you're acting normal, but you did change, you did change. Well, the problem is if you answered "yes," they would put you in the hospital for thirty days for observation. If you answer "no," you get to go home.

Well, which way do you think they answered? Everybody wants to go home.

I can give you a whole list of stuff that bothered me. Here's one, heavy rain. When we were at firebase Fox, a South Vietnamese Army base, the NVA moved troops through the jungle and nobody knew it because the rain covered up any noise. They set up during the night. Nobody heard them. When the rain ended they came. There were a lot of them.

They (counselors) picked through my memory trying to get me to remember all that went on that day. According to what the doctor told me at the Cleveland Clinic, "Your mind shut it off." He said whatever happened was so horrific that your mind blocked it. He said, "I don't want to try to bring it back because I don't know what it's going to do to you."

All I remember was that in the morning there were about nine guys sitting on a pile of sandbags, and I was holding an AK-47 in my hand and I had blood on my uniform. What did I do? I don't know. So they put all of us on a helicopter and flew us out to the ship and we washed up and everything, and we hung out during the rest of the day and that was it.

I think the suicide rate is so high for guys when they come back because when you kill somebody it's not something that you forget. You're not brought up like that. It's not the way we're brought up in America.

The North Vietnamese? Well, they fought the French. They fought the Japanese and then they fought us guys. To them there were only two ways to get out of the war. One was to die and the second was to win it.

Us? We rotated home. But we brought the war back with us.

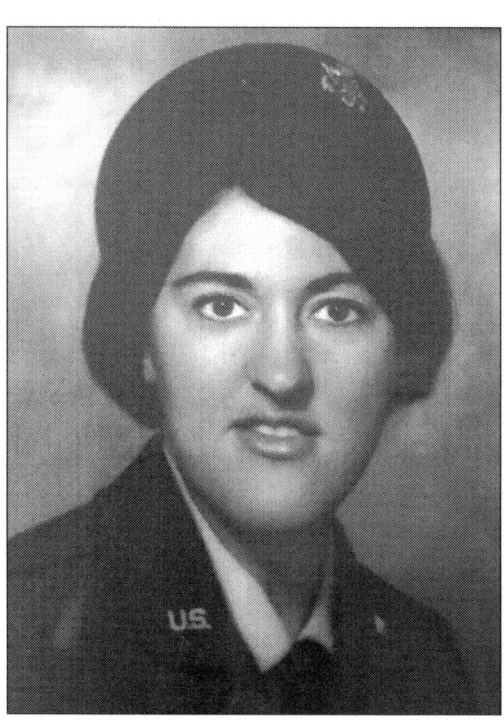

COL. JUDITH LISA, RET.

Nurse Corps
US Air Force
Vietnam War

The final days before South Vietnam fell under Communist control were truly chaotic. Panic had set in for both soldiers and citizens who knew what awaited them once North Vietnamese troops took over.

In an effort to help save the lives of some of the most vulnerable, the US began flying out babies, children, and families of those who had worked for the Americans.

A flight nurse from Negaunee, Michigan was thrilled to take part in this historic, humanitarian endeavor. It was a heroic effort, but one that had an absolutely tragic beginning.

I received my nursing diploma at St Joseph's Hospital in Hancock, Michigan, and was recruited to work at the University of Michigan hospital in Ann Arbor. It was really great, just a great experience. There were four of us who were recruited and shared an apartment. Things were going really well. I even bought a new car, a Corvair. One night my roommate and I went out and were on our way back to the apartment when my car hit a patch of black ice. Which honestly I had never experienced before; I didn't know what black ice was. We skidded head-on into an oncoming car.

Long story short, I didn't walk again for six months. I had broken both of my femurs. After four months my dad came down and flew home with me in an air ambulance. My mother took care of me until I could walk again. I had a lot of time to think about what I wanted to do with my nursing career.

Once I recovered I got a job at a local hospital, Bell Memorial, near my hometown of Negaunee. There was an Air Force base nearby, K.I. Sawyer. I had some friends who lived there. I would go there and watch as the C-9s would come in for landings. I saw the nurses who worked on the flights. I found it all very impressive. So, I made up my mind to join the Air Force. I just felt like it would be a great opportunity for me.

I actually waited until my parents were in Italy visiting family before I joined. I did that so they wouldn't be able to talk me out of it. They wouldn't have wanted me to leave. I passed my physical and took my oath in October of 1970.

For Air War College I did my thesis on Rolling Thunder, the bombing campaign in North Vietnam. I found that subject very interesting. I truly believe the war was run by the White House and not the military. I believe we would have won the war if it had been conducted by military strategists rather than politicians. What really happened, in my opinion, is that the North Vietnamese outsmarted us. They knew we weren't going to bomb certain areas and they took advantage of that. They used the Ho Chi Minh trail to a great advantage in overcoming South Vietnam on land.

My first assignment was in the hospital at Travis Air Force base in California. I remember reporting there in January of 1971. I enjoyed working in the hospital. Over the years I was trained in pediatric care, adult care, and flight nursing.

From the moment I joined, I always hoped to become a flight nurse. In 1973 I was selected. I went through a very good six-week course and was then assigned to flights to the Pacific. I trained in a C-141. My route was Travis to Hickam Airfield in Hawaii, Guam, and then the Philippines, which is where we would pick up patients and fly them back.

The Vietnam War was still going on at this time and I hoped I would be lucky enough to fly there. I really wanted to do that. If you're a flight nurse, you want to go where you are needed the most. You didn't have a choice; you were sent where they told you to go. I was fine with that; this is what I signed up for.

In April of 1975, a program was started to get as many Americans and their families out of Vietnam as quickly as possible. They also wanted to get as many orphans and children who had an American parent out of there. It was assumed that kids who may have been the child of a GI would be killed once the North Vietnamese took over. The name of the program was Operation Babylift. Obviously, my parents were very worried that I was going to be a part of this.

On the first flight of evacuations from Saigon, a very horrible thing happened. The plane being used was a C-5. It wasn't designed for transporting passengers. It had two separate decks, the upper and lower. The bottom deck was filled with wives of embassy workers and other people who had worked in American government offices. The babies and children were on the top level. Food and formula for the babies were brought onto the plane. Shortly after the plane took off something caused rapid decompression. The plane crash-landed in a rice paddy. Everyone in the lower deck was killed.

Editor's note: *Because there was no flight manifest, an exact number of deaths is impossible to say, but published crash reports cite seventy-eight children and at least fifty adults killed. More than 170 passengers, presumably all of them having been on the upper section survived. During the three-week mission, over 3,000 babies and children were evacuated to the United States.*

I had two friends die in the crash. My friend Mary Klinker, I had been her flight instructor. She was on the bottom level and was killed. Another good friend, Regina Aune, had left the bottom deck and gone upstairs to get her flight kit. That's what saved her. She did end up with a broken leg but was very lucky to survive. One of the other medical crew members who died, I will never forget, Sergeant Padget. He was just the absolute nicest man. He sent me cards with scripture notes on them. I'm glad I saved every one of them.

When my parents heard about the crash, they were obviously very concerned because they knew it was from my squadron. I called them as soon as I could and told them I was fine. I did make sure to call them as soon as I got back to Travis after each trip from then on.

We would fly from the Philippines to Saigon on C-130s. It was a smaller cargo type of plane. It didn't have seats or anything like that. We had to configure the aircraft. Then from the Philippines to Travis, we would fly on C-141s.

Once we landed at Tan Son Nhut Airport in Saigon, we would wait for transportation that would take us to a shack. I don't remember if they even had bathrooms in them. We would wait there for the orphanages to bring us the children that needed to be evacuated. On the early flights that I did, it was mainly the babies they were trying to get out first.

The babies would be lined up in boxes. The first thing we did was to go around and feed them and then change them. Whatever orphans they brought we took. Most of the children didn't speak English, or if they did I never heard them. In fact, they spoke very little, even to themselves. They were just very, very quiet.

After the crash of the C-5, we were no longer allowed to take baby formula that the orphanage was giving us for the flights. There was suspicion that one of the boxes on the C-5 had been sabotaged; that an explosive may have been buried in one of the boxes which detonated and caused the swift decompression. I don't believe they ever proved it, but that definitely was a theory.

Unfortunately, the babies were not accustomed to our formula and got very sick with diarrhea. We had to be concerned with dehydration. It's very sad to say, but not all of them survived the trip from the Philippines to the United States.

We had a flight crew and a medical crew which consisted of nurses and medical technicians. The North Vietnamese hadn't taken over Saigon yet, but the South Vietnamese feared for their lives. There were a number of boats filled with people trying to escape; they were running scared. They knew that if they had helped the Americans in any way the North Vietnamese would kill them.

The South Vietnamese Army had artillery set up all around the flight line and some of the planes were actually shot at, but I don't believe any were hit. Their Army was just scared crazy and acting that way. But I never feared for my life. I felt that we would make it out each time.

I thought the South Vietnamese were good people who appreciated the United States. I felt so bad for them when I left for the last time knowing some of them were going to have a very hard time or even be killed.

My thoughts at that time were simply that I was given a mission and it was my duty to serve that mission to the best of my ability. That was it. I felt these children deserved the opportunity to come to our country, to be safe. Even if the children did not look American at all, the thought that they may have an American parent would have led them to be killed. I'm proud of having been part of that.

Years later there was an effort by some parents in Vietnam who wanted to get their children back. I guess I can understand their feelings.

In Michigan, I go to a Vietnamese nail salon and when I tell them I was a flight nurse in and out of Saigon they treat me like gold. The ones who speak good English will ask me all sorts of questions about my time over there and then share it with all the others. They would tell me stories of how they got out of the country on boats. They very much appreciated the fact that they were able to come to the United States.

I feel privileged to have served in the Air Force. It continued my education, I've traveled the world, made incredible friends. I have nothing but good things to say about serving my country. Between active duty and reserves, I spent a total of twenty-seven years in the Air Force and retired as a full colonel.

I will admit though that there was a time when I was pretty upset with my country. It was when we were flying those missions and no one seemed to care. All those people killed in that horrible crash and hardly anyone said a word. You would see the demonstrations on TV; I still have no use for Jane Fonda. Maybe those people didn't appreciate the fact that we were risking our lives. If they were not in favor of the war, fine. But the protests are what bothered me.

Our country's attitude has certainly changed. I believe the people who served in Vietnam helped pave the way for our current vets. Back then you never heard anyone say, "Thank you for your service." I think Vietnam vets showed everyone else how returning vets should be welcomed home and respected.

Passing the word: Paul and Donna Boehm, chapter leaders of Vietnam Veterans of America, work together in the basement of their home to put out a newsletter for Vietnam War veterans. The publication is called *Free Fire Zone*, carrying items of interest to vets.

Paul and Donna Boehm were featured for their work with the local Vietnam Veterans of America chapter in the Green Bay Press-Gazette.

DONNA AND PAUL BOEHM

Vietnam Veterans of America

One of the constant themes shared by Vietnam vets is the lack of counseling or organized support once they returned home. Donna Boehm and her husband, Paul, an Army veteran and a two-time Purple Heart recipient, saw this need and took it upon themselves to remedy the situation.

Starting at the grass-roots level and working out of their basement, they formed Vietnam Veterans of America Chapter 224 which has become one of the largest Chapters in the state of Wisconsin.

DONNA: It really started on Veterans Day 1984. We were in Washington, D.C., for the dedication of the Fighting Man statue at the Vietnam Memorial. We were just walking around with a Vietnam Veterans group from La Crosse, Wisconsin, and they just started telling me their stories. It was just out of the blue. This group of four guys and me were talking as we walked along. One of them started talking about his brother being on the Wall and how they had both been in Vietnam. It was block after block of conversations like this. I don't know why he picked me to open up to, but I just felt like it was a sign that we needed to do something. We needed to start a Vietnam Vets chapter back home.

We were on the plane heading back to Green Bay the next day and I turned to Paul and said, "We're going to start one of those chapters in Green Bay." He said, "No we're not." I said, "Yes we are." He said, "No we're not." I said. Yes, we are." He said, "It's a lot of work." I said, "I don't care. We will do it together. I can't do it myself. You're the veteran. I need you. We can do this."

Paul Boehm collection

I just felt that the guys in our area needed a way to meet together and share their stories. I didn't know of any other way of getting them together than to go back home and start a chapter.

PAUL: Donna won the argument. I figured it was better to agree. She wasn't going to quit. She was going to spearhead this. So I got going and we started connecting other Vietnam vets in town to see if they were interested in something like this, and they were.

DONNA: It all began in our basement. We started out so small. We had a little can, a lard can to collect donations in.

PAUL: We still have that can. We put it in our museum.

DONNA: We also had a copy machine in the basement that we would print the newsletter on.

We would call and call and call people. Paul called all the people he knew from high school who had been in the service. We would have little meet and greets. We would go wherever we could get a free venue and maybe have some hotdogs and beer donated. That's how we would get them to sign up. And then Paul found a way to raise money so those guys could become lifetime members and not have to pay dues.

It took a while to really get going, but after about two years we got up to 500 members. We ran it until 1994 and then backed off and let others run it.

The timing, when we started, was perfect. The guys were finally ready to talk. The media was also suddenly interested in Vietnam and guys felt like they were finally allowed to talk about it.

PAUL: A lot of the guys though were still pretty leery about talking to anyone other than other vets. It was hard for some of those guys to come out because they had always been depicted as crazy, long-haired lunatics. What we wanted to do was show that we were regular people. We were Catholics or Lutherans or whatever religion there is. A lot of us went to church. We had jobs and we raised our families. We weren't all crazy. The great majority of vets were normal citizens.

Our first official gig was at the National Railroad Museum (Green Bay, Wisconsin). There were four of us that showed up and marched in their ceremony. We carried a flag on a pole that one of the guys had taken off the wall from his work. The knob on top of the pole was loose and kept coming off while we were marching and someone would have to go over and pick it up. The American Legion guys were laughing at us.

DONNA: I'm sure they were thinking, *Typical rag-tag Vietnam vets*. For some, the recognition was good, for others it wasn't. We had many guys crying in our basement. They didn't want to be in the news. They didn't want to talk about Vietnam. They were wondering why they had to keep being reminded of it. There were some that just wanted it buried. None of their experiences with the media up until then had been good.

We just tried to help coach them through it with a lot of beers and a lot of tears. Mainly we just listened. For some reason, guys would open up to me, share their deepest memories. Many of the stories were horrible, just horrible. Stories they had never told anyone before, not even their wives. Some of them hadn't even told their wives they had been in Vietnam. Which is incredible.

PAUL: We were always depicted as losers, as baby-killers, many had terrible homecomings. I mean, these were guys who, many of them, had put their friends in body bags. And they still weren't accepted back home.

I was at a VFW for a buddy's wedding reception one time and we were at the bar to have a drink and I was talking about joining and one of the guys said, "No, you can't join up here. You weren't in a real war." Vietnam wasn't a real war? Okie-Dokie.

DONNA: Many of these guys felt that by the end of the war, the American people not only hated the war but hated the veterans too. They believed that anything the news reported would be negative. So they didn't say anything to anybody.

As Paul said, some of them had picked up their friends in pieces and then within twenty-four hours went from the mud of Vietnam to their hometowns. They had no counseling, nothing. So, like any painful episode, they buried it. But then with the anniversary of the fall of Saigon, the memories started coming to the surface and they were a mess, just a mess.

PAUL: There was one vet that I partied-hardy with. But then one night he sat down in our basement and told his story. One member of his group had accused him of being a coward. He said that he had hidden during an attack and that's the only reason he was one of the few survivors. He was living with that every day. He sat there and cried and cried and cried.

DONNA: Survivors' guilt was huge, huge with many of them. It didn't matter where they served or what they did. They just felt they didn't do enough.

In the late 1980s, we went to the Chicago Welcome Home Parade. That was the first big one in the country. It was an awesome experience, unbelievable, a once-in-a-lifetime thing. It was really the first public thank you these guys had gotten. It helped so many guys so much.

PAUL: We were marching down the street and they would be throwing confetti out of the tops of these high-rise buildings. By the time the parade was done the stuff was up to our knees.

DONNA: Afterwards a lot of guys who hadn't seen each other since Vietnam reconnected at the park. It was really something special.

PAUL: You're bringing a tear to my eye right now. Another thing we could sit and talk about for hours is the Wall. (Vietnam Veterans Monument, Washington, D.C.)

DONNA: That's a sacred place. It's just sacred. Everyone who is connected to it in any way experiences something spiritual when they go there. We have been there at least ten times. We would go there

Paul Boehm (left) leans on a shovel as he and a buddy take a break while in Vietnam. (Paul Boehm collection)

---

anytime day or night. It didn't matter. There were times we went at midnight just to connect with the guys.

When the artist that designed it decided to cut the earth to open the wounds so they could heal properly, well, she had to have had some sort of spiritual guidance.

I know some people didn't like it, but I think she had it down perfectly. She got it.

PAUL: When we went there we told guys who hadn't been before to bring their Kleenex. We knew guys would cry. Let it out. But when you go there, you don't just go there. You have to sneak up on it, start where it's low, and go from there. And then when you get down into the hole at the bottom everyone is quiet as church mice.

I remember one time a school bus pulled up with a bunch of kids on a field trip. You know how kids are on a field trip. Well, those kids were so quiet, so respectful. That was really something.

You didn't have to have been in the same place over there to form a bond, a brotherhood. It's just sharing the same experiences. It's like you were together even though you weren't physically together. You could have been with the 101st or The Big Red 1, and experienced the same exact things. The hardships, the being gone at Christmas, being away from your family. It was just all the experiences put together and that creates a camaraderie of brotherhood. It's just what we endured that kept us together.

DONNA: Paul still has nightmares. He still has flashbacks.

PAUL: You never know what will trigger them. It might be a smell, a sound, a helicopter flying over with that hum of the rotor. I will get flashbacks just cutting the lawn from just the smell. Not terrible thoughts, just fleeting thoughts.

You know, once we started getting vocal with our groups and everything, some of the Korean War vets started speaking up. They were kind of treated like us when they came back. They didn't lose their war. They didn't tie their war. Everyone just called it quits. It was exactly the same in Vietnam. They just quit. Fifty-eight thousand dead Americans and then they quit. That bothered some guys, you know? At least blow the frickin' place up before you leave. Bomb Hanoi, drop a big frickin' bomb down the biggest chimney in the middle of the place before you leave.

DONNA: Not all the Vietnam vets want the attention. There was a time the city of Green Bay wanted to feature the Vietnam vets in its Fourth of July parade and a lot of them said no. Too many years had gone by and it was not their time anymore. They didn't want to do that. It was the young guys' turn, like the 432nd (Civil Affairs Battalion) when they came home from Iraq. It was their turn to be welcomed home.

The planning committee couldn't believe it. They were dumbfounded. We were still in it, just not in the front. I drove a cute convertible with the Gold Star mothers, in the rain. They loved it.

We did have a great time with the 432nd when they returned home. We had so much fun with them. There was a parade that was going to end at the Brown County (Veterans Memorial) Arena. We made them a banner in our basement that went all the way across Oneida Street.

PAUL: Our basement smelled like magic markers for a month.

DONNA: Our guys said that no one is coming back from anywhere anymore without a proper welcome home.

PAUL: When they got a few blocks from the arena, we went out with beers and everything and welcomed them home right in the middle of the street. People were like, "You can't stop a parade." The hell we can't. "But they will be late getting to the arena." Yeah well, that's too bad. We had a great time with them. We welcomed them home in our own way.

DONNA: One of our long-term goals was raising money to build memorials around Green Bay. For the first one we were hoping to raise $18,000 and we raised $25,000. We gave it everything we had. Paul and I each worked forty hours a week at our regular jobs and we both spent at least forty hours a week with the chapter.

Sometimes I think we had to be getting help from up above. We just had to be. There's no other way we could have pulled this off. But we could tell we were making a difference. Guys would say, "Finally we have somebody to talk to about this."

And then the guys in the group would form new friendships among themselves. You would have lawyers and your everyday workers and in this group, they were all equal. No one was above anybody else. It was really something special to witness.

PAUL: The best result from starting up the chapter? Brotherhood.

DONNA: Now I'm tearing up, but yes the camaraderie. It was just awesome to witness. It didn't matter what you did for a living, what you did in the service, what you did in Vietnam, none of that mattered.

PAUL: Back then we could go to a bar. Well, now it might have to be old folks' home, but we could play one song and if there were Vietnam vets there we would have people hanging on to one another, swaying to the music and singing. And some probably would shed a tear. The song would be *Goodnight Saigon* by Billy Joel.

DONNA: I'm proud of how far we advanced as far as raising money to build three memorials. We have the All Service Memorial, the Vietnam Vets Memorial, and the POW Memorial.

But honestly, in the beginning, bringing all these guys together was my biggest goal. That's what I really wanted to do and it's still what I'm most proud of.

PAUL: I always tell people and my kids if it wasn't for Donna, I would be dead. I would be a dead man and I believe that. The only thing we had before the chapter was to self-medicate and taverns seemed like a good place to do it. Donna found a way to give us another option.

GOLD STAR FAMILIES

I've always felt that the most underappreciated aspect of those who fight in wars is the effect it has on the ones they leave behind. The pain of seeing a man in uniform at the front door about to deliver the terrible news is, I'm quite certain, a nightmarish experience that never truly goes away.

With the greatest respect, four Gold Star families share not only the immediate pain, but the lifelong effects of losing a beloved family member in the war.

DAVID DELLANGELO

8th Cavalry Regiment
1st Air Cavalry Division
US Army
Vietnam War
KIA October 3, 1968

David Dellangelo's story is as heartbreaking as they come. After completing his tour in Vietnam with the 1st Air Cavalry, the wheels of his transport plane were off the ground. The first leg of his journey to his hometown of Negaunee, Michigan, had begun. He had to be euphoric. This is a moment he surely dreamed about during every unbearably hot, wet, miserable day in his combat zone.

He was minutes into his trip to freedom, on October 3, 1968 when absolute catastrophe struck. It would lead to him being the only service member from his hometown to die in Vietnam.

His younger brother Andy, sixteen at the time, recalls the terrible night they were told of the incident and the lasting effect on his family.

ANDY DELLANGELO:

After high school, Dave went to Northern (Northern Michigan University) for a year, but he didn't like it. My dad was telling him to stay in school, but he was drafted as soon as he dropped out and, after training, was sent straight to 'Nam.

He was in Vietnam from the fall of 1967 to the fall of '68. I know there was some heavy fighting going on there, but he never really shared anything with us. Maybe he told my mom in the letters he sent her, but she didn't really share too much with us. Later on, she ended up burning the letters to try to put it behind her. I've got some of his air medals for the number of times he flew into combat. He must have done a lot of flying in choppers in and out of the jungle. I think it took 25 missions to get one medal.

It was kind of tense having a brother over there. I kind of went about my business with sports and high school, but you would hear about it every night on the newscasts. They would be talking about so many casualties and everything. You couldn't really get away from it.

He was right near the end of his tour when he decided to stay for an extra month. They had a deal where if you volunteered to extend, you would be able to get out of the Army as soon as you got back. So he stayed for the extra month and got set to come home.

He got on the transport plane to take him out of the field. There were 10 other guys on there with him. I guess they were about 1,100 feet in the air when a chopper came in and collided with the plane. From what we heard the blades of the chopper came through the windshield. They both went down. There were thirteen guys on the chopper. Everybody was killed, twenty-four guys.

Editor's note: *A summary of the official report of the accident states that the CH-47 helicopter, commonly known as a Chinook, was on a routine flight delivering troops and supplies to Camp Evans. The base was located less than twenty miles north of the city of Hue and very near Highway 1 which was one of the main highways in South Vietnam.*

At roughly the same time the Chinook was descending to land, a C7-A transport plane which David Dellangelo and ten others were on, was taking off from that same field. Investigators determined that the two aircraft collided with the rotor blades of the Chinook slicing through the windshield of the airplane killing both pilots instantly. The plane spun out of control and crashed. All on board were killed. The damage to the Chinook was also catastrophic leading to a similar crash and the loss of all eleven men on board.

I remember it was at night and there was a knock on the door so I answered it. There was a guy standing there in uniform. I knew what that meant. He told my parents what happened. It was a nightmare. I ended up calling some neighbors that were close friends to come and sit with my parents. It was bad.

It killed my dad. It killed him. He started getting dementia and then I think he just gave up. He closed the bar he owned two years later. My mom was a tough old bird, but it was tough on her. She didn't talk much about it, but she was a mess. My sister was only ten. She was a mess too. It was bad, it was really tough. I guess I had to be the strong one. It definitely toughened me up mentally, you know. I was only sixteen years old. I was young and had my life ahead of me so I tried to go on.

I was in a bar in Gwinn, (Michigan) one time and a guy asked me my name and I said Dellangelo. He said, "Any relation to Dave?" I said that was my brother. He started to cry. He was there when it happened. He said he was sitting at the bar on base. I asked him why he wasn't on the plane. He said he was in no hurry to get out of there. He said he was all done with the fighting and was in a safe area. I guess he wanted to hang out with his buddies. But he said Dave was in a hurry so he jumped on the very first plane he could get on.

I wasn't really into politics, but I wasn't really for the war. You think of the people over there, even the Vietnamese people. We bombed the hell out of them. It wasn't just the Americans, the Vietnamese were suffering too. I just wish we could avoid those kinds of conflicts. I feel bad for families that have gone through something like that. Just like the guys in Iraq and Afghanistan. They get hit with those roadside bombs and are losing legs, or getting killed and leaving a wife and kids behind. It's just sad. Too bad countries can't find a way to get along.

They always say leaders don't fight, soldiers do. That's the truth.

JOHN GMACK

8th Cavalry Regiment
1st Cavalry Division
US Army
Vietnam War
KIA May 28, 1970

If anyone thought turbulence on the streets in the US or bloodshed in the jungles of Southeast Asia would begin to subside in the new decade of the 1970s, they were sorely disappointed. The two in fact would go hand-in-hand.

1970 will be remembered for the US military making its first official forays into Cambodia, attacking the Communist forces before they could cross the border and stage attacks in South Vietnam. While many military strategists applauded the decision, huge numbers of college students and regular citizens alike saw the move as an escalation of the war and protested in numbers never before seen.

What may have been overlooked were very young, very brave, very frustrated GIs such as John Gmack of Green Bay, Wisconsin, who just hoped to make it home from a war he believed had become pointless. His sister, Jill Gmack Amel, details this young soldier's life and the struggles to see him recognized for his sacrifice.

Jill Gmack Amel:

John was two years older than me. In looking back I wish we were closer, but he was just that big brother who did his thing at Premontre High School. He played hockey and loved the outdoors, hunting and fishing. His girlfriend was a cheerleader at St. Joseph Academy. I was going to Green Bay West and had my circle of friends. He used to try and set me up with some of his buddies, but I didn't want any part of those guys. I was too shy and introverted. They would have run roughshod over me.

John Gmack
(Gmack family collection)

He wasn't a bad guy in any way, just mischievous and was known for having bad luck. I remember he used to make fake IDs for his friends. Another time my mom found a bottle of alcohol in the closet that he was going to be taking out; so she filled it with a nasty mixture of who knows what. One day he was practicing casting with his fishing pole in the yard and broke a window on our house. We had cousins who invited us over for the opening of their pool. It was still frigid cold, but my aunt dared John to jump in for five dollars. He did, with all his clothes on. That was John.

One night he was out with his friends and someone sucker-punched him over a girl, knocking out his front tooth. Then when he was out with his buddies he would take out his plate and secretly put it in their pitcher of beer. He had a great sense of humor.

But he also had a very serious and quiet side. He dreamed of being a doctor. We had an uncle who was a doctor and John wanted to follow in his footsteps in the worst way. But when he tried enrolling at UWGB he was told he didn't have enough science classes or the right kind to get in. My dad was not happy with the admissions office that they wouldn't at least try to find a way to make it work. My dad still holds a grudge over them for not letting him make up those classes he needed.

So because of that, the whole military thing started. I think he had a low lottery number so a friend of his convinced him to avoid the draft and join the Army. That gave him a chance to go to officers training school, which is what he wanted to do.

The morning he left for Vietnam is kind of hazy. He had been home on leave. I do recall he only wore his uniform one time while he was home, and that's only because someone asked him to. I just remember that he left really early, like 5:00 a.m. I heard my parents get up and the normal commotion, but I just stood in the background. I think I was a little afraid to face reality. Also maybe a little afraid to intrude on my parents' goodbyes. So I just stayed in the background. That's all I remember about that day. I believe it was Valentine's Day of 1970.

John sent a lot of letters. At the time I read them, but I don't remember too much about them. I should pick them up and reread them now. When you're that age, sixteen, you just don't think anything bad could happen. You just felt like, *He will be back, he will be back, we don't have to worry about him.* I did write to him, but I regret that I didn't write to him more.

I think my mom saved every one of them. He would ask about things back home, about the political situation with protests and everything. He just said, "From my standpoint, whatever they do to protest the war, more power to them. This is not something we should be in. Let them protest. Let them do whatever they can to get us out of here." He wanted people to know that it wasn't right to still be fighting over there.

Looking back now I can see that he was still himself in a lot of ways. He would ask us to send him Kool-Aid and things like that. He was always appreciative of what we sent and he always wanted to make sure he said hello to Grandma. But he was also very honest about what they were going through. He hated being there: the heat, the rats, the jungle rot like he got on his thumb that wouldn't go away, many of his friends were being killed or wounded. Other than being with what he said were a really great bunch of guys, there wasn't one good thing about it.

***

March 10, 1970
Dear Mom and Dad,

I thought I'd better write today because tomorrow we get logged and the mail goes out and comes in.

Well, we left the LZ the day before yesterday and came out in the field on a not too good of a mission. These are the details, the 8th E company (30 men) made contact with the gooks in a bunker complex and were outnumbered. Around 3:00 p.m. that afternoon we got the word to be ready to go out and help them. But because it was so late only one platoon got out. E company had already had 3 killed and 8 wounded. So our only platoon got there with only 15 minutes of daylight left and went into the bunkers. They got 6 wounded alone that night.

Today I walked point and was shaking a little but we only heard the gooks moving ahead of us, nobody shot. Am glad this day is over with.

Well anyway, I'm still alive and healthy but we still got to get to that bunker complex. Probably tomorrow or the day after...

So any word on my re-up yet? In your next letter, send a pin for my watch, I lost one.

Gotta go now, Love John

P.S. Don't worry. (Yet)

***

When John enlisted he was promised his choice of jobs in the Army. Infantry definitely wasn't one of them. He asked my dad to contact Senator Proxmire, which he did, about a rule that if you weren't given the job you were promised that they would take, I believe, a year off of your service time. If that didn't work he wanted to re-up with the hopes of getting a different job and out of the infantry right away.

***

March 18, 1970
Dear Mom and Dad,

This is going to be short but to the point because of lack of paper and daylight. As of now I have made up my mind about re-upping and I think my decision will stand. My answer is yes, I'm going to re-up for the following reasons.

1. *On the last 11 days we have had 3 killed and 17 wounded.*
2. *I lost a friend today-killed-shot in the head. Goes with #1*
3. *Everybody, including my squad leader, says to re-up.*
4. *If I stay 11-B (11 Bravo infantry) I'll probably end up here for a second tour.*
5. *I WANT TO STAY ALIVE!*

The car deal sounds good. What's the price? Any extras? My vote is for a boat.

The guys here are all real nice, you couldn't find much better. I suppose because we're all in the same boat. I really can't tell you where I am in relation to a city. All I know is that we're about 10-15 miles from Cambodia and our rear is in Song Be.

I did get Grandmas package almost 2½ weeks ago.

Gotta go, Write soon,

Love, John

P.S. Letters may be coming further apart because of contact.

John Gmack heads out on a five-day patrol into the jungles near Song Be, South Vietnam. (Gmack family collection)

March 24, 1970
Dear Mom and Dad,
   This is going to be real short but can't be helped. Just a brief news letter. I'm alive although action has been heavy. We lost 7 more. So our total is 4 KIA and 21 wounded. No need to worry for 3 days anyway. Tomorrow we go on a 3 day R&R cause we are in such a hurt, mentally and physically. You wouldn't believe the strain.
   So for now, write soon, Love John

March 29, 1970
Dear Mom and Dad and fam,
   Finally now I can write some letters.
   I just finished my 3½ day R&R in Bien Hoa and it was great. All

the cold beer and pop and good food we wanted. Needless to say I wasn't in much shape for writing letters.

The total for our 16 days in the boonies ran 32 people, 4 dead, 28 wounded.

Storm lost 2 fingers. I saw him at the airport. He was on his way home and smiling all over the place. I hope this time the area is better. Now I'm about 6 miles west of Song Be.

I got 3 packages in Bien Hoa, 1 from you and 2 from Grandma. So tell her thanks. (the cake was spoiled.)

I sent 3 rolls of film home. So get them developed and send back with 2 envelopes big enough to put them in, ok?

On one of the rolls there's some pics of a show we had in Bien Hoa. It was good, everybody went crazy and everybody was smiling for the first time in a few days.

Well gotta go, Love, John

April 1, 1970
Dear Mom and Dad,

Just a short note, I just remembered something about my re-up. So goes the army that if you were guaranteed something and are a three-year man, but don't get it, they chop one year off the time. I was guaranteed my choice of schools but didn't get it. So maybe you can work something on that. If it happens that they will take a year off I will stay out here.

Not much more to say.

Love, John.

April 6, 1970
Dear Mom and Dad,

I got your package a couple days ago and the watch pins. Also a box of gum from Grandpa-thanks.

I also got a letter from Proxmire.

So I wrote him back and told him the story and asked him if I could change my MOS without re-upping, or if I could get a year taken off. He sounded pretty interested.

***

I believe John felt like he had to do something. That if it stayed the way it was, he was not getting out of Vietnam alive. I know my parents wanted to do anything they could to get him out of there. He felt they didn't have a cause to fight for anymore.

The last letter he wrote was three days before he died. He wrote of finding a big enemy cache. Finding that would lead to everything else

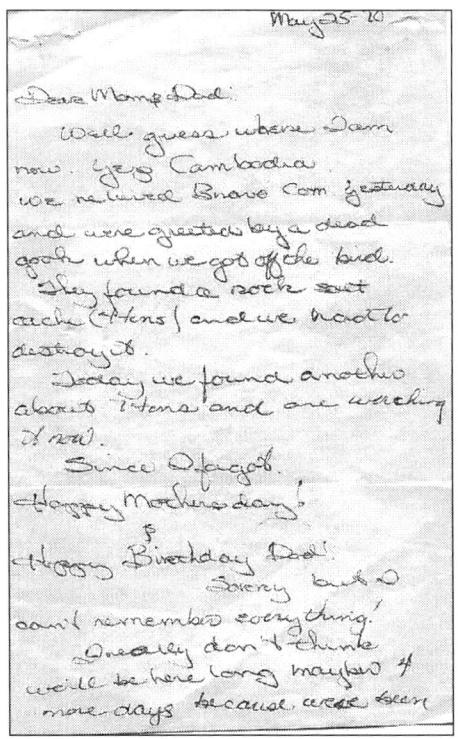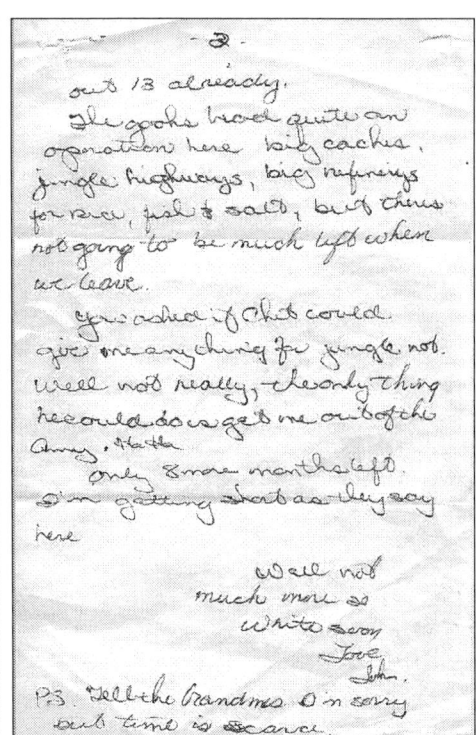

John Gmack's final letter home arrived the day after the family was notified of his death. (Gmack family collection)

that has happened since. We received the letter the day after we were notified that he had been killed.

***

May 25, 1970
Dear Mom and Dad,
Well guess where I am now. Yes Cambodia.
We relieved Bravo Company yesterday and were greeted by a dead gook when we got off the bird.
They found a rock salt cache (4 tons) and we had to destroy it. Today we found another, about 7 tons and we are watching it now.
Since I forgot, Happy Mother's Day! And Happy Birthday dad! Sorry but I can't remember everything!
I really don't think we'll be here long, maybe 4 more days because we've been out 13 already. The gooks had quite an operation here, big caches, jungle highways, big refineries for rice, fish and salt, but they're not going to be much left when we leave.
You asked if Chet could give me anything for jungle rot. Well not really, the only thing he could do is get me out of the army. Ha ha.

John Gmack works a weapon while bandaged up to protect the jungle rot on his left thumb. (Gmack family collection)

Only 8 months left. I'm getting short as they say here.
Well not much more so write soon.
 Love John
P.S. Tell Grandma I'm sorry but time is scarce.

***

He was killed on Memorial Day, May 28, 1970.

The day we were notified is extremely fuzzy to me. I think my mind went into a shell and repressed my memories. Anyway, this is what I have in my memories of that day.

We lived right behind St. Agnes Church in Green Bay. My mom went to church every day. She had wanted to become a nun when she was younger.

She was walking home from church when she saw a strange car drive by. She got a feeling that this was not good, that something wasn't right.

My dad was golfing. Someone got a hold of him at the golf course. When he got home mom was lying on their bed crying. My parents were normally very stoic, very stoned face. I had never seen them cry.

I just remember going to my room to get out of the way. My brother Jim was there. He remembers it much better than I do.

Jim Gmack:

It was a beautiful sunny day. I was twelve years old. My mom had gone to church to pray for John's safe return, as she did on a regular basis. While she was gone an Army officer came to our door. I opened it and he asked if my mom and dad were home. I told them no, but that my mom should be home soon. He said thanks and that he would be back later. I didn't think anything of it. I figured maybe it was one of John's friends coming over to visit.

When my mom came home I told her a guy from the Army had been there. She looked at me and I saw the life drain right out of her eyes. She knew exactly why he had been there. I will never forget that.

When the officer came back she went to the door and received the news. She dropped to the floor, just collapsed. I can still see it like it happened yesterday. I felt terrible. It was very tough to see. I was very concerned as to whether or not she would be okay.

Losing John was devastating, just brutal. He was the firstborn. We all looked up to him. We knew he had a great future ahead of him. My mom was a very tough lady and didn't show too much emotion, but I know she never got over it.

Jill Gmack Amel:

I do remember the funeral mass, it was at St. Agnes Church. It was absolutely overflowing. The visitation was at Coad Funeral Home, right across from our family appliance business. His girlfriend, Kathy, and I hadn't really been close but we definitely supported each other that night. Neither one of us wanted to be in the room when they closed the casket. We just hung on to each other in an adjacent room.

Interment was at Fort Howard Cemetery in front of the little chapel. John was always late for everything and my dad used to say he's going to be late for his own funeral. Well, the hearse overheated and broke down on the way there. So yes, you could say John was late for his own funeral.

My mother was very stoic until they played taps and did the twenty-one-gun salute. That was hard for her. Hard for everyone.

It was such a terrible, terrible thing that he died. But to see how much he was loved by the number of people who came out was at least a very good feeling. Even fifty years later his old friends and classmates still remember and honor him.

On June 24th, 1970, a little less than a month after John died, one of his close friends from Vietnam wrote to my parents and described what happened:

Mr. and Mrs. Gmack, I'm one of the grunts from the second platoon of Alpha company. I've been in either Vietnam or Cambodia for five months now. John and I got along quite well together and I considered him one of my best friends. We went through the bad times as well as good times together.

I really didn't know at first if I should tell you how he died because it was just an ironic accident, but who has a better right to know than you?

Here it is exactly as it happened. We found an unusually large cache of NVA field gear. It took most of the day to uncover it and take an inventory of the items found. We were going to bring in engineers to blow up and extract the cache, but it was too late to get them in that day.

To make sure the gooks didn't try taking it away, the first platoon put an automatic ambush on the trail. An automatic ambush is several claymore mines on a tripwire.

John's position was the next one to the left of mine. Two people from my squad went out to put out trip flares and John went out with one other man from his position. Remember, it was 8:00 and already dark when we got there. The 4 men were walking towards each other when a man from our squad tripped the ambush. The blast was about 20-30 feet away from me and it was absolutely deafening. Trees and bamboo were flying around and 3 big balls of fire and smoke rose above the treetops.

This is the worst part, two of them we couldn't even find in the darkness. When the sun came up we did find what was left of them. When we found John he wasn't in too bad a shape at least not that any of us or the medics could see. We called in a medevac bird to take him out.

That next morning word came over the radio that he had died in the early morning hours. This was really hard to take and it really hurt. I knew I had lost my best friend. But then I would think about it and find myself not believing it. Almost as though it's all a bad dream and someday I'll wake up and it will be over. But when the AK-47s start and the B-40 rockets start coming in I know it's no dream.

At times I get so sick of seeing gooks, watching my buddies die, the mud and the rain, the jungle and the bugs, that I feel like throwing down my weapon and quitting everything.

Such is the life of the grunt. The people who are actually fighting this war; the people who search the jungles for the enemy and fight him face to face on his own ground. And what do we get for it? Quite a bit! We get our buddies killed and the chance to do it all over again tomorrow and the next day for 364 days.

I am truly sorry this had to happen and I'm sorry for you people too. I hope I never have to see this type of thing again.

Sincerely...

***

My mom was very upset that John didn't receive a Purple Heart. She tried contacting our State Representative, Toby Roth, to help but they didn't get anywhere with the Army.

I tried hard twice, through different channels including Representative Mike Gallagher of Green Bay's office to get him one. His assistant Kerry did everything she could for us but no luck. The Army kept saying his death wasn't because of enemy contact.

Here's part of one of the letters we got back:

Department of the Army
Awards and Decorations Branch
1-3-18

...pursuant to Department of Defense and Army regulation, award of the Purple Heart is authorized only to Soldiers who are wounded as a result of enemy action. Based on review of official casualty rolls from the Vietnam era, he was killed on May 28, 1970 as a result of non-hostile circumstances...he does not meet the strict regulatory criteria for award of the Purple Heart...

Another excuse they gave was that there was "No enemy presence." Well, as we tried to point out, there were enemy weapons in the cache, and I read one letter that there were enemy footprints all over. How can you say the enemy didn't have a presence?"

One of the hardest things I ever had to do was call his former captain. He was not well-liked in our family. My parents really resented the fact that those guys were sent out at night, pitch dark, in the rain, weren't even told exactly where they were supposed to go, and besides that, John could basically only use one hand.

The captain did write a letter supporting John getting the medal. But told me he still supported sending them out on that mission, said it was something that he believed had to be done.

EXCERPTS: "...*I firmly believe that US soldiers, sailors, airmen, and Marines serving and fighting in direct combat - as was the case with PFC Gmack - earned their Purple Hearts when wounded or killed in the line of duty against enemies of the United States. I hope the re-*

view of the just request will agree with me that he earned this and will at last present this award to his family on behalf of a grateful nation."

They told us we would only have two shots at it, but we're not going to stop trying. We are allowed more attempts but only if we come up with new viable information.

For years we would take my parents to the Vietnam Memorial in Green Bay on Memorial Day. My mom so respected the Vietnam vets that were there. She knew they were a family. That they had to form a family among themselves because the country had turned against them.

When mom passed we asked, instead of flowers, to make a donation that would go to the Vietnam Vets Association and the Disabled American Vets. We gave them over $4,000. Mom would have been so happy with that.

My husband and I have property near Mountain, Wisconsin, and have an agreement with the DNR to log the property. We decided that when they logged it, we would cut trails in so we could use our ATVs and kind of explore the area.

We name them all, trying to be clever, like "Blackberry Trail, "Loggers Lane," "Pine Cone Pass." We had signs made for each of them.

There was one place on the property we called, "Hunters Hill." On the top was a clearing that headed toward a deer stand. I said to my husband, "You know what? That looks like a good place for a landing zone, a safe spot." We named it, "LZ John."

Every time we go up there and see it I think of him and how much he would have loved it. I feel his spirit there like it's his comfort zone. A peaceful place for him to be.

This sign honors the memory of John Gmack on property in northern Wisconsin owned by John's sister, Jill, and her husband.

MIKAL SULLIVAN

2nd Marine Regiment
3rd Marine Division
US Marine Corps
Vietnam War
KIA June 6, 1968

While there may not have been what could be considered a "safe" time to enter the military during the Vietnam War, the years of early 1967 through 1968 were, without question, the most lethal.

Body counts, broadcast nationwide on network newscasts, brought the stark news into living rooms on a nightly basis. Over 28,200, nearly half of the 58,220 killed in the 11-year-war, lost their lives during that two-year period.

Undeterred, two brothers from De Pere, Wisconsin, Patrick and Mikal Sullivan, just over a year apart in age, enlisted. Mikal, a proud determined Marine, would become the first person from his hometown to lose his life in Vietnam.

Patrick Sullivan, an Army veteran, recalls the brother he so admired.

Patrick Sullivan:
From the time Mikal was ten or eleven years old, he subscribed to *Leatherneck Magazine*. That was his dream, to be a Marine. Why, I don't know, but that's what he wanted to do. It's not like my family pushed him or anything. In fact, my dad did not like the military at all. He had been in the engineers during World War II in the Philippines and hated being bossed around and told what to do.

Mikal Sullivan poses with his rifle in a river in Vietnam. (Sullivan family collection)

The funny thing is I felt the same way that Mikal did. I felt a need to serve my country. In April of 1967, I enlisted in the Army. In May Mikal and a buddy skipped school and joined the Marines. In fact, we have another brother, Jim, who spent twenty-eight years in the Army and retired as a command sergeant major. So we definitely felt a sense of duty in our family to defend our country.

The weird thing about Mikal is that he had rheumatic fever five times. Two of the times were so severe that he was in the hospital. He must have lied to the recruiter and they didn't find anything when they gave him a physical. When he was in Vietnam, the state health department came looking for him. They had declared him handicapped because they saw in his records that he had rheumatic fever so many times.

He was a good kid. A tough kid but a good kid. He was friends with everybody. We had so many laughs. We worked at a pizza garden together. It was called "The Scroll," on Main Street in West De Pere. It was mostly kitchen work and deliveries. I remember one time he came back from a delivery and told me about a famous Packers player who was having a party at his house when he was supposed to be at training camp. The funny thing is, that player had talked to Mikal's class about staying out of trouble and things. He asked Mikal, "You're not going to say anything to anyone are you?" We got a big kick out of that.

Mikal was a heck of a football player. He was a halfback. I would go watch him play at old Minahan Stadium. I remember one time he had a pulled groin and they basically taped his legs together so he could play. He played all four years in high school. At his funeral three of the six pallbearers were his high school football coaches. I thought that really said something about the kind of guy and the kind of football player he was. The coaches loved him.

When he wrote to me from Vietnam he didn't say anything about how bad it was. He didn't want me to worry. Years later when I found out what it had been like for him, I felt worse than ever. I know I would have been scared shitless. They were in Quang Tri Province near Con Thien. I found out that a lot of people in his platoon were getting killed right alongside him. They were going out on patrols every couple of days. The day he was killed, they were in a battle for five-six hours.

In 1991 one of his guys wrote about what it was like.

Editor's note: *In a thorough twenty-one-page first-person account of the battle, one member of the platoon, Jim Kaylor, a friend of Mikal and later of the Sullivan family, described what started out as a routine patrol on an exceedingly hot day in June 1968. The following is a summarization of that account.*

The platoon, which included Mikal Sullivan, had been patrolling a dry rice paddy when suddenly near 11:00 a.m. a tremendously well-concealed and numerically superior force of NVA soldiers sprung an ambush from bunkers and firing holes. During the intense fighting, the corporal directing the fight asked for a volunteer to go in search of a squad on the right flank with whom they had lost radio contact. Both Kaylor and Sullivan volunteered. Mikal was selected. It's the last contact any of the survivors had with him. After the battle, Kaylor helped recover Mikal's body and carry it to the waiting Huey helicopters. Kaylor realized that the roles could very easily have been reversed.

According to Kaylors' research, the platoon had fourteen killed during the nearly six-hour battle. He also cites statistics that on that day alone, forty-five Marines were killed in action in Quang Tri Province.

Patrick Sullivan:

In late May of 1968 I was sent to Germany. I hadn't been there long before my parents received a telegram telling them that Mikal had been killed in action. It was June 6, 1968, the same day that Robert Kennedy was assassinated.

I made it home before his body arrived. It took over three weeks for it to make it back. There were so many people getting killed in Vietnam at that time that they were backed up processing them all.

He was sent to California, then Dover, Delaware. That's where they fixed him up in his dress blues uniform and placed a plastic shield over him. Then he was sent to Ryan Funeral Home in De Pere.

Before he was sent to Vietnam I had actually tried to see if I could take his place, but they just laughed at me and said no way. I had a job most people would have loved. I was a cartographer. I was sitting in an office or a big tent, making maps. On other days we would go out in the country and set up communication sites. At the same time he was getting shot at with AK-47s and mortars and his guys were being overrun. Plus, he was married and had a daughter. She was born in September of 1967. He and I both came home for the baptism. That's the last time we were together. Right after that he got shipped out to Vietnam.

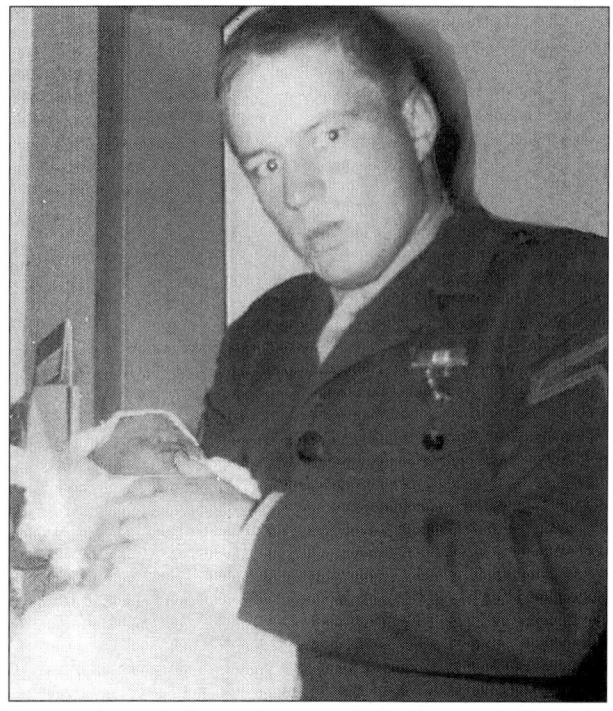

Prior to leaving for Vietnam, Mikal Sullivan came home on leave for his daughter Christine's birth and baptism. (Sullivan family collection)

1968 was a sad time for military people. You kept hearing that the people back in the states hated you. When I was on my way back for the funeral and stopped at Ft. Dix, New Jersey, somebody said I would be smart to wear civilian clothes on the rest of the flight home.

When I got home, I partied a lot just to try and get rid of the bad feelings. We were all heartbroken. A lot of us were wondering why it had to happen to him. Those were hard times. As proud as I was to serve my country, I didn't talk about being in the Army. Nobody talked about it back then. Years later I found out that guys who I had hung around with and went to school with had been in the service, but you didn't know it because nobody ever brought it up.

My brother Jim asked me one time, "Did you guys have a welcome home parade when you got back, the way they do now?" I said, "No, we didn't even tell anyone we were in the military because of the antics of some of the people out there."

Years ago I worked at a job in Ashwaubenon. We had some Vietnamese working there. This one girl asked me one day, "Why don't you ever talk to me?" So I told her the story of my brother being killed in Vietnam and told her I still had problems with it.

She said, "Thank you. Thank you for you and your brother's service." She then told me her background. She grew up in a village in

Bereaved Widow — Family and friends of Lance Cpl. Mikal Sullivan, 19, De Pere's first battle casualty in Viet Nam, attended burial rites Monday at Mt. Calvary Cemetery. An American flag which draped military coffin is given to widow by a Marine Corps officer. Mrs. Sullivan is the former Janice Olmsted. An infant daughter, Christine, also survives.

South Vietnam. At night the VC would come in and torture people. She said they would string people up and cut their arms or legs off with machetes. The VC were terrible to them. She said people have no idea how bad it was for the Vietnamese civilians and that the only people that gave them hope were the Americans.

Her family: father, brothers, and sisters escaped from Vietnam by going out in the ocean and sitting on a raft for like two weeks until they were picked up by a US military ship. She said if it wasn't for the Americans, she wouldn't have anything.

She was the first person to thank me for serving in the military.

Things have changed so much over the years. I personally never resented the government or the military. I still have nephews who serve. But now when you go to speak at a school or for a ceremony, they all applaud you and the kids ask really good, interesting questions. It was never like that before. There are some middle school teachers who have done a really good job of teaching kids about our veterans.

A few years ago a 50th-anniversary ceremony was held to honor Mikal. I couldn't believe even after that many years how many of his friends came out.

We all feel terrible about what happened to him, but there's something else you have to remember. His dream, his entire goal from the time he was ten years old, was to be a Marine. I honestly think he was willing to accept whatever came with that. So no matter what, he accomplished his lifetime dream. Not everyone can say that.

If I could have one more day with him, I would give him a big hug, tell him I loved him, tell him I miss him. And I would thank him for being someone I am very, very proud of.

1ST LT. TOM SHAW

129 Assault
Helicopter Company
US Army
Vietnam War
KIA April 27, 1972

Describe the characteristics of what might generally be considered an "All American Boy," and chances are Tom Shaw of Fond du Lac, Wisconsin, would fit the bill. A star athlete and honor student, this college graduate, with an extremely low draft lottery number, decided to enlist rather than be drafted.

His passion to fly, much like his father's during his time as a Navy pilot in World War II, helped fuel his decision. His brother Kevin, six years younger, recalls life before, during, and after his big brother's experience in Vietnam.

Tom was the oldest of us five kids and it just seemed like he had everything in the world going for him. He was an excellent athlete, a great student, had the quickest wit, and everyone looked up to him. He was always kind. To me, he was larger than life.

There was one basketball game that was probably emblematic of his life. Our school, little Fond du Lac St. Mary's Springs, was playing gigantic Fond du Lac Goodrich High School in their brand new gym. It was November 24th, 1964. It seemed like the whole community was there. It was an amazing game and so loud you couldn't hear yourself think.

He didn't start the game, but came in off the bench and scored 24 points. The score was tied with five seconds left. He drove the lane, was fouled, and sank two free throws to win the game. That was my brother. Cool as a cucumber.

He graduated in 1966 and went to St. Norbert College. The war was obviously very much in the news during the entire time he was in there.

I became very vigilant regarding anything concerning Vietnam. I would watch Walter Cronkite with my dad and pay attention to all the grim

Tom Shaw's basketball heroics were highlighted in the local newspaper. (Shaw family collection)

statistics about American casualties. From the fourth grade, I thought about the Vietnam War a lot. I remember vividly the news about things like the '68 Tet Offensive, and people like LBJ, Robert Kennedy, and Robert McNamara. I followed the news very closely. I always loved the sports page, but I recall turning first to the obituary listings to see if any local boys had been killed in Vietnam.

I remember during his sophomore year in college when he got his draft number, which was three, I recall him saying that if the war didn't end while he was in school there was a good chance he would be going to Vietnam.

He became very interested in flying and joined the ROTC. My dad had been a Navy pilot during WWII and supported it. Everybody thought that was a good route to go. We did not realize how treacherous it was for helicopter pilots in Vietnam, however. We prayed constantly that the war would end before he would be sent there.

He married his high school sweetheart, Ann, right after he graduated from St. Norbert in 1970. On the day of the wedding, they drove to Ft. Eustis, Virginia, to start his training. Then from there he went to different flight training schools in Texas and Georgia. He left for Vietnam on January 10, 1972. He would spend 105 days there.

Tom and Ann had a son while he was in training so I'm sure it was very, very difficult to leave his family, but he never showed it to us. I remember him joking to me that maybe the hippies and yippies would scream loud enough so that Nixon would bring all the soldiers home. He was very patriotic, but he understood the complex viewpoints about the war.

I was in tears when he was getting set to leave. I told him I was worried about him. He hugged me and said, "It's a piece of cake. I will be back before you know it."

Maybe I watched all the stuff that was going on in the news too closely because I had a lot of sleepless nights and nightmares about him being over there. I never admitted that to anyone, not even my parents. But it really haunted me, the thought that he might not come back.

We received many good, positive letters while he was there. He was always optimistic. He didn't talk about being shot at every day. He really loved to fly. It's not for the faint-hearted, but that was him.

Editor's note: *Bernie Hernandez from Ogden, Utah, was one of the two door gunners on the mission in which Tom and three others were killed. He recounts that fateful day, April 27, 1972.*

Bernie Hernandez:

I had flown with Lt. Shaw on some maintenance flights but this was our first combat flight together. So I didn't really know him all that well. What I do remember is that everyone just considered him a good dude, respectful and friendly to everybody. I also heard he was religious.

Mr. Shaw was going to be flying our ship, number 426. Bruno Sanchez and I considered it ours because we crewed it; we were the door gunners. Mr. Shaw was taking the place of our regular pilot who was grounded because he was over his allotment of flight hours.

Our main missions were supplying South Korean troops around the An Khe Pass. This was always a dangerous area and now the NVA had circled five separate areas to attack in what was then known as The Easter Offensive. Their objective was to cut off the supply lines to outposts in the region.

I can recall flying over the area on other missions and one time seeing the tail fin of a C-130 cargo plane sticking out of the jungle ground. There were burned-out trucks from hitting land mines or getting attacked by RPGs. There was one area where the NVA had a .51-caliber machine gun set up that caused so much damage to choppers and was so hard to hit that they had to call in an F-4 and bomb it out of action.

Another thing the NVA were very good at was mortaring choppers that dropped off supplies. They seemed to have incredible timing and accuracy. I remember on one mission, dropping off the ammo and other supplies, and looking out the back and seeing a mortar hit inside the perimeter. We got out of there and it wasn't ten seconds later that a mortar hit right on the landing pad we had been sitting on.

On the night of the 26th (April 1972) I came back from a mission, had chow, and went to get some sleep. I had terrible dreams. I dreamed that something bad was going to happen the next time I went out.

The next morning I went down to get my guns set up in the bird, but I still didn't feel right. I still felt weird. Call it a premonition or whatever, but I had never felt that way before.

We did our inspections and pulled pitch (took off) at 7:00 a.m. It was the two pilots, Bruno and myself, and two South Korean RTOs (radio-telephone operators.)

We headed up the An Khe pass to Ridge 26 which is at the base of the valley. We were to land there, load up supplies, and get instructions. Our mission was to supply hill number 638.

Just before 11:00 a.m. we were flying low following a logging road that I hadn't even noticed before. It was very tight on both sides. I remember thinking it was like the *Twilight Zone* in there. Just before we got to a clearing we heard what sounded like a "tick," almost like the sound of a BB going through a Coke can. I heard the copilot, Mr. Claud Strother, (chief warrant officer) over the intercom say, "Pull up!" just before we hit the ground. We bounced up. I remember seeing all the C-rations, ammo cans, water cans sliding forward to the back of the pilot seat. The two Korean soldiers had also been flung forward. After we touched the ground, Lieutenant Shaw pulled back. We kind of backed up, did two 360 degree circles. I imagine we got up to about 1,000 feet in the air. I remember thinking that I was going to die. I had a daughter who was born three weeks before I went to Nam. I remember thinking that I would never see her again.

The next thing I remember was heading down doing approximately ninety knots. I remember thinking about jumping out, but before I could we crashed into the side of a hill.

I remember waking up on the ground outside of the chopper. I looked into the cockpit. Lt. Shaw and Mr. Strother were slumped forward in their seats.

I looked over at Bruno who was also on the ground and I thought he was dead. Then I passed out. In the meantime, Bruno woke up, looked at me, and thought I was dead. This happened several times. Finally, Bruno got up, went into the cockpit, and turned off the engine to keep it from exploding.

We wanted to get away from there. We knew the NVA had seen us go down. I don't know if someone had gotten to us while we were

Tom Shaw (second from right) poses with his crew. (Shaw family collection)

knocked out, but my machine gun, M-16, ammo, and helmet were all missing.

We were both pretty messed up. My tibia and fibula were broken, a piece of my hip bone was chipped off, my eye was swollen shut, I had a bunch of cuts. Bruno had a broken femur and some other injuries. I don't remember this, but Bruno told me I carried him out of there. I honestly don't remember that. We went about seventy-five yards to a clearing and waited for a rescue team.

Captain Alan Jones landed first and walked up the trail. We were going to light him up, but he yelled, "Cease fire! Cease fire!"

I remember them bandaging us up and then going to the crash site to get the bodies out and look for the Korean bodies. They also found them outside of the chopper, but I'm not sure how far away they were.

After bandaging up Bruno and me and giving us a shot of morphine, they medevacked us out to Quang Youn MASH unit.

That day was exactly the type of thing I had dreamed about the night before.

Note: *Kevin Shaw continues from the time he learned his brother was killed.*

Kevin Shaw:

It was 6:35 p.m. on the last day of April 1972. It was a really cold, nasty Sunday night. My brother Dave and I were sitting in the living room. He was facing the street, I was facing him. All of a sudden I saw him turn white. I turned and looked out the window. Walking onto our parents' front porch was our parish priest and a guy in a long, green coat. Dave and I looked at each other and instantly we knew.

We answered the door. I can still see my fifteen-year-old self, crying in the mirrored sunglasses of the officer at our door.

The Army officer couldn't tell us what had happened. He had to deliver the news to the first of kin, which was Ann, Tom's wife. She was at her parents' house five blocks away. My mom kept begging him, "Can't you please tell us what happened? But he couldn't so we quickly drove to Ann's parents' house.

We walked up to the door of their beautiful old house on Division Street. When Ann's mom saw us she said, "Oh how nice you all came to visit." Then she looked down the driveway and saw the Army officer and the priest and let out a scream, falling to her knees. It was a heartbreaking night as my parents also called my brother Tim and sister, Mary, who were students at St. Norbert at the time. Seeing my mom tell my grandparents about the loss of Tom, their oldest grandchild was especially tough.

The funeral was held a week later on a beautiful May day. The church was so packed people had to stand outside. There was a total cross-section of people which is what you would expect with Tom.

I remember when my Dad met the undertaker to receive the casket at the airport, Tom's roommate from Vietnam, Jim Crigler, and Ann went along. At some point, early on during the drive, there was what sounded like three knocks from the casket. The undertaker quickly explained that sometimes there is settling with the casket after long flights. But Jim and Ann, both knowing Tom's sense of humor, looked at each other and said, "That's Tom. He's letting us know he's here."

My parents were incredible examples of how to handle a loss like this. They were always proud of him. They flew the flag every day on our front porch. I know it affected them both, but back then you just kind of dealt with it and didn't show much emotion. They were very faithful and calm people, and their constant focus was to raise five kids in the best way possible and they stayed that way.

I remember Christmas that year was hollow. The ironic thing is that I never had another nightmare about Tom or Vietnam. The strong anxiety I had while Tom was in Vietnam seemed to leave me. After Tom was

Saturday, April 29, 1972

Copter Crews Running the Big Risks in War

By Peter Arnett

An Khe Pass, Vietnam–AP–Since the start of the recent enemy offensive, more Americans have died in downed helicopters than from any other cause.

Some helicopters fall prey to the sophisticated antiaircraft fire that the North Vietnamese have introduced in their thrust into South Vietnam. Others crash into mountainsides, victims of rifle fire, as they make daring, low level flights to aid embattled fire bases.

Some go down for reasons never to be fully known.

Pinpoint Fire

In the last hours of the two week battle for An Khe Pass, the crash of a UH-1E helicopter this week ended the lives of two American pilots and two Korean observers. Two crewmen were injured.

The Huey crashed without a word from the pilots.

During the battle, every flight below 3,000 feet was a nightmare for the Americans. No Vietnamese or Korean helicopters were available to help.

The helipad of the An Khe outpost atop the pass came under pinpoint mortar fire. When a helicopter approached to drop supplies and drag wounded aboard, a North Vietnamese mortarman would throw a shell into his tube. He hoped the helicopter would still be on the pad when the round exploded eight seconds later.

The American pilots would make cunning approaches, racing over and between trees, out of view of that gunner until the last moment. They would dip onto the pad and hope to be away before the round exploded.

Help Arrives

The enemy and fate never caught up with those Americans until the end of the battle. A surviving member of helicopter crew said he thought he heard rifle fire as he leaned over his machine guns staring into the elephant grass below. A split second later he was half conscious below the broken helicopter.

He heard a cry. Despite a broken hip he staggered through the brush and saw his fellow gunner.

He was still standing dazed when Lt. Col. A. A. Niyamoto, an American liaison officer with the Koreans, approached, followed by Maj. Allan Jones, commander of the 129th Assault Helicopter Company.

A rescue team flew overhead. Without a thought to danger, the team landed just below the wreck.

Niyamoto bandaged the injured gunners. Jones and a Korean radio operator knelt in the grass, calling for a medical evacuation helicopter and gunships for protection.

Jones and Korean soldiers pushed up to the helicopter and dragged out the four broken bodies.

Minutes later a white helicopter painted with a red cross fluttered into the pass. The wounded were carried down the hill on litters.

The Koreans went back to their base. Within 90 minutes, the books were closed on this episode in the battle of the An Khe Pass.

This Associated Press article described the circumstances surrounding the incident that cost Tom Shaw his life. (Shaw family collection) killed my concern was with my parents along with Ann and their son. I just wanted to make sure I was a good, caring son.

Losing Tom left a big hole in our hearts. I know I went through the motions for a good part of my high school years. I probably needed to talk to someone about what I was going through, but you never thought about doing something like that back then.

The high school board came to my parents to ask if the school could start an award in Tom's name. Since 1973, the Tom Shaw Memorial Award has been presented to the senior male athlete based on adherence to Christian ideals, and excellence in leadership, academics, and athletics. Tom always talked about becoming a teacher, counselor, and coach. He had been accepted for the school counselor program at the University of Wisconsin, to start when he came home. I think he would have followed through and, as in everything else he pursued, he would have succeeded.

It's hard to believe it's been fifty years since Tom has been gone. He lives deep in our hearts and we remember him and all who serve the USA.

ACKNOWLEDGEMENTS

This is the absolute hardest part of writing a book because there is always that fear of missing someone who helped along the way.

To Randy Scannell, an incredible friend and the stepfather of Benjamin Edinger, a proud, courageous Marine who lost his life from wounds suffered in Iraq in 2004. This man has been the first and last person to look at every word. If it were back in my day, he would have worn out a year's supply of red pens. Corrections, suggestions, and many, many hours of hard work for little reward. I cannot thank this man enough.

To Mike Dauplaise and his wife/business partner, Bonnie Groessl. I first rubbed shoulders with Mike, literally, while jostling for position during Forrest Gregg press conferences when Forrest was head coach of the Green Bay Packers. Okay, if that does not make us both feel old, nothing will. His guidance and expertise during the book development and layout process have been extraordinary.

To Ron Christensen, former Marine drill instructor and current head of the Oconto County Veterans Affairs Office. This gentleman helped in numerous ways with anything and everything dealing with the Marine Corps. From research and finding authentic battle documents to jargon, to candidates to profile, he did it all. I value his guidance and friendship. But most of all am very thankful that I never had to face him as a DI.

To Rich Appel, former Lt. Colonel with the 432nd Civil Affairs Battalion and now superintendent of the Horicon School District, a gentleman who did not hesitate to help in numerous ways when it came to writing about his beloved US soldiers.

To Craig Salo, Director of the Marquette County Veterans Affairs office, for his help in putting me in contact with Vietnam vets from his region. If you think I'm going to write a book and not include veterans from the Upper Peninsula of Michigan, you are sadly mistaken.

To Major General, (Ret.) Daniel Ammerman, a true treasure trove of information who never hesitated to help with any questions I had, no matter how big or how small.

To Rich Karki and his remarkable wife Karen. They not only shared their own compelling personal story but also provided me with names of others to interview and became a sounding board on so many other issues it would be impossible to list them all.

To my wife Julie and son Dominic. I realize computers have been around for about twenty years, but there were several-errr...many-err.... an incredibly large number of times when I would tap into their advanced computer knowledge for assistance in a variety of ways. I honestly believe they will miss my cries - day or night, of - "Julie, Dom... would you come down here (lower level office) and help me with something. Ok, actually, I am very, very certain they won't miss that for a second.

To the families of not only the veterans profiled in this book, but also to the innumerable number of people who have encouraged me to keep the memories and experiences of our veterans alive. My greatest reward is when they tell me they can actually hear their grandfather, father, uncle, neighbor, or whoever, speaking the exact words that are on the pages. It may not always be in the most precise grammatical form, but their words came straight from the heart and I didn't change a thing.

And finally and most importantly, to the veterans and their families. The gratitude I have for you, for sharing your experiences with me, which, in more than a few cases, were extremely personal and sometimes painful. Hopefully, it was also somewhat cathartic. Whether it was over coffee, over something a little stronger than coffee, in your living room, kitchen, garage, patio, or over the phone, my appreciation for you taking the time and your willingness to share your incredible experiences for future generations is immeasurable. This book belongs to you.

ABOUT THE AUTHOR

John Maino

Fifty Strong is John Maino's fourth book featuring the stories of military veterans. The others (*Frontlines, The Pacific,* and *ETO-European Theatre of Operations*) dealt with World War II veterans of Wisconsin and Michigan. Maino spent over thirty-five years in radio and TV. He embedded as a reporter with the 127th Infantry at Camp Navistar, Kuwait, and with the 432nd Civil Affairs Battalion at both Camp Liberty in Baghdad, Iraq, and Camp Nathan Smith in Kandahar, Afghanistan. He is a native of Negaunee, Michigan, and is extremely proud of his Yooper heritage.

Made in the USA
Middletown, DE
13 May 2021